Civil Rights Era Plays From Alabama

Flawed Good People | HUBERT GRISSOM

© Copyright 2023 By Hubert Grissom.
The performance of each play is subject to royalties.
For more information and performance licensing consult playwright
at hubertgrissom@gmail.com

Book design by Shawn Wright, shawnwright.net

ISBN: 979-8-9882325-0-6 (paperback)
ISBN: 979-8-9882325-1-3 (hardback)

All Rights Reserved

No part of this book may be reproduced in any form or by any electronic or mechanical means, including information storage and retrieval systems, without written permission from the author, except for the use of brief quotations in book reviews.

"To err is human."
Alexander Pope

"Perfect is the enemy of the good."
Voltaire

"[P]eople who do really good stuff have flaws."
Barack Obama

*For my children, Leeth, Lauren and Christopher,
who many years ago shared their playroom
on the top floor of an old house in Birmingham
and who watched cartoons to the
click, clack of my old Selectric typewriter.*

Contents

FOREWORD Lorian Hemingway 7

INTRODUCTION 11

WINSTON DRIVES BIG JIM 15
Winner 2019 Southern Playwright Competition, Jacksonville State University, Jacksonville, AL.

WEDGES 89
Produced 1990 Terrific New Theatre, Birmingham, AL

WATERIN' HOLE 145
Produced 1991 Terrific New Theatre, Birmingham, AL

JAMELLE, ALABAMA'S TEENAGE FIRST LADY 199
2016 Reading with Marsha Folsom, also an Alabama First Lady, Cullman, AL

CODE BAPBOMB 237
Produced 2007 Stageworks & Gorilla Theatres, Tampa, FL

BACKSTORY 295

ENDNOTES 325

ACKNOWLEDGEMENTS 333

ABOUT THE PLAYWRIGHT 335

ACCLAIM FOR PLAYS 336

ACCLAIM FOR PLAYWRIGHT'S EARLIER WORK 336

Foreword

HUBERT GRISSOM'S MOVING AND STUNNING COLLECTION OF CIVIL RIGHTS PLAYS is a long overdue paean to the incomparable spirit, indelible soul, and profound courage of Black Americans during one of the most horrific periods in American history: Grissom's *Flawed Good People* spans the '50s and '60s in the Deep South, most notably in his home state of Alabama.

The collection addresses, among so many mortifying trials and welcome moments of pure humanity of that era: the rise and fall of former Alabama governor and Black sympathist Big Jim Folsom; the dignified heroics of Rosa Parks as she softly, but with an iron will, refused to give up her seat on a bus in Montgomery to a white man; the Ku Klux Klan bombing of the 16th Street Baptist church in Birmingham that obliterated the lives of four young Black girls; and in stark contrast the often congenial relationships between Blacks and whites when the outside world was not privy. Although the latter, historically, is far more the exception than the rule.

Perhaps the most sympathetic character of all, and much to the surprise of this reader, was Folsom himself. A man torn by his basic honor and decency and his wish to make Alabama great as much or more for the Black man as for the white, he is the embodiment of the title of the collection: a flawed good person. He comes across, behind the scenes with his Black chauffeur, Winston Craig, as a man of transparency, curiosity and humanity. And given the times during which he reigned as governor, this is akin to a small miracle.

As a whole, the collection stirred deep memories in me, ones that came quickly and unbidden, and as stark and grotesque as they were when they first made their mark in my life. While Grissom grew up in Alabama, I grew up one state over in Mississippi. My childhood heroes were two: Dr. Martin Luther King, Jr. and Muhammad Ali, and they remain so to this day.

My first (and last) Ku Klux Klan meeting took place in a cow pasture across the road from my Aunt Faye's house. My older cousin took me by the hand and led me toward the flaming crosses — there were three — that filled the already hot humid night with the smell of creosote. I remember my aunt running from the house yelling, asking my cousin what did he think he was doing, dragging me to that meeting. And I remember him turning to look at his mother straight on.

"Mama," he said evenly, "How else is she gonna learn what these bastards do if she don't see for herself."

As we carefully picked our way through the barbed wire fence my cousin whispered in my ear. "They hate us, too," he told me. "Why?" I asked. "Cause we're Catholic. They hate Black people, Jews and Catholics." No, I was not a "white savior," but I was a kid filled with fire and spit, and an oddly well-formed and distinct hatred for injustice in any form. Or maybe, I have told myself in later years, I just liked a good fight.

There were TV cameras that night, broadcasting live from the field filled with manure and dozens of Klansmen in their full white robes, faces hidden, burning crosses staked to form an arc around the back of the stage, which was nothing more than a quickly tacked together plywood box. It was hot as hell. Faces hidden except for the one on stage. He spat out words I had been raised never to say, made to swear never to say because my own family, only a generation back, had tried, and often failed, to pass for white. We were mostly Cherokee, but there was Black in the mix, too. My mother never let me get too dark in summer. But there was one word that caught me quick that night, pulled me up straight and tall as I felt my hands clench into fists. "You want your children goin' to school with them burr heads?" The unmasked one shouted this from the stage, dared people to think of such an abomination. He had the piggish eyes of a wild boar.

Something broke in me in that instant, the kind of instinct you have when you see a rattler about to strike and you just happen to have a gun in your hand. I kicked and pushed my way through the crowd so I was right at the foot of that crummy plywood stage, right up tight near the TV cameras, and then when I made sure they had caught me I made a big huge sign of the cross, the way Catholics do before they genuflect, so there was no mistaking what I was doing, and the one onstage stopped for one shocked moment, long enough for me to hear my Aunt screaming from across the road to my cousin to get me out of the crowd. "Now!" Her voice was panicked. "Now!" She had been watching us live on TV.

My cousin pulled me with no small effort from that cow pasture, kicking and screaming all the way. Words were all jumbled up in my mouth. I remember screaming "stupid, stupid, ignorant, STOP!." I remember saying I was going to kill someone, I remember my aunt putting a cool cloth on my forehead as my cousin now carried me limp in his arms. I remember crying.

And another memory: A chance ride with homegrown white civil rights workers from Birmingham who asked if I would help them to register Black people to vote in exchange for a partway ride across the country. I rode in the back of their truck as we drove the backroads of Alabama in deep darkness, many of the roads unpaved because they snaked through cotton fields. We'd pull up to a sharecropper's house in the middle of the night, and there would be a lantern burning, someone waiting on the sagging porch. I remember one particular stop. I peeked out from the truck and saw an old Black woman, and even in that light I could see her eyes were scarred over with cataracts. Those all-white milky eyes in her beautiful Black face, unseeing, but her smile was like fireworks going off in that deep night when she felt the hand of the driver touch hers. I remember touching my own lips, tracing the smile that had formed there, and I spoke out loud, not caring who heard, because we were among friends here. "She's gonna vote. Hell yeah, she's gonna vote!"

This is what *Flawed Good People* brought up in me. Memories. Raw boiling emotion. And memories pass for religion in my book any day, for they are the vault and burial ground of the past upon which we perform the mutable ritual of scrutiny. I hope we never stop looking, never stop remembering, never leave our conscience at the door for the sake of appearance. And I hope like hell writers like Hubert Grissom never stop spreading the gospel. Amen.

Lorian Hemingway

Lorian Hemingway is the author of three critically acclaimed books: *Walking into the River*, *A World Turned Over*, and *Walk on Water*. She is the director and final judge of the Lorian Hemingway Short Story Competition.

Introduction

MAKE AMERICA 1955 AGAIN? SERIOUSLY? 1955 was the year Emmett Till was tortured, then lynched in Mississippi. That year Congressman Adam Clayton Powell visited Alabama and the Montgomery Bus Boycott began with the arrest of Rosa Parks. 1955 also marked the beginning Alabama Governor James E. "Big Jim" Folsom's second term, the year he asked the teachers of Alabama for wisdom, tolerance and objective thinking in light of the Supreme Court's decision in *Brown v. Board of Education of Topeka, Kansas* that desegregated public schools. Six years earlier near the end of his first term, Governor Folsom called for racial equality in his 1949 Christmas Message, over a decade before the school children and Dr. Martin Luther King, Jr. faced Public Safety Commissioner Eugene "Bull" Connor's police dogs and fire hoses in Birmingham.

Flawed characters in conflict are important links in the dramatic arc that keep theatre patrons from leaving at intermission — we hope. Then, there is the age-old debate as to whether history repeats or merely rhymes, with the giant among southerner writers, William Faulkner, suggesting that the past is not even past. In addition to his comedies and tragedies, William Shakespeare saw a need to put history on stage.

Historically, these plays begin with Governor Folsom's first term, a time when the Dixiecrats walked out of the 1948 National Democratic Convention in Philadelphia, because, *inter alia,* Hubert Humphrey had introduced a civil rights plank in the platform. (WINSTON DRIVES BIG JIM.) These plays end in the late 1980s when investigators were reopening the Klan bombing of the 16th Street Baptist Church in Birmingham that killed four young girls. (CODE BAP-BOMB.)

As a southerner, I first started writing these plays as an apology, suggesting that not all white southerners were of one mind, one loud voice, that is, Confederate-flag-waving, forget-hell, sore-losing potential insurrectionist. During this process, I tentatively defined "Jim Crow Liberals" as natives who lived among those loud voices but were different. Flawed perhaps but tending toward progress, toward our elusive "New South."

Growing up a North Alabama Appalachian-foot-hillbilly I did not think I was privileged but I was with a dose of white blindness. These plays reflect that journey and with limited exceptions have not been edited to reflect political correct wokeness as it has evolved. For good or ill, plays over a span of time become a biography of sorts. See: Terrence McNally, SELECTED WORKS, A Memoir in Plays (Grove Press 2015).

As his name suggests Governor Big Jim Folsom was physically large and as a human he was larger than life with an ardent belief in democracy, yet flawed, an individual who could drink most under the table and who could teach King Lear and Willie Loman a thing or two about aging awkwardly.

The Folsom family house was across the street from my elementary school in Cullman, Alabama, an all-white Sundown Town, and my sister Dr. Jenny Folsom married Big Jim's son Jack. I was a student at Birmingham-Southern College in 1963 when Dr. King came to Kelly Ingram Park in Birmingham and the 16th Street Baptist Church was bombed. After law school out-of-state I returned to Birmingham.

WEDGES features a young lawyer who encounters an African American domestic on his volunteer Saturday at legal aid. Years earlier the maid "found" some diamonds in a potted plant after a drunken brawl on the governor's yacht and immediately got a one-way bus ticket north. At the time of the play she is older, disable and returns to Birmingham to confess and rid herself of her "wedges of sin."

In WATERIN'HOLE Black and white railroad workers drink together after work in a barroom near the tracks in Birmingham. In the late 1950s, blue-collar buddies ignore the prevailing Jim Crow laws, plot a union strike, listen to football on the radio and hoot it up under the watchful eye of the bar's owner/operator an African American female.

JAMELLE, ALABAMA'S TEENAGE FIRST LADY features Big Jim's bride when she is older having matured into a steel magnolia. In this mostly one-woman play, Jamelle chats with an original (or want-to-be) Strawberry Picker who plucks out music that includes early country, blue grass, folk and old campaign stumps songs.

BAPBOMB (renamed CODE BAPBOMB) is timed, circa1988, with the reopening of the 16th Street Baptist Church bombing that killed the four young girls and the accidental opening of secrets found in an old law firm safe. As a young lawyer in a politically aware firm, I learned that everyone, e.g. the Klan, police, FBI, newspapers, etc. wiretapped everyone else; ergo, the powerful knew of plans to bomb the church and no one tried to stop it. In CODE BAPBOMB the characters are fictional, but for those wishing to know more, I recommend: **BEHIND THE MAGIC CURTAIN**, Secrets, Spies, and Unsung White Allies of Birmingham's Civil Rights Days, Thorne, New South Books, 2021.

The lead play WINSTON DRIVES BIG JIM won the 2019 Southern Playwright Competition at Jacksonville (Alabama) State University and delves into the friendship between Big Jim Folsom and Winston Craig, his African American chauffeur-valet-confidant-assistant. Winston Craig studied agriculture at Tuskegee Institute during Professor George Washington Carver's tenure, served in the Navy during World War II, and was a friend and parishioner of Dr. Martin Luther King, Jr. attending Dexter Avenue Baptist Church in Montgomery at the time of the Bus Boycott. The play also features Ruth Craig, who was a cousin of Rosa Parks also of Montgomery at the time of the Boycott. The Craigs were unsung, low profile civil rights activists, while forming a true bond and friendship with Alabama's most powerful politician. This friendship yielded some positive changes and lasted as political power waned seeing Big Jim appear drunk/drugged on television the night before he lost an election to George Wallace.

His flaws notwithstanding, Big Jim Folsom was ahead of his time in Alabama when he called for racial equality in his 1949 Christmas Message that has been memorialized thanks to Birmingham-reared and Pulitzer Prize winner Howell Raines, who recommended the Message to his *New York Times* colleague William Safire. (LEND ME YOUR EARS, GREAT SPEECHES IN HISTORY, Norton, 2004, page 718.) But, years after his Message, Folsom gave lip service to segregation after George Wallace set a race-baiting tone in Alabama politics of the 1960s.

Why does our "New South" regress as if it is mimicking a backward dramatic arc, e. g. Harold Pinter's BETRAYAL? Is this just the Make American Great Again (MAGA) crowd looking in the wrong direction as their name suggests? May 2023, Alabama Senator Tommy "Three Branches of Government?" Tuberville in an effort to keep white nationalist in the military, proclaimed them to be good Americans, Trump Republicans and MAGA people. The Senator's proclamation came on the heels of Alabama journalist Kyle Whitmire wining a Pulitzer Prize in Commentary for "State of Denial" a year-long exposé of how the state whitewashed Alabama history making sure that white supremacy was taught and preserved through its education system.

What is the place, albeit duty, of "The Whites" as Dave Chappelle might call us? Do the Jim Crow Liberals in these plays risk becoming part of a backward arc? Once I attended a lecture at the University of Alabama, Birmingham (UAB) about the civil rights era. During the talk, I stood in the back of the auditorium next to an "angry Black man" who muttered loud enough for me to hear: "White man profiting off Blackman's plight!"

In 2018 after I wrote WINSTON DRIVES BIG JIM, I saw the movie GREEN BOOK. While I adored the film, that Black man back at UAB continued to haunt me. Later watching the Oscars, I was embarrassed that all the white guys who had produced GREEN BOOK crowded out the few Blacks on stage as they congratulated themselves on winning Best Picture. Such is Hollywood, I thought, and I understood when Spike Lee and others reviewed the movie harshly. But, should it along with THE HELP, THE BUTLER, DRIVING MISS DAISY be banned? Or do we put them in the context of their time and try to learn something? White saviors? Critical race history?[1] The messy middle of politics? Even Birmingham-reared comedian Roy Wood, Jr. pokes fun at white folks suggesting "nuance" while at the same time riffs that not all Blacks were part of the "struggle."

Flawed: Over the years when not wanting to confront a racist directly I'd hide within my skin color — that is ruddy pink and prone to little skin cancers. Back then I had a conceit: "You did not tell your barber you were an 'integrationist' for fear he'd do a Van Gogh on your ear." Cue a sinking feeling and banjo music: While reading Birmingham-reared Diane McWhorter's Pulitzer Prize winning CARRY ME HOME, Simon & Schuster, 2001, there in print was the name of my barber as head of a local Birmingham area Klan. No it could not be? The name is quite common and I still have both ears.

Watching the televised murder of George Floyd, I had another sad, sinking yet familiar feeling harkening back wondering how much and if anything has changed. On MSNBC Joy Reid reflected on racism in 2020 and rhetorically asked if it had ever been this bad? Voila, a metaphorical light bulb appeared as she answered herself: "The Sixties just called and said hold my beer!"

My personal history of coming of age and later practicing law in Birmingham during the civil rights era produced these characters both hooligans and heroes, both real and fictional. Hence, I give you my plays begging that they be put in the context of their time and their Alabama with a hope for a future that if history insists on rhyming it quits repeating the horrific!

Hubert Grissom
Spring 2023

DRAMA
JACKSONVILLE STATE UNIVERSITY

WINSTON DRIVES BIG JIM

BY HUBERT GRISSOM

WINNER 2019 SOUTHERN PLAYWRIGHTS COMPETITION

October 3-4th, 2019

Ernest Stone Center for the Performing Arts
Jacksonville State University

WINSTON DRIVES BIG JIM

DEVELOPMENT HISTORY

STAGEWORKS, TAMPA, FL
On March 24, 2019, the play was first read at Stageworks Theatre and was directed by James Rayfield. The cast:
- **Winston Craig** – Bob Devin Jones
- **Big Jim Folsom** – Jim Wicker
- **Ruth Craig** – Fanni Green
- **Jamelle Folsom** – Michele Young
- **Southern Male** – Richard Coppinger

JACKSONVILLE STATE UNIVERSITY, JACKSONVILLE, AL
Staged readings of WINSTON DRIVES BIG JIM were presented on October 3 & 4, 2019 at the Ernest Stone Center for the Performing Arts, Jacksonville State University. The Artistic Staff: Michelle Tailor, Director; Eric Wilkerson, Asst. Director; Ashe Fadely, Stage Manager; Cheyenne Oliver, Lighting Design; Alli Angel, Sound Design; John Davis, Tech Dir.; Light Board Operator, Sean Golson; and Sound Board Operator, Dylan Curvin. The cast:
- **Winston Craig** – Jake Lewis
- **Big Jim Folsom** – Lawrence Mason

Ruth Craig – Dominique Canzater Cheney
Jamelle Folsom – Chloe Barnes
Southern Male – Andrew Alan Harp, Jr.

A special thanks to Joy Maloney of the Department of English, Jacksonville State University, who coordinated the Southern Playwright Competition.

TIME & PLACE

Act One
- **1963** Prologue: Lake Guntersville near Buck's Pocket, AL.
- (Governor George Wallace "Segregation Forever" beginning.)
- **1947-49** Montgomery, AL and Lake Martin.

Act Two
- **1955-57** Montgomery, AL.
- **1963** Epilogue: Lake Guntersville near Buck's Pocket, AL.
- (Dr. Martin Luther King, Jr. "I Have a Dream" ending.)

CHARACTERS

Winston Craig (WINSTON): Chauffer/valet/confidante (ages 30-46). Dapper African American who knew MLK, Jr., Rosa Parks, E.D. Nixon and other civil rights leaders and was the chauffer to four governors of Alabama.

James E. "Big Jim" Folsom (BIG JIM): White progressive populist tall two-term Governor of Alabama (ages 40-56). Sometimes called "Kissin' Jim" because of his love of women and corn whiskey.

Ruth Biggs Craig (RUTH)[2]: African American female, (ages 30-46) cousin of Rosa Parks, a beautician, educated by nuns in Cincinnati, Ohio and holds a teacher's certificate from Alabama State (Teachers') College (now ASU).

Jamelle Moore Folsom (JAMELLE): White female (ages 19-31) becomes Alabama's Teenage First Lady. Also, female inaugural dancer in silhouette.

SOUTHERN MALE (multiple)[3]: George Wallace, Gen. Graham, Bull Connor, Handy Ellis, Dixiecrat, Gov. Dixon, State Rep., rioter, news reporter & Klansman.

SETS (MINIMAL & FLUID[4])

- Dais/lectern: Capitol Steps for inaugural addresses and other speeches.[5]
- Upstairs dressing area with suit caddies converts to lake house bedroom.
- Car/Cadillac limo, front bench seat only.
- Study/office desk with phone and "window" flanked with flags of USA & AL. (Christmas tree/decor, Act I, Sc. 9, 1949 Christmas Message, Act II, Sc. 4, December 1955 Bus Boycott, Act Two.) Microphone for 1949 Message.
- Craigs' kitchen table, phone, radio, coffee pot & two chairs.
- Porch/patio chairs & small table at houses on Lake Guntersville and Lake Martin; area doubles as patio overlooking swimming pool at Governor's Mansion.

Winston Craig with a state car.

Courtesy of the Montgomery People Collection, Alabama State University Archives, Levi Watkins Learning Center

Jim Folsom

Courtesy of the Folsom Family

WINSTON DRIVES BIG JIM   19

George Wallace at State Capitol.
Courtesy of the Alabama Department of Archives and History

ACT ONE, Scene One

At rise: *George Wallace at dais & on T.V. plays portions of his January 1963 Inaugural Address. WINSTON & BIG JIM in rockers on porch in half-light watching T.V.*

SOUTHERN MALE (George Wallace)[6] In the name of the greatest people that have ever trod this earth, I draw the line in the dust and toss the gauntlet before the feet of tyranny, and I say segregation now, segregation tomorrow, segregation forever."

(Dark at dais.)

WINSTON *(As lights come up he turns off T. V.)*

BIG JIM They'll be replaying that speech long after George is dead and gone.

WINSTON Governor Wallace knows his audience.

BIG JIM Why are they replaying that speech now? His inauguration was back in January.

WINSTON Couple of Colored students gonna enroll down at the University.

BIG JIM And, he's gonna stand in the schoolhouse door. Didn't know it was today. *(Beat.)* We should've beat that little piss ant.

WINSTON Governor, it wasn't exactly your fault.

BIG JIM Exactly whose fault was it, if it wasn't mine?

WINSTON Last election, things had changed on you ….

BIG JIM What'd you mean things?

WINSTON Things were just different.

BIG JIM Goddamn it Winston, speak up! I got drunk on T.V.!

WINSTON That too. But …

BIG JIM But what?

WINSTON *(Pause, conflicted.)* You didn't know what was in that whiskey?

BIG JIM I knew it was whiskey. *(Pause.)* I have only myself to blame.

WINSTON Governor, go easy on yourself. The time was …

BIG JIM Time was? Things were? The finish line was in sight. If only …

WINSTON If?

(They laugh.)

BIG JIM I know, if a frog had wings.

WINSTON It would not bust its fanny when it jumps.

BIG JIM When did you start finishing my sentences?

WINSTON Figure, 'bout seven, eight years ago Governor.

BIG JIM I'm getting old and my guard was down. Don't remember much … (lights fade).

SOUTHERN MALE (Political Bad Guy) *(Upstage, with flask, speaks to "off-stage" BIG JIM.)* Jim, here, drink this. *(Pause.)* There's nothin' we can do about that strike. Gotta drive down to Montgomery. *(Pause.)* I know you're tired. (Pause.) This will help. *(Pause.)* Just a little swig to calm you down. Here. *(Extends flask.)*

JAMELLE *(Enters upstage, confronts Southern Male.)* What are you doing?

SOUTHERN MALE Governor's tired. *(Pause.)* This will help.

JAMELLE Are you out of your mind? He cannot drink that.

SOUTHERN MALE We gotta switch T.V. stations. Drive down to Montgomery.

JAMELLE No booze! *(Reaches unsuccessfully for flask.)*

SOUTHERN MALE He needs this to relax.

JAMELLE He does not!

SOUTHERN MALE Look, Jamelle, we didn't know about the strike. Not gonna cross a picket-line.

JAMELLE You can run some campaign footage?

SOUTHERN MALE Folks want to see the Governor live on T.V. the night before they vote.

JAMELLE Live! Not if he drinks that stuff!

SOUTHERN MALE Look little lady, you calm down. We barely got time to drive to Montgomery.

(Dark upstage. Lights up downstage.)

WINSTON Believe you said it was the Wallace Boys.

BIG JIM Wallace Boys?

WINSTON You know, the ones who put a mickey in that bourbon. The Wallace Boys.

BIG JIM Boys?

WINSTON That's what you said.

BIG JIM *(Laughs.)* You better not call 'em "boys" … they'll cut your nuts out.

WINSTON Ouch! Thanks for the warning. *(Pause.)* You're pulling my leg.

BIG JIM Oh, sure, I knew 'em. They were just hangers-on. Toadies.

WINSTON With a pint of whiskey in their hip-pocket.

BIG JIM You should have stopped me.

WINSTON I wasn't driving you anymore, remember?

BIG JIM As I said, I don't remember much about that last day. Like I was sedated ….

(Dark downstage.)

SOUTHERN MALE (T.V. Reporter.) *(Lights up. Reporter with microphone.)* June 1962 reporting form WSFA Montgomery. We are talking to Jamelle Folsom, former First Lady and wife of defeated candidate former Governor Big

Jim Folsom.

JAMELLE Thank you for having me.

SOUTHERN MALE Mrs. Folsom, what happened during those last days before the primary?

JAMELLE First, let me thank the people of Alabama for all the support you have given us over the many years of serving you. It was a long hard fought campaign and we must move on.

SOUTHERN MALE Everyone wants to know about that last day.

JAMELLE It was a long hard fought campaign and Jim was tired.

SOUTHERN MALE He was in pretty bad shape when you all got to Montgomery.

JAMELLE I said he was tired.

SOUTHERN MALE Governor Folsom appeared intoxicated on television and could not even remember the names of your children.

JAMELLE We are blessed with many sweet children.

SOUTHERN MALE But he mixed-up their names.

JAMELLE He did okay naming Jim, Jr. and Jack but did have difficulty with Josh and the girls.

SOUTHERN MALE He appeared intoxicated.

JAMELLE We believe someone gave him a sedative by mistake.

(Dark upstage.)

BIG JIM *(Lights up downstage.)* Sedative? Sounds like they wanted me dead.

WINSTON You had no idea —

BIG JIM One of them boys did high-tail-it to Mexico right after the primary.

WINSTON You don't remember any of this?

BIG JIM T.V. showed me messin' up Jamelle's hairdo like I was wooing her into the bedroom.

WINSTON That too.

BIG JIM Beverly Hillbillies ain't got nothin' on us.

WINSTON Not the kindda T.V. show you needed the night before the primary.

BIG JIM If I'm not laughin', I'm cryin' in my … *(looks in glass)* … my friggin' ice tea.

WINSTON As you say, we take one step forward and two backwards. *(Points to T.V.)*

BIG JIM I say a lot of stuff. *(Beat. Points to T.V.)* That racist piss ant. He's running out of gas. That crap at the University is staged ….

SOUTHERN MALE (George Wallace) *(At Dais & via T.V.)* "I stand here today as Governor of this Sovereign State and refuse to willingly submit to the illegal usurpation of Power by the Central Government."

BIG JIM See, he's hiding behind states' rights. Just watch, Wallace will step aside when Kennedy federalizes the Guard like Ike did out in Little Rock. Watch!

WINSTON You lost that election before you ever went on T.V. *(Pause.)* Wallace ran those ads that had you drinking Scotch whiskey with Congressman Powell.

BIG JIM Scotch whiskey tastes … ugh … and smells like old shoe leather.

WINSTON It wasn't what you were drinking. It was who …

BIG JIM Heard Congressman Powell had some moral charges against him.

WINSTON That's not it. Congressman Powell is as black as I am and some folks (can't get past) ….

BIG JIM Wallace had his White Citizens booing my name like I was a stray dog, forgettin' that I paved their God-forsaken dirt roads. *(Pause.)* Yes, your Buddy Congressman Powell was the Hottest Tater of all.

WINSTON Hot Potatoes … Outside Agitators are bad to tell Southerners what to do.

BIG JIM Telling Southerners what to do is like teaching a pig to sing.

WINSTON It aggravates the pig.

BIG JIM And it's a waste of my time!

(They laugh. Big Jim abruptly stops.)

BIG JIM Winston, God help us we already fought one Civil War. (Beat.) Look!

(Points to T.V.)

SOUTHERN MALE (Gen. Henry Graham) *(In front of dais with back to audience & on T.V. in National Guard fatigues.)* "Sir, it's my sad duty to ask you to step aside under order of the President of the United States."

U.S. Attorney General Nicholas Katzenbach confronts Governor George C. Wallace on June 11, 1963 in front of Foster Auditorium, University of Alabama, Tuscaloosa, AL. as President Kennedy federalizes the Alabama National Guard and General Henry Graham ask Governor Wallace to step aside.

ACT ONE, Scene Two

At rise: *After dimming of lights[7] RUTH downstage as WINSTON walks to Limo, putting on a chauffeur cap and jacket, picks up newspaper and checks out limo.*

RUTH *(To the audience.)* That gentleman is Winston Craig, my husband of seven years, and he is the Chauffeur to the Governors of Alabama. Winston grew up near Selma and his Auntie says we're kin to the Air Force Base Craigs. *(Laughs.)* We don't tell the white folks that. Anyway, Winston attended Tuskegee Institute for a couple of years where he studied agriculture and spent two years in the Navy during our recent War with Japan. Winston has a lot of down time and reads every chance he gets. *(To WINSTON.)* Winston, paper boy came by yesterday wanting us to start taking the *Journal*.

WINSTON *(Looks at Newspaper in hand.)* Ruth, Honey, he throws the *Advertiser* every morning.

RUTH That's what I told him.

WINSTON It's not the first time, he's tried to get us started taking the afternoon paper.

RUTH Just passing on what he said.

WINSTON Last time he tried, I tell him by the afternoon, I already know what's going on driving the Governors and all. *(Lingers at Limo.)*

RUTH *(Points upstage.)* It's January 1947, and here in Montgomery "Big Jim" Folsom is about to give his Inaugural Speech as the 42nd Governor of Alabama. He fancies himself, a Populist. *(To Audience.)* Listen.

Governor Folsom at Alabama Capitol.
Courtesy of the Folsom Family

BIG JIM *(At dais on Capitol steps, in Morning Coat with Top Hat removed.[8])* "Now I am *your* Governor. From this day on I will be the trustee of your power. I want to be, and I am going to be, the faithful servant of all the people."

RUTH *(Crosses arms.)* Does all the people include us?

JIM BIG "I believe in the kind of democracy that touches the home of the average man. The kind of democracy that goes back to the branch-heads and the bush-arbor gathering places. Now that's the kind of democracy that give the average man and woman more to say about the way our government is run. It means we want to get rid of worn-out restrictions on voting."

RUTH Poll tax affects poor whites, as well as us Coloreds.[9] There were only 60 of us registered Colored voters in Montgomery for the election last year. *(Shakes head.)* That's not 60 percent Black. No, that was only 60 of us singular souls.

BIG JIM "The kind of democracy that I believe in, is not the kind that says there is a North Alabama, a South Alabama, a Wiregrass or a Blackbelt."

WINSTON Governor Folsom grew up in the Wiregrass and his adopted home is in North Alabama. So he has the advantages of being from two regions of common folks, neither region known for big industry nor the plantations with slave labor.

BIG JIM "It is the kind of democracy that says we are all working together here in Alabama for the best interest of the whole state. It's the kind of democracy that says every section of the State shall have fair representation in our government."

RUTH In the Blackbelt, they vote cows, pine trees and white folks living and dead but not us.

WINSTON The Blackbelt, where I'm from, is known for its rich black soil and plantations. But, it's not lost on politicians that the Blackbelt has more Negroes than whites.

BIG JIM "Another thing that needs to be done to make Alabama more democratic is to open the way for women to have a full share in our government."

RUTH Women got a long ways to go, and Lord help us Black *women!*

(Overlap the word "Women".)

BIG JIM "*Women* have had a full and equal share in building our State. They have been leaders in building schools and churches and communities. They have not had as much chance to add their inspiration to our political affairs. The more part they have, the more honesty and the more democracy we're going to have in government."

WINSTON The newspapers call him the "bachelor governor."

RUTH He's not exactly a "bachelor." No, he's a widower with two small girls. Got his Sister Ruby tending the children while he was out gallivanting and running for Governor.

BIG JIM "There are those who are frightened by real democracy. They have always worked to trim it down a little here and trim it down a little there.

They want to keep power in the hands of a few. I am not afraid of too much democracy. I am afraid of what happens to people when they have too little democracy."

WINSTON When Big Jim Folsom campaigned he held his rallies outside the Courthouses instead of inside like the other politicians.

RUTH By him speaking outside, meant we could gather across the street from the Courthouse Square, and listened to his every word.

BIG JIM "I start this new day in Alabama as your governor with malice toward none and good will toward all. I want to be and I am going to be the governor of *all the people*."

(Overlap.)

RUTH *All the people*, Governor, I hear you? *(Pause.)* Gonna hold your feet to the fire.

BIG JIM "I need your prays, I want to be the best governor I can be for you, and you and you and you. I thank you and may God bless every one of you."

(Exits to applause.[10] Dark.)

RUTH *(Walks to and sits at kitchen table. Lights up.)* The Inauguration was something else. Longest parade we'd ever had. I believe, the Governor invited the whole state and promised to kiss all the ladies. *(Shakes head.)* For those of us who live in Montgomery seems like they all showed up.

WINSTON *(Joins Ruth at kitchen table while reading newspaper.)* Newspaper said the Inaugural festivities were Jacksonian, to say the least. And the Inaugural Balls were something else.

JAMELLE *(In silhouette wearing full skirt and bobby socks jitterbugs across stage.[11])*

WINSTON & SOUTHERN MALE (as Newspaper Man) *read.*[12] "3,000 jammed Hanger 6 out at Maxwell. Big Jim's hillbilly band, the Strawberry Pickers, tried to organize square dances and the big dance bands played swing. Teenage girls in slacks and bobby socks danced next to socialites in long gowns and evening gloves. Big Jim tried to kiss all the young ladies most of whom arrived single."

RUTH I suppose, the young ladies were trying to snag the *(quote)* "bachelor" governor.

WINSTON & SOUTHERN MALE (as Newspaper Man) *reads.* "You could smell dime-store perfume on the bobby-soxers and the latest numbered fragrances out of Paris, France on the social ladies. The dances went on to the wee hours. It was a funny sight. All those single young ladies ended up doing the jitterbug with each other. Even had a one-legged man doing a jig all by himself. It was quite the show. Not to be out done, the Governor ended the evening in the wee hours, attempting the jitterbug, himself."

RUTH Still, most of us had to watch from the side lines or behind a serving tray. So, we got a new populist governor and, Winston, you got a new boss.

Big Jim and the Strawberry Pickers.
Courtesy of the Folsom Family

ACT ONE, Scene Three

At Rise:[13] *Upstairs dressing room morning light WINSTON fusses with two handsome, double breasted suits — one white linen, one blue serge — hung on valet caddies. Bottle of Early Times bourbon on nightstand. BIG JIM enters from tub bath with only a towel drying himself. WINSTON is not accustomed to BIG JIM's lack of modesty.*

BIG JIM Those are some fancy duds.

WINSTON Yes, sir, Governor. Gotta keep you dressed up for the Ladies.

BIG JIM Ladies will be the death of me.

WINSTON Yes, Sir.

BIG JIM Winston, you attached?

WINSTON Married Miss Ruth Biggs back in '40. We have a boy, Winston, Jr., age five.

BIG JIM Kids around here are about the same age.

WINSTON Yes Sir.

BIG JIM My sister giving you any trouble?

WINSTON No Sir, Miz Ruby runs things just fine and little Miss Cornelia is a charmer.

BIG JIM First time you have had to deal with a First Sister and a house full of little girls?

WINSTON Yes Sir, that's new but we get along just fine.

BIG JIM Especially after the cocktail hour. *(Pours a shot of Bourbon.)* Your wife religious?

WINSTON Yes, Sir. Ruth educated by the nuns up in Cincinnati. Says, woman needs three things, her Bible, her Jesus and her own money.

BIG JIM And, your money too. *(Laughs.)*

WINSTON Yes, sir, Governor. *(Pause.)* My Ruth got her teaching certificate, but can't find a teaching position here in the Montgomery schools.

BIG JIM That's gotta change.

WINSTON Ruth also trained to fix hair.

BIG JIM That's a good skill. Women like their hairdos.

WINSTON Sure do.

BIG JIM How about you?

WINSTON Sir?

BIG JIM Did the nuns teach you too?

WINSTON No, sir, I go to Dexter Baptist.

BIG JIM I'm a Baptist, too, when I go. *(Pause.)* I'll work on gettin' us a proper First Lady.

WINSTON Yes Sir, I learned, you been a widower for a few years now.

BIG JIM I'm lookin'. *(Winks.)* Sometimes the fishin' is more fun than the catchin' *(Beat. Checks out suits.)* Looks like my size. Where did these come from?

WINSTON Yes Sir, took the liberty of picking these out down at Fannins.

BIG JIM That pricey store, downtown?

WINSTON Yes Sir, they like to keep the measurements of our Governor.

BIG JIM Recon they do. *(Pours another shot of Bourbon.)* You want one?

WINSTON No Sir, I'm fine. I'm driving you later this morning.

BIG JIM *(Throws back shot.)* And, you gonna "Sir" me to death.

WINSTON Yes. Governor.

BIG JIM Now, Fannins' not handing out suits free of charge?

WINSTON No Sir, Governor, I have an account at Fannins and took them out on approval. If you like them, I'm sure they'll give a good discount.

BIG JIM A Governor discount? *(Puts on boxers.)* Everybody sure nice to me now that I'm Governor. But, I can't get too fancy for the dirt road crowd.

WINSTON Sorry. Governor, I can return them.

BIG JIM No. No. I was kidding … there'll be times we'll slip off to the big cities and I'll need to dress up … for the ladies.

WINSTON Sir, I did not mean …

BIG JIM Quit "Sir-ing" me.

WINSTON Yes … okay. *(Presents shirt, tie to BIG JIM.)* I believe *Life Magazine* wants to do a spread on our new Governor.[14]

BIG JIM So you think I should dress up for the slick magazine? *(Laughs)* They'll be looking for the hillbilly Governor. Fannins got any bib overalls?

WINSTON Sir?

BIG JIM Just pullin' your leg. I appreciate these outfits. You know, I lived in New York City for a while and because I'm so tall I got a job barking at Radio City Music Hall. They dressed me up in a tuxedo and we'd hawk 'em in off the street.

WINSTON Again Sir, Governor, I didn't mean.

BIG JIM It's all theatre. I need to look nice for the general public, if not for *Life Magazine* and the ladies.

WINSTON Again, I did not mean to be presumptuous.

BIG JIM Quit apologizin'. As my old basketball coach said, we put our britches on the same way, on leg at a time.

WINSTON Yes, Sir. *(Hands him his pants.)* I mean Governor.

BIG JIM Winston, look, in this room and in the car when we are by ourselves, you can say anything you want to me. I'm big enough to take it. *(Pats stomach.)* After getting elected, I don't need one more yes-man blowing smoke up my ass.

WINSTON Yes, Sir. Governor.

BIG JIM Winston, I'm not a whole lot older than you.

WINSTON Yes, Governor. It's gonna take some doing, to change my upbringing.

BIG JIM I figured, our upbringins not a whole lot different. We both had a little college, like to read and have sailed the seven seas.

WINSTON I was only in the Pacific. Took my submarine training up at the Great Lakes.

BIG JIM Another thing, the color of your skin does not matter to me. We're all black in the dark.

WINSTON Sir, I know my place.

BIG JIM You're missin' my point. When I was in the Merchant Marines, down in the ship's hole up to my ass and elbows in grease and grime, it didn't matter the color of a mate's skin.

WINSTON Yes …

BIG JIM I worked with all kind of folks down in the ship's belly. And, I suspect when the Japs were shootin' torpedoes and droppin' depth charges, didn't matter the color of your skin either.

WINSTON Sir, I'm not accustomed.

BIG JIM Accustom to what? Folks tellin' it like it is? You know, FDR integrated some facilities, like out at Maxwell.[15]

WINSTON Yes, Governor, I know.

BIG JIM The War is over and you served. *(Pause.)* I also know you spent some time up in Birmingham a few years back.

WINSTON I did. That's when Governor Dixon asked me to start driving for him down here.

BIG JIM In the Steel Mills, Coloreds and whites work side-by-side, doing the same job.

WINSTON Had a neighbor who worked at T.C.I.

BIG JIM Big Mules make an issue of race just to divide and conquer and keep the unions out. *(Pause.)* Did you ever hear of that Conference on Human Welfare?

WINSTON Was that when the Coloreds and whites got together back in the '30s?

BIG JIM So, you heard about it?

WINSTON You might say that. *(Pause.)* That's when Commissioner Connor got upset.

BIG JIM Heard Old Bull made 'em separate. Enforcing some local segregation ordinance.

WINSTON That's what he said.

BIG JIM But the meeting went on as planned.

WINSTON With Coloreds and whites sitting on opposite sides of that center aisle. *(Laughs.)* With Mrs. Roosevelt sitin' squarely in the middle of that center aisle.

BIG JIM She's stubborn as a mule and Bull knew not to mess with Eleanor. *(Laughs and shakes head.)* And, the Meetin' went on as planned?

WINSTON Yessir, you heard right. They came from all over the South. Senator Peppers from down in Florida. I believe Governor Graves set up that Human Meeting.

BIG JIM Did you know Bibb was Ku Kluxer back in the '20s?

WINSTON Heard something like that.

BIG JIM Back in the '20s, some of them boys joined the Klan like it was the Rotary Club.

WINSTON Rotary Club don't hang my people from trees!

BIG JIM Good!

WINSTON What?

BIG JIM No, no. Not good that the Klan hangs folks from trees. Good you're talkin' honest.

WINSTON You a different kind of Governor.

BIG JIM Let's hope so. We got to remember our history or we're doomed to repeat it.

WINSTON History rough on my people.

BIG JIM Took the New Deal and the War to get us out of the Depression.

WINSTON Not much been coming our way even after the War.

BIG JIM Believe it was Eleanor who persuaded Bibb to set up that meeting … after he denounced the Klan.

WINSTON Never did get to drive for Governor Graves. He died too soon.

BIG JIM He did die too soon. *(Pause.)* I hear you got some good ears, hearing stuff like you do, 'specially down at Dexter Avenue Baptist. So, when I need some advice, I'll just ask you, "What would Governor Bibb Graves do?"[16] We can speculate what Bibb would do.

WINSTON Yes, Sir. I mean Yes Governor.

BIG JIM Back in '44, I met a Colored porter on the train, when I was coming back from the Democratic Convention and we got to talking about things.

WINSTON Was that Brother Nixon?

BIG JIM You kin?

WINSTON No Sir. No, we not kin. I just know E.D. from church and such. He'll talk some politics.

BIG JIM He was talking about the Negro's right to vote … not that I need any more votes.

WINSTON Excuse me for saying so, but we have not had a Governor like you before.

BIG JIM Let's hope not. Now, how's things going on here around the Mansion?

WINSTON Everything is fine. But …

BIG JIM But, what?

WINSTON Well, it's not that important.

BIG JIM Come on. Try me.

WINSTON Well, Miss Rachel allowed as how she does not want me driving her to school in the state car.

BIG JIM Little too fancy for her?

WINSTON You know how school children are?

BIG JIM Thought I did. Maybe, I don't.

WINSTON My time can better be spent arranging your schedule first thing.

BIG JIM Just make sure Ruby gets 'em to school on time.

WINSTON Yes, Governor.

BIG JIM We got a lot of work ahead of us. *(Offers handshake.)*

WINSTON *(Beat. Stares at Governor's hand. Then joins handshake.)*

ACT ONE, Scene Four

At Rise: WINSTON and RUTH at kitchen table, with coffee and newspapers.

RUTH Sounds odd to me. "What would Governor Bibb Graves do?" I mean, how would you know? He's dead.

WINSTON I figure, the Governor is really asking me what a good Democrat would do.

RUTH Democrat? *(Beat.)* Like up North?

WINSTON Mentioned Mrs. Roosevelt some.

RUTH Winston go slow. I mean, telling him what you really think.

WINSTON I know. I know. But, when I give a proper answer, he pushes for more.

RUTH We can know too much. *(Pause.)* You know, Rosa and E.D. are just back from that meeting up in Tennessee. Said, they are talking about some real change.

WINSTON That's what the Governor says. Said New Deal got us out of the Depression.

RUTH Did you tell him, some of us are not out of it yet?

WINSTON I did. But you just told me to go slow.

RUTH So, he knew about that meetin' up in Tennessee?

WINSTON Yes.

RUTH And, he knows about that Committee out at Maxwell?

WINSTON He does.

RUTH Should I mention it to Rosa?

WINSTON She probably knows. But, why don't we *all* slow down.

RUTH So, the Governor rides up front when it's just you two?

WINSTON He likes the company, and, yes, I plan on telling him about the roads out here.

RUTH Won't matter much. *(Looks at newspaper.)* Legislature plans on blocking all his programs.

WINSTON Looks that way. *(Takes last sip of coffee.)* I gotta run. Love you. *(Kisses Ruth goodbye. Crosses to Limo.)*

RUTH Love you too. Drive safe.

(Dark on Ruth.)

WINSTON *(Opens Limo door.)* Morning Governor.

BIG JIM *(Enters, sits shotgun in Limo.)* Good day for some Legislating.

WINSTON You're not serious? *(In Limo, drives.)*

BIG JIM 'Course not. Knuckleheads don't like me or the turnip wagon I came in on.

WINSTON Was that turnip wagon pulled by a Big Mule?

BIG JIM Hell no … just a scrawny old gray donkey. That's what has 'em pissed off.

WINSTON But, *you* are the Governor.

BIG JIM Why don't *you* tell 'em that.

WINSTON If they are not listening to you, they won't be listening to me.

BIG JIM They not listenin' to nobody but their Bosses … the Big Mules.

WINSTON Gotta dance with those who bring you.

BIG JIM I'm dancing my ass off.

WINSTON I know. *(Beat.)* Some say they lookin' to run you with Truman next year.

BIG JIM Ticket could use some life … but we got our hands full down here. *(Car bounces.)* Where the hell are we going?

WINSTON Thought I take a short cut through my neighborhood.

BIG JIM This ain't no short cut, it's in the opposite directions from the Capitol.

WINSTON No time to stop by the Capitol, you got that talk up in Birmingham.

BIG JIM Still, you're drivin' in the opposite direction.

WINSTON Wanted you to see my neighborhood.

BIG JIM And, you wanted to jar my eye teeth, to loosen up my oratory skills?

WINSTON No, Sir. When you're paving roads, thought these here in Mobile Heights could be put on the list.

BIG JIM Okay, okay, just get us back on the main highway.

WINSTON We could use some help with the roads.

BIG JIM Okay, I'll do what I can … just remind me.

WINSTON Yes, Governor. *(Pause.)* Remind me again why we going up to Birmingham?

BIG JIM Though you knew?

WINSTON I sorta do, but we don't spell it out … I mean, list the "C.I.O." on your schedule.

BIG JIM It is vague and off-the-record? *(Pause.)* The Congress of Industrial Organizations is a progressive labor union. Big Mules call 'em Communist.

WINSTON That's what they call Northern Democrats.

BIG JIM "Communism" has become a dirty word after we gave Stalin half of Europe. *(Beat.)* This trip is off the record … like when I meet unannounced with the Coloreds. No need to give the Press too much to talk about.

WINSTON I'm catching on. *(Beat.)* You staying at the Tutwiler Hotel?

BIG JIM Yes, *we* are staying at the Tutwiler.

WINSTON I'm just as happy staying at the Dunbar. It's just a few blocks to the west and the Dunbar is in the Book.

BIG JIM You don't need no goddamn Green Book … you're traveling with the Governor.

WINSTON I know but …

BIG JIM No buts about it. You are on the Governor's staff and I might need some advice on short notice.

WINSTON Does Commissioner Connor know about these hotel arrangements?

BIG JIM Bull don't mess with me. And, Winston, you worry too much. *(Beat.)* Just the same, when we get to the hotel, pull down the alleyway and we'll go through the service entrance. The meetin' is confidential.

WINSTON We'll be hard to miss in this car.

BIG JIM Service entrance is a political tradition. *(Laughs.)* Entrance supposed to be "off-the-record" even after Bull got caught during his afternoon delight.

WINSTON Huh?

BIG JIM Yes. Old Bull and a lady of the evening. I should say a lady of the mid-afternoon decided to visit the Tutwiler via the service entrance. And, somehow Bull's political enemies got word and had a private investigator bust in his room and snap a photo while Bull was about to enjoy her lips on his. *(Laughs. Points.)* On his member.

WINSTON Are you sure the service entrance is safe?

BIG JIM We're not having sex, we're just meeting the CIO, which may be worse. *(Laughs.)* They tried to prosecute Bull on morals charges. And, you know what the Judge said after he heard the charges and reviewed the photographic evidence?

WINSTON No, I suppose I don't.

BIG JIM Judge said, it's her mouth, she can carry coal in it for all I care.

WINSTON *(Muffles laugh.)*

BIG JIM Now let me rest my eyes. *(Puts hat over eyes, to nap.)*

   (Dark. BIG JIM exits. WINSTON stands by car.)[17]

WINSTON After Birmingham, I drove the Governor all over Alabama and the South beyond. It's February 1948 and we're headed down to Wakulla Spring, Florida for the Southern Governors Conference and I suspect to integrate another hotel while the distinguish Governor of South Carolina proposes a resolution to perpetuate the Jim Crow South. *(Beat.)* Governor had a long night writing his speech, so he'd been napping since we left Montgomery. Then, we drove by this farm house *(points)* with a lady and her children out front, drawing up some well water. Governor was thirsty, so we stopped.

BIG JIM *(Enters refreshed and gets in Limo. They drive.)* Sure are some nice people back there and that water hit the spot. Nothing like cool well water after a long night of speech writin'. *(Beat.)* Winston, you know, we ought to do something for that nice community back there and them good folks … maybe pave a road or build a new school. Something nice.

WINSTON Governor, we've been in Florida for about forty miles now.

ACT ONE, Scene Five

At Rise: *WINSTON at limo reading newspaper. BIG JIM in dressing area in boxer shorts talking on phone.*

WINSTON Governor and the Legislature don't get along. Last election, a Self-Starting Segregation Amendment was on the ballot that would let the Legislature block any civil rights progress by calling itself into session on a whim and against the Governor's wishes.[18] Governor told the white folks the power grab by the Legislature would halt his road program but let us Coloreds know that the Legislature wanted to pass literacy tests and have us guessing how many jelly beans in Mason jar if we wanted to vote. That Segregation Amendment lost by 20 percentage points. Newspaper man said, *(Reads newspaper.)* "A javelin was thrust at Folsom, he caught it in his paws and snapped it in two." *(Pause.)* Governor began feeling his oats. He rejected the idea of running as Truman's Vice President in 1948, and started seriously running as a Favorite Son from Alabama. *(Exits to dressing area.)*

BIG JIM *(Talking to phone.)* I'll keep that in mind, Judge. Do take care and regards to your lovely bride. Good-bye, now. *(Hangs up and laughs.)* That's something else.

WINSTON *(Enters on last line.)* Sir?

BIG JIM That was the Probate Judge speaking for the Democratic Party.

WINSTON Which Democratic Party?

BIG JIM Judge is a Loyal. He was warning me about our worthy opposition.

WINSTON The Big Mules?

BIG JIM Big Mules … the Bolters … the old State's Righters? Call 'em what you will. *(Shakes head.)* Judge said, everybody knew I was bad to be Kissin' on the Ladies.

WINSTON Magazines have you dating a lady out in California.

BIG JIM Governor Warren's daughter Virginia. *(Winks.)* We just went dancin' and you are readin' too many magazines. *(Begins to dress.)*

WINSTON I got a lot of standing around time. *(Beat.)* This new yellow tie will look nice.

BIG JIM Ladies? Can't live with them and can't live without them. *(Pause, points to phone.)* Judge, on the phone just now said the Big Mules had gone out and rented them a woman of the evening. She's the prettiest thing they could find in New York City. And, dressed her up, looking like next year and smelling of Paris France.

WINSTON Must be quite the lady.

BIG JIM And, Judge said, that my political enemies had planted her on the streets of Montgomery and she'd be lookin' for Old Kissin' Jim. *(Beat.)* But, Judge seemed to be warning me.

WINSTON Warning?

BIG JIM Yes. And, you know what I told the Judge?

WINSTON No?

BIG JIM I said, Judge, sounds like that's quite a woman and the Big Mules went to a lot of trouble to find such a fine lady, dressing her up fancy and all, Judge says yes. And, have her smelling real good and sweet. So, I say to the Judge: They went to a lot of trouble just to set a trap for me? Judge says yes, that they did. And, I say Judge they went to all that trouble to set a trap for Old Big Jim. Well, Judge, I say, they gonna catch this Old Boy every time.

WINSTON *(Timid laugh. Beat.)* Governor, have you ever thought of taking up with Miss Jamelle?

BIG JIM Taking up with Miss Jamelle? *(Half-light on dressing area, as BIG JIM finishes dressing.)*

JAMELLE *(Lights up at Limo.)* I'm Jamelle Dorothy Moore, and I took a ride with Big Jim, when I was still in high school. Said he got the name "Kissin' Jim," because he kissed so many babies on that campaign trail, or that's what he told me. One night after one of his rallies, I did take a ride with Big Jim and we talked and talked to the wee hours. *(Smiles.)* Nothing romantic took place at all … not even a goodnight peck on the cheek. *(Laughs.)* Lot of talk went on inside that car, getting to know each other. And, I'm sure a lot of talk went on outside that car. *(Winks.)* I didn't even know the Governor was courting me, me being so young and him being a widow-man with two young daughters. Lordy, he was almost twice my age. *(Pause.)* After graduation from Berry High, I moved to Montgomery and got a job at the Highway Department. *(Exit.)*

BIG JIM Taking up with Jamelle? She does stand out in a crowd. Her parents' let her go to a party after one of my campaign rallies. The host was real nice and said Jamelle could have anything to drink that she wanted. *(Laughs.)* You know what she asked for?

WINSTON No?

BIG JIM Chocolate milk shake. *(Laughs.)* She asked for chocolate milk shake.

WINSTON I'm talking about settling down.

BIG JIM Her Mama even moved to Montgomery just to keep an eye on us.

WINSTON Governor, I've been picking her up at the Highway Department for a year or so now.

BIG JIM So what are you saying?

WINSTON Y'all should think about gettin' married.

BIG JIM Her parents have not warmed up to the idea.

WINSTON Governor, she doesn't need her parents approval, she's over 18.

BIG JIM Just barely.

WINSTON Well, marriage would help. *(Pulls out newspaper.)* The local paper reprinted that story from the *New York Daily News*. *(Glances at paper.)* Quoted from that paternity law suit, like it was Gospel.

BIG JIM Not sure I even knew that Putman Lady.

WINSTON Says here, she gave birth to your son.

BIG JIM I don't have a son. It is a smear campaign.

WINSTON So, she was just another lady of the evening walking the streets of Montgomery?

BIG JIM You think that'll work?

WINSTON Settling down would help a lot more than another one of your *stories*.

BIG JIM I know, I know. *(Pause.)* church folks frown on a bastard ... a love child?

WINSTON I would not blame it on church people.

BIG JIM Jamelle and I have talked about marriage. *(Beat. Deep breath.)*

WINSTON And?

BIG JIM Before we get too serious, I need to clean up that law suit. And, we got that trip to Washington and New York.

WINSTON So, let's get you packed.

ACT ONE, Scene Six

At Rise:[19] *BIG JIM in white suit, waving to "crowd" as flash bulbs pop. RUTH at kitchen table with coffee and newspaper. WINSTON off stage within earshot of RUTH.*

RUTH *(Reads, then shouts off stage)* Winston, who's gonna take care of that child? Says here the Governor got that law suit served on him and he jumps on an airplane and goes off to New York to take up with some more women.

WINSTON *(Enters.)* He already had the trip planned. Those modeling ladies up in New York named him 1948 Leap Year Bachelor.

RUTH How can he be a "bachelor" when he's a widower with two small daughters?

WINSTON Governor says he don't write the news, just wants his name spelled correctly. Besides, those young ladies at that Barbizon School are heavily chaperoned.

RUTH I don't know. He ought to be home tending to his mess instead of high-tailing it up to New York and risk making more mess. Says here ...

RUTH & SOUTHERN MALE (Newspaperman) *(Read.)* New York City. Barbizon School. Governor Folsom was met by 100 girls who he began kissing in rapid succession. A crowd of twenty five hundred gathered and backed up traffic for blocks. Folsom even tried to kiss on a woman reporter. The police asked the Governor to move his show inside, where he continued to kiss on the young ladies.

WINSTON Sounds like the newspaper don't appreciate the Governor's being "Leap Year Bachelor." Gotta run. *(He kisses Ruth, exits to Limo.)*

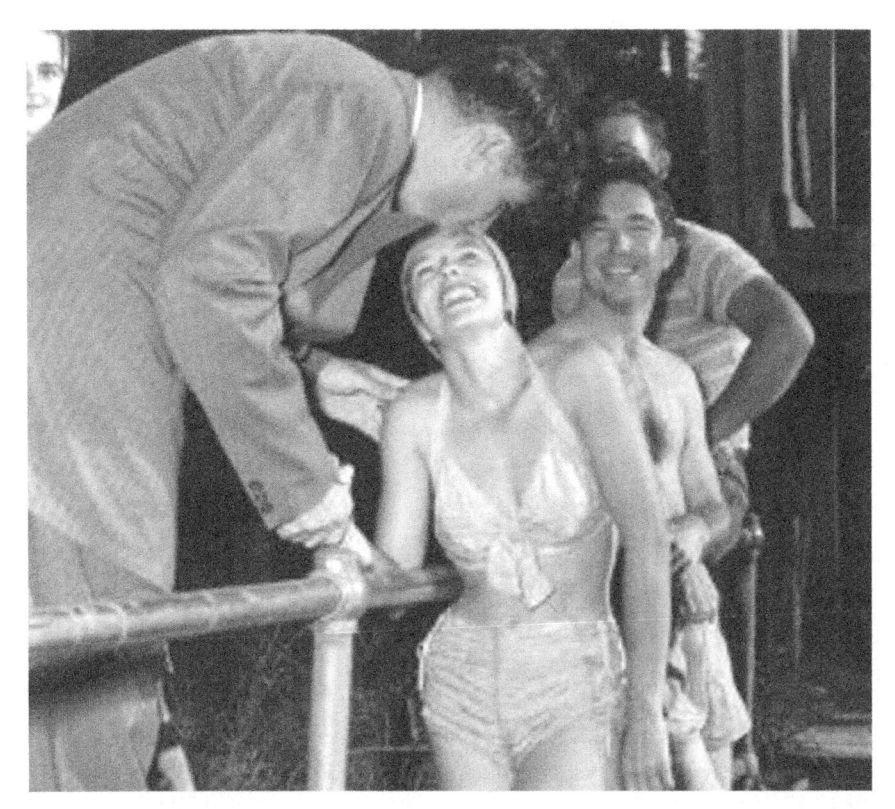

Kissin' Jim with unidentified bather.
Courtesy of the Folsom Family

BIG JIM *(Smiling and waving, as flashes go off. Then, lights down.)*

WINSTON *(At Limo with Newspaper.)* That spring, after the paternity suit made headlines, the Governor's favorite son candidacy for President *faded* …

WINSTON & SOUTHERN MALE (Newspaperman) *Faded,* then "melted like a snow flake falling in a river."

WINSTON But it got worse, in the primary that May the Governor, as a Loyal Democrat, did not even win a delegate position to the Democratic Convention in Philadelphia. Voters don't approve of a child out of wedlock.

BIG JIM *(In dressing area, undressing to boxers.)* It's good for a fellow to get a spanking once in a while. It helps him keep his feet on the ground.

WINSTON The day after the Governor lost being a Delegate to the Democratic Convention, he married Miss Jamelle Moore. It was a small private ceremony at the Rockford Baptist Church in Rockford, Alabama. *(Laughs.)*

The Church even had a rock façade. Anyway, the couple honeymooned at a borrowed cabin on Lake Martin. We were to keep their Honeymoon plans confidential, but ... *(Lights fade on Winston.)*

BIG JIM *(in boxers)* & **JAMELLE** *(in bridal negligee) (Lights up with couple in a pre-consummation embrace.)*

THUNDEROUS NOISE: ROCKS ON A TIN ROOF, BEATING POTS & PANS, SHOUTS, SINGING 'HERE COMES THE BRIDE' AND 'Y'all COME.'

JAMELLE *(Frightened.)* Jim, what's that?

BIG JIM I'll check. You stay here. *(Kisses Jamelle. Crosses to porch and looks offstage. Beat.)* What are you boys up to?

SOUTHERN MALE (Political Friend) *(Offstage)* Celebrating your wedding night.

BIG JIM Some celebration. *(Looks in direction of noise.)* My God, you all showed up.

JAMELLE Jim, Honey, whats going on?

BIG JIM Nothing Honey, just a wedding night serenade. I'll be back in a minute. *(Picks up bottle.)* Okay, just one round and you boys will be on your way. *(Exits.)*

JAMELLE *(In dressing area.)* That tin roof sounds real nice in a soft rain. Lordy, that racket nearly scared me to death. We were getting ready for our wedding night, when the racket started. Sounded like the Fourth of July and World War Two all at the same time. Jim's cabinet members said they were serenading us with those and pots and pans ... and rocks on that tin roof. *(Sighs.)* They are just a bunch of over grown boys. Believe he is pouring 'em a shot of whiskey, trying to get rid of them. I hope.

ACT ONE, Scene Seven

At Rise: **WINSTON** *at Limo waiting on Governor.*

WINSTON When word of the marriage got out, wedding gifts poured in by the truckloads. Big heavy tea sets and serving pieces. The staff at the mansion griped and griped about all the extra silver we had to polish. *(Beat.)* It's July 1948 and I'm waiting for Governor Folsom to return from the Democratic

Convention in Philadelphia that he attended as a faded favorite son, not as a delegate.

BIG JIM *(Enters in rumpled white suit with luggage.)* Hell of a trip. I've been to some goat ropins' and a few cow fuckins' and I ain't never seen nothin' like that.

WINSTON *(Helps with luggage. Then drives.)* I read it was quite the show.

BIG JIM Circular firing squad by the gang that can't shoot straight! *(Beat.)* Old Bull was frantic trying to get recognized after they passed Hubert Humphrey's Civil Rights Plank. *(Laughs. Pulls flask from pocket and takes a drink.)* They just ignored Bull and gaveled the Convention closed for the afternoon session.

WINSTON I read all about it.

BIG JIM When we reconvened after supper, the Chairman recognized your friend Handy Ellis.

WINSTON Not exactly my friend.

BIG JIM During roll call, Handy interrupted and led the revolt. Charge!

SOUTHERN MALE (Handy Ellis) Mister Chairman! Mister Chairman! "At this time, without fear but with disillusionment, we are carrying out our pledge to the people of Alabama. We bid you good bye."

WINSTON That was it? They just walked out.

BIG JIM Little over half our delegation walked ... just the Bolters ... excuse me they now call themselves "The States Rights Democratic Party!" *(Beat.)* Up north they call 'em "Dixiecrats."

WINSTON Dixiecrats?

BIG JIM Yes, Dixiecrats. The entire Mississippi delegation walked. Fools even refused to ride in the limousines provided by the convention. Paid for the taxis outta their own pockets.

WINSTON So, half the delegates stayed on as regular Democrats?

BIG JIM Just under half. Your friend George Wallace stayed.

WINSTON Not exactly my friend. I find him to be shifty and he likes to grandstand.

BIG JIM Winston, all us politicians like to grandstand. *(Clears throat, takes a swig; then emotes.)*

BIG JIM & SOUTHERN MALE (as Wallace) The Honorable George C.

Wallace of Alabama seconds the nomination of the Honorable Senator Russell of Georgia.

BIG JIM Even the southern loyalist tried to put some distance between themselves and Truman and that Civil Rights Platform.

WINSTON But Truman got the nomination.

BIG JIM Truman didn't need the South. *(Beat.)* Dixiecrats gonna hold a meeting up in Birmingham later this summer.

WINSTON Splitting up the party?

BIG JIM Believe the party has done split.

WINSTON Have the Dixiecrats forgotten about the Depression?

BIG JIM Oh, they belly-ache about the central government as they lap-up their New Deal handouts. *(Pause.)* Their memory is as short as their dicks.

WINSTON *(Laughs, politely.)* I would not know that.

BIG JIM All them fat fuckers, got little nubs down there. *(Laughs. Takes another drink.)* I'm gonna either sleep it off or continue to drink it off, probably both.

WINSTON We're almost to the house.

BIG JIM *(Confused, looks out window.)* This ain't the mansion?

WINSTON Want you to say hello to Ruth and maybe get you a cup of coffee.

BIG JIM Not gonna ruin a two dollar buzz with a nickel cup of coffee.

WINSTON Not gonna charge you for the coffee. *(Struggle slightly assisting BIG JIM from limo to the Craigs' kitchen table.)* You need to freshen up before I drive you to the mansion with your new bride waiting.

RUTH *(At kitchen table, looks up at commotion.)* What have we here? *(Stands.)* Afternoon Governor.

WINSTON Governor wanted to drop by and say hello.

BIG JIM I did?

RUTH Heard you been up in Philadelphia?

BIG JIM I have? *(Pause.)* Yes, I was. *(Pause.)* Not the City of Brotherly Love. *(Pause.)* Dixiecrats were in town.

RUTH Winston, I just made a fresh pot. *(Points.)* Heard Truman got the nomination.

BIG JIM He did? *(Pause, realizing where he is.)* Yes, Ruth Honey, he did.

RUTH Paper said our delegation walked out of the convention.

BIG JIM Half did? *(Pause.)* Just the Dixiecrats. God help 'em! God help us!

WINSTON *(Pours coffee for BIG JIM.)* Governor said there's a Civil Rights plank in the platform.

BIG JIM I did? *(Pause.)* Yes they ... we did. Good for us!

RUTH You think it'll do any good down here?

BIG JIM Your guess is as good as mine. *(Beat.)* Got a cock fight going on in the Party and the old white Rooster is in trouble. *(Sips with disdain some coffee. Pulls out flask and pours shot in coffee.)* Ruth, Honey, you know the difference 'tween a cannibal and a Democrat?

RUTH Governor, I guess, I don't.

BIG JIM Cannibal does not eat family members.

RUTH Hard to be a Democrat down here.

BIG JIM Thatta girl! *(Pause.)* What? *(Pause.)* You not still votin' for Abe Lincoln and his boy Herbert Hoover?

RUTH My vote is my business.

WINSTON Ruth? Please? *(Removes spiked coffee & takes Governor by arm.)* Governor, you need a nap.

BIG JIM I do not! *(Struggles with Winston, struggles to act sober and then to Ruth.)* Ruth Honey, we gotta start somewhere.

RUTH Start? My vote counts for nothing.

BIG JIM No. Not nothing. *(Confused.)* Yes, it does. We need you ... *(Struggles against Winston's guiding to nap.)*

RUTH Will Truman even be on the ballot down here?

BIG JIM What? *(Pause.)* Dixiecrats gonna fight us at every turn.

WINSTON Let's get you a nap. *(Struggles to off-stage.)* You, need to get that Convention out of your head. *(Off stage.)* Miz Jamelle can't see you like this. *(Long pause with noise while Winston settles Big Jim. Then Winston re-enters.)*

RUTH He's not gonna get sick on my good sheets, is he?

WINSTON No, he holds it down pretty good. *(Beat.)* Ruth, Honey, you need to go easy on the Governor.

RUTH He's not going to remember much. Besides it feels good to speak up for a change.

ACT ONE, Scene Eight

At Rise: *WINSTON at Limo with newspaper.*

WINSTON Later in the summer of 1948, the Dixiecrats held their convention in Birmingham, the pre-eminent city of the so-called "New South." Birmingham is growing so fast they call it the "Magic City" and only New Orleans boasts a larger population. *(Beat.)* My former boss Governor Dixon was the Keynote Speaker.

WHITE SOUTHERN MALE (Governor Dixon) *(At Dais.)* The South will not stand alone and right thinking people everywhere will rally to our cause. The States' Rights movement will prevent the establishment of a "Federal Gestapo" and will serve as a defense against those who would destroy our civilization and mongrelize our people.

WINSTON Odd, when you drive someone for years, you may not know his heart. *(Pause.)* Then the Dixiecrats nominated Strom Thurmond for President. *(Pause.)* Governor Folsom said he tried to hide-out, but during a lull in the proceedings, he welcomed the delegates to Birmingham and Alabama as his official duty.

BIG JIM *(At dais.)* As the Governor of this Great State, I welcome you to our Magic City and the New South. While I opposed Truman's nomination on several grounds, I stand for every man and woman's right to vote their convictions. Welcome to Birmingham.

WINSTON In the fall of 1948, Truman was not even on ballot in Alabama but he did not need Alabama to win a close race against the Republican Dewey. Dixiecrat Strom Thurman got less than three per cent of the popular vote and only 39 electoral votes. Dixiecrats got so angry, a Blackbelt Representative from Selma took after the poor whites too.

SOUTHERN MALE (Dallas County Representative.[20]) *(At dais.)* "The trend in Alabama at the present time is towards turning our government over to the masses, and in my opinion if we do not place restrictions and qualifications on a voter in this session of the legislature, we will have seen our last election in Alabama where the people who carry the burden of taxation would have any voice in our State government.

***

It is time for the thinking people of Alabama to rally together and get behind a movement that will protect the interest of the people who *made Alabama great*. This is our last chance if we turn the ballot box over to the uneducated masses of this State we can expect nothing but chaos in the future." *(Dark at dais.)*

BIG JIM *(In office decorated for Christmas with microphone on desk. Musing.)* Legislature starting to sound like Hitler, lettin' only their Master Race vote.

WINSTON *(Enters on BIG JIM's musing.)* Alabama's Jesse Owens put a dent in that Master Race stuff back in 1936 in front of Hitler, himself. *(Walks to desk area, and finishes decorating Christmas tree.)*

BIG JIM Dixiecrats always run their mouth before they stick their foot in it.

WINSTON It's their mouth, they can carry coal in it, for all I care.

BIG JIM Touché *(Laughs.)* You getting' riled up?

WINSTON Governor, you know we've been riled up. But, I'm not gonna burden you.

BIG JIM Burden me? You'd have to stand in line and wait your turn.

WINSTON I know. *(Beat.)* What are you working on?

BIG JIM Year end talk ... my Christmas Message on the radio for the good people of Alabama.

WINSTON '49 was a little better than '48.

BIG JIM Let's not fool ourselves. *(Looks at notepad.)* Pay raise for teachers, 1,408 miles of newly paved roads, higher old age pensions and record breaking state revenues. But, that's only a drop in the bucket, compared to what's needed.

WINSTON Not like you're getting a lot of help from the gentlemen on Goat Hill.

BIG JIM They still want me impeached.

WINSTON Will they ever give up?

BIG JIM I doubt it. *(Beat.)* I was able to sign that bill that made the Klan take off their masks.

WINSTON That was a step in the right direction. *(Laughs.)* But, we always knew who they were, because we could see their shoes.

BIG JIM *(Laughs.)* Kluxers not the brightest torches in the parade.

WINSTON I'll leave you to your Christmas Message.

BIG JIM I believe you'll like what I got to say. Make sure you and Ruth tune into the radio. And, tell Ruth I'm thinking about her and the children at this holy time.

WINSTON We'll be listening. And, Merry Christmas. *(Winston exits to kitchen table joining Ruth to listen to Message, in half light.)*

BIG JIM *(At desk with microphone.)*[21] "I am happy to have this opportunity to talk to the people of Alabama on Christmas Day. This is the greatest day, the most revered day, of our entire calendar.

"It is good at Christmas for us to turn our thoughts to the neglected because Christmas is a time to think of others and not of ourselves. It is a time for us to ask questions of our inner self.

"Our Negroes, who constitute 35 percent of our population in Alabama — are they getting 35 percent of the fair share of living? Are they getting adequate medical care to rid them of hookworms, rickets, and social diseases? Are they provided with sufficient professional training which will produce their own doctors, professors, lawyers, clergymen, scientists — men and women who can pave the way for better health, greater earning powers, and a higher standard of living for all of their people? Are the Negroes being given their share of democracy, the same opportunity of having a voice in the government under which they live? As long as the Negroes are held down by deprivation and the lack of opportunity the other poor people will be held down alongside them. There are others, too, who should share in our thoughts of the neglected — wounded veterans, the blind, the shut-ins, the crippled, and on and on. The job for us here in Alabama is a *positive* attitude toward our fellowman. Let's start talking fellowship and brotherly love and doing-unto-others, and let's do more than talk about it — let's start living it.

"We must all constantly strive to put our democracy to fuller service for our people in order that all may be more richly rewarded with the fullness of the earth.

"And now, this is your governor, wishing for each and every one of you a goodly share of Christmas spirit, a table filled with the fruits of the earth, and a heart filled with love of the little babe of Bethlehem."[22]

End of Act One

ACT TWO, Scene One

At Rise: *WINSTON at Limo, JAMELLE in hat, gloves with Bible near dais.*

WINSTON Last year, 1954, Governor Folsom ran for a second term, defeating all seven opponents in the Democratic Primary without a runoff. *(Laughs.)* Not many Republicans in Alabama, so the Democratic Primary elects the Governor. He loved campaigning. Governor would get on that flatbed truck with his Strawberry Pickers and they'd have a hoedown.[23] *(Spoofs hillbilly foot-stomping.)* His song "Y'all Come" invited everybody to come see him, with a special invitation to the northern industrialist to come to the New South.

JAMELLE *(Holding Bible as lights come up.)* Jim and I have been married, almost seven years, now. Since we left Montgomery last term, we've been blessed with Jack, Bama, and Thelma, we call her Scrappy. Governor is bad to say he keeps me barefooted and pregnant. I let him say what he wants to, and you good people of Alabama should thank me for settling him down. Today, I held the Bible *(lifts Bible)* while Jim was sworn in.

WINSTON Today, we could mingle in the crowd and listen to the Governor's inaugural address. But, as we waited for the Governor to proclaim our rights as American Citizens. He wasn't as clear as he had been during his first term. *(Beat.)* Nine days after the Primary last spring, the Supreme Court stirred up the Dixiecrats with that School Board case about Colored children going to school with white children. *(Exits to dressing area.)*

JAMELLE It's a glorious day in Alabama, but they got me busy changing outfits, with a Mansion full of children to tend to. Remember y'all are invited to the Mansion for tea this afternoon. And, tonight we got inaugural balls all over Montgomery. Y'all come! You hear! *(Lights fade.)*

BIG JIM *(In dressing area removing morning coat.)* Well what did you think?

WINSTON *(Brushing a "modern" suit & tux jacket.)* The weather held out, nicely.

BIG JIM It was a little chilly in that convertible.

WINSTON Longest parade inaugural history.

BIG JIM Did you see that float about Big Jim's road program?

WINSTON The jalopy stuck in the mud on one end —

BIG JIM Brand new car and sooth-pavement on the other end. *(Changing clothes.)* This new mansion is nice.

Big Jim in the inaugural parade.
Courtesy of the Folsom Family

WINSTON More spacious.

BIG JIM Your previous boss nearly choked on the $100,000 price tag, but he knew Ike's freeway would clip that old brownstone. *(Beat.)* How's Ruth and your family?

WINSTON Ruth's fine and we had another baby girl, Regina.

BIG JIM We both got us a house full of children.

WINSTON We 'bout to bust out of our little house.

BIG JIM When Jamelle was in the hospital with Scrappy, I got sick as a dog. Had to be hospitalized myself.

WINSTON Y'all okay now?

BIG JIM Guess so. *(Shakes head.)* Women got their hands full.

WINSTON I hear you. Ruth fixes hair and runs the house too.

BIG JIM You heard me when I said, "Women deserve full citizenship."

WINSTON Yes, Governor I did.

BIG JIM Remember when I appointed Judge Price?

WINSTON First lady judge on the State Appeals Court.

BIG JIM Well, she turned out to be my canary in the coal mine.

WINSTON Judge Price didn't die?

BIG JIM No. No. She won statewide last election. Let the Big Mules know Folsom-ites are here to stay. *(Pause.)* Time we put women on juries.

WINSTON Don't know when they'd find time to sit on juries.

BIG JIM They say that Ginger Rogers does everything Fred Astaire does …

WINSTON Only she does it backwards in high heel shoes. *(Polite laugh, but flat.)*

BIG JIM I like this new suit, more modern.

WINSTON Got it down at Fannin's.

BIG JIM That pricey store that likes to keep the Governor's measurements? *(Pats stomach.)* Did they allow for my new girth?

WINSTON You know they did.

BIG JIM Is something wrong?

WINSTON No, Governor.

BIG JIM You don't seem yourself with all the festivities coming up this evening.

WINSTON Sorry, Governor.

BIG JIM What is it? Did you like my speech?

WINSTON It was a *nice* speech Governor.

BIG JIM Nice? That's horseshit. Come clean. What would Governor Graves say?

WINSTON You sure you got time for me?

BIG JIM Goddamn it, Winston!

WINSTON He'd say, you left out a mention of the Negro's rights when you were reapportioning the Legislature and putting women on juries.

BIG JIM I called for all counties to have a Public Defender.

WINSTON We're not all criminals. And, when would Public Defenders get around to representing Coloreds?

BIG JIM Liberty and justice means —

WINSTON That sounds good, but we still got a lot of Jim Crow left on the law books.

BIG JIM I know. And, you know, I know it! Goddamn it!

WINSTON Sorry I brought it up.

BIG JIM No. No. You were supposed to bring it up. And I asked for *(Beat.)* That School Board case brought out the fanatics and the Kluxers. Had to say I would not force a Negro child to go to school with the white kids.

WINSTON You twisted the words up but some of us are not laughing. Out in Kansas, Little Linda Brown walks past the white school just a few blocks from her house on her way to her Colored school two miles away. Sometimes she doesn't make it because of the snow.

BIG JIM Even her lawyer. Little Linda Brown's lawyer?

WINSTON *(Irked.)* Attorney Thurgood Marshall.

BIG JIM Yes. Even Lawyer Marshall said the Court ought to start with older college students.

WINSTON He said college graduate students. *(Pause.)* Linda Brown is the same age as your girls …

BIG JIM Do Colored children really want to go to school with white children? They even talkin' about bussin' children way across town.

WINSTON Colored children tired of getting hand-me-down books and walking past better …

BIG JIM I'm gonna tear down all those shot-gun school houses and put in the best supplies.

WINSTON Yes, Governor, but …

BIG JIM Build sturdy structures every child will be proud of.

WINSTON Colored children will have to wait for their turn, which …

BIG JIM You know, I take care of your children.

WINSTON I meant all Colored children will have to wait on new facilities even if the Legislature lets you build them.

BIG JIM Legislators are arguing that if we implement that School Board case, Colored families will lose jobs by lettin' their children go to school with white children.

WINSTON The Court said that "separate but equal" was not the same as equal.

BIG JIM I've been preaching that the Supreme Court is the law of the land, but they screwed up putting school children ahead of lettin' everybody vote.

WINSTON I can vote, but not many of us can.

BIG JIM Democracy takes care of itself, if everybody can vote. Little children should not be used as a political football.

WINSTON Yes, but …

BIG JIM Politicians need time to figure things out.

WINSTON It's been a long time already.

BIG JIM Goddamnit Winston. *(Pause.)* Dixicrats already formed that Interim Committee to keep Alabama segregated.

WINSTON I know you can't just snap your finger.

BIG JIM Did I ever tell you about the time I was out 'coon huntin' with my cousins?

WINSTON Sir?

BIG JIM No. No. Raccoon huntin'. With a 'coon dog.

WINSTON 'Coon hunting also meant hunting for escaped slaves.

BIG JIM Goddamn it! I can't even open my mouth around here anymore …

WINSTON That size sixteen is too big to fit in your … (mouth) .

BIG JIM Speaking of mouths, I rue the day I asked for your smart lip. *(Smiles.)* Nobody I knew wanted to kill and eat a *rack-coon*. On the contrary, 'coon huntin' was just an excuse to go out in the woods, build a camp fire, drink some whiskey, shoot the shit while listenin' to the dogs run.

WINSTON That's good to know.

BIG JIM Quit messing on my story. Anyway, we'd build us a campfire, and put some sweet taters in the coals to cook while we passed the bottle and listened to the "rack-coon dogs" run, chasing rack-coons. One time my cousin got hungry and impatient and pulled one of them taters out of the fire early. It was hot as hell-fire and he juggled it like. *(Thinks.)* Well, he juggled it like a hot tater and when it burned his fingers he threw that tater up 'side the head our other cousin. He didn't mean to but that tater stuck to our cousin's ear. Got a scar to this day.

WINSTON Sound dangerous.

BIG JIM Yes, and handling hot sticky issues is like handling Hot Taters. Need me some deflecting time.

WINSTON Governor it's been too long …

BIG JIM Goddamn it, Winston, I can't do it all.

WINSTON Sorry, I brought it up.

BIG JIM No, I'm tired before we even get started. *(Pulls out wad of cash, counts out several big bill and hands to WINSTON.)*

WINSTON What's that for? *(Pause, hands money back.)* That's not necessary. My state salary is good.

BIG JIM *(Laughs.)* Here take it. I'm not trying to …. Here take it. *(Forces on WINSTON.)* It' not what you think.

WINSTON *(Stares at cash.)* Well, what is it?

BIG JIM Heard you been registering folks to vote. This'll help pay for some of our goddamn Poll Tax. *(Smiles.)* Let me know if any of them registrars give you trouble.

WINSTON Thank you. *(Pause.)* We good. *(Pockets cash. Looks at watch.)* Governor, they're waiting on you downstairs.

BIG JIM You ready for the festivities? *(Puts on jacket.)*

WINSTON We'll be at that "Separate but Equal Inaugural Ball" at Alabama State this evening.

(They Laugh.)

BIG JIM Good. I'll drop by late and dance a jig with all deliberate speed.

Act TWO, Scene Two

At Rise: *RUTH & WINSTON at kitchen table with newspaper spread out. JAMELLE in ball gown & BIG JIM in tux waltz across stage.*

RUTH New Alabama? *(Shakes head.)* At least we had our own dance. Governor looked a little tired when he dropped by and tried to dance.

WINSTON Said he had to make the rounds. Listen to what reporter Hall wrote up:

WINSTON & SOUTHERN MALE (as news reporter) *(Read from newspaper.)* "Folsom, winner in the one-lick primary victory, brought whale-tailed Cadillacs parked beside high-cabbed pickup trucks and banging tailgates;

Calico rubbing against mink; Overalls and tobacco juice seated with Brooks Brothers flannel and filter tips; Unified applause from card-carrying C.I.O. organizers and open shop operators'. Sin-hating fundamentalist cheek-by-jowl with liquor agents. But much more remarkable — and we believe unique in the line of Southern mob spellbinders --- is the appeal of Folsom to both the *(quote)* 'nigger hater' *(quote)* element and the Negro himself." [24]

RUTH Governor was not as clear as he was last time.

WINSTON That's what I told him.

RUTH You did?

WINSTON *(Irked stare.)*

RUTH Well, I'm proud of you.

WINSTON Don't be. Governor's got his hands full.

RUTH He seems to enjoying dancing ... especially around school integration.

WINSTON He lets me fuss at him, but then explains what he has to do out in public. Said he swept in a lot of his Legislators in the last election, but most of them still oppose integration.

RUTH Did you tell him some of us don't want to wait much longer?

WINSTON He knows. And he knows about those meetings out at Maxwell.

RUTH Should I let Rosa know?

WINSTON I'm sure E.D. has told her. Governor even asked about our new preacher.

RUTH I doubt you Baptist will lead the way. Up North the priest lead ...

WINSTON We are not up North.

RUTH You Baptist don't rock any boats. Besides, you said that new preacher of yours left Atlanta for some peace and quiet so he could finish his thesis or some such.

WINSTON Martin did say he appreciates our smaller church.

RUTH Martin? Y'all on first name basis, now?

WINSTON He's more down-to-earth than some preachers and he needs some time to finish his Ph.D. Gotta run. *(Kisses Ruth goodbye. Exits.)*

RUTH Love you and drive safe. *(Picks up phone.)*

ACT TWO, Scene Three

At Rise: *In patio chairs, Jamelle and Big Jim in swim suits overlook children splashing in pool. Pitcher of iced tea with glasses on table. Winston enters.*

JAMELLE Winston your children are so well behaved.

BIG JIM Wish we could say the same about our boys.

WINSTON Ruth really appreciates letting the children swim.

BIG JIM Children need to learn to swim. Right Winston, you're an old Navy man.

WINSTON Navy don't give you much of a choice. *(Beat.)* Ruth said to thank you.

JAMELLE How is Ruth?

WINSTON Just fine, Ma'am. She's waiting in the car. We're gonna take the children to buy some shoes for school.

BIG JIM Waitin' in the car? Go get her and bring her here for a glass of tea.

WINSTON She's not dressed.

BIG JIM Not dressed? *(Laughs.)* Bet she'd got on more clothes on than we do. Now go get her.

WINSTON I'll see what she says. *(Exits.)*

JAMELLE Jim, what on earth? If a woman is not presentable …

BIG JIM Presentable? We're half naked.

JAMELLE This is the Governor's Mansion and not everyone is comfortable. Besides …

BIG JIM Besides what?

JAMELLE I'm not presentable either. We need to present proper …

BIG JIM We're not royalty. Besides I got an announcement.

JAMELLE You don't understand. *(Pulls on beach robe.)* Not everybody thinks like you do.

WINSTON *(Enters followed by Ruth.)* Y'all remember Ruth.

JAMELLE	**BIG JIM**
Yes. Hello Ruth.	Of course. Sit down, Honey.

RUTH *(Does not sit.)* Governor, Mrs. Folsom, we appreciate you letting the children swim.

58 FLAWED GOOD PEOPLE

JAMELLE Ruth it was our pleasure. Happy to share our new swimming pool.

BIG JIM Shaped like the State of Alabama *(points)* and your tax dollars paid for it.

RUTH *(Looks at children playing.)* It's nice and it's so important that children learn to swim.

JAMELLE Growing up we girls didn't even go down to the river.

BIG JIM Nobody had a swim suit back then. Boys swam naked as a jay bird.

JAMELLE Jim?

RUTH I feel better knowing the children can swim.

BIG JIM Have a seat and pour yourself some tea.

WINSTON We really can't stay. *(Shouts.)* Children come on. Time to get dressed.

OFF STAGE CHILDREN VOICES *(Cacophony of overlapping responses over splashing water.)* Why? No! Can't we play? Watch. No you're it! Please. Watch!

BIG JIM *(Shouts.)* Five more minutes. I need to talk to your Mama and Daddy. *(To Ruth and Winston.)* Now have a sit.

RUTH Governor, you'll have their vote when they are old enough. *(Politely sits.)*

BIG JIM Now you're talking.

JAMELLE Governor spoils them and leaves me to raise 'em. *(Laughs.)* Then he goes off riding around with your husband.

BIG JIM Easy ladies. It's all state business. *(Points.)* Winston you too. Have a seat.

JAMELLE Tea?

RUTH	**WINSTON**
No, thank you.	No, Ma'am.

BIG JIM Ruth, what do you think of that School Board Case?

JAMELLE Jim? Please?

BIG JIM Jamelle? It's just a question.

JAMELLE Ruth, Honey, don't let him put you on the spot.

RUTH We want what's best for our children.

JAMELLE All parents do.

WINSTON Governor, Ruth may not feel as comfortable speaking up …

RUTH I feel comfortable saying what's on my mind, if the Governor asks.

BIG JIM Good. Women make more sense when it comes to their children. *(Pause.)* Ruth I understand you got your teaching certificate.

RUTH Yes, but I was not able to get a position in the school system here.

BIG JIM I know and that needs to change. *(Pause.)* Now, what was education like for you growing up?

RUTH I was educated Catholic in Cincinnati and education was the primary focus.

BIG JIM When the nuns weren't whacking your knuckles with a ruler. *(Laughs.)* Did you go to school with white children?

JAMELLE *Jim, please?*

> *(overlap.)*

RUTH *Sometimes.* But, it's not so much who you sit by in school.

BIG JIM I thought so.

JAMELLE Jim, not everybody is comfortable talking …

RUTH It's important that a child is told that she is getting the best and can be the best.

BIG JIM That's what I thought.

RUTH Children are like sponges, they soak up everything.

JAMELLE Jim, please?

BIG JIM What is it Jamelle?

JAMELLE Do we have to go there?

BIG JIM Yes, we need to go there. Ruth is an educator.

JAMELLE But?

BIG JIM No buts about it. Jamelle, remember when I watched the neighborhood boys playing in the street back home?

JAMELLE Jim?

BIG JIM Our house in Cullman is across the street from the elementary school.

JAMELLE I've heard this before. Now y'all excuse me, I need to change.

(Exits.)

BIG JIM Back home there's this pack of neighborhood boys. I call 'em the East Elementary Gang. After school they run off a lot of pent up energy on their bicycles and such. *(Laughs.)* They have pine cone battles using garbage can lids as shields. Then one day, I noticed they got organized by Joe Lewis.

RUTH Joe Lewis, the boxer?

BIG JIM His namesake, I suppose. This Joe Lewis is just a kid and his Mama works for the local judge … only Colored kid in town.

WINSTON *(To Ruth.)* Cullman is all white.

RUTH We know.

BIG JIM It's not all white. We got a Colored bootlegger, but that's another story.

RUTH We also heard about that sign.

SOUTHERN MALE (Klansman shouts and holds sign.) *"Nigger don't let the sun set on you here!"*[25]

BIG JIM We got rid of that sign.

WINSTON It's still in the Book.

BIG JIM One of the few Sundown Cities in the South.

WINSTON You're right, most Sundown Cities up North.

BIG JIM Back home, we got a Grand Cyclops of the Klan living just across town in the projects.

RUTH That's a switch.

BIG JIM *(Laughs.)* Ruth, Honey, you catching on.

RUTH Sure you want to hear from me?

BIG JIM Yes, I do. *(Pause.)* What I was getting at with Joe Lewis. *(Pause.)* The town ladies take turns tutoring Joe Lewis in the mornings, so he's finished around lunchtime. Since he's the only one being tutored no need for homeroom, recess, gym, or such.

RUTH Just the basics?

BIG JIM Yes. Well, with this extra time after lunch, Joe invents these clubs that the white boys try to join when they get out of school around three. He's got a bicycle club. *(Laughs.)* Leans a two by ten on a saw horse and gets the white boys to race their bikes up the ramp and out into thin air. *(Laughs.)* Some of our white boys not too smart and risk leaving their future manhood on them handle bars.

WINSTON Governor, we best be going. *(Shouts to pool.)* Children! Time to go!

BIG JIM *(Shouts to children in pool.)* Hold on kids. I'm not finished just yet. Few more minutes.

OFF STAGE CLILDREN VOICES *(Cacophony children responding over splashing water.)* Yipee. Thank you Mr. Governor. Yea. Your it. Watch! Yipee.

BIG JIM *(To Ruth.)* Joe Lewis also formed a weight lifting club and his Mama bought him a guitar. My point is, look at the kids. *(Points.)* They're just playing. It's natural.

WINSTON Governor we know.

BIG JIM Joe Lewis taught the white boys doo wop on that electric guitar.

RUTH Doo wop? *(Laughs.)* Governor are you not getting down on it? Are you?

BIG JIM You could hear that racket a block away. *(Shakes head.)* Education is where you find it.

RUTH I agree. But, a child also needs to feel special ... feel safe as they learn. Children absorb everything, including hurtful insults ... whether we adults think so or not. Society lets my children know they are less than. *(Quiet anger.)* And adults are supposed to be surprised when they don't grow to their full potential. So, yes, it was about time for that School Board Case!

WINSTON Ruth Honey?

BIG JIM Winston told me about little Linda Brown and how she'd walks past the white school on her way to the Colored school. We need better schools?

RUTH It's not just the buildings. *(Pause.)* Dignity is as important as arithmetic.

BIG JIM Y'all know I got a problem with what I can say in public and what I believe.

WINSTON Governor, we need to get going.

BIG JIM I preach that the Supreme Court is the law of the land. But ... *(Pause.)* I even told the teachers last spring that we needed more wisdom and tolerance. Unfortunately, we hear more noise from those who are blinded by prejudice and bigotry.[26]

RUTH Those are wonderful words, but did they listen?

BIG JIM Some of the teachers heard me, I suppose. But the ones who need to hear it, don't listen. *(Pause.)* You know Tuskegee Institute *(points)* just forty miles as the crow flies. Yes, it has produced and nurtured some of this State's most prominent educators and scientists, George Washington Carver, Booker T. Washington. *(Pause.)* I made sure Tuskegee was fully funded.

RUTH *(Facetiously.)* We thank you. But, that's just one institution.

BIG JIM I still need to get elected. *(Pause.)* Don't want to be a sacrificial lamb?

RUTH A sacrificial bull? *(Laughs.)*

BIG JIM *(Laughs with RUTH.)* Thatta girl.

WINSTON *(Uncomfortable.)* Ruth we need to be going.

BIG JIM Hold on Winston. You know how hard it is to come by the truth when you're Governor?

WINSTON Yes, but that shoe store won't stay open for y'all to solve the school situation.

BIG JIM I said, I had an announcement. And, I'm not much on the school situation. *(Stands, puts his arm around Winston and speaks to Ruth.)* But, I'm going to appoint our Mister Winston Craig to the Board of Trustees of Tuskegee Institute to carry on its grand tradition of education, science and agricultural progress. We'll have a proper announcement at the Capitol in a few days. *(Pause.)* Ruth, this knucklehead will need your help when it comes to educational progress.

ACT TWO, Scene Four

At Rise: *WINSTON at Limo with newspaper. JAMELLE in office. BIG JIM offstage within hearing of office. SOUTHERN MALE at dais.*

SOUTHERN MALE (Blackbelt State Senator.) "We don't want the Black Bastards to learn to read and write."[27]

WINSTON Civil Rights leader E.D. Nixon invited New York Congressman Adam Clayton Powell to Montgomery to help advocate for Negro rights. Governor said for me to meet the Congressman at the airport and bring him by the Mansion for cocktails.

JAMELLE *(Speaks to BIG JIM off stage.)* Jim, I'm not sure it's a good idea, entertaining a Colored Congressman.

Congressman Adam Clayton Powell and Reverend Martin Luther King, Jr.
Associated Press; restored by Adam Cuerden

BIG JIM *(Enters.)* Jamelle a member of Congress is always welcome here at the Mansion.

JAMELLE If word gets out. *(Pause.)* And, what will we serve?

BIG JIM Let the staff handle it. Remember you ordered a milk shake at your first cocktail party.

JAMELLE Camellia may not feel comfortable serving a … one of her own.

BIG JIM She might surprise you. Just have her put out some cheese and crackers. Winston will figure out what the Congressman likes to drink.

JAMELLE I'm still not sure this is a good idea.

BIG JIM They'll come and go before you know it.

JAMELLE I don't know, when you get to talking.

BIG JIM Jamelle, Honey, please?

JAMELLE Do you know how many will be in the Congressman's party?

BIG JIM A car full. Half of New York. How am I supposed to know? This place is big enough to handle it. Again, Jamelle, if a gentleman is a member of Congress, he is welcomed here at the Mansion, regardless of his suntan. *(Winks.)* It'll be okay.

JAMELLE *(Gives him a kiss.)* You big lug, I still don't know why Mama let me marry you. *(Exits.)*

WINSTON I met Congressman Powell and his entourage at the airport in the State car and took them by the Mansion for cocktails. *(Beat.)* Later, I drove the Congressman to his speaking engagement at Alabama State College and parked out in front of the gym for all to see. Congressman Powell delivered a powerful message on voter rights and publicly thanked me and the Governor for our hospitality. *(Exit to office/study.)*

BIG JIM *(To phone, looking out window.)* That's right Judge, he can post bail. *(Pause.)* Yes. Yes. *(Pause. Laughs.)* You know I don't drink Scotch whiskey on the front porch of the Mansion, I drink bourbon … cheap, rot-gut, corn whiskey on the back porch. *(Pause.)* That's right, take care. *(Pause.)* And, hello to your lovely bride. Bye, now. *(Hangs up.)*

WINSTON *(Enters.)* Afternoon, Governor.

BIG JIM Goddamn it, Winston, your brother Tom would fuck up a one car funeral.

WINSTON Sir? I usually do the driving.

BIG JIM What's going on out at Mobile Heights? Aren't you the Mayor out there?

WINSTON That's what they call me. Nothing official. It's mostly just a name.

BIG JIM Okay, Mayor, what's going on?

WINSTON Klan been driving through and some neighbors followed them. It's calmed down some.

BIG JIM Your brother was trying to get a neighbor[28] outta jail.

WINSTON Governor, I can explain.

BIG JIM Let's hope so. Between Congressman Powell and the Klan, y'all got me dancing a jig.

WINSTON Tom was down bailing out a neighbor.

BIG JIM Remember, I'm the one who sent in the unmarked car.

WINSTON I wasn't at liberty to tell the neighbors there was an unmarked car in the neighborhood. They were scared enough as it was.

BIG JIM The cross burnings?

WINSTON We got use to that. We'd put the fire out with a garden hose and when the wood dries we use it for kindling.

BIG JIM But what's this talk about illegal firearms?

WINSTON They're legal.

BIG JIM Sounded excessive to me.

WINSTON We can put out them crosses, but we can't stop bullets with garden hoses.

BIG JIM So, your neighbors organize as vigilantes.

WINSTON It's not all that organized. But …

BIG JIM But what?

WINSTON You should've fired me.

BIG JIM For what?

WINSTON For driving Congressman Powell.

BIG JIM You had permission. Hell, I recall asking you to meet him at the airport. *(Pause.)* Didn't I?

WINSTON Yes I know. But that's why the Klan started driving by my house.

BIG JIM So the Klan got pissed. What's new?

WINSTON Scared the daylights out of some of my neighbors.

BIG JIM I told you, I'd take care of it.

WINSTON No way to tell who was Klan and who was law enforcement in that unmarked car.

BIG JIM We all look alike?

   (They laugh.)

WINSTON We can joke up here in the mansion, but in my neighborhood …

BIG JIM The plainclothes officers said you neighbor had quite an arsenal.

WINSTON Just a couple of shotguns and a .45.

BIG JIM That's a lot of fire power. *(Laughs.)* Officers overheard Tom saying he was a property owner and wondered if the "birds" would let him post bail.

WINSTON He's sorry he called the officers "birds." He didn't mean *to* …

BIG JIM *To* be over heard.

WINSTON He's sorry.

BIG JIM If they'd call me a "bird" that would be a step up.

WINSTON Again …

BIG JIM We handled it.

WINSTON But, Sir …

BIG JIM Hold you horses. It's okay. Hopalong Cassidy been past this rock before. I send in the good cops and all of a sudden I don't know who to trust. *(Looks out window.)* Remember last summer when our kids played in the pool?

WINSTON Yes.

BIG JIM Back in the '40s when our ship stopped in Hawaii, I learned the Australian crawl from Duke Kahanamoku …

WINSTON What? Who?

BIG JIM Duke Ka-han-a-mo-ku, the Olympian swimmer from Hawaii. And, he wasn't exactly white.

WINSTON We appreciated your letting the kids come over to swim.

BIG JIM When the kids played last summer, if they had a spat, they'd work it out. Didn't worry too much about skin color.

WINSTON They are just kids.

BIG JIM Some adults seem to be the problem.

WINSTON Some adults?

BIG JIM Okay most adults, but we are spending too much time, money and energy on separate everything.

WINSTON You know how I feel.

BIG JIM But your friend Congressman Powell did us no favors.

WINSTON Do you need my resignation?

BIG JIM Hell No! But why the devil did he brag about coming by the Mansion?

WINSTON You know, you have my resignation, if it will help.

BIG JIM Bullshit! I do not want your resignation. But the Congressman was a little uppity, made it sound like he was royalty, drinking Scotch whiskey on the front porch.

WINSTON I'm sorry.

BIG JIM I'm just pissed at the whole situation. We got our hands full.

WINSTON Congressman was grateful … He was bragging on you.

BIG JIM I didn't need it.

WINSTON Do you have any idea what you did for the kids?

BIG JIM Kids? It was just the Congressman and his fancy entourage.

WINSTON More than that. I mean treating a visiting Colored Congressman with dignity. In his speech, he told the college kids he would not have been chauffeured in a New York State-owned limousine. Nor, would he have been invited to have a cocktail with the Governor of New York, in his very own state.

BIG JIM I enjoyed his company. *(Pause.)* But, he spouted off too much to the press and I suppose to anyone else who would listen.

WINSTON It wasn't just anybody. Governor, you extended to Congressman Powell all the courtesies due a visiting congressman. You should have seen those college kids listening. You could have heard a pin drop. Something changed in that moment. *(Pause.)* They'll register to vote when the time comes no matter how difficult it may be. *(Beat.)* When they walked outside after the assembly, they looked at me and the limousine, like someday, just someday, they'd get to ride in a state-owned car. Not as a chauffeur but as a dignitary. You have no idea what you did for those kids.

BIG JIM Not sure I needed that. But why did he have to say we drank Scotch whiskey.

WINSTON I believe that's what I poured him.

BIG JIM And I drink Early Death with my Hot Taters.

WINSTON Hot Taters? *(Beat.)* Recall Miz Jamelle put out some nice pimento cheese and crackers.

BIG JIM You two will be the death of me. *(Beat.)* Congressman Powell is a sharp dresser. Perhaps we should update our outfits to New York standards.

WINSTON I'll see what I can do.

ACT TWO, Scene Five

At Rise: *RUTH at kitchen table with WINSTON offstage, but within ear shot.*

RUTH *(On phone.)* Lord have mercy. *(Pause.)* I see. Did she call the Lawyer? *(Pause.)* Minding her own business? Do tell. *(Pause.)* Moved the sign on her? *(Pause.)* She did? I see. *(Pause.)* Will she go to jail? *(Pause.)* When will you know? *(Pause.)* Yes. Yes. I'll tell him. *(Pause.)* Let us know what happens. God Bless. *(Hangs up. Shots off stage.)* Winston, they done arrested Rosa!

WINSTON *(Enters.)* Not Rosa. Where?

RUTH On the bus when she was leaving work. One of the ladies she works with saw the whole thing.

WINSTON What? I thought …

RUTH She was riding home after work. Sitting in the Colored Section minding her own business, when the bus got crowded and the bus driver moved that sign on her.

WINSTON Moved the sign?

RUTH You been driving the Governor too long. You know that sign that says: Colored Section and we are supposed to sit in the back behind that sign.

WINSTON Everybody knows about the sign. Didn't recall they moved it around.

RUTH *(Laughs.)* You hadn't been on a bus since you started with Governor Dixion. Driving around in fancy cars. Lord Honey. When the bus gets crowded with Coloreds they move the sign up toward the driver to make more room for us. But when the whites crowd on like after work, they move that sign toward the back to make room for the whites. Sometimes Coloreds have to stand up 'cause the white folks got all the seats.

WINSTON Thought they quit moving that sign around after that teenage girl[29] got arrested last spring. *(Pause.)* So, that happened to Rosa?

RUTH This very afternoon. Rosa was sitting just behind the sign. The white section got crowded. So the driver gets up and puts the sign on the back of Rosa's seat and told her to move behind the sign so a white man could have her seat.

WINSTON She didn't move?

RUTH No she did not move. That's what they told me. Then, the bus driver called the police and they arrested her. Just like that.

WINSTON Did she resist?

RUTH She didn't want to be arrested. Told the police she was tired and politely refused to get up and move. Then they haul her off to the jail house, we think.

WINSTON I mean, did she put up a fight?

RUTH You know Rosa is not the type to put up a fight.

WINSTON I know she's not. Just hope she was polite to the police.

RUTH Imagine it's hard to be polite when you are getting hauled off to the jail house.

WINSTON I worry about resisting arrest.

RUTH She was Rosa. You know her.

WINSTON Haven't they been waiting on something like that? I mean, Rosa is the nicest of all your cousins and to catch her sitting there, minding her own business.

The arrest of Rosa Parks
Associated Press; restored by Adam Cuerden

RUTH You know, I don't go to those meetings.

WINSTON You might-as-well, with that grapevine of yours. *(Points to phone.)* Is she okay?

RUTH Okay? *(Incredulity.)* She's been arrested. *(Pause.)* Believe they gonna take her fingerprints and throw her in jail. We just hope she was able to call Lawyer Durr. But still they still want you to tell the Governor.

WINSTON Supposed to drop by the Mansion on my way downtown. *(Beat.)* Earlier today I picked up one of Miz Jamelle's boxes from the department store. Didn't see Rosa, she must have been in the back.

RUTH Wish somebody would box me up pretty outfits, with a hat and gloves to match, and have them delivered by such a handsome man. *(Smiles.)* Not even Christmas yet.

WINSTON It's almost Christmas, but it's more than that. You know the Governor won't let Miz Jamelle shop downtown with all the tension. Governor says she don't have time with a house full of babies but we all know it's the tension downtown.

RUTH Tension or no tension, must be nice getting them matching outfits hand delivered. You can tell the Governor, we got us a house full of babies too.

WINSTON He knows. You tell him every chance you get.

RUTH He asks. Oh, yes, before you go to the Mansion, E.D said to drop by.

(Lights fade on Craig kitchen and up on Governor's office.)

BIG JIM *(In office, watching Jamelle decorate Christmas tree.)* Looks like we're starting Christmas early this year.

WINSTON *(WINSTON enters with package.)* Miz Jamelle that's a nice tree. *(Hands box to Jamelle.)*

JAMELLE Winston, thank you for picking this up. *(Takes box.)* How's Ruth and your sweet children?

WINSTON They're fine.

JAMELLE Hope you are planning a big Christmas. *(Pause.)* Can't wait to open this. Thanks again. *(Exits.)*

BIG JIM Jamelle appreciates you picking up her outfits. Still fusses that she can't go downtown.

WINSTON That may be the last package for a while.

BIG JIM You know we can't let her go downtown with all …

WINSTON Tension is gonna get worse. They arrested Mrs. Rosa Parks ….

BIG JIM I know. But, there are other seamstresses at the department store?

WINSTON Yes. But …

BIG JIM But? But what?

WINSTON *(Stare at Governor.)*

BIG JIM Okay. Arresting her was a fool's errand. It was already tense downtown …

WINSTON It's more than Miz Jamelle not getting her outfits properly fitted and boxed up.

BIG JIM Rosa Parks is already out of jail.

WINSTON I know E.D. posted bail.

BIG JIM Heard Clifford and Virginia both showed up at the jail. Must have been a real hootenanny. *(Pause.)* They just booked Mrs. Parks and let her go home.

WINSTON Believe that young lawyer Gray gonna handle her case from now on.

BIG JIM But, Lawyer Gray can't prevent her from getting' fired.

WINSTON We know, but there is more. *(Hands BIG JIM a leaflet.)* The Women's Council is calling for a boycott.

BIG JIM *(Reads.)* It was a matter of time, but do they have any idea the consequences?

WINSTON E.D. Nixon is calling for a meeting.

BIG JIM I met E.D. a few years back.

WINSTON You mentioned that. And, he speaks highly of you.

BIG JIM Give him my regards. *(Pause, reads leaflet.)* Now, what's going on?

WINSTON Sunday all the preachers are taking to their pulpits and talking about that flyer.

BIG JIM Dexter Avenue Baptist?

WINSTON Yes, Reverend Martin seems a little slow to come around, but most of the other Preachers are on board. Mount Zion. Holt Street Baptist.

BIG JIM Is your Reverend Martin still working on his Ph.D?

WINSTON Believe so.

BIG JIM Did you tell him to read Gandhi?

WINSTON He's pretty well educated.

BIG JIM Whatever happens, we don't need any violence. Look at what they did to Emmet Till over in Mississippi.

WINSTON Emmet Till was not violent. He was just a kid.

BIG JIM Violence will cause the Klan to double down. And, cops may become part of the problem.

WINSTON We know.

BIG JIM Peaceful protest only. *(Pause.)* Did Martin read Gandhi?

WINSTON Martin thanked you and said for you to read Dante …

BIG JIM Dante? That goes back a ways …

WINSTON Said, "The hottest places in hell are reserved for those who during times of great moral crisis, maintain their neutrality."

BIG JIM Is he trying to out-smart me?

WINSTON No, Governor.

BIG JIM Sounds like he might win. Tell him I'm not all that neutral.

WINSTON We know. *(Pause.)* You know, Rosa was minding her own business.

BIG JIM Rosa? How well do you know her?

WINSTON Rosa is Ruth's cousin. We see her from time to time. Family gatherings.

BIG JIM Ruth's Cousin Rosa was an excellent choice. That teenager last spring …

WINSTON Miss Caludette Colvin.

BIG JIM What? Who?

WINSTON That teenager last spring had a name … young Miss Caludette Colvin.

BIG JIM Anyway, she was too young … too risky. *(Pause.)* I told the cops Rosa was an excellent seamstress. But Department store may still fire her.

WINSTON She knows the risk.

BIG JIM *(Looks at leaflet.)* When's that boycott supposed to start?

WINSTON They'll know by Monday if it works or not.

BIG JIM How you gonna keep the white folks from firing their maids?

WINSTON Gotta take some chances.

BIG JIM Walkin' in this cold weather?

WINSTON You always say, freedom is not free.

BIG JIM The ills of democracy are best cured by more democracy. Courts made a mistake in that Brown Case … starting with school children. Just little pawns in an Old White Man's game.

WINSTON Governor, you are a white man.

BIG JIM Not that old and got some Choctaw in me.

WINSTON I probably do too.

ACT TWO, Scene Six

At rise: *WINSTON at Limo waiting for BIG JIM. Southern Male near dais with rebel flag and sign "Forget Hell!"*

WINSTON Bus boycott going on for a couple months now. Just last week, they bombed the Kings' house. Threw the bomb right up on the porch with Coretta and the baby at home. Martin was out at a speaking engagement. So Coretta called me at the Mansion. She and the baby were scared to death, but not hurt. They saw a man leave in a light colored car, but nobody got the tag number. Thank God no one was hurt. *(Beat.)* Ready or not, Reverend Martin got right in the middle of the bus boycott. Lawyers say they made a mistake charging Rosa under Jim Crow instead of "refusal to obey" an officer or some-such. They fined her $10, but now they've got themselves a federal law suit challenging old Jim Crow.

SOUTHERN MALE *(Rioter with sign.)* Autherine Lucy, Autherine Lucy, you so big and black and juicy, that's why I want me some Autherine Lucy. *(Sensual hip thrust.)* Forget Hell!

WINSTON Governor says, when it rains, it pours. A few days ago, a Colored lady, Miss Autherine Lucy, sat in on some classes at the University over in Tuscaloosa. It went okay at first with her professor and classmates, but over the

Autherine Lucy with Attorneys Thurgood Marshall and Arthur Shores.
Alabama Department of Archives and History

weekend, there were riots. *(Reads paper.)* So Miss Lucy will withdraw from the University for her own safety. Governor also says when the going gets rough, the tough go fishin'.

BIG JIM *(Enters with fishing gear and empty cooler. Shrugs.)* Not bitin', too windy.

WINSTON *(Helps with gear, etc. They get in car.)* But, it was good to get away? And, stick your head ... I mean, toes in the sand.

BIG JIM Winston, go easy. *(Pulls out flask.)* Cold and windy. *(Inverts empty flask, laughs.)* Guess, I finished it off.

WINSTON Governor, there's a lot going on.

BIG JIM Tuscaloosa?

WINSTON Miss Lucy withdrew for her own safety or so they say.

BIG JIM Young bucks had to get it out of their system.

WINSTON What?

BIG JIM The "Forget, Hell" crowd came from off campus. They yelled and screamed and burned themselves out. But on Monday they all went back to their shit jobs.

WINSTON It's more that screaming and yellin'. Governor, you can't ignore violence in the street?

BIG JIM Watch me. *(Pause.)* You don't fight wars on too many fronts. Ask Hitler.

WINSTON Now, we're supposed to consult Hitler for advice?

BIG JIM Winston, don't push me.

WINSTON Sorry. But a lot coming at me too.

BIG JIM What?

WINSTON I'm getting it from both sides.

BIG JIM You seem upset?

WINSTON I do my share of jitney for the boycott, but my neighbors see me in this nice car and I still have my job at the Mansion.

BIG JIM You've earned it.

WINSTON Klan wants me fired, and I'm supposed to do more jitney driving for the neighbors.

BIG JIM Welcome to the one-man island. I should have stayed in Gulf Shores. *(Awkward pause.)* How are things at the Mansion?

WINSTON They're fine.

ACT TWO, Scene Seven

At Rise: *In dressing area, BIG JIM changing into formal wear.*

WINSTON *(Enters to assist.)* Photographer waiting downstairs.

BIG JIM Heard Jamelle is none too happy about this?

WINSTON Governor, I've never see her this up(set) …

JAMELLE *(Enters abruptly, angry, in inaugural ball gown, unzipped in back.)* … Jim I can't believe this.

BIG JIM It's *National Geographic*, Honey … they just want a few snap shots.

JAMELLE No notice! Winston, how can y'all schedule this on short notice? No, notice!

WINSTON Ma'am, I …

BIG JIM Winston had nothing to do with it.

JAMELLE I'm nursing Josh, and can't even zip up this damn dress. *(Turns back to BIG JIM.)*

BIG JIM Huh?

JAMELLE Help me with this.

BIG JIM I said it would be okay and forgot. Winston had nothing to do with it.

JAMELLE Forgot?

BIG JIM *(Fumbles unsuccessfully with zipper.)* You filled out since the inauguration.

JAMELLE Shut up! They're your babies too! I can't believe you.

BIG JIM That was the office doings. Forgetting to let you know. *(Fumbles with zipper.)* Winston can you help?

JAMELLE *(Turns back to WINSTON.)* Winston, I thought you ran the office?

WINSTON They don't tell me everything. *(Stares at Jamelle's back.)*

JAMELLE Okay, you've been spared. I'm only gonna kill the Governor. *(Points over shoulder to zipper.)* Can you help?

WINSTON *(Awkward.)* Yes, ma'am. *(Tries to zip dress.)*

BIG JIM You'll have to stand in line.

JAMELLE & WINSTON What? *(Both awkwardly reposition as if to form a line.)*

BIG JIM Not that. You'll have to stand in line to kill me.

JAMELLE Jim, I can't believe you. Winston, tell him …

WINSTON Governor's right. Lot of folks out to get him. *(Struggles with zipper.)* Zipper is a little stubborn.

BIG JIM Photographer is not gonna shoot your backside.

WINSTON *(Finishes zipping.)* There, Miz Jamelle, you'll be fine.

BIG JIM He can shoot up from the bottom of the staircase … up under that pretty chin. *(Runs finger under JAMELLE's chin.)* It'll be over before you know it.

JAMELLE *(Pushes him away.)* Let's hope so. Thank you, Winston. Jim we'll talk later.

BIG JIM Jamelle I love you.

JAMELLE Oh. You. I keep lettin' you off the hook. But not this time. *(Exits.)*

BIG JIM You're right, don't believe I've ever seen her this mad. *(Pause.)* I'll shoo the photographer off as soon as I can. We need to get back to the Capitol.

WINSTON Heard something about the bus case?

BIG JIM Frank held bus segregation to be unconstitutional.

WINSTON Judge Johnson is a good man … isn't he a Republican?

BIG JIM Rare as hen's teeth. Ike had to turn over a lot of rocks, but he found him a Republican up in Winston County. *(Pulls on Tux jacket.)* Now, let's get this show on the road. *(Exits to neutral space.)*

WINSTON *(Tidies up desk and checks some papers.)*

JAMELLE & BIG JIM *(In neutral elevated area to mimic National Geographic photo. Flash bulbs pop as BIG JIM extends a hand to JAMELLE in her inaugural gown.[30])*

Jamelle and Big Jim in Governors Mansion
Courtesy of the Folsom Family Collection

78 FLAWED GOOD PEOPLE

ACT TWO, Scene Eight

At rise: *RUTH at kitchen table with newspaper talking on phone. WINSTON at limo with newspaper. Klansman in hood. Big Jim in office. All in half light.*

RUTH *(Lights up. Speaks to phone.)* That's right. That's what the Governor told Winston and I'm reading it right here in the paper. *(Pause.)* You're asking too many questions. *(Pause.)* Yes. Yes. They gonna get rid of those signs all together. Not just move them back and forth. *(Pause.)* That's right. There won't be a "Colored Section." *(Sighs.)* Someday. *(Pause.)* That too. *(Pause.)* I got no business riding to town just to sit up in the front of the bus. Winston drives me where I need to go. *(Pause.)* Be careful on that bus and God bless. *(Hangs up. Lights fade on RUTH.)*

WINSTON The boycott ended last December and Martin, E.D. and Rosa ceremoniously rode a bus for the first time in the 381 days that the boycott lasted. It all came with a price well beyond worn-out shoe leather ... several churches and homes were bombed and snipers fired on the buses. It's September 1957 and Klan acting like sore losers.

SOUTHERN MALE *(Klansman)* Boy! Why they call you Judge. You ain't no judge. *(Holds up razor.)* You niggers have raped your last white woman. Pull the Judge's britches down. We gonna relieve this nigger of his desire for our white women. *(Goes through castration. Muffled scream.)* There. *(Holds up bloody testicles.)* Pour the turpentine where his manhood was. *(Laughs. Dark.)*

BIG JIM *(At desk, on phone.)*[31] So, he was a good Colored man? *(Pause.)* I see. I see. He didn't smart off to a white woman? *(Pause.)* How many did you interview? *(Pause.)* I see. No white woman was involved ...they just cut his nuts out? *(Pause.)* You still got your marching orders. *(Pause.)* Go back up to Birmingham, and tell them Kluxers they better find a goddamn rock to hide under ... we coming after 'em. *(Pause.)* Clear you schedule. *(Pause.)* I'll handle the Captain. *(Pause.)* Keep me posted. Bye. *(Hangs up.)*

WINSTON *(Enters.)* Afternoon, Governor.

BIG JIM Can you believe it? Klan cut the nuts outta of a Colored man up in Birmingham.

WINSTON What did he do?

BIG JIM Best we can tell, he was walkin' on the side of the road while Black.

WINSTON My God!

BIG JIM Klan boys left him on the roadside, to bleed out.

WINSTON Where?

BIG JIM Birmingham ... near Tarrant City. *(Pause.)* Labor Day, six Klansmen grabbed a man, who goes by the name of Judge Aaron. *(Pause.)* Turns out he was a fine citizen.

WINSTON Jesus!

BIG JIM They cut his nuts out ... castrated him, scrotum and all ... with a razor and poured turpentine in the wound. Found him on the side of the road. Turns out the turpentine probably save his life.

WINSTON That's hard to believe. But ...

BIG JIM I sent some investigators up there and the dumbass Kluxers are bragging about it.

WINSTON They got a confession?

BIG JIM Apparently, it's public knowledge. Kluxers figure they'll get off like they did over in Mississippi. *(Pause.)* Dumb asses.

WINSTON *(Disbelief.)* They'll get off ... just like Mississippi.

BIG JIM Not this time.

WINSTON Says who?

BIG JIM I do, Goddamn it! I'm the Governor! *(Beat.)* My investigators checked with folks in Union Springs ... where Judge Aaron was from. *(Pause.)* Wanted to see if he was uppity, and maybe brought it on hisself.

WINSTON Uppity? What if he was a little uppity? Still, to be castrated?

BIG JIM Turns out Judge Aaron was a fine citizen ...

WINSTON *(Anger.)* A white folks' nigger ...

BIG JIM Hold on, Winston. *(Pause.)* He did nothing to provoke ...

WINSTON Sorry, but what does it take to provoke a castration?

BIG JIM Winston, I'm on this. No, man deserves ...

WINSTON Governor, when is enough ... enough?

BIG JIM Enough is enough! But there's plenty of blame to go around. Nobody is signing on to my Bi-Racial Commission ... including your people.

WINSTON My people? White folks not signing up either.

BIG JIM Two wrongs do not make a right. George is out there stirring up fear and hate. Some folks are only happy when they are angry.

SOUTHERN WHITE MALE (George Wallace.) Your Governor Big Jim Folsom is soft on the nigger question.

WINSTON He's running for Governor next year. What's new?

BIG JIM George has turned on me big time. (Laughs.) Last election, we were campaigning down in Barbour County, George was kissin' my ass and kissin' the ass of some Judge. *(Beat.)* So, I make the mistake of getting' out on the wrong side of the car and shaking the hand of the first fella I met.

WINSTON That fella was a Colored Janitor according to the newspaper.

BIG JIM I suppose. But to hear George tell it, you'd thought it was Nat Turner hisself.

WINSTON Is that why the whites are not joining your Racial Commission?

BIG JIM Bi-racial Commission. And, yes, whites are shootin' themselves in the foot. *(Pause.)* Northern industrialist not coming down to hicks-ville.

WINSTON So it's just about attracting new industry?

BIG JIM Folks need a pay check before they can enjoy your precious civil rights.

WINSTON Sorry for wanting my *precious* civil rights.

BIG JIM Winston cut me some slack! *(Pause.)* Goddamn it! We spend too much time proving we are not as bad as Mississippi. And, that's a low fuckin' bar.

WINSTON Governor?

BIG JIM Y'all just like to boycott?

WINSTON Governor, c'mon?

BIG JIM And march. But nobody wants to sit down and work things out.

WINSTON I wouldn't say that.

BIG JIM What would you say?

WINSTON What would Governor Graves say?

BIG JIM Okay Winston, I'll risk it. What would Bibb say?

WINSTON He'd say, you deflecting too much on the school question.

BIG JIM Goddamn it, I can't do it all.

WINSTON Gotta start somewhere.

BIG JIM Little school children are not the problem. Adults are!

WINSTON Maybe so, but folks not gonna keep settling for half a loaf. When they took those signs off the bus seats … we hoped it was a beginning, not an end. We want our *precious* civil rights!

BIG JIM I know. I know. *(Pause.)* I'm just tired of being on this One Man Island.

(Phone rings.)

BIG JIM *(Answers phone.)* Yes. *(Pause.)* Um …Um …I see. *(Pause.)* Are they sure? *(Pause.)* Goddamn it. How do they know? *(Pause.)* Again, are you sure? *(Pause.)* Yes. Yes. Send 'em over. *(Cups phone, to Winston.)* Winston, we got a bomb threat.

WINSTON Bomb threat? Where?

BIG JIM Here at the Mansion. Go get Jamelle! *(Points.)*

WINSTON Yes, Governor. *(Exits.)*

BIG JIM *(To phone.)* You sure they know how to disarm a bomb? *(Pause.)* You're right. You're right. Not much choice. *(Pause.)* You're right. We'll hurry. *(Pause.)* You Hurry! *(Pause.)* No, don't call the Highway Patrol. Don't need a bunch of flashing lights and blocked off roads. *(Hangs up.)*

JAMELLE *(Enters Frantic.)* Jim! Oh, my God! Winston said …

BIG JIM Calm down, it's just a threat.

JAMELLE Just a threat? What do you mean? Just a threat! The Children?

BIG JIM They're sending over some bomb experts.

WINSTON They sure it's a bomb?

BIG JIM Pretty sure. I mean they're sure about the phone call, tipping 'em off. *(Beat. To WINSTON)* You seen any strange folks around here?

WINSTON Governor there strange folks all over this place.

BIG JIM *(To Winston)* Send the staff home for the day. Don't scare 'em. *(Pause.)* Tell 'em we're exterminatin' for termites.

WINSTON Yes, Governor. *(Exits.)*

JAMELLE Jim, what are we gonna do?

BIG JIM *(In deep thought.)*

JAMELLE Jim? *(Pause, shakes him.)* Jim, what are we gonna do?

BIG JIM Get the kids dressed up ... we're going to the Zoo.

JAMELLE What?

BIG JIM Bomb squad is coming over. And, we don't want any panic. Get 'em dressed up for the Zoo. Now, hurry.

Coutesy of the Folsom Family

ACT TWO, Scene Nine, Epilogue

At Rise: *WINSTON at Limo in casual attire. JAMELLE & BIG JIM on porch.*

WINSTON It's the dog days of August, 1963, and I'm again visiting the Governor and Miz Jamelle at their summer house on Lake Guntersville. Hot as Hades. *(Fans self with newspaper.)* At least there is a breeze off the Lake. *(Pause.)* The very next day after Governor Wallace stood in the school house door at the University of Alabama last June, Meager Evers was shot dead in his driveway over in Mississippi. *(Beat.)* Lord, we've been through a lot. The bomb threat at the Mansion turned out to be a prank call, thank God. Authorities never did find out who bombed Coretta and Martin's house. *(Beat.)* Governor is still hurt that he lost his run for a third term and George Wallace was elected Governor. *(Pause.)* Anyway, I like to visit with Governor Folsom and Miz Jamelle, just as friends.

JAMELLE *(On porch with pitcher of iced tea.)* Jim Honey, wake up. I believe I heard Winston drive up.

BIG JIM *(Stirs from dozing.)* Winston, oh yes.

WINSTON *(Enters.)* Afternoon, Miz Jamelle. Governor.

JAMELLE Winston, you're a sight for sore eyes. Give me a hug.

WINSTON *(Awkward hug avoiding tea pitcher.)* Miz Jamelle you are lovely as ever.

JAMELLE You say that to all the ladies.

BIG JIM You lookin' none the worse for the wear.

WINSTON Good to see you too, Governor.

JAMELLE Winston, how's Ruth?

WINSTON She's good. Still operating her beauty shop out of the front room.

JAMELLE We love our hair dos. How's your children?

WINSTON Winston, Jr. thinks he's a grown man. Rita and Regina getting excited about the new school term.

JAMELLE Winston, you have not changed a bit. Handsome as ever. *(Places tea on table.)* Now, I'll leave you boys to catch up. Pass on my regards to Ruth and your sweet children. *(Exits.)*

BIG JIM *(Slowly stands and gestures to chair.)* Make yourself at home. *(Awkwardly picks up pitcher of tea.)* Glass of tea?

WINSTON Let me get that. *(Reaches for pitcher.)*

BIG JIM You're my guest. Now sit. *(Awkwardly sloshes tea toward glass.)* How's things?

WINSTON Gas station business is good. *(Pause, stares at tea pouring.)* Let me get that. *(Takes pitcher, pours glass, and tops Governor's glass.)* Family healthy. You?

BIG JIM 'Bout the same around here.

WINSTON How's the children?

BIG JIM They're all over the place. I can't keep track.

WINSTON Children grow up fast.

BIG JIM Jim, Jr. took up the guitar.

WINSTON The guitar?

BIG JIM Don't ask him to play that Puff Dragon song.

WINSTON Doubt he's gonna hang out with us old folks.

BIG JIM Only song he knows.

WINSTON He's just learning?

BIG JIM Drive you crazy.

WINSTON *(Beat.)* Look at that boat coming in the cove … yonder. *(Points.)*

BIG JIM That's Melissa water skiing …

WINSTON She's real good and on just one ski.

BIG JIM Practicing to get a job skiing down at Cypress Gardens with Ruby's girl Cornelia.

WINSTON I remember Miss Cornelia. *(Pause.)* Water skiing, huh?

BIG JIM Yep. Nowadays girls get paid to water ski. Go figure? *(Beat.)* How are thing down in Montgomery with your new Governor?

WINSTON It's a mess. You know 'bout as much as I do. Governor Wallace is using his new Pardon and Parole Board like never before.

BIG JIM Like never before? I doubt that.

WINSTON It's more than just the pay-offs. They're gonna undo just about everything you accomplished. Word is that when the Board meets in October their first order of business will be to pardon the Klansmen who castrated Judge Aaron.

BIG JIM They elected a racist. What did they … we expect?

WINSTON One step forward, two steps backwards as somebody once said. *(Reaches for T.V.)* Mind if I turn this on?

BIG JIM Suit yourself.

WINSTON They're televising Martin's March on Washington.

BIG JIM Heard that was today.

WINSTON March for jobs and freedom.

BIG JIM Good thing he's in Washington and not Montgomery. Up North is where the jobs are. *(Looks.)* That's a helluva crowd.

WINSTON Yes, it is.

BIG JIM Guess, Martin gave up on Alabama after Bull turned loose his goddamn dogs and them fire hoses. *(Shakes head in disbelief.)* Water blast coming out them hoses enough to scoot little children across the sidewalks.

Dr. King at the Mall, Washington D.C.
U.S. Marines Public Affairs Office

WINSTON Say, those fire hoses can take bark off trees. *(Points to T.V.)* They're calling it a Movement now … more than just Alabama. Listen.

Voice of Dr. Martin Luther King, Jr. via T.V. "I still have a dream, a dream deeply rooted in the American dream – one day this nation will rise up and live up to its creed. 'We hold these truths to be self-evident: that all men are created equal.' I have a dream."

BIG JIM We should've done more.

WINSTON Times were tough on you. *(Points to T.V.)* Listen! Martin's gonna preach to that crowd.

Voice of Dr. Martin Luther King, Jr. via T.V. "I have a dream that my four little children will one day live in a nation where they will not be judged by the color of their skin, but by the content of their character, I have a dream today."

BIG JIM It's all about the children. As it should be. *(Beat.)* See that boathouse down there? Early one spring the kids wanted to get the ski boat out. Why I don't know. It was cold and windy, but they were kids. Rather than argue with 'em, I fumbled with that old rusty hoist and finally got the boat in the water.

Then with one foot on the boat and one foot on the dock, I got distracted as the boat floated out ... *(Lost in thought.)*

WINSTON Governor, the boat floated out from the dock?

BIG JIM *(Snaps out. Laughs.)* When it floated out from the dock, I was straddle-legged. Splash! Coldest friggin' dip, I ever took. *(Pause.)* Yeah, a moderate segregationist is like being a little bit pregnant? *(Pause.)* One foot on the boat and one foot on the dock. *(Lost in thought.)*

WINSTON Governor?

BIG JIM Goddamnit, Winston, time caught up with me.

WINSTON What are you talking about?

BIG JIM Drunk on T.V. Losing the election. You name it.

WINSTON You did not know what was in that whiskey.

BIG JIM I knew it was whiskey! Goddamn it! *(Beat.)* Problem is, I no longer gave a shit. I'd been off the booze the whole campaign. Then the election turned on me. Hell, everybody turned on me.

WINSTON Not everybody?

BIG JIM Wallace had his white citizens booing my name like I was a stray dog. I'd meet a shift change at the steel mill and white union men would not shake my hand ... just drop their eyes and walk away.

WINSTON Got hateful toward the end. But, that was nothing new for us.

BIG JIM Winston, a politician is a lot like a snake oil salesman. On the back of that flatbed bed truck we ride on with our sales-pitch and a big smile. *(Beat.)* When the crowd stops smiling back ... that's a tornado ripping your heart out.

WINSTON You didn't lose everybody.

BIG JIM Only a handful ...

WINSTON We voted for you.

BIG JIM I appreciate the loyalty but only you and a handful can vote.

WINSTON *(Beat.)* Believe Martin's dreaming about voting rights too. *(Points to T.V.)*

BIG JIM You told him to resist violence at all cost?

WINSTON Believe he knows that. And ...

BIG JIM And?

WINSTON And, he knows the Movement is more than just riding a bus around downtown Montgomery.[32]

Voice of Dr. Martin Luther King, Jr. via T.V. "I have a dream that one day in Alabama with the vicious racist, with its governor having his lips dripping with the words of interposition and nullification, one day right there in Alabama little Black boys and little Black girls will be able to join hands with little white boys and little white girls as sisters and brothers. I have a dream today."

~ END OF PLAY[33] ~

TNT presents a F.A.S.T. production of

WEDGES

a new play by Hubert Grissom

starring
Donna Thornton • Steve Stella
Ruth Speake • John Batson

Directed by Carl Stewart

May 3-26, Thursdays, Fridays and Saturdays
8:00 pm, $9.00

Terrific New Theatre
101 21st Street South, 328-0868

Wedges

Produced May 3 - 26, 1990 Terrific New Theatre, Birmingham, Alabama, and directed by Carl Stewart, designed by Steve Stella and stage managed by Cari Gisler Oliver. The cast:

Sadie Belle Graham - Donna Thornton
Smith (narrator) - Steve Stella
Governor - John Batson
Governor's Wife - Ruth Speake

SETTING

Act One - Shotgun house on the banks of Village Creek, Birmingham, Alabama.

Act Two - Parlor, Governor's house, a town in North Alabama.

TIME

Three days in August in late 1970s. (Act Two, Scene Two – A year later.)

CHARACTERS

SMITH - The narrator, lawyer is in his late thirties with a little gray at the temples. He wants to do good but gives the impression he'd rather be somewhere else.

SADIE - An aged African American female who uses a walker. She was the Governor's former cook and is getting old and making things right.

GOVERNOR - Seventy plus, white, tall and stately, but awkwardly dressed. He is recently blind and has dressed himself. Played with a sense of history, more precisely his place in history.

WIFE - Early fifties, white and a former beauty queen with fashionable daytime attire. Her stark beauty and friendliness give the impression that she has some flirt in her. (Southern charm, not clichéd flirt.)

ACT ONE (one continuous scene)

AT RISE: *Just past noon on Saturday in the dog days of August. Smith enters with a briefcase, and on daybed, Sadie sits, humming Sweet Hour of Prayer.*

SMITH *(On stoop, wiping brow.)* August in Birmingham… it ought not take place. You can even smell it. The pavement is melting and Village Creek could cough up rotten eggs and no one would ever know. *(Wipes brow.)* I'm Smith Wakefield and this is my volunteer Saturday at the Legal Aid Office. I know it doesn't look much like an office. I can't figure why it always happens to me. I volunteer for some greater good and I get stuck making house calls in this section of town when I should be at the lake with Alyce water skiing or making love. *(Knocks, looks and waits.)* Alyce and I have only been married since Christmas. *(Pushes hair.)* No, it's just my first marriage … and she is more than half my age but not my much … I did deb parties for ten or fifteen years and then decided to settle down. You see, my volunteer Saturday ends at noon and it was almost noon and I was headed out of the door when the phone rings. Well, I just can't walk out when the phone is ringing. Oh, there were two other volunteers and I should have kept on going. But, not me. *(Shakes head.)* No, I

WEDGES 91

told myself that it might be Alyce wanting some fresh limes for the gin and tonic or maybe the ski rope finally broke. Then the receptionist at Legal Aid hems and haws to the caller about it having to be a legal problem and how the woman will have to come by the office. Apparently, the woman gets a little excited and this excites the receptionists. *(Shrugs shoulders.)* My coming out here was like giving Don Quixote a new set of windmills. I don't know why I even bother to volunteer; I'm not very good at it. *(Knocks.)* And, this is the elderly woman, who telephoned at the last minute and we're not even sure she has a problem, but she can't get around too good. Even if she has a problem, what am I supposed to do on Saturday afternoon?

SADIE *(Clumps to door.)* Yes?

SMITH *(Adjusts tie.)* Well, here goes.

SADIE *(Opens door.)* Yes, sir?

SMITH I'm Smith Wakefield from the Legal Aid Office. You called?

SADIE Why, yes, come in here Lawyer Smith. I'm Sadie Belle Graham. Do come in out of the heat. *(Turns in walker.)* Make sure you close the door behind you. *(Looks at broken fan.)* Breeze box don't work, but at least we're out of the sun.

SMITH *(Runs finger under collar.)* What seems to be your problem?

SADIE Do have a seat we'll get to that. *(She gestures to chair.)* Would you care for some tea?

SMITH Yes ma'am that would be fine.

SADIE Could I take you coat?

SMITH How would you manage?

SADIE I manage just fine. Your coat?

SMITH No, I'm fine. Just some tea, that would be nice.

SADIE Good, folks don't know how to live in this heat. Why take them A-rabs[34] they don't run around half naked. No, they cover their-selves up. Folks open up the windows and doors looking for a breeze. And, I tell you, during these dog days they can forget about any breeze. What breeze you get smell like the Creek. *(Points to window.)* All you get if you open the windows and doors be the hot sun, the flies and the mosquitoes and the criminal element. *(She turns toward the hot plate.)* It'll be a minute. The water is about to boil.

SMITH Could you put some ice in my tea?

SADIE Place didn't come with no Frigidaire. Anyway, not too good drinking real cold things in this heat. *(She slides to the hot plate and fiddles with the tea.)*

SMITH *(Mops brow and feels the uncertainty of the chair.)*[35] Mrs. Graham, what's your legal problem?

SADIE Lawyer Smith could you come help with the tea? *(As he walks to the hot plate, she lifts a square of sugar from the Burger King.)* Sugar?

SMITH No, thank you. *(Helps with the tea as she makes way to daybed.)* Now what's the problem?

SADIE *(Smiling with a teatime presence.)* Lawyer Smith, how many children do you have?

SMITH I don't have any.

SADIE Oh.

SMITH Just been married since Christmas. *(He straightens in wobbly chair.)* Now what's the problem?

SADIE Well, don't wait too late. Women nowadays waits too late to have their babies. And, that down drome gets to my babies. They done quit taking my starch that I gets down below Bessemer. And, when me and the doctor tells them to take to their bed you'd think we's trying to punish a spoiled child. *(Sips her tea.)* Yessir Lawyer Smith you mustn't wait too late. No babies yet?

SMITH My wife is just twenty-six. *(Uncomfortable.)* And, we're trying

SADIE Good.

SMITH I mean I married late but you don't have to worry about my wife.

SADIE What's her name?

SMITH Alyce with a "y". I mean what's my wife got to do with your legal problem?

SADIE That's a pretty name. It would sure look pretty on announcements and such. You all still announce special events, don't you?

SMITH Well, yes, I suppose we do. But, Mrs. Graham ...

SADIE I never did have me any babies of my own flesh, but I figured I had me close to fourteen all told. *(Smiles.)* Yessir, Lawyer Smith, I had me the Governor's babies. Two by his first wife and four or five by his second wife. He even kept on having babies after he lost that election and I had to get me a one-way to New

Jersey. *(Serious.)* Had to get me one of them one-ways outta the want ads and take that bus up to Newark when the Governor lost that race.

SMITH Mrs. Graham …

SADIE *(Smiles.)* The Governor, he was something else. Every morning the Governor would wake up at dawn and come down to the kitchen wearing just his shorts and them air conditioning boxes running at the window and killing us all. Anyway, when he got down to the kitchen I'd have his coffee ready in that mug what had his name on it. *(She lifts hand to indicate how big the mug was.)* I'd fix him a half dozen eggs sunny side up. And, my angel biscuits and fry a rasher of bacon. Good, thick bacon… not that puny supermarket bacon. *(Smiles as if to smell the bacon.)* Waiting on his breakfast, he'd stand with his foot propped up on the kitchen counter like it was a foot stool. Yessir, the Governor was a tall man, six foot, eight inches and his shoes when he wore them, was a sixteen. Soon as he hit that door them shoes come off. And, he was a smart man, standing there in front of them air conditioning boxes near naked and calling his cabinet members and wakin' um up telling them that that bonded whiskey was turnin' um sorry. *(Smiles.)* While he ate his breakfast, he'd tell me 'bout the plans he had for the poor people and when he'd get a little tipsy at night he tell me it didn't matter whether you was white or Colored or part Choctaw Indian, poor folks was poor folks just the same. *(Pulls a square of tissue from her robe sleeve.)* The Governor was part Choctaw Indian … that's what made him so tall.

SMITH Mrs. Graham, why do you need a lawyer?

SADIE Governor called his whiskey, Early Death, but it looks like he might out live them all. Not the age, it's the mileage.

SMITH Mrs. Graham …

SADIE I has me a bunch more children up in Summit, New Jersey. *(Picks up pace.)* My real love is the Mister Marriam Family. Boy and two girls. They from Valdosta originally, but now he puts together insurance companies all over the world. Lawdy. It scared me to death when he told me that sometimes insurance companies go broke and have to be put back together, 'cause I be counting heavy on that policy Jeb was to leave me. Worked for Mister Marriam on Tuesdays and Thursdays, even after the arthritis got my knees. I'd make pancakes using a half dozen of them fresh eggs. Mister Merriam would say, "Sadie Belle, why, you can sit right there on that kitchen stool and mix up them pancakes the rest of our life." Worked some on the weekends before I came back south. Mister Merriam like having me around. His wife be always out working on a charity and I'd keep track of my childrens. Don't know why folks go out working on a charity when they don't take care of things at home.

SMITH I know the feeling.

SADIE I bet your wife is a pretty thing.

SMITH Well, yes, she is.

SADIE Healthy?

SMITH Mrs. Graham could we get to the reason you called?

SADIE Called?

SMITH The Legal Aid Office … you're supposed to have a problem.

SADIE *(Rocks forward and stands.)* Please, call me Sadie Belle.

SMITH *(Polite exasperation.)* Okay, Sadie Belle do you have a problem? Otherwise, I've got to go take care of things at home, as you put it.

SADIE *(Clumps to cans.)* Yes, me and the Governor ahead of our times. We's worried about the environment long before it became the thing to do. You let the industry suck the elements out of the earth and who you thinks gonna put the elements back?

SMITH Alcoa?

SADIE No siree, God and another million years.

SMITH You may have a point there.

SADIE I don't know about you, but I don't figure me and my childrens have got another million years. But, I'm turning the corner.

SMITH The corner?

SADIE I figure when you get all this mess straightened out, me and God will be on real good terms.

SMITH You may be asking too much.

SADIE While we talk, would you mind stomping a few cans? Had me a neighborhood boy, but he wanted in on the profits. You know how to turn them up on their top and flatten them all in one stomp. It's not at all pleasant. *(She clumps to chifforobe.)*

SMITH Things seldom are in my business. *(Starts stomping cans.)*

SADIE You should have been a doctor.

SMITH *(To audience.)* I know a baby doctor.

SADIE Some counties down south of here don't even have a baby doctor.

SMITH I'm not a doctor. I'm a lawyer. Why am I here?

SADIE I don't think of you as a lawyer.

SMITH Thanks, I think. Could we get to your problem? After all it's Saturday afternoon and my wife's biological clock is ticking.

SADIE Lawyer Smith, why do you come down here to the Creek to help us?

SMITH It's not healthy, I know.

SADIE Health? Sure ain't, but what's health got to do with it?

SMITH Being an aberrant caretaker, people pleaser

SADIE Now you ain't sounding so good.

SMITH Just thinking out loud.

SADIE Sounds like tongues to me.

SMITH Tongues?

SADIE You know crazy stuff ... but it's better to get that stuff out than to lets it stay pens up inside. That stuff inside you is what kills you. Wedge you from around here to New Jersey.

SMITH No, it's strange you asking me just now, why I come down here? You know, I haven't asked myself that question in years.

SADIE Figure. You don't take time for nothing. Don't even take time to come outta of your coat. *(Pause.)* Now, that's good for you, but you don't know it. People all the time doing the right thing for the wrong reasons. But I guess, I shouldn't oughtta complain.

SMITH *(Mumbles.)* Right thing for the wrong reasons?

SADIE You okay?

SMITH You know, I almost forgot. It's been a long time since I thought of why I do what I do.

SADIE Lord, Honeychild, when I'm thinking for myself, I'm in enemy territory.

SMITH No, you dug up a root.

SADIE Family roots don't grow on trees. Speaking of which, you ought to be home with that bride of yours.

SMITH *(Off guard.)* That's private

SADIE Didn't mean to pry, but we needs our future generations. And, I can't help it if procreation and animal lust looks alike.

SMITH I guess, it's no accident that I happened by here.

SADIE Nothin' ever happens in God's world by accident … but we sure got a lot of folks makes it look like a heap of accidents all the time…

SMITH No. No. It's funny.

SADIE Ain't so funny to me.

SMITH I don't mean ha ha funny … funny like in coincidence …

SADIE Coincidence is God's way of keeping quiet. *(Quickens pace.)* Lawyer Smith could I trouble you for some help? *(Opens door to chifforobe.)*

SMITH Sure. *(Stands to help with grocery bag.)*

SADIE *(Positions herself on daybed. Pulls a roll of letters from bag.)* My Jeb passed in July and I got on the bus to come down here and tend to his affairs. He'd promised me that insurance policy. Now, we never got married like we always planned to, but Mister Merriam says we common law husband and wife. Is that right, Lawyer Smith?

SMITH Depends on the facts. Did you live together as man and wife?

SADIE Well, yes, we did ever four years, steady, when the Governor was out of office and I'd move back to Birmingham. Every four years. And, I's already pretty old when I took that one-way to Newark.

SMITH Mrs. Graham …

SADIE Off and on, I'd say about twenty years.

SMITH Mrs. Graham…

SADIE Sadie.

SMITH Okay, Sadie, I don't know.

SADIE Whadda you mean you don't know? You the lawyer.

SMITH I know I'm the lawyer, but …

SADIE You sure?

SMITH Yes, I'm sure.

SADIE Good.

SMITH But, I'm not so sure of the law.

SADIE I's afraid of that.

SMITH How long did you say you lived together?

SADIE Off and on about twenty years ... when the Governor was out of office. *(Fumbles with letters.)*

SMITH That's what I don't know. I mean, I don't know if it's long enough. It may have to be continuous.

SADIE *(Opens piece of paper.)* It's long enough. You ought to try to live with Jeb. Honey, every day is forever.

SMITH Continuous. That's important, to make sure you were not living with somebody else.

SADIE I told you I's living in the Mansion with the Governor.

SMITH Mrs. Graham ... I mean Sadie.

SADIE The Governor was married part of his first term and all of his second term in office. *(Smiles.)* Oh, he was always talking about night time integration. You don't think me and the Governor getting' it on?

SMITH Oh, no. Of course not.

SADIE He's jes laughing about those Blackbelt boys and how they was trying to keep the Negros from votin'. Governor said they voted pine trees and tombstones but was afraid of my people. Governor, would always say they Colored folks outside of Selma didn't get them blue eyes by lookin' at the sky. That's what he was referring to when he be talking 'bout nighttime integration.

SMITH I see.

SADIE That was different times and the Governor was way ahead of the times.

SMITH *(Impatient.)* That is all very interesting...

SADIE Don't you know it. *(Lifts papers.)* Look what I found. I helped him write it. *(Squints at papers.)* Yeah, me and the Governor got a lots done over breakfast. Did I tell you about my biscuits ... I put a little yeast in them to push the buttermilk and soda along. Drinkin' man sure likes the taste of yeast of a morning. *(Squints at the papers again.)* This was the Governor's nineteen forty-nine Christmas message. Governor always said he couldn't think of nothing worse than slavery. Said that's why he was for one man, one vote, the right of the Colored man to vote and puttin' women on juries. Called him the Kissin' Governor… he sure knew where his votes were coming from and for that matter the Governor knew where his kisses coming from too. *(Smiles.)* Look here. *(Holds up papers.)* Read this… it was nineteen forty-nine over thirty years ago. *(Hands the papers to Smith.)* Now, read that.

SMITH *(Reads to himself and it takes Sadie a few beats to notice.)*

SADIE No, no. Read it out loud. I helped him write it, right there in the Mansion while he took on his breakfast.

SMITH Mrs. Graham, I know I started all this, but we don't have time.

SADIE Time is all we got … and the right to vote and the right to sit on juries … and that speech is more precious than the air we breathe… specially this stinkin' air down here by the Creek.

SMITH *(Stares at papers.)* Mrs. Graham, it's a couple of pages … could we?

SADIE I can't read it for myself no more, Baby, the milk done got my eyes.

SMITH Milk?

SADIE Clouds up, real bad. You gonna get old one day, Sugar. I's already old and I sure would appreciate it if you would read me a bit of my speech.

SMITH *(Thumbs pages.)* How much?

SADIE All of it. *(Looks at him.)* You wouldn't say just half of the Lord's Prayer? Now, would you?

SMITH Well, no, ma'am.

SADIE Well, go on.

SMITH *(Clears throat.)* I am happy to have this opportunity to talk to the people of Alabama on Christmas Day.

SADIE Skip down to what's marked.

SMITH Okay. Okay. *(Glances down and straightens in chair.)* It is great to live in America, with all of its plenty and bounty… yet it behooves us not to forget…

SADIE Skip on over to where it says, "Our Negroes…"

SMITH *(Looks down page and turns to next page.)* Our Negroes who constitute thirty-five percent of our population in Alabama…

SADIE That's right Governor. *(Starts circling room in walker as if in the presence of Governor.)*

SMITH *(Looks up, then continues.)* Are they getting thirty-five percent of the fair share of living?

SADIE *(Excited.)* No way.

SMITH Are they getting adequate medical care to rid them of hookworms, rickets and social diseases?

SADIE Are you kidding … no way … Governor raised barefoot and poor and he's always worried about them social diseases … for poor folks, of course. *(Looks at Smith.)* Now go on.

SMITH Are they provided with sufficient professional training which will produce their own doctors, professors, lawyers, clergymen, scientist…

SADIE Still not.

SMITH Men and women who can pave the way for better health, greater earning …

SADIE Still not.

SMITH Men and women who can pave the way for better health, greater earning powers and a higher standard of living for all of their people.

SADIE Who you kidding, Brother?

SMITH *(Distracted by Sadie's participation, but anxious to finish.)* Are the Negroes being given their share of democracy?

SADIE *(Sternly.)* You still kidding.

SMITH The same opportunity of having a voice in the government under which they live?

SADIE No way.

SMITH As long as the Negroes are held down by deprivation and lack of opportunity…

SADIE Right on.

SMITH The other poor people will be held down alongside them.

SADIE That's right. That's right.

SMITH Let's start talking fellowship and brotherly love …

SADIE A-men. Brother.

SMITH *(Reluctantly gets in swing of things.)* And doing unto others...

SADIE As they do unto you ... Golden Rule ... Governor left the whole thing out, figured folks knew about ... always said folks smarter than you give 'em credit. That's right ... read on Brother.

SMITH And let's do more than talking about it, let's start living it.

SADIE I hear you.

SMITH In the past few years ...

SADIE He talking about forty-nine.

SMITH I know. *(Continues to read.)* In the past few years, there has been too much negative living.

SADIE Don't you know it.

SMITH Too much stirring up old hatreds...

SADIE A-men.

SMITH And prejudices ...

SADIE That's right.

SMITH And false alarms.

SADIE All the time.

SMITH The best way in the world to break this down is to lend our ears to the teachings of Christianity ...

SADIE A-men.

SMITH *(Admires words.)* And the ways of democracy.

SADIE A-men Brother. *(Smiles.)* We did us a pretty good job for back then.

SMITH I'd say you did for back then. Sorta unbelievable.

SADIE What don't you believe?

SMITH I mean, I believe it all. It was unbelievable for nineteen forty-nine. I was only eight years old. I thought the world was crazy until nineteen sixty.

SADIE It was. What's that got to do with it?

SMITH It all started when I went to college ... it was 1960. *(Points.)* Right up on the hill, not far from here. We were stuffing phone booths and hiding beer cans from the Methodist preachers ... Wham-o! The world changed right before my eyes. It didn't happen far off somewhere and I read about it ... no, all I had to do was to walk to the edge of campus and look across the street. And, there were rednecks, the Klan with Confederate flags protesting the integration of Graymont School. Hate for the sake of hate.

SADIE I think I hear what you're trying to tell me.

SMITH No, I don't think you do. I mean, I'm not talking about race relations as much as I'm talking about ignorance ... ignorance and the human condition.

SADIE Honeychild, lets me tell you we didn't have much of a human condition.

SMITH I'm not talking just about you and your people. I mean, you don't have to be Black to call Legal Aid.

SADIE But, let's face it, most of us down here are Black. And, when you look close like, we's shades of brown anyways.

SMITH Well, I got angry about the human condition whatever color it was.

SADIE Might do you some good to stomp a few 'luminum cans, it's good to get that stuff outta your system.

SMITH The world had to change, but why did it have to change while I was in college? I felt robbed.

SADIE You kids watching too much television back then anyways. If you gonna be aggravated; at least the good Lord done aggravated you in my direction.

SMITH Live and learn.

SADIE Speaking of learning, I never did learn if me and Jeb was common law husband and wife.

SMITH I said, I didn't know.

SADIE Figures.

SMITH Is there anything else in your shopping bag? *(Points.)*

SADIE It's full. *(She laughs.)*

SMITH I was afraid of that. *(Laughs.)*

SADIE Anyway, Jeb always said I had me a ten thousand dollar insurance policy. He worked at T.C. and I. and he was pretty good to me, but he never did give me a dime. And, I figured if I had to work, I might-as-well get me a good job, like with the Governor. But, my Jeb always said that that insurance policy be right here waiting on me. *(Crosses to chifforobe and notices Smith watching her.)* What you looking at? You not suppose to be looking where I keeps my stuff. *(Fumbles with stuff and returns to daybed.)* I should have known him being so crazy with his money and all. Lawyer Smith do you have any sisters?

SMITH No, I was an only child.

SADIE That's not too good. But, I reckon it's good you didn't have any sisters.

SMITH I didn't have a lot to do with it.

SADIE When I gets down here to Birmingham, Jeb is already buried, but he's not cool in his grave, and his no-count sister just laughs at me. He's done took my name off that policy and put hers on it and that insurance company said it was gonna pay her the money. I wrote Mr. Merriam about what the man said and he don't reckon we can do much about it. *(She hands him a letter.)*

SMITH *(Reads letter.)* The letter appears to be correct. And, a change of beneficiary is always permissible unless under duress.

SADIE Well, she duress him all right, the way she took him into her place after he took on the black lung. Even the black lung folks down at the government building says I'm not his wife.

SMITH *(Looks back at the letter.)* Have you spent the three hundred dollars Mr. Merriam sent you?

SADIE It run out last week. Why, this place ain't fit to live in and it's forty-five dollars a week. *(She blots a tear.)*

SMITH Do you need money to bet back to Newark?

SADIE Reckon that be all that's left for me to do. *(She bends over to bag and picks up a tobacco pouch.)* Can you give me a hand?

SMITH Sure. *(He reaches for the pouch. Struggles to untie strings.)*

SADIE Last time I got 'em out to look at 'em, my foolishness pulled a knot in the string. My fingers not too good anymore. *(Pulls Bible out. Gives Smith the Bible and takes the pouch.)* When I gets shed of 'em, God gonna give me life in the hereafter. Is that what it says?

SMITH I don't know.

SADIE Open it up to Romans, Chapter Six ... it's talking about the law and you the lawyer.

SMITH I'm not that kind of lawyer.

SADIE What kind of lawyer is you? *(Struggles to untie pouch.)*

SMITH Bond lawyer. You know, municipal bonds, industrial bonds and junk bonds … that sorta of thing.

SADIE Governor use to say God didn't make no junk. But, my heart has been a mess ever since I come across these things. *(Points.)* Romans, Six, Fo-teen.

SMITH Huh?

SADIE In the Bible there, Romans, Six, Fo-teen.

SMITH *(Thumbs Bible and reads.)* You're right the law does die when we do. *(Reads.)* "For sin shall not have dominion over you: for ye are not under the law, but under grace."

SADIE Now, Six, Twenty.

SMITH *(Reads.)* "For when ye were the servants of sin, ye were free from righteousness."

SADIE Now finish out the Chapter.

SMITH "For the wages of sin is…"

SADIE Wedges.

SMITH *(Looks up, gives up.)* The wedges of sin is death; but the gift of God is eternal life through …"

SADIE Do you think I got a chance? *(Finishes untying strings on pouch.)*

SMITH At what? Righteousness?

SADIE Well, no, I's more interested in sanctification and eternal life.

SMITH *(Holds Bible open.)* Mrs. Graham, I can't help you with that.

SADIE (Slowly spreads diamonds on Bible.) First time I've seen them in in a while. I be so foolish pulling that knot too tight.

SMITH *(Awe struck.)* Are these real?

SADIE Of course, got me a Bride's book down at Sears and Roebuck. *(From the bag she lifts a book, Owning Your First Diamond.)* When, I walk through Sears and Roebuck, I stop at the diamond counter and I reckon that they worth about fifty thousand dollars by now.

SMITH *(In a trance.)* At least.

104 FLAWED GOOD PEOPLE

SADIE But, I can't live with 'em no longer.

SMITH Are these the problem? *(Points at diamonds.)*

SADIE Holy Book says "the wedges of sin be death." Them things made me a slave of sin and now I got to go face Him. I needs to be a slave of righteousness and gets me some sanctification. Got to get shed of them things.

SMITH Is that where I come in?

SADIE The law only got a hold on me while I living, the Holy Book says. *(She points to Bible and diamonds.)* But what did I gets out of them things? Shame has been wedging me from Mobile to Newark.

SMITH Whose are they? *(Lights fade on Smith.)*

SADIE *(Spot on Sadie.)* Lawdy, you wouldn't believe it. I told you about the Governor and some of them parties he'd throw. Well, during the Governor's second term the State had three yachts … the Alice, the Dixie and the Jamelle Two. Sorta like Columbus … three of 'em. The Dixie looked like an old snapper boat. *(Pause.)* Of the three of them, I likes Alice the best… solid mahogany… a pretty thing, over a hundred feet long. The Governor would take me on all the trips. I think of the Coloreds that worked at the Mansion, I's his favorite. Believe it was my angel biscuits, the way he always bragged on 'em. Well, that spring around nineteen fifty-seven, they this big group of important folks from Detroit be coming down to look about to relocate their factories. Lawdy, one night one of them womens from De-troit go so mad and drunk at her husband she went into a rage. Her night nerves got her. They'd just announced that airbrakes factory moving down around Opelika and the Governor ordered out that French champagne and we be pouring in them little glasses that don't hold nothing and the Governor pouring champagne over the heads of the men folks and baptizing them Alabamians and Choctaw Indians. And, the men folks they be laughing like they had figured out how to laugh again. And, them women folks they as tight as spool thread. You could tell, all you had to do be look at they eyes. *(Sigh.)* That one woman, what worried me the most, her night nerves get her and she kicked in the front of the drum what had the band's name on the front of it. The Midnight Brothers and they could make them trumpets sound like your soul in pain, but that drum kept your spirit throbbing. *(She bounces lightly on the bed.)* Once that saxophone player hit one of them high notes and it made me cry out loud for my Jeb. The Governor didn't care none if the Coloreds stayed around when we not needed and he come over that night and put his arm around me and pulls his handkerchief from his coat pocket and let me cry in it. The handkerchief smelled like the laundry room at the Mansion. That was back when Duz soap was Duz soap and Faultless starch was Faultless starch. And, the Governor wore pure white raw silk suits, and he didn't mind no Colored crying into the side of his coat. *(Laughs and lists her head as if into the Governor's silk suit.)* Lawdy, ain't nobody tall enough to cry on the Governor's shoulder. Well, that woman from De-troit ripped that diamond butterfly off the shoulder of that thin dress, material and all. I be pouring a pour of champagne and I just lifted the bottle and let it run all over the front of my uniform apron and watched her get at that microphone and call the Governor an Indian hick. Goshamighty, she didn't need to come all the way down from De-troit, Michigan to figure that out, for that's what the Governor called hisself. *(She laughs.)* That diamond brooch be shaped like a butterfly and she wore it on her shoulder, just on the titty side of her shoulder seam. She screaming and everybody got real quiet and she threw the brooch toward her husband. But, it went over his head. He had silver hair and was a happy man when he wasn't around that woman. Well, throwing that pin must of made that woman feel good cause she started laughing, but it was a crazy laugh. Them night nerves. And, her husband being a good man went to her and everybody else must of thought it was paste diamonds being a butterfly and so big and all. But, I saw it land in one of my split-leaf dildrons, a tall one, the one I rubbed with mayonnaise to make it shine. With all the commotion at the bandstand and the Governor ordering real whiskey broke out, I slip over the dildron and there it be. With all the commotion, I just put it in that towel, I had wrapped around that champagne bottle. *(Sighs.)* I's younger and foolish and I knew there was a big world out there and there was a better life than waiting on white folks, even the Governor as good a man as he be. I's younger and wasn't worried about no sanctification and the life in the hereafter. And, waiting out Jeb's life on that insurance policy, just confused my thinking, so I slip that butterfly into the pocket of my uniform. They be looking for it, but they all confused by the whiskey and champagne. *(Pause.)* Early before dawn just after the last noise quieted down in the ballroom, I took the diamonds outta the butterfly with my tweezers and threw the set in Mobile Bay. Then, I hid the diamonds in one of them egg poachers in the galley. No one would ever cook the Governor's eggs in one of them contraptions. *(She smiles.)* He eats 'em fried sunny side up. Lawdy, the next morning they told what them things worth. *(She points to the diamonds.)* Forty-eight in all, mar-keets, pear-shaped, teardrops, bag-u-ettes mostly and that center emerald cut better than three carats. Now, them ain't no Sears and Roebuck diamonds, but they'd bring close to thirty or fifty thousand. Why, no telling how much even at Sears they bring. *(She takes a swelling breath.)* Lawyer Smith, all I want is a one-way ticket back to Newark and get them off the wedges of my sin. *(Lights slowly come back up on Smith.)* Why, within a day we all over the Mobile papers ... about them important factory folks throwing diamond brooches at one another on the State yacht. Even had to go take a 'dector test where they strap things around your arm and ask you questions real slow and they just want a "yes" or "no." Now, Lawyer Smith, that scared me. Not 'cause I'm afraid of no jail ... they got trustees from Kilby Prison working at the Mansion and it ain't no bad life. *(She lowers head.)* Don't let no thief work at the Mansion, though. Governor always choose those what kill love ones outta passion. Says, when they come outta of the passion, they okay. And, I afraid the Governor would turn me out and I waited too long to tell the Governor about the diamonds. Even wished of hiding the butterfly back in the 'dildron. But, my foolishness done broke it down. And, them highway patrolmens done turned the dirt out looking for that thing. Well, I just took the detector test and thought about my Jeb back at T.C. and I. in Birmingham. And, I passed it. I mean with articles in all the Mobile papers, and that all the papers we got. Why, no telling what all else we's in. Now, Lawyer Smith, all's I want is a one-way back to Newark I've been paying my wedges of sin and gonna die and the Governor never did find me out. Why, I was gonna tell him, and I thought he'd laugh about it, but I couldn't t take them chances.

SMITH Mrs. Graham, you know, you could be put in jail for all this.

SADIE Jail? What kind of lawyer is you?

SMITH Not much of one today.

SADIE Jail? I be an old woman and all I wants is a little sanctification and a one-way back to Newark. *(Looks at the diamonds.)* They worth sixty thousand dollars.

SMITH It only takes a thousand.

SADIE For a bus ticket? Lordy. I get a senior citizen discount.

SMITH No, for first degree theft.

SADIE I ain't interested in no degrees.

SMITH Mrs. Graham, this is serious. First degree theft is a Class B Felony and carries two to twenty.

SADIE Two to twenty?

SMITH Years in the penitentiary.

SADIE I ain't interested in no penitentiary, I'm too old. I just want to go work out my days for Mr. Merriam and then gets me a little bit of that eternal life.

SMITH I'm not a preacher, I'm a lawyer. And, I got to tell you these things.

SADIE Let me tell you a thing or two. The Governor walks around with a pocket full of pardons.

SMITH He's not ...

SADIE That Nixon went out of office pre-pardoned, and I figured as old as I am and as much as I done, I'm pre-pardoned too.

SMITH ... not Governor any longer

SADIE Once Governor, always Governor. Figures, if I make it to New Jersey, the Great State of Alabama ain't gonna extra-flight me just to put me on welfare. Mr. Merriam says I could sit right there on that kitchen stool and mix up them pancakes the rest of my life. And, he ain't even had my biscuits yet.

SMITH *(Re-loading paper bag.)* Mrs. Graham let's pack We'll get you a bus ticket or something.

SADIE *(Swells with courage.)* That ain't all Lawyer Smith.

SMITH What?

SADIE Got me something else been wedging me around,

SMITH *(Beat.)* Even Jesus took forty days in the wilderness.

SADIE Them diamonds ain't nothing compared to my final sin.

SMITH What?

SADIE Drugs ... *(Shakes head and tears up.)* ... I caint.

SMITH Drugs?

SADIE You know about drugs?

SMITH *(Subtly runs finger to side of nose.)* Some.

SADIE These was knock-out drugs.

SMITH Most of them are.

SADIE Ain't talking about that stuff out yonder in the street. *(Points.)* I's talkin' professional drugs.

SMITH Professional?

SADIE You know, like on tee vee.

SMITH Tee vee?

SADIE Television.

SMITH I know.

SADIE Don't sound like you do.

SMITH Columbian cartel?

SADIE Columbiana Karl? Not him. He was on radio in nineteen forty-six. Not tee vee in sixty-two.

BOTH What are you talking about?

SMITH Where do the drugs come from?

SADIE Store as far as I know.

SMITH You said television.

SADIE How did you know?

SMITH *(Puzzled.)* I don't know.

SADIE Don't know what?

SMITH What you are talking about.

SADIE Sounds like you do. *(Looks sternly.)* How much do you know?

SMITH All I know is that you said something about professional drugs on television. And, I asked where they come from.

SADIE How do you expect me to know that?

SMITH Could we start over? What are we talking about? Television? What kind of drugs?

SADIE You know, like when the Man pulls the pill apart and pours the powders in the coffee. Don't you watch television?

SMITH *(Relieved.)* I see.

SADIE Only it was my lemon water.

SMITH Lemon water?

WEDGES 109

SADIE I can't go into it.

SMITH I'd say you are doing a pretty good job of not going into it.

SADIE No sir, Lawyer Smith, I can't.

SMITH Mrs. Graham, it's better to get that stuff out of you than to let it stay penned up inside of you. *(Listens to himself.)* That stuff inside of you will kill you. Wedge you all over the place.

SADIE I know, that's what I say. But, I just can't. *(Starts to cry.)*

SMITH Please. Please, Mrs. Graham.

SADIE Sadie.

SMITH Sadie. What's lemon water?

SADIE *(A laugh through tears.)* I make a big to do about it. Just get me some spring water out near Bessemer where I get my clay and I get me some real big lemons at Hill Grocery sto and only half squeeze 'em.

SMITH Clay, water and lemons?

SADIE No, clay starch is for my babies and the lemon water is for my stomachs ... those acid-i-fied stomachs.

SMITH I thought lemon was an acid.

SADIE Counter acid.

SMITH I should have known. *(Pause.)* Mrs. Graham, why do I have the feeling we're going backwards?

SMITH We is?

SMITH Is that a question or an answer?

SADIE I just caint ... lets me call you next week when I gets my nerves back up.

SMITH No. No. I only do this on Saturday.

SADIE You do?

SMITH Whatever it is, Mrs. Graham, we've got to go into it now.

SADIE Sadie.

SMITH I mean, Sadie. Either, we buy the ticket or we get out of line.

SADIE Reckon, I ought not wait until I meet my Maker.

SMITH At this rate we may meet Him about the same time.

SADIE Rates?

SMITH I'm free on Saturday ... special one day only offer.

SADIE You ain't gonna trick me.

SMITH Mrs. Graham ... Sadie ...

SADIE What's it take to set the Governor's race aside?

SMITH I don't know ... fraud, I suppose.

SADIE Is that anything like duress?

SMITH More like stealing votes.

SADIE They stole 'em alright after we drugged the Governor.

SMITH Drugged? When?

SADIE Sixty-two.

SMITH That was over ten years ago.

SADIE Banty Rooster Wallace still Governor, what's left of him, and the Governor ought to be Governor.

SMITH Governor ought to be Governor, makes sense to me.

SADIE Them was tough times.

SMITH I know, I was ...

SADIE A college boy chasing skirts ... that ain't what I'm talking about.

SMITH No. No. You don't understand.

SADIE Understand? Governor didn't need my lemon water... he just wanted me in Montgomery to break it to me gent-ly. Yeah, I understand all too well... Governor was runnin' behind because of the Out-Nigger boys.

SMITH The out what? I thought that was a pejorative term.

SADIE It ... been jarring me around all my life. But, it got real bad in nineteen sixty-two. You see, we had them demonstrations held up until after the Governor's race.

SMITH I had two college friends sit-in at the Woolworth's lunch counter.

SADIE I'm talkin' big time, serious demonstrations. Like here in Birmingham ... Martin, Reverend Fred, Ralph ... the whole bunch.

SMITH Why were you holding *up* the demonstrations?

WEDGES   111

SADIE The nineteen sixty-two Governor's race, you ain't been listening.

SMITH Demonstrations? Governor's race? Didn't know they were connected.

SADIE You not supposed to know. But, they was. See the Out-Nigger Boys, the segregationist, they all out runnin' for Governor and the Freedom Riding folks get on them buses and come to town about a year too early. Governor called them the Outside Hot Taters.

SMITH Outside Agitators?

SADIE That's what the Out-Nigger Boys called them.

SMITH I see.

SADIE Governor fell behind in that primary race.

SMITH I thought it was because he got drunk on television.

SADIE Drugged. Governor would not sling mud with the rest of them. Says you lets the mud dry and you can just brush it off. *(Turns sad.)*

SMITH Mrs. Graham are you saying …?

SADIE Sadie saying the Governor sends for me the day before the election … he's down in Montgomery. The Man comes right up to my front door in a big long Cadillac convertible and saying the Governor needs me cause he's crying in his Early Death and the enemies got to him.

SMITH Enemies?

SADIE Everybody runnin' for Governor got enemies right under their noses like spies … worse than the Russians.

SMITH Russians?

SADIE That Cold War. Only, the war in Alabama was hot. And, I didn't know the Man was mean spirited. Probably one of them spies.

SMITH What are you talking about?

SADIE Listen. I gets in that convertible and the tops back and the Man he's so worried he don't put the top back up and we fly down the highway towards Montgomery. Only, we stops by Hill Grocery Sto … for some lemons.

SMITH Let me guess. Lemon water.

SADIE Governor got an acid-i-fied stomach and a bruised brain, buts we don't know it yet.

SMITH Bruised brain?

SADIE Hem-a-something ... clot on the brain. Cut it out two years later after I left town. *(Pause.)* I was worse than Judas ... doing what I did.

SMITH What did you do?

SADIE Where was I?

SMITH Purgatory, on the highway to Montgomery.

SADIE They puts me in a room at the television station ... just me and my lemon water. Governor comes in and he's worn out and he's sad and he gives me a big hug and thanks me for holding up them demonstrations and said our pensions in a heap of trouble ... them Outside Hot Taters. Governor real sad. *(Shakes head, perchance to cry.)* And, I tell him he did all he could do and I tell him we voted for him. You see he'd come to the Colored churches before he announced for governor and tell us that he was for us though the Out-Nigger Boys had him up a tree and he have to tell white folks what they want to hear.

SMITH Like my professor said, it was the race issue after all. I thought it was because he got drunk on television.

SADIE Drugged. Everybody use to his Early Death... but that night was different... his doctor give him his vitamin shot and he was run down from running.

SMITH Running?

SADIE For Governor. You ain't been listening.

SMITH Mrs. Graham you are telling me things people don't really know.

SADIE People ain't supposed to know Miz Sadie's business ... that's between Sadie and the good Lord and the free Lawyer what the dog days done drugged in.

SMITH *(Laughs.)* I guess I asked for that.

SADIE Talking to you gets pretty easy ... after a while. *(Serious.)* That's when the Man axed me for my lemon water when I was trying to talk the Governor outta of going on television because Governor don't look too good. Governor saying he's fine. Governor asking me to pray for a miracle and out of the corner of my eyes I see the Man puts the powders in the lemon water. I tell the Governor not to drink it, but he does anyways. I tell him not to gets on television, but he does anyways. I'd make Judas look like a sissyboy. And, you know something else?

SMITH Very little.

SADIE My Jeb back in Birmingham says that they was something wrong or the Man won't give me no hundred dollar bill just for a jug of lemon water.

SMITH You and your little cottage industry.

SADIE Don't charge the Governor. But, around election time, everybody handing out large bills, and change hard to come by in a television station.

SMITH Never thought about it that way.

SADIE Governor gets on television and the rest is history. Real sad.

SMITH I know.

SADIE You don't know the half of it. I mean it wasn't nothing to see the Governor miss the names of his childrens … I mean, I seen him stone sober go through the whole list before he gets the one standing right before his eyes.

SMITH *(In a daze of recall and talks at the same time as Sadie.)* I felt robbed.

SADIE We all do that, when our mind be on something else. Governor's brain is bruised and them drugs makes it go crazy.

SMITH Why did it all have to happen while I was in college?

SADIE Hot Taters hard to handle and there goes my pension. Television will kill you.

SMITH One of my professors left town about that time … joined a long line of expatriates.

SADIE Governor didn't even make the runoff in that primary. Well, the Governor turns to Early Death and disappears, the Man and his buddy head to Mexico and I gets me a one-way to New Jersey … I had it with the whole rotten mess.

SMITH You go to New Jersey a lot.

SADIE Just a few times and I need to be there now.

SMITH Last one out of Alabama turn the lights out. I went out of state to law school for much the same reason, and, of course, the Viet Nam War was heating up.

SADIE You was in the War?

SMITH I was definitely not in the War. A law school draft dodger.

SADIE Call yourself a conscience rejector it sounds better.

SMITH Let's pack. *(Puts suitcase on daybed.)*

SADIE Been saving my angel biscuits in case Mr. Merriam gets put out with me. *(Fumbles in papers.)* But, he just as happy as a pig in sunshine with my pancakes.

SMITH Miz Sadie ...

SADIE Hadn't had to use my angel biscuits yet. *(Hands Smith the index card.)* Save my biscuits for folks like the Governor.

SMITH *(Looks at card.)* What's this for?

SADIE That's my special recipe for angel biscuits. I'm sending it home to your bride.

SMITH What for?

SADIE *(Looks puzzled.)* It's my only copy and I got it in my head if I needs it.

SMITH My wife ... bride doesn't cook much.

SADIE In that case, why don't you take her a small diamond.

SMITH Oh, no, I cook some. *(Reads recipe.)* Thank you. *(He starts to put card in pocket.)*

SADIE When you dissolve the yeast in warm water, be sure to put a pinch of sugar in and get it started real good. That's not written down. And, make sure the yeast is good. Don't pay no attention on the package about how old it is. Just make sure it works. Foams up like dirty soap suds. *(Goes behind screen to put on hat and fur.)*

SMITH I made some rolls once.

SADIE I's afraid of that. While you sittin' there pack my stuff outta the chifrobe into my grip. You see I didn't write it all down, my little secrets. If you could get some fresh churned butter to spread on the dough before you fold it and cut out the biscuits ... fresh butter hard to find these days ... you better use that sweet butter from the grocery sto.

SMITH Is that the white butter in the aluminum foil?

SADIE You catching on.

SMITH *(Puts recipe in pocket.)* Mrs. Graham, I'm really touched by this.

SADIE Don't be. Just make sure the butter is soft and not melted when you spread it on. *(Steps into room.)* God, them things melt in your mouth and melt any man you want 'em to. *(Looks at Smith.)* Say you do the cooking?

SMITH Some. Mostly, it's my wife's Mama and our family's cook. I cook some on the weekends.

SADIE What's her name?

SMITH My wife's Mama?

SADIE No, the cook's name?

SMITH Sarah Slossberg.

SADIE Where she go to church?

SMITH She's German and it's a long story.

SADIE We got time on the way to the bus.

SMITH *(Aside whisper to audience.)* Or, jail.

SADIE Do I qualify?

SMITH Qualify? Qualify for what?

SADIE For the legal aid. Do I have me enough problem?

SMITH Fifty thousand in missing diamonds and throwing the nineteen sixty-two Governor's race and setting Civil Rights back a decade or so ... I'd say that qualifies.

SADIE Seventy thousand ... diamonds got to be worth seventy thousand by now. *(Hands Smith the diamonds.)* Already feels better just being shed of them.

SMITH What am I supposed to do with 'em?

SADIE You the lawyer. *(Directs loading of grocery cart.)*

SMITH Yes, I keep forgetting.

SADIE *(Pulls a scrap of paper from the pocket of her coat.)* Here, I scribbled Mr. Merriam's address down for you. Figure if there's any of that reward money left after your fee, you might send me a little.

SMITH Reward?

SADIE Five hundred or maybe a thousand dollars. And, that was way back then. No telling what it might be worth now.

SMITH When you get sanctified, you don't waste any time.

SADIE You talking crazy.

SMITH I needed the break.

SADIE Sure you okay with them diamonds?

SMITH Somebody's got to do it and I'm the lawyer.

SADIE *(Looks at audience.)* You can't get good charity no more. *(Swings walker to top of load in grocery cart and uses cart as a walker.)*

SMITH What?

SADIE I said I want to clarify… since you come for free, when you talk to the Governor, you best hold off on that nineteen sixty-two Governor's race and my lemon water.

SMITH I suppose you are right.

SADIE History gonna have to take its course and it's about time history learned to get along without me and the Governor.

SMITH History will never be the same. *(Fumbles in pocket.)* Here's my card.

SADIE *(Reads card and laughs.)* Lord, I ain't seen so many funny names, since I tried to look up a number in that Manhattan telephone book.

SMITH *(Picks up brief case and anything not loaded in cart.)*

SADIE Now, when you make my angel biscuits be sure to cut them on the angle and they'll look like little pillows. *(They start to exit.)* Now, don't overcook them. They suppose to turn just a little brown around the edges. Don't want you burning my biscuits. Eats them with some mountain honey or some strawberry jam. You eat them while you and your bride are still in your morning robes and don't worry about them dripping. *(Smiles.)* Now, when you see the Governor, don't tell him I gave you my biscuit recipe … he's been trying to get it for years and in my business that's what I call job security.

End of Act One

ACT TWO, Scene One

AT RISE: *Smith on stoop of Governor's house and Governor's Wife tidying up parlor, and adjusting her hair while singing You Are My Sunshine.*

SMITH This is the Governor's house, a little rough for the wear. *(Knocks.)* I put Sadie Belle … I mean, Mrs. Graham on the bus. She sent me back to the ticket counter twice to make sure I had squeezed the last penny out of her senior citizen discount. And, she got on the bus pretending to know everybody just like you do at a family reunion. She told everybody that I was the best lawyer in Birmingham and then she made me hand out my card for a few laughs. *(Knocks, again.)* It all seemed worth it when Sadie gave me a big kiss with fresh lipstick on. *(Pause.)* Sunday morning, I made Sadie's biscuits … cut them on the diagonal like diamonds. My yeast must have been old. Biscuits came out a little flat, not like little pillows. *(Shrugs.)* I didn't go to the D.A. No, I came here to the Governor's house hoping for a solution or perhaps to joust with another set of windmills.

WIFE *(Opens door.)* Good Moan-ing. *(Looks past him.)* Good Lord, it's gonna be another scorcher. *(Looks at Smith.)* You're not another bill collector, are you?

SMITH No. I'm Smith Wakefield.

WIFE Wakefield … let's see, Wakefield. *(Points finger.)* Republican fund raiser from Birmingham.

SMITH My uncle.

WIFE Republicans treat a woman like a princess, but Democrats more fun. Come on in.

SMITH I'm mostly a Democrat, if that counts.

WIFE Honey, it all counts. You look like one of them love children from the Sixties who makes plenty of money. I bet going in the voting booth for you is like going into a room of pretty women. *(Adjusts hair.)* Republicans have to first decide if they are going out to play. Democrats just have to decide who and how many they are going to play with. *(Pause.)* What business you in?

SMITH Lawyer.

WIFE Governor's not too big on lawyers these days. You not in the Legislature, are you?

SMITH Well, no.

WIFE That's a mixed blessing. We're trying to get the Governor's pension plan beefed up and the Legislature is playing games with us. Supreme Court too. It's not blind justice; it's just blind period. If you're shot in a shopping center parking lot while you're off on a lark running for President, they'll give you all the pension money you want, but if you just get old and go blind, that's another story.

SMITH Well, they say, legislation is like sausage, if you like sausage you sure don't want to watch it being made.

WIFE It was mostly the Supreme Court that did us in.

SMITH At least the Supreme Court has the good graces to do it in chambers.

WIFE *(Laughs.)* You sorta cute in your own little way. *(Picks up a piece of paper.)* This is our poop sheet on the pension bill. They may go into Special Session this fall and if you could put in a good word for us.

SMITH *(Looks at paper.)* I don't know …

WIFE Growing old ain't no fun. Just do what you can. *(Pats him on arm and leads him to a chair.)* Reckon you didn't drive all the way up from Birmingham just hear me talk about that pension bill.

SMITH I would like to speak to the Governor, if that's okay?

WIFE *(Shouts upstairs.)* Governor, Honey, company. *(Turns to Smith.)* Is there anything wrong?

SMITH No, it's just about an old friend of his.

WIFE He'll love that. He's got plenty of time for old friends … I just wish more of them were in the legislature. Dying off.

SMITH Yes. Ma'am.

WIFE You know he's blind since that last stroke.

SMITH Yes, ma'am, I heard.

WIFE Could I get you some tea or coffee? It'll have to be instant.

SMITH No ma'am, I'm fine.

WIFE Yesterday, he just talked the ears off one of them graduate students from the University. I think that he senses he's getting old and his days are numbered. Lord he's been through brain surgery, open heart surgery and no telling how many minor strokes. *(Sighs.)* But, he bounces back. *(Points to sofa.)* Have a seat.

SMITH Thank you. *(Sits.)*

WIFE You say you know an old friend of his?

SMITH Well, yes.

WIFE Might I ask who? Governor is friends with just about everybody.

SMITH Mrs. Graham. Mrs. Sadie Belle Graham.

WIFE Oh, Sadie, how is she?

SMITH Pretty good.

WIFE Lord, we loved Sadie, she sorta ran the Mansion. *(Points.)* That's her in this picture here.

SMITH Yes, she has one just like it.

WIFE You've seen her recently? Thought she was in New Jersey.

SMITH She's on her way back there. Her husband died.

WIFE Sorry to hear about Jeb. Just between the two of us, he wasn't much of a husband. *(Sits on sofa.)* Lord, I guess I should be grateful that the social situation was what it was back then, because the Governor loved that woman. Of course, the Governor loved all women. *(Thinks.)* There was no hanky panky that I know of, but they sure did spend a lot of time together talking… taking on advice as the Governor calls it. Always talking about her biscuits… I caught her slipping a little yeast in them to make them rise real pretty and give it that little taste nobody else could figure out. *(Pause.)* Now, the kitchen wasn't my favorite room. And, Honey, the Governor didn't marry me for my cooking. They still laughing at me about the time all the help left and I tried to cook. Kitchen like walking through a mine field to me. Tried to cook the Governor's breakfast. I used them Pillsbury biscuits that come in a can and I popped them open and ran them under the broiler. *(Laughs.)* Burnt on top and dough on the bottom. *(Pause.)* That kitchen is not for me. Sure you wouldn't like some coffee?

SMITH I'd better not risk it.

WIFE *(Smiles and nods approvingly.)* Yes, you are cute. Let's see, you're a half ass Democrat and sorta look prosperous. I might have a daughter about your age. *(Sighs.)* Course, I got a daughter just about everybody's age.

SMITH Oh, I'm married.

WIFE That's good. Any children?

SMITH First one just on the way. *(Pause.)* You're the first person I've got to tell. Just found out about it on Saturday. My wife had some tests done last week and she was pretty sure she was pregnant. But, she didn't want to disturb my Saturday at the Legal Aid Office. We were at the lake when out of the blue, she said, "I'm pregnant!"

WIFE Great!

SMITH She was out across the lake water skiing… going through the slalom course when she slid right up to the dock without getting wet.

WIFE All my girls skied … never did get wet … mess up their hair. *(Adjusts hair.)* Gonna have a baby, that's great! You'll make a great daddy. This calls for a celebration, but we don't have much to celebrate with around here. Would you like a Seven-up?

SMITH No thanks. I really need to get back to Birmingham after I talk to the Governor.

WIFE Honey, you being a lawyer, you gonna have time for a Seven-up. Besides, you gonna be a daddy.

SMITH Could you make it Diet?

WIFE Don't you love them. Taste like they got real sugar in them. *(Exits to kitchen.)*

SMITH *(To audience.)* Saturday afternoon Alyce and I went for a swim, just the two of us. Have you ever seen someone so full of life that it's radiant, like sun on a summer lake. *(Pause.)* We made love on an air mattress in the boat house … simply could not wait. Afterwards, we lay there listening to the water wash under the boat house. Then, out of the blue, she said: "I'm pregnant!" Just like that, "I'm pregnant!" And, I said something dumb like, "how can you tell so soon afterwards?" She convinced me that it was official. Then, I got up and started making a fool of myself, trying to make her comfortable in a boat house of all places and telling her she shouldn't be skiing or making love, I headed out of the boat house to get her some ice cream and dill pickles and she told me to put my swim trunks on.

WIFE *(Enters with Seven-ups on tray with goblets.)* You sure are in a good mood. *(Pours.)* Enjoy.

SMITH What's me being a lawyer and having time for a Seven-up got to do with anything?

WIFE You may need several Seven-ups. Something about one of the boys, a lawyer in the legislature, taking the last pension bill to the Supreme Court after the Governor signed it into law and then it wasn't law anymore, Blames you boys … lawyers.

SMITH I didn't really follow it but seems like I read …

WIFE All I do know the very day that the Court said we don't get any more pension, that blood clot run to his head and explode right behind his eyes… blind as a bat. Guess it's good he doesn't read any more, he's got enough rolling around in his head to keep three graduate students and a professor busy … only ones that come around much anymore. (Pours more Seven-up.) Enjoy!

SMITH Thank you.

WIFE *(Points to regular Seven-up on tray.)* This is his. He'll know it's here … anything cold to drink in the room and the Governor knows it. What they say about a blind man and the senses is true… sure is.

SMITH I see. *(Pauses.)* I mean, I understand.

WIFE I got to be going. The Governor will want to know if I checked your credentials. Just tell him yes. *(Points to phone.)* If the phone rings, just answer it, Governor still has a hard time getting around.

SMITH *(Looks at pay telephone.)* I didn't know they put those in residences.

WIFE Had to Honey. Governor said it was the children and me that was running up the long-distance phone bills. So, he up and calls the phone company and has one installed like we's a truck stop or something. But, let me tell you it was the Governor all along. He'd forget whether that pension bill was in Washington or Montgomery, and he'd call all over the place. Yeah, you might say we had to put a governor on the Governor.

SMITH How do I answer it?

WIFE Just say Governor's retirement villa.

SMITH If my office tries to reach me can they?

WIFE Sure Honey, we listed. *(Shouts upstairs.)* Governor, Honey, Company. *(She points to large chair.)* This is his chair. You'll need to talk a little loud and in his left ear. He should be down any minute. Tell him I went to the bank. Nice to meet you. *(Turns at door.)* Sure, you won't stay for lunch, me and the Colonel know how to fry us up some chicken.

SMITH No ma'am, I can't.

WIFE Good luck on that new baby. And, y'all come back, you hear. *(Exits.)*

SMITH *(Looks around room. Phone rings. Looks at audience.)* Wouldn't you know it? *(Goes to phone and answers.)* Governor's retirement… villa. *(Nods.)* His wife told me to. *(Nods.)* No, I'm just visiting. *(Pause.)* He's upstairs. *(Pause.)* I see. Should you be telling me this. *(Pause.)* I'll be sure to tell him. No more bacon and eggs and leave the butter off his biscuits. *(Pause.)* Sure thing. Well, thank you. *(Hangs up.)* *(To audience.)* That was his doctor… the Governor hasn't taken his medicine as directed and he gets a friend to take him down to the truck stop for breakfast. When I asked the doctor if he should be sharing the Governor's medical status, he said neither he nor the Governor had time for protocol. *(Continues to look around.)*

GOVERNOR *(Noise at top of stairs, cane clanking against stairs and banisters. Prolonged. Heavy uncertain steps descend the stairs. Cane loudly scraps banisters. At landing Governor stands erect and stately.)* Yes.

SMITH *(Standing.)* Sir. I'm Smith Wakefield, a lawyer from Birmingham.

GOVERNOR Pleased to meet you. *(Extends a groping hand.)*

SMITH *(Shakes hand.)* Your wife's gone to the bank.

GOVERNOR Don't know how she piddles so much with that mite the legislature doles out. *(Points with cane.)* Have a seat.

SMITH Thank you. Your doctor called.

GOVERNOR I've heard everything he's got to say. Not interested. *(Takes seat carefully and cocks hearing aid toward Smith.)* Say, you're a lawyer?

SMITH Yessir. But, your doctor called.

GOVERNOR One pocket lawyer or two pocket lawyer?

SMITH *(Puts hand on coat pocket.)*

GOVERNOR You in the legislature?

SMITH No sir.

GOVERNOR Good.

SMITH I never ran for the legislature. My uncle tried.

GOVERNOR Republican.

SMITH My uncle is a Republican, but I'm mostly a Democrat.

GOVERNOR When you gonna make up your mind?

SMITH What?

GOVERNOR It's just as well. It's the two-pocket lawyers in the legislature that's got the whole state screwed up. Why take the way they jerked that pension bill around. Like a city boy trying to ring the neck of a chicken. Say you're not in the legislature?

SMITH That's right. Never ran.

GOVERNOR Reckon, that makes you a one pocket lawyer.

SMITH *(Feels pocket and looks at audience.)*

GOVERNOR Three branches of government set up by the constitution. Right?

SMITH *(Perplexed.)* Well, yes.

GOVERNOR Judicial. Executive. And, legislative. Right?

SMITH Yes.

GOVERNOR Lawyer's officers of the court?

SMITH Yes.

GOVERNOR Judicial branch?

SMITH Right.

GOVERNOR *(Takes a drink of Seven-up.)* Now, when a lawyer gets elected to the legislature, he ought to resign his judicial license. Otherwise, it violates the separation of our three branches of government.

SMITH I see.

GOVERNOR Unconstitutional, to pocket money from two branches of government at the same time. *(Rests chin on cane.)* Problem's been around since 1803, but the people ain't done a damn thing about it.

SMITH 1803. Louisiana Purchase?

GOVERNOR Now, that was a hellva of a land grab, Executive Power at its best. No, I was talking about Malbury verses Madison… thought you was the lawyer.

SMITH Judicial review.

GOVERNOR That's the fancy word for it. I call it two fisted stealing.

SMITH Never thought of it that way.

GOVERNOR Sounds like you one of them love children that ain't missed nary a meal.

SMITH Well, no.

GOVERNOR Don't know why I still get so bent out of shape.

SMITH Fat love children?

GOVERNOR Two fisted stealing. Only two ways you can change it is by legislation or the courts. And, my friend you boys… and girls in control of both of 'em.

SMITH Never thought of it that way.

GOVERNOR Not thinking much today? You see when you set yourself up to be God, it's hard to see what's right in front of you. Like them Tee Vee preachers … all the money and women they could hope for. They just work about an hour on Sunday and spend the rest of the week dipping their fist in the till and their pecker in the congregation. *(Drinks Seven-up.)* Yeah, I'm afraid that we are not leaving this place better off than we found it. I paved a road to every working farmer's front door. You ever been stuck on the other side of a sea of mud?

SMITH *(Aside to audience.)* Not literally.

GOVERNOR We let the Big Mules suck our earth and we don't charge 'em enough.

SMITH A Big Mule? Charge for what?

GOVERNOR Aluminum! Soda pop cans! That's what your automobiles are gonna be made of one of these days… soda pop cans.

SMITH *(Looks at can.)* You may have a point there.

GOVERNOR When you finish with your cold drink, I'd appreciate if you'd stomp the can and put it over yonder by the telephone. *(Hands Smith his can.)* And, while you're up, if any need stomping, I be much obliged. You turn blind and it's hard to stomp cans.

SMITH *(Collects cans and goes to area near telephone.)*

GOVERNOR You know how to turn 'em up on their top end and flatten them all with one stomp?

SMITH Yes, I've got some practice in recently. *(Stomps.)*

GOVERNOR Good, neighborhood boys be by to pick up this afternoon. Little bastards cuttin' in on the profits, but we are building the cars of the future.

SMITH *(Stomps more cans.)*

GOVERNOR You sound like you're about forty; guess you been around the block a couple of times.

SMITH Thirty-seven.

GOVERNOR You got too many worries for a young man.

SMITH You think so?

GOVERNOR Remember yesterday you asked me to tell about that time down in Montgomery when I was running for my second term.

SMITH Yesterday?

GOVERNOR Well, it come to me this morning while I was in the shower. I's running for my first term or maybe it was my second term and we had that caravan going all over the state, and this judge down in Montgomery, who probably knew me better than God.

(Phone rings.)

SMITH Governor's Retirement Villa.

GOVERNOR What did you say?

SMITH It's your wife.

GOVERNOR It always is.

SMITH *(Into receiver.)* Yes ma'am. Yes ma'am. *(Cups phone.)* Your wife says she's at the bank and just ran across Senator Hargrove and wants to know if she should get him to add an amendment to the pension bill that'll let you hire a full time nurse.

GOVERNOR Don't need no nurse, but it is a paycheck. Come to think of it, it's not a bad idea. But, it's an appropriation bill and that has to be introduced in the House and not the Senate.

SMITH *(Into receiver.)* It needs to be introduced in the House and not the Senate. *(Pause.)* I see. (Turns to Governor.) She says the only House member she can locate is Representative Boyd and he is speckle trout fishing down in Biloxi.

GOVERNOR Tell him he might ought to do his fishing in Alabama if he's looking to run for higher office.

SMITH *(Into phone.)* Did you hear that? *(Pause.)* I really can't stay. No, really. If you must know, I like the original recipe.

GOVERNOR Tell her to do what she can with Senator Hargrove. And, that I'm tired of chicken.

SMITH *(Listens.)* I don't think it would hurt either. Sure. Sure. Goodbye. *(Hangs up.)*

GOVERNOR Where was I? Oh, yes. Well, my first wife had died and I was gettint a reputation for strong drink and even stronger women. Lord, I even went out to Hollywood, and they seemed to take a likening to this big ole half breed ... but that's another story. Well, the Judge he takes me in to his chambers and give me some fatherly advice. He knew my Daddy and my father-in-law and I guess he figured I was in need of some fatherly advice. He up and tells me that the opposition has done gone to New York City and hired them the prettiest woman they could find. She's gonna be smelling like Paris, France and looking like next year. *(Pauses as if to smell and see.)* And, my worthy opponents were gonna plant this woman on the street of Montgomery, Alabama, and she's gonna be looking for me. The Judge he's mighty worried and I appreciated his concern ... course he wouldn't be opposed to moving up a notch in judging if a vacancy were to come open while I was Governor. I prop my feet up on his desk, and say, Judge, let me get this straight. Well, Judge, I say, if my worthy opponents spend that kind of money setting a trap like that ... and baiting it with that kind of bait ... they gonna catch this ole boy every time.

SMITH (Laughs.)

GOVERNOR When you boys write your books, I wish you'd go easy on my love for women folks and strong drink.

SMITH Books? Governor, I'm not ...

GOVERNOR Dont t y'all generally turn that stuff into a book?

SMITH Governor, I'm afraid ...

GOVERNOR Even had a story going around about me entertaining Congressman Adam Clayton Powell. We were supposed to be on the front porch of the Mansion drinking Scotch whiskey. That's where they made their mistake. All I had to do was to get on the back of that flatbed truck and tell the good folks of Alabama that in the first place, I don't drink Scotch whiskey, I drink bourbon or good white lightn' when I can get it, and two, everybody knows the Governor don't entertain on the front porch, I entertain on the back porch. *(Smiles.)* Never did get caught in a lie, you have to re-invent those damn things every morning.

SMITH I'm no good at lying either. *(Puzzled.)* Congressman Adam Clayton Powell?

GOVERNOR Good, you just write it down like I tell you. And, that Powell fella was pretty good company. He's just like me: grew up without a pot to pee in. And, he just wanted a better cut for his people. I told you that I was part

Choctaw Indian ... but it would be nice to list me as a Native American ... that way, it reaches more people and I don't have to worry about what boat I came over on.

SMITH Governor, I'm not ...

GOVERNOR Lord, son, I've survived a lot. Like that time that scalawag newspaperman broke that story in New York City 'bout that woman claiming to have me a boy out of wedlock. *(Pause.)* Some University fella came through here the other day saying that boy was the prettiest child that I ever sired. I figured that University fella was a little light in his loafers, because my daughters are real beauty queens. *(Tilts head toward Smith.)*

SMITH So is my new wife.

GOVERNOR You got any children?

SMITH *(Starts to speak but hesitates.)*

GOVERNOR Guess, you hadn't had time, since you just got married last night.

SMITH Governor, you've got me confused.

GOVERNOR You're a half-ass Democrat who's writing a thesis... a book or some such.

SMITH No, I'm a lawyer, but I guess you're right about being a half-ass Democrat.

GOVERNOR Why is a lawyer writing a thesis?

SMITH I'm not, but I do have a child on the way, just found out about it. In fact, your wife was the first person I got to tell.

GOVERNOR Boy, you don't waste any time, do you? Way I see it, you turned heterosexual, got married and sired you a baby overnight. That may be an indoor record and you talking to the pro.

SMITH Sir, I'm Smith Wakefield a lawyer from Birmingham.

GOVERNOR Republican?

SMITH No that's my uncle. I'm a half-ass Democrat. I thought we had established that.

GOVERNOR You in the legislature?

SMITH No, but I'll do what I can for your pension bill.

GOVERNOR Good. Three branches of government and it's unconstitutional to steal from two branches at the same time.

SMITH I know. I know.

GOVERNOR How you gonna help with the pension bill if you're not in the Legislature?

SMITH Friends.

GOVERNOR Talk to some of them Republican relatives of yours, We need all the help we can get.

SMITH Sure.

GOVERNOR *(Sits upright and eases depth of chair.)* Since you tre not writin' a book, reckon you didn't drive all the way up from Birmingham to hear the old Governor rant about something that's been going on for damn near two hundred years.

SMITH Well, sir. *(Takes a breath.)* I represent a former employee of yours.

GOVERNOR Who's that? State did most of the hiring.

SMITH Mrs. Sadie Belle Graham.

GOVERNOR I'll be damn, how's she doing?

SMITH She has a little trouble getting around, but she's in pretty good spirits.

GOVERNOR Lord, we all got trouble getting' around. Last I heard, she's up in New Jersey.

SMITH I assume, she's back up there now.

GOVERNOR Assume… that's an ass before you and me; you lawyers always ass-uming. Don't you know?

SMITH Well, I put her on the bus on Saturday.

GOVERNOR Saturday? You sure had a busy weekend.

SMITH I suppose, I did.

GOVERNOR How did you run across Sadie Belle?

SMITH I was working at Legal Aid as a volunteer.

GOVERNOR You sure was busy, but good for you. If you don't help poor folks, you can expect revolution… and you never know when you'll need their vote. *(Pause.)* Sadie Belle. *(Smiles.)* You ever taste her biscuits?

SMITH No. She didn't have an oven.

GOVERNOR Sadie Belle without an oven? That's like Bobby ... Al ... What's-his-name without a race car.

SMITH Made Sadie... Mrs. Graham's biscuits this weekend.

GOVERNOR Sure wish you would share Sadie's recipe with my wife.

SMITH They didn't turn out too good.

GOVERNOR Sadie probably held out on you. Wouldn't do no good to give my wife the recipe. Did she tell you about the time she set the Pillsbury Doughboy on fire?

SMITH Well, yes.

GOVERNOR Did my wife offer you something to eat?

SMITH I'm not hungry and she sorta talked me out of it.

GOVERNOR Good thinking. *(Nods.)* Bet my Sadie Belle never did get a dime of that insurance policy.

SMITH Well, no she didn't, but I came upon a bigger problem.

GOVERNOR That lemon water wasn't her fault although she's claimed it was all the way from Montgomery to Newark. Every now and then, outta of the blue, I'll get a letter from somebody saying they's sorry about me gettin' drugged up on Tee Vee and how things would have been better off if I'd been elected governor. *(Pause.)* We wouldn't have no Civil Rights if that Kennedy boy hadn't got shot... folks nowadays only listen to death and destruction ... nothing else gets their attention. I forgave Sadie Belle years back. *(Pause.)* We's just ahead of our time. Yeah, you got to forgive those around you, so as you and the good Lord can get around to forgiving your own self.

SMITH I suppose that election is pretty much history, but your stand was important and will be in the history books.

GOVERNOR Them history books don't vote and hand out pensions. *(Smiles.)* Funny, you calling it a stand. After all them drugs they pumped in me, it took quite a man to stand at all.

SMITH Mrs. Graham has something else on her mind.

GOVERNOR She ever get shed of that butterfly pin?

SMITH Sir?

GOVERNOR You know about that butterfly pin?

SMITH Well, yes.

GOVERNOR She must be gettin' ready to meet her Maker. You see, I knew she had it all along. *(Rubs chin.)* It was the way she talked the next morning. Chatting like a dodo bird. Well, I knew she's the only one sober when that woman let go of that thing. Sadie's religion won't let her drink, but she don't have any problem holding on to hope in the form of that diamond butterfly pin. *(Pause.)* Well, Sadie has the diamonds. Just what's in all this for you, anyway?

SMITH *(Antsy.)* Well, Governor, I don't know. I guess like everybody else Mrs. Graham grows on you and I really don't want her to go to prison ... or even have the hassle of our courts ... judicial branch.

GOVERNOR Don't worry about the courts. I asked what's in it for you?

SMITH Like I said, I was just volunteering at Legal Aid, and she was one of my cases. I mean, I was on my way to procreate and bingo I go get stuck in the Sadie Belle Graham tar baby.

GOVERNOR You did have a busy weekend. But, you are not answering my question. *(Points cane.)* What's in it for you? You can start off with the big picture and assume ... you boys are good at ass-uming... assume that life is a terminal illness and we all are gonna die. Now why did you spend your Saturday chasing after poor folks and not playing with the baby's mama?

SMITH You mean, why do I volunteer?

GOVERNOR I suppose. You see I don't really know who you are, except you been beating around the bush since you got here. Bet my wife didn't check out your credentials either.

SMITH I didn't know it was I who was beating around the bush.

GOVERNOR Let's put the hay down where the goats can get it. I don't trust many folks since they turned on me and are jerking my pension around. I figure you're not with the D.A. Office or you'd walked in flashing badges and such. But, I need to know what's in all this for you.

SMITH This may sound corny.

GOVERNOR The corny-er the better. That's what's wrong with folks, they spend too much time thinking about what they are going to say. Corny is good.

SMITH Maybe, I'm here because I can't forget where I was when Kennedy was shot. *(Pause.)* I cried.

GOVERNOR Yeah, I cried too … in my Early Death.

SMITH We were having exams. I know it was just November. But, it seems like we were having exams … you know, the cafeteria was filled in bunches … like it is with exams. And, Maxene from Selma came in like nothing had happened. We'd just all heard that Kennedy had been shot … hadn't even heard about the death yet. And, Maxene says in a loud voice: "It's about time they shot the nigger loving sonofabitch." I just stared at her and walked down the hill to the fraternity house and finished off my crying. But, a couple of weeks later I got drunk at her … we were all dressed up at the fraternity formal and I cursed her with all I had in me … use to get real brave when I got drunk.

GOVERNOR Drunk man's tongue speaks a lot of truth.

SMITH Earlier, that semester, during rush week, the bomb went off. It was Sunday morning and we just thought it was another foundation over on Dynamite Hill. But, it was the four little girls.

GOVERNOR Children are something else. We grownups can decide to step out there and take our chances with the crazy folks… the freaks… the giraffes with the short necks. Grownups can get shot at and stuff, but them children they are a different story. Pisses me off!

SMITH I don't know if that's why I went to law school or that's why I'm here or not or if it has anything to do with it. I mean, I can't help my name, my birth right, my whatever, but I can make a little bit of difference. *(Pause.)* At least, I thought so at one time.

GOVERNOR The Pea River flooded when I was in College. Unfortunately, it takes a human catastrophe to wake young folks up. When you get to be my age, you learn that the only way to take the clout out of death is to live in the here and now and do the next right thing … some folks call it moral courage … yeah, you'll do.

SMITH Well, when I got back to Birmingham after law school, young lawyer's salaries were going up and I was going to a debutante party twice a weekend and I sorta forgot that down at the end of the Valley by the steel mills things weren't so good. *(Pause.)* I hadn't done a damn thing with my life … I mean like give back. And, besides that if you didn't volunteer for the Legal Aid office, they'd assign you a pro bono criminal case, I have a fear of incompetence and if I was going to be incompetent, I had rather do it at Legal Aid where people didn't go to jail. Of course, Mrs. Graham came along. And, yes I'm a white liberal, and yes, I was in college in Birmingham when the church was bombed ... even heard it down the Valley at the fraternity house. And, yes, I saw you on television when you lost that election ... it was my first time to vote ... and I voted for you anyway.

GOVERNOR Yeah, I did get a few votes and you sure know how to win the trust and confidence of the old Governor ... even if you are peeing on my leg.

WIFE *(Enters with two buckets of Kentucky Fried Chicken and speaks to Smith.)* You like crispy fried or original recipe?

SMITH I really can't stay.

GOVERNOR She didn't ask you that.

WIFE Can't make up your mind, just like a Republican.

SMITH Original recipe.

GOVERNOR Chicken is chicken.

WIFE Had a special on wings. *(Serves the Governor.)*

GOVERNOR Always do. I was raised on necks and backs.

SMITH I couldn't ...

GOVERNOR Dust to dust. Necks and backs to necks and backs ... and wings?

WIFE I'll just put it out and you can eat what you want. *(Pause.)* Started to go by Captain Ds after I talked to Representative Boyd ... fish sure sounds good for a summer day.

GOVERNOR The Queen of Fast Food Alley.

WIFE They all got salad bars now and it sure beats being in the kitchen in this heat.

GOVERNOR Honey, you only went into the kitchen to dry your fingernails.

WIFE I know when to volunteer. *(Holds up one hand as if to dry nails.)*

GOVERNOR Speaking of volunteers ... might ought to let this one finish, feed him and send him back to Birmingham.

WIFE It'll be a minute. Got to heat up the biscuits. *(Exits.)*

GOVERNOR Where was I before Julia Child came through?

SMITH The butterfly pin.

GOVERNOR *(Laughs.)* Well, I told you everybody pretty well in the jug drunk, even the help. That leaves Sadie Belle sober. Right?

SMITH Her religion. Right.

GOVERNOR Come to think of it, her religion sure is convenient on her. You see, I use to talk to Sadie Belle early of a morning. Cause, not much ever got by that woman. I figured that butterfly pin didn't either. Yeah, you could put what got by her in a snuff box. *(Thinks.)* She ever sell that butterfly pin?

SMITH Well, no. That's why I'm here.

GOVERNOR Never did sell it?

SMITH No, I have them. They started bothering her.

GOVERNOR Well, she took her own sweet time. And, she knew that I'd let trustees work at the mansion but couldn't be no thief.

SMITH They had to kill loved ones out of passion.

GOVRNOER They're a safe bet. Just like a mean drunk, the morning after ... sweet as a little wet puppy. I covered the error of Sadie Belle's ways with a little wager. Couldn't afford to let her get away seeing as much as she saw and while taking on my advice might as well eat me a good breakfast. *(Pause.)* You ever taste her biscuits?

SMITH No sir. No oven. Made some myself.

GOVERNOR Oh, yeah? Well, you ought to before she gets away *(Runs fingers through hair.)* Ole Sam Womble and the Governor, we made us a wager back then. You know, he's the one with that airbrakes factory. Alabama's been good to him. He's might-near all over the world with them factories. Has his private plane fly me in a whole crate of oranges every Christmas. Used to be a case of Wild Turkey back when I was a drinking man. *(Pauses as if to taste the whiskey.)* Ole Sam has got more money than God, and he was about to go broke 'fore he came to Alabama. Well, that Development Board just up and give him enough land for that factory, and he was possum eatin' happy. Reckon that crazy wife of his, the one that threw that butterfly pin at him ... reckon she never did get over her nerves. *(Shakes head.)* But, the Alabama sun done shine up that ole dog's ass a couple of times. He broke up with his crazy wife and married him a little Maid of Cotton from Wetumpka, I believe, 'bout half his age. You know about takin' on a child bride. *(Pretends to wink at Smith.)*

SMITH Never thought about it that way.

GOVERNOR Don't you go to thinking again.

SMITH She is a lot younger than I.

GOVERNOR Child brides always are. That one back in the kitchen was just nineteen and couldn't make a biscuit with an act of Congress and four chapters of the FHA. But, love should be innocent.

SMITH I never thought about it that way.

GOVERNOR Is there an echo in here? What did I tell you about thinking?

SMITH Sorry.

GOVERNOR Yeah, I figure that you and ole Sam and the old Governor here, done belong to the same club. And, that little Maid of Cotton could walk across a room. *(Smiles vicariously.)*

SMITH *(Laughs.)* Sounds like you did more than a little kissing.

GOVERNOR Boys gonna be boys … at least they use to be. And, I did my share of gambling… hell, my whole life was a gamble … come to think of it. Yeah, I covered the error of my Sadie Belle's ways with a little wager. Bet ole Sam she'd come clean with that butterfly pin… way she liked to work around the Mansion and all. (Pause.) God-a-mighty, she took her own sweet time. *(Laughs.)* Where's that thing now?

SMITH *(Pulls pouch from his pocket and hands it to the Governor.)*

GOVERNOR *(Fingers pouch.)* Thought that thing was a butterfly.

WIFE *(Enters.)* Did I smell diamonds?

GOVERNOR You got the timing of the Hong Kong flu.

WIFE Figured she had them all along. Every woman at the party eyeing that butterfly.

GOVERNOR Thought that damn thing was a butterfly.

SMITH She broke it down.

WIFE Shame. *(Reaches for diamonds.)*

GOVERNOR Ain't gonna let the goat guard the cabbage patch.

WIFE I just wanted to look.

GOVERNOR My crown is in my heart, not on my head. Not decked with diamonds. *(Puts diamonds out of reach of wife.)*

WIFE You wouldn't have believed the way Sadie acted until she passed that lie detector test. That day, I could cook about as good as she could. She put half a box of salt in the broccoli … Brought the broccoli to the table looking like little trees with snow on them.

GOVERNOR Hard to pass them test when you lying.

WIFE Had to take my test twice … those diamonds stole my heart, pulse, blood pressure and all.

GOVERNOR Take them test with your head not your heart.

WIFE Looked for them diamonds for three days. Sadie even let the pressure cooker explode with a pot roast in it. I put two and two together. Sure glad she passed that lie detector test or we'd all starved to death.

GOVERNOR Kitchen like a war zone. Sadie left the powder or some such outta my biscuits. Hard as wood and chewed like rubber.

WIFE Kitchen ain't safe … you can get hurt.

GOVERNOR Now leave us be.

WIFE Just one last look.

GOVERNOR Eyes too big as they are.

WIFE More Seven-up? *(Exits.)*

GOVERNOR *(Fingers pouch.)* She broke 'em down?

SMITH Hid them in the egg poacher in the galley of the state yacht.

GOVERNOR Which one?

SMITH Which egg poacher?

GOVERNOR Yacht?

SMITH The Alice.

GOVERNOR Solid mahogany and one hundred feet long. But, I eat my eggs fried

SMITH Sunnyside up.

GOVERNOR When Sadie Belle passed that lie detector test, Sam just let the bet drop. Everybody, after things settled down figured that woman just threw it out the door, across the deck and into Mobile Bay. Except a few of them newspaper reporters seemed to know better, but they done figured we'd quit talking. *(Pause.)* Shouldn't been leaked in the first place. *(Thinks, then smiles.)* Ole Sam never did call that bet. Course, back then nobody much called a bet on the Governor. Bet him the value of them things. And, I guess there's a reward due Sadie Belle. Believe it was five hundred dollars and that's at six percent interest since nineteen-fifty-seven. Interest alone six hundred dollars. Believe my bet was for ten thousand. Reckon, I won't claim interest. My best guess is them things worth four or five times as much now. Alabama sun done shined up Sam's ass one more time. Sam owe you anything for that one pocket of yours, Lawyer Smith?

SMITH *(Puzzled.)* No, I was working at Legal Aid, as a volunteer. I couldn't charge.

GOVERNOR You know, I believe you.

SMITH Thanks.

GOVERNOR And, that's mighty nice of you. If you don't help out the poorfolks…

SMITH … You can expect revolution.

GOVERNOR I'm seeing more Democrat in you and I figured you to be just a paycheck Republican anyway. Yeah, you sorta grow on a fella. How many children you got?

SMITH One on the way.

GOVERNOR They make life complete.

SMITH I almost talked myself out of getting married.

GOVERNOR I thought so.

SMITH I met Alyce at my last debutante party… of course, I'd been calling it my last debutante party for five years. *(Pause.)* Governor, you've had a lot of babies, do you know the moment of conception?

GOVERNOR I'd usually had me a nip or two when I did the conceiving. But, they say the mind plays all sorts of tricks on you.

SMITH Seems like I remember the exact time and I felt a real extension of myself.

GOVERNOR When I get them feelings, I go sit in the closet until they go away.

SMITH Sir, what should we do with the diamonds?

GOVERNOR I'll get the wife to send them to ole Sam and collect my bet. *(Pause.)* Wife might hold one out for a Christmas present … last few years been lean.

SMITH *(Gives Governor the diamonds.)*

GOVERNOR You got Sadie Belle's address?

SMITH A friend of hers.

GOVERNOR Sure you won't stay a while?

SMITH I really need to get back to Birmingham.

GOVERNOR Eat you a bite. *(Starts to eat.)*

SMITH I do need to get back.

GOVERNOR *(Waves chicken wing as he talks.)* Life is what passes you by, while you're trying to be someplace else. It's a shame. I believe it was down in Mobile back in the forties that somebody said I was going places. I said, "Hell, I am places."

SMITH Governor, take my word for it I feel like I am someplace right here and now, but I do have to get back to Birmingham.

GOVERNOR On your way out leave Sadie's address over there by the phone.

SMITH *(Walks to telephone and leaves address.)* It's right here by the phone.

GOVERNOR Lawyer Smith.

SMITH Yessir?

GOVERNOR You say you have a baby in the hopper?

SMITH Yessir.

GOVERNOR Well, when it gets here, you play with it like you was a kid yourself.

SMITH A kid?

GOVERNOR Like I said, you play with it and let somebody else do the raising. Do you both good. Offer you a drink of whiskey but hadn't been a drop in the house since they laid open my heart years back. *(Smiles.)* Hell, my heart always been laid wide open. Doctors worse than lawyers.

SMITH Governor, many thanks. *(Grabs his hand and shakes it.)* I really hate to leave, but I must. Thanks again. *(Starts exit.)*

GOVERNOR You ought to eat some chicken. We might solve some more problems. Hell, we might even dig up some problems we didn't know we had.

(Telephone Rings.)

SMITH *(Looks in direction of kitchen and then answers telephone.)* Governor's residence. *(Pause.)* Speaking. Good, I was hoping you could find me. *(Pause and turns serious.)* What? What? How bad was she hurt? How's the baby? *(Pause. Gets excited.)* Yes. Yes. She was pregnant. We just found out about it this weekend. What hospital? I'll be right there. *(Hangs up. Turns to Governor,)* My wife fell water skiing. She had an accident. Jumping the ramp like she wasn't pregnant.

GOVERNOR If she don't want that baby, it ain't none of your business.

SMITH How can you say that?

GOVERNOR 'Cause, my son, somethings we ain't got no control over. You wound up tighter than fishin' line on a fifty-dollar reel with your whole life planned out. *(Points.)* Good Lord ain't up in heaven just sittin' on his hands.

SMITH I've got to go … thanks. *(Exits.)*

GOVERNOR *(Shouting.)* Get your butt back in here!.

SMITH *(Reappears.)*

WIFE *(Reappears, with Seven-up.)*

GOVERNOR Ain't a damn thing you can do runnin' down the road half crazy. And, when you get to the hospital, you'll just be in the way. Only time the doctors let me in the operating room was when they wanted to cut me open. *(Senses that Smith is calmer.)* You need another Seven-up?

WIFE Here it is. *(Offers Seven-up.)*

SMITH No, thanks.

GOVERNOR Too bad, we need the aluminum.

SMITH What am I supposed to do? *(Ire.)* Stomp some more cans?

GOVERNOR You're suppose to collect yourself. You know how many times entire nations go off half-cocked and crazy? *(Brief pause.)* All the time. You need a plan and that plan is to calm down. Then, we're gonna get on that telephone over there and call the hospital. We spend most of our life in a catastrophe that never takes place. Now take three deep breaths.

SMITH *(Breathes.)*

WIFE Honey, this is serious. *(Touches Governor's shoulder.)*

GOVERNOR I know it is.

WIFE But …

GOVERNOR Now leave us be.

WIFE *(Exits.)*

GOVERNOR *(Points to Smith.)* Now you get on the telephone over there and tell the operator you with the Governor and to put you through. *(Pulls quarter from change purse.)*

SMITH *(Fumbles for quarter, then takes quarter from Governor and dials the operator.)*

GOVERNOR Tell her it's an emergency.

SMITH *(Waits.)* Yes, operator. I'm with the Governor and we have an emergency. *(Pause.)* She says all your calls are emergencies.

GOVERNOR Hold your own.

SMITH Seriously, my wife just had an accident and she's at University Hospital in Birmingham. *(Pause.)* My name is Smith Wakefield and my wife's name is Alyce. *(Pause.)* No, I don't have the number. *(Pause.)* I know there are a lot of numbers. Try emergency. *(Pause.)* Yes, my calling card number is 205-323-1803…

GOVERNOR *(Mumbles.)* 1803. Malbury versus Madison.

SMITH *(Waits.)* Tracy asked how you getting along today.

GOVERNOR Tell Tracy just fine. Tell her when I'm next elected I'll put her pay raise in the rate structure.

SMITH She's putting the call through. *(Pauses.)* How do you get a real operator and not a recording?

GOVERNOR Telephone companies good to the Governor. Special light goes off when I pick up the telephone and put in a quarter.

SMITH Yes. Yes. I'm Smith Wakefield. Are you the doctor? *(Pause.)* Yes. Yes. My wife is Alyce Wakefield. *(Pause.)* How is she? *(Pause.)* I don't care who the attending physician is. *(Anger.)* How is she?

GOVERNOR Calm down.

SMITH *(Into telephone.)* I'm sorry. How's the baby? *(Pause.)* What baby? *(Pause.)* Yes. Yes. She pregnant. We just found out about it. *(Pause.)* What was she doing going over the ski jump?

GOVERNOR None of your business.

SMITH Yes. I know they are supposed to exercise.

GOVERNOR Still none of your business.

SMITH Why can't you give out information over the telephone?

GOVERNOR That should be obvious.

SMITH I'm with the former Governor and I'll be there in an hour.

GOVERNOR Once a Governor, always a Governor.

SMITH *(Hangs up telephone.)* Hospitals ... they won't tell you anything ... she was in satisfactory but guarded ... then I told them she was pregnant and they moved it to critical. Hospital words ... I don't know a thing.

GOVERNOR You are not supposed to know that which is none of your business. Only thing I do know is you flying down the highway and stirring around is not gonna help. Everything is gonna be okay and it may take place without you. *(Pauses.)* Time you sat down and let the old Governor tell you what you can and can't do in this lifetime ... specially with them women folks. You see, the South is really a materialistic society ... always has been ... always will be... They only let us think we are running the show ... doing the strutting like a peacock with its feathers spread out. Yeah, them women folks they are something else. *(Pause.)* If that baby does get here, you just play with it and quit fussing over everything.

SMITH *(Grabs Governor's hand and shakes it and begins exit.)* Governor, thank you for everything. Sadie's address is right there by the telephone. *(Exits.)*

GOVERNOR *(Comes out of deep thought,)* Y'all come back, you hear. And, don't go in that delivery room, you'll just be in the way. *(Pauses, thinks and stands.)* Talking to that boy was like trying to teach a pig to sing. It aggravates the pig and it's a waste of my time.

ACT TWO, Scene Two
(a year later)

AT RISE: *Smith on stoop of Governor's house with coat over arm and with book and reading glasses. Lights down on Governor in his chair, Wife on telephone and Sadie down stage facing opposite of Smith.*

SMITH *(Spot. Reads from book.)* "Resolve to be thyself and know that he who finds himself loses his misery." Matthew Arnold. *(Reflects and closes the book.)* The trip back to Birmingham that day was both the longest and shortest trip I have ever made. All I could hear was the Governor saying that my stirring around wasn't going to help much. Then, I thought that all I have ever done was stir around like a squirrel in a cage. *(Pause.)* When I got to the hospital, Alyce and the baby were okay. Alyce slowed down and had the baby … a little girl, who we call Sunshine. She is truly a miracle. The Governor and Sadie found me in my squirrel cage and grabbed me by the nape of my neck and made me slow down and try to live in this lifetime … one slow easy step at a time. *(Pause.)* When I last heard from the Governor's wife, it was just after Sunshine was born and the Governor had announced that he was running again. At first I thought it was sad that the Governor was running again … his being blind and all, but then his words came back that running for public office was a privilege … almost as sacred as the right to vote. *(Pause.)* I keep in touch with Sadie. She is in New Jersey and has it set up so she can talk into Mr. Merriam's speaker phone in the kitchen and through the magic Mr. Merriam's dictating machine and his secretary Sadie sends me a letter from time to time. *(Pause.)* That spring, the rivers and lakes were filled to overflowing and everyone talked about the weather.

Lights fade on Smith

WIFE *(Spot and telephone rings. She answers.)* Headquarters. Re-Elect the Governor, you hear. *(Pause.)* Lawyer Wakefield, how's that baby? Hope y'all are high and dry. Governor always says little boys carry the name, but little girls carry the heart. How's that bride of yours? Good. Good. *(Pause.)* You read it right, we announced for Governor. Nothing like a campaign to make the sap rise, if you get what I mean. *(Laughs.)* Says, he is getting old enough that he doesn't have to lie about tax cuts … says tax cuts takes all the vision out of being Governor. *(Pauses and fingers diamond stud in ear.)* Diamonds? Why, yes, Sam Womble sent me some diamond studs for Christmas, along with the reward money. Kept the real big ones for himself and that little Maid of Cotton. *(Picks up scarves, one blue and one green.)* It's the running that's fun. We're gonna figure out who the winner might be and throw our support … get a VIP table at the inaugural ball and maybe a car in the parade. *(Signs.)* And, our state pension needs renewing every four years. Do you think I look better in blue or green? *(Pause and holds both scarves up.)* Never could make up my mind. You can have them parades … a convertible in Montgomery in January is not my idea of fun. A VIP table is nice and we are living on that pension money. *(Pause.)* Give that bride and baby a big hug and kiss for me. And, y'all come, you hear.

Lights down on Wife

SADIE *(Lights up. She sits with a mixing bowl.)* Dear Lawyer Smith, Glory be and hallelujah. I be surely blessed about the news of my Sunshine. When the good Lord give me my sanctification and righteousness, I didn't expects Him to send me another baby. Yeah, the Good Lord sure knows how to shower down the blessings. I be surely blessed. *(Pause.)* Burp my Sunshine real good and get my Baby off that titty milk as soon as you can, 'cause no telling what some of the mamas takin' for them night nerves. They say, some of them mamas got 'em a valium deficiency. Now, that Dr. Spook didn't have him any babies of his own flesh, but he was like me he knows a lots about babies. You hug 'em when they hurts and hug 'em when they happy. And, don't ever lets them fall too hard on they heads. Don't let them climb loose bookshelves. *(Pause.)* I was thinking about applying for a job raising my baby back down there in Birmingham. But, Mr. Merriam real good to me and he got me in a home just around the block form where I gets my co-balt treatments. I'm afraid more than the arthritis done got after ole Sadie Belle's bones. Lord. Lord. If I had known giving up on sin was so easy, I'd done it years back. I even got me a nice set of ear bobs outta my sin. *(Holds ears.)* But, I guess I had to let the misery wedge me all over the place. Got to go put Mr. Merriam's pancakes on the griddle. Hadn't had to use my biscuits on him yet. I see on the television where the rivers are about to crest down there in Alabama. Gets that bride and my baby and heads for the high ground. Love, Sadie Belle.

Lights down on Sadie

GOVERNOR *(In silhouette, in chair, making a political speech.)* We need to control the high waters of spring and make this world a better place for our citizens and other living things. It's gonna cloud up, but it's not gonna rain. And, folks during my several campaigns for governor, it has been cloudy many times. Now, that reminds me of the time when I was a boy and I had rather go fishing than to plow ... now the only time I got to go fishing was when it was too wet to plow. One day I was plowing along and out of the south a little thunderhead cloud sprung up and got mixed up with another thunderhead and both of them thunderheads got together turned the sky awfully dark. As the thunder rolled across the sky, I just knew it was gonna rain. *(Pause.)* Yes, sir, I could already feel the catfish a-biting on my hook. So, I stopped the mule and started out for the house. *(Slowly stands.)* From across the field I saw my Paw coming in a trot ... he was waving his hands. And, he was shouting something, but I couldn't hear him at first. Then, about that time a little breeze come up out of the west and that big bad cloud began to break up and that breeze brought the worst message a young fisherman ever heard ... by that time my Paw was in hearing distance ... I could hear him say, "Boy keep that mule hitched up ... it ain't gonna rain."

Lights down on Governor

SMITH *(Optional) (Lights up on Smith.)* Sadie and the Governor are no longer with us ... died within a month of each other a few months back. Their funerals were sad at first, but for some strange reason turned joyous. They should have been at their own funerals ... maybe they were ... but I haven't figured all that out yet. *(Pause.)* The Governor's funeral was in a large Baptist church ... large Baptist church ... now that is a redundancy? His funeral was on a bright fall day and the church filled up to overflowing. The choir loft squeezed in all the state dignitaries and the small airport north of the town was filled with planes from Washington D.C. The crowd outside the church waited with the television cameras on the sidewalk. At the cemetery a single bagpipe wailed on a small knoll under a solid oak tree. The Governor should have been there ... maybe he was. *(Pause.)* Just a few days later Sadie died. I didn't think Sadie had any family or friends, because when I met her on that stifling August day, she seemed so alone with her sins. The service was in the funeral home across from Elmwood Cemetery ... you know the one with the mosaic of the Black Jesus over the altar ... the cemetery where they recently buried Coach Paul "Bear" Bryant. Let me tell you, Mrs. Sadie Belle Graham had some family and friends ... they came from all over ... and she had her share of state dignitaries too. All of her children were there, including Sunshine. Again, I was only sad that she wasn't there to see all of them ... all of us, but knowing Sadie, she probably was there. *(Pause.)* It's gonna cloud up, but it ain't gonna rain.

~ END OF PLAY ~

TERRIFIC NEW THEATRE
(*Birmingham's only self-supporting theatre.*)

presents

Waterin' Hole®
a new play by Hubert Grissom, Jr.

directed by Carl Stewart
with Design by Steve Stella

May 16 through June 8
Thursdays, Fridays and Saturdays
at 8:00 p.m. *** Tickets $10

FOR RESERVATIONS CALL
328-0868

starring:
Donna Thornton
John McGiboney
Mark Lawrence
Phil Robinson
Dwayne Johnson
Steve Stella

featuring:
The Voice of Alabama
John Forney

Waterin'hole

Waterin'hole was produced May 16 - June 3, 1991, Terrific New Theatre, Birmingham, Alabama. It was directed by Carl Stewart, designed by Steve Stella and stage managed by Cari Gisler Oliver. The cast:

Avery (A.J.) - John McGiboney
Minnie Mae - Donna Thornton
Cleo (C.D.) - Mark Lawrence
Buck (B.J.) - Phil Robinson
Foil - Dewayne Johnson
Deputy Doyle - Steve Stella
Voice of Sports Broadcaster - John Forney

TIME

Act One - Spring of 1959
Act Two - Fall of 1959

SET

The Waterin'Hole is an ordinary bar with pinball machine and jukebox near the railroad yard in North Birmingham. Jukebox plays early Rock 'N Roll, early Johnny Cash under the Sun label and Hank Williams, Sr. TRAIN OF LOVE[36] is played for transitions. Jars of pickled eggs and sausage are on the bar. There is a window near an exterior door. There is an upstage exit to kitchen area behind bar and an upstage booth. Downstage, there are tables and chairs.

CHARACTERS

AVERY (A.J.): White conductor, who talks a lot and has two wives, with a son by each and each son plays football on opposing teams.

MINNIE MAE: Black bar owner, bartender and cook. Late 30s or 40s.

BUCK (B.J.): White engineer, the fanatic (Klansman) with a modern wife.

CLEO (C.D.): Black cub railroad worker-brakeman. Early 20s.

FOIL[37]: James Dean lookalike, high school dropout.

DEPUTY DOYLE: Deputy Sheriff, Elvis lookalike.

RADIO ANNOUNCER: Off stage male voice from '50s sportscast.

(Foil and Doyle may be same actor. The extent of the characters' smoking and drinking has not been written into the script, but it should be heavy. While there is a lot of drinking, there are no "drunk" scenes.)

ACT ONE, Scene One

AT RISE: *Jukebox playing TRAIN OF LOVE by Johnny Cash and noise of pots and pans being washed. Enters Avery, Cleo and Buck, dressed in RR bib overalls and period RR caps. Avery carries a bag of explosives and two boxes of Easter candy.*

AVERY *(Shouts toward kitchen noise.)* Minnie Mae, it's an emergency! We just run over a drunk hobo ... one of them new diesel engines and forty cars ... got us a bad case of the nerves. Nurse!

CLEO *(Excited.)* Aunt Minnie, you would not believe it. Hobo was a army vet. Just broke his ankle and skin'd his nose ... believe I need me a shot of whiskey, after all.

BUCK If he'd been sober, he'd be dead.

CLEO Minnie Mae, make mine a double shot. *(Pause.)* But, just one.

AVERY Minnie Mae, it's a goddamn emergency ... need it bad ... a shot of your fine medication. White whiskey, anything. *(Pats bib pocket and pulls out roll, placing money on bar.)* I'm dying of thirst. Minnie Mae, please?

MINNIE MAE *(Enters drying hands.)* Hold your horses ... Avery, Baby, you gonna drink all I sell you anyway.

AVERY Nurse, thank God, you've arrived. If I'm lying, I'm dying.

MINNIE MAE What's the big hurry?

BUCK His craving done hit him real bad.

MINNIE MAE *(Looks at Cleo.)* Cleo, Sugar, you supposed to be coming in the side door to make Old Bull happy, and white whiskey is a little too strong for my Baby.

BUCK See, Avery, I told you even the niggers are not comfortable ...

MINNIE MAE Colored ...

BUCK Colored not comfortable coming in the front door.

MINNIE MAE Comfort not got a thing to do with it.

CLEO *(To Buck)* Thank you. Which door was that? *(Points in different directions.)*

AVERY Buck, you can hold your high horses. If you ask me a door is a door. Ain't like Cleo is gonna steal the fuckin' door. What's the big deal? *(Grabs his throat and looks around.)* When we gets rid of these social issues, still stay this would be an ideal place to open a Waterin'Hole for the dispensing and purveying of spirituous liquids, for all of God's children. *(Places bag under table.)* Minnie Mae, Baby, I'm dying, and I ain't lying.

MINNIE MAE *(Pops tops off three long neck beers and pours shots of white whiskey from a Mason jar.)* Don't want no trouble ... them new Supreme Court laws have not made it all the way down here to Birmingham.

AVERY It just a matter of time.

MINNIE MAE Tell Miss Autherine Lucy that. She didn't last a good week at the University.

BUCK See, Avery, whadda I tell you. Coloreds know their place. Right Minnie Mae?

MINNIE MAE *(Hateful.)* Not exactly.

AVERY This money is Union made and collected. *(Proudly, hands Minnie money. Throws back whiskey and chases with beer.)* You talking to the newly elected Recording Secretary of the Local Brotherhood of Railroad Trainmen and Yardmen ... number 402 ... in charge of the social fund if we go out on strike. As a union official, it's my job to be social. Money is money, whether we go out on strike or not. *(Pats money on bar.)*

MINNIE MAE They letting the goat guard the cabbage patch.

AVERY Yeah, we'll have us a party after I take out that trestle down near ....

BUCK Speaking of party, Minnie Mae, guess who married his turnaround woman over in Attalla last weekend? That was the woman who gave him a son back during the war.

MINNIE MAE Avery, Baby, thought you was already married? And, calling a woman a turnaround woman worse than calling a woman a you-know-what. *(Pause.)* And, Avery Baby, you already married.

CLEO What's this turnaround stuff ... I looked it up in my Safety Rules and it ain't there.

AVERY Cleo, it's a dictionary word meaning where a beast of burden or a cargo vessel gets shed of one load, turns around, takes on another load and heads home. When we had the mighty ladies... the steam engines... it was done in the roundhouse with respect... turning around, that is. Pissant diesels do it out in the open yard.

BUCK Since the Union done got us a mandatory eight-hour rest period, fellow can get lonely waiting to come home. Only, some of us get more lonely than others. Avery, you like I Love Lucy going through revolving doors.

MINNIE MAE And passing out boxes of chocolate candy. *(Shakes head.)* Why on earth did you decide to marry a second lady?

AVERY Hush. My boy over at the turnaround needs a legal Daddy. They say he's good enough to play ball for the Bear.

BUCK Yeah, and you be on the sideline helpin' Bear coach. *(Laughs and turns to Minnie Mae.)* Avery's got double the problems and he messed up the Easter candy too. Double dipping ain't easy.

MINNIE MAE Buck, what you talking about?

BUCK Tell her Avery.

AVERY Well, Thelene down in Oak Knoll… she's my regular wife… she don't like nuts in her Easter candy. *(Picks up or points to Easter candy boxes of different colors.)* While Eilene, my new wife, over at the turnaround … over in Attalla … just loves nuts in her candy …

MINNIE MAE And, nuts in her bed too.

AVERY You know, it gets lonely waiting for the train to get made up over at the turnaround.

MINNIE MAE And, when you bite into the candy, you don't know what nut you gonna git.

BUCK That's part of the fun. *(Laughs.)* Still say it'd be cheaper to pay for it … than to marry it.

AVERY That takes all the romance outta of it.

BUCK Romance? Nuts ain't only in the candy if you ask me.

AVERY Minnie Mae, could you get the kettle going and steam open those boxes … the lady down at the Mary Ball Candies didn't mark them boxes … don't know the nuts from the creams. And, let me tell you if I take the wrong candy to the wrong wife, they'll know there is a rabbit in the wood pile.

MINNIE MAE Avery you a mess. Lonely over at the turnaround… and down at the regular house, too. *(Shakes head and makes ready to steam open boxes.)*

BUCK You can't be the Daddy to all of North Alabama … just 'cause the kid knows how to play football. *(Laughs.)* You going to need some of that up-front football money from one of them rich alumni the way you are sinking into debt.

AVERY Got plenty of money.

BUCK You just bought two Chevys and you owe your paycheck to the bookie.

AVERY Chevys are two years old… still say they'll never make a Chevrolet as pretty as they did in fifty-seven. And, he's not a bookie… he runs the Pure Oil Station.

BUCK If he'll take either side of a game and charges juice money, he's a bookie. *(Shakes head.)* Betting on Kentucky to win the basketball tournament… just 'cause Kentucky number one team in the nation, don't mean they crap in the S.E.C. I told you Mississippi State's basketball team had it all.

AVERY I'm still gonna bet on 'em Wildcats out in Wichita.

BUCK Yeah, Mississippi State got the good sense not to go out to Kansas and play basketball with a bunch of niggers … *(Notices stares.)* Excuse me Coloreds. Bill Hilburn knows what he's doing. Defending our way of life from outsiders. I don't care if it is the NCAA tournament.

MINNIE MAE Didn't think you knew what that N double A was.

AVERY He's talking about the National Collegiate Athletic Association … not the National Association for the Advancement of Colored people. And, how Mississippi State won the Southeastern Conference Basketball Tournament and refused to go to the National tournament because some of the teams out in Wichita, Kansas will have Coloreds playing on the team. *(Throws back another shot.)* I seen some little Negra boys down in the projects playing basketball and if you ask me, that seems to be their sport … right Cleo …

CLEO (Nods.)

BUCK Ain't right. White chickens don't mix with the speckle chickens in the barnyard.

AVERY That's bullshit. Make that chickenshit. And now you're the authority on barnyards. Who do you think you are? George Washington Carver?

CLEO Who is Bill Hilburn?

BUCK President of Mississippi State. He knows our southern ways … not likes that fella they got down in Tuscaloosa.

CLEO Well, we can play some ball … speckled or not.

AVERY Not going to the National tournament. That's like folks saying, "I'll show you, I'll shoot myself in the other foot." Some ball players would give a left nut to go the national tournament, but Mississippi State afraid of the Nigras … like their dicks are too long or their sweat will stink … right Cleo.

CLEO We can play some ball, alright. *(Pretends a jump shot. Laughs.)* If I's Buck, I wouldn't be talking too much … bout how we different. *(Throws empty beer bottle to Minnie Mae.)*

MINNIE MAE *(Catches bottle.)* Two points.

BUCK Avery, you just using that mouth of yours to cover up 'cause you lost so much money on that game and if you spend a dime of the Union money, I'll turn you in.

AVERY And your ass will be walkin' home.

BUCK As soon as we get the Frigidaire paid for, I'm gonna get Debbie Lou her own car to drive down to them beauty shows. I just soon walk home now that you lettin' Cleo ride in the front.

AVERY He's always rode in the front. *(Looks at Cleo.)* First one to the car rides where they want to, right Cleo?

CLEO *(Nods.)* That's what you say.

AVERY When my back went out just after the War and I was in that back brace … Cleo's Daddy … Big Cleo … didn't think twice about doing my heavy liftin' for me. *(Pauses and bends over as if to give into back.)* Everybody loved Big Cleo. Didn't they Minnie Mae?

MINNIE MAE Sure did. And you had some back trouble. More than just heavy lifting? *(Laughs.)* Big Cleo said sometimes he had to lift you up on that caboose your back in such bad shape.

BUCK If the dispatcher knew you couldn't even climb on the caboose, he'd …

AVERY Big Cleo saved my job. And his boy can ride anywhere he wants to … and now that my brakeman here can read as good as you can … he's going to be taking the Safety Rules Test pretty soon and he'll be a Conductor in charge of the train … including your pink butt.

BUCK That day will never come.

MINNIE MAE Already come as far north as Montgomery. My cousin says they can ride in the front of the bus, but most Coloreds still go to the back. They say it's what you gets use to. *(Pause.)* And, they say you don't want to sit with your back to just anybody. *(Laughs and looks at Buck.)* Course they say most of the whites done quit riding the bus.

AVERY Yeah, another case of "I'll show you, by God, I'll shoot myself in the other foot while I walk to work." *(Polishes off drink and motions for another.)* And, when Bear Bryant finds him a good ball player, he'll call him an Indian, if he has to. My boys say he's already sent some scouts out to some Colored schools. Ball players are ball players, right Cleo?

CLEO That's what they say.

BUCK Yeah, what you gonna do next fall when you got one of your boys playing nose guard, head-on against your other boy?

AVERY You just jealous 'cause you got a house full of girls.

BUCK At least, they all in the same house.

AVERY You know they tell that story about the time a rich doctor had his wife in the West stands out at Legion Field and the good doctor had his girlfriend in the East stands. He had 'em keep on paging him and he kept changing sides of the field. Worked out for him.

BUCK Oak Knoll stadium ain't no Legion Field and you ain't no doctor. Paging Avery Joe Johnson ... time to switch tracks ... I mean, sides of the field now.

AVERY Like that Hobo we run over today, I guess we gonna need me a little luck.

BUCK Make that a lot of luck. Enjoy it while you can.

AVERY Yeah, lucky like Ole Bull when they caught him at the Tutwiler Hotel.

BUCK You gonna make up some stuff, now. *(Laughs.)*

AVERY No, it's the truth ... I got a brother-in-law that works for that piano company and their loading dock backs up to the service entrance to the Hotel. Say if you stand there on the loading dock, scratching you ass long enough you'll see every politician and every turnaround woman in the state pass through that service entrance. He ought to know, been working there since before the War.

MINNIE MAE What's this got to do with Lady Luck?

AVERY Well, ole Bull got some enemies in the po-lice department.

MINNIE MAE That ain't the only place.

AVERY A set of detectives broke in on him at the Tutwiler, and his turnaround woman had his pecker in her mouth. *(Laughs.)* And, when it came out in the Courthouse …

BUCK Good, God, he must have a long one for it to come out at the Courthouse. *(Laughs.)* That's a block or two away from the hotel.

AVERY *(Frustrated.)* His pecker didn't come out at the Courthouse. It was a morals charge.

BUCK Makes for a better story if it did come out at the Courthouse.

MINNIE MAE Tell your story, Avery Honey, you going to anyway.

AVERY Where was I?

CLEO Ole Bull gettin' him some joy.

MINNIE MAE Hush, let the white folks slander they own selves.

CLEO Remember when Reverend Jones of the Village Creek AME went to Chicago?

MINNIE MAE That's something the congregation does not speak about.

CLEO I heard that he got one of them Chicago women to do what y'all talking about that woman did to Bull with her mouth, and that woman in Chicago wanted Reverend Jones to kiss her after it was all over. Reverend Jones said, "Unh, unh, unh. Only the words of Jesus tur-ch my lips." *(Laughs.)*

MINNIE MAE Cleo Baby you listening to the wrong folks. Besides, that Sunday after he got back from Chicago, Reverend Jones preached his best sermon. You Can't Walk with Jesus, If You Run With the Devil. *(Shakes head and laughs.)* If we didn't need men to have babies, they'd be a bounty on them.

AVERY Bounty?

BUCK You better stay away from them Chicago women.

MINNIE MAE Best stay away from turnaround women, period.

AVERY Where was I?

BUCK Something about Ole Bull and how his goober come out at the Courthouse.

AVERY Oh, yeah, testimony come out at the Courthouse on that morals charge.

BUCK When the Judge found out she had his goober in her …

MINNIE MAE Lord, Child, she done gone after the Judge too?

BUCK No. No. Not the Judge. I mean, the Judge said, "It's her mouth, she can tote pig iron in it if she wants to."

AVERY *(Deflated, because they stole his joke for him.)* The Judge said, "It's her mouth, she can tote coal in it if she wants to."

CLEO Was that before or after she go after the Judge? *(Laughs.)*

AVERY Y'all sure know how to jump on another fella's joke.

BUCK That's just a story ... Bull is an honorable, church going ...

AVERY ... Racist. Church going racist.

BUCK Bull and that nice lady were fully clothed when the detectives went in on them.

AVERY Sure thing, Buckaroo. And it ain't even much of a story after you finish jumping around on it.

MINNIE MAE Ain't nothing much to talk about.

CLEO Hear tell, turnaround women something else.

MINNIE MAE You just watch out, Cleo, Baby.

BUCK Wait 'til you make Conductor, you might be able to afford you a turnaround woman. *(Pause.)* God, they sure do smell good and they fix their hair up real pretty.

AVERY Ain't none of them affordable. But, I tell you some women are good at going to Church and some women are good at ... I mean ... smelling good and looking pretty.

MINNIE MAE And, some women good at both ... we just hard to find.

AVERY Not many of 'em these days goes both ways. *(Receives stares.)* You know, some of 'em do Church real proper like with choir and circle meetings, and, I hear tell, some of 'em also like their sweet-smelling fun too. But, you can't prove it by me.

MINNIE MAE You boys gettin' to be over forty and you still chasing that Tally Whacker around like you just discovered it and its magic tricks.

BUCK We boys ain't the only-est ones. Debbie Lou bought me some of that new French under wear down at Blach's Department Store. Debbie Lou is something else.

AVERY And, them French drawers is the funniest things I ever saw ... not bigger than a sling shot. Drop your overalls and show Minnie Mae. *(Reaches for Bucks shoulder strap.)*

BUCK Hush, at least I wear underwear.

AVERY Can't afford no underwear, I'm paying for my boys' Chevrolets. Course, I wore my last pair of drawers out ... taking them on and off.

BUCK And, you got two houses and a bookie on your payroll, too. Wonder you can afford britches. *(Pause.)* My Debbie Lou stays abreast of the latest fashion. You would not believe it ... but she said at the Tutwiler Beauty Shows it ain't no longer just blondes, brunettes and redheads. No, she was telling me, they got cherry-silver, russet-beige and spring-lavender hair colors.

CLEO She work at the Tutwiler?

MINNIE MAE That's not a proper question.

BUCK Beauty shows at the Tutwiler. No, she goes to beauty school down by the Terminal Station, but she goes to the Beauty Shows at the Tutwiler. Beauticians come in from all over for the Shows ... Demopolis, Leeds, and as far away as Selma, Anniston and even Florala. That platform artist from Low-Real was demonstrating that new frosty look.

MINNIE MAE Frosty look? You know what you talking about?

BUCK I do. It's where they just bleach out every other little wad of hair.

CLEO Why they want to do that?

BUCK Beats me, but it sure is pretty.

MINNIE MAE How they manage to do that?

BUCK They got this bathing cap with holes in it and they pull out little wads of hair. Sometimes I go with Debbie Lou just to watch. They turns out real beautiful.

AVERY No wonder you need them French underwear to keep up with all that high fashion.

MINNIE MAE *(Looks a roll of money on bar and helps herself a twenty-dollar bill.)* This will cover last week's tab. I'd better collect while I can. With everybody talkin' fashion, I might buy me a new skirt and sweater set. And, maybe a new hairdo. Frosty look? Do tell. *(Shakes head.)* Every other wad of hair? Do tell? I bet them hairdos cost a pretty penny.

AVERY Money is just part of it. If we do go out on strike this time, we're gonna be ready... come over here you might as well learn about this stuff too. *(Sits at table and is joined by Buck and Cleo. Avery pulls bag from under table.)* The latest.

CLEO That stuff scares me to death.

BUCK And, I'm gettin' too smart to mess with that stuff.

AVERY Einstein you best listen. Got me issued some of the latest plastique... *(Fiddles in bag amongst fuses and bars of explosives.)*

BUCK What's plastic gonna do?

AVERY This is plastique explosive ... not plastic. French invented it before the last real war to get after the Algerians. *(Pulls package from bag and puts on table.)* Its pliable, like putty. *(Holds up cord.)* They make these things in short, medium and long. *(Laughs and ties an over hand knot in cord.)* Praise the Lord for nitro starch.

BUCK That looks like that silly putty, I bought my youngest daughter at the ten-cent store.

AVERY This stuff is the latest. See this knot you just wrap the plastic around the detonation cord or rig you up a blasting cap and some wire. And, bingo, there she blows. BOOM! *(He wraps the plastique around the detonation cord leaving a long tailing cord.)* Or, you can light the end of it and run like hell. If the cord is long enough, you can be in the next county before it blows.

CLEO Don't mess with that stuff in here.

AVERY Stuff just as good as TNT and a whole lot easier to work with.

BUCK Wish you'd be careful. You sure you know what you doing?

AVERY Einstein, what kind of question is that?

CLEO No offense Mister Avery, but it sounded like a pretty good question to me.

AVERY Drop that Mister stuff ... we all good Union men now. That Waxahachie Creek trestle bridge be a whole lot easier to knock out this time around. You just press one of these little babies on one side of the rail and one on the other side near where the rails join ... and you might press a few in the girder ... about midways between the pilings. Bingo! There she blows. BOOM!

BUCK That trestle bridge is one hundred, four foot long ... you ought to remember that from the last time.

AVERY Shut your trap about last time … we fightin' for our living right now and them new hairdos. The bridge is a hundred and three foot long. And, everybody needs them a little excitement ever now and then.

CLEO Not me Man, I don't even like cap pistols.

BUCK If I'm gonna blow something up, ain't gonna be no bridge during no strike.

AVERY After a hop, skip and jump there she blows. BOOM! BOOM!

FOIL *(Enters, collar turned up on his red windbreaker, like James Dean. Looks around and says nothing.)*

BUCK *(Sees Foil, but Avery does not see him.)* Boom! Boom! That's the best duck huntin' story, I've ever just about heard.

AVERY Wasn't talking about no duck huntin' story.

CLEO Boom! Boom! Yes, you was.

AVERY I's talking about that railroad trestle bridge down at Waxahachie Creek.

CLEO Good place to hunt ducks?

BUCK How do you call a deaf duck?

AVERY What?

BUCK DUCK! *(Points out stranger.)*

MINNIE MAE *(Enters and looks at stranger.)* What'll it be?

FOIL Pabst.

MINNIE MAE You twenty-one?

FOIL Yeah.

AVERY Minnie Mae give the boy a Pabst on the Union … the law is, at best, relative with all that white whiskey you passing out. *(Catches on and hides explosives.)* As I was saying that if they get that Landrum-Griffin Bill through Congress, it'll set Unions back fifty years.

CLEO Readin' in the newspaper where it says that new law just gonna get after hoodlums in organized labor… the Unions.

BUCK Organized, hell, it looks unorganized to me.

AVERY Ain't no hoodlums in organized labor, and it's gonna do a lot more than get after union bosses. It's gonna get after honest, dues paying, Union members, like us. Them diesel engines cuttin' out jobs and now the rich Republicans gonna cut out Unions altogether. Featherbedding, bullshit.

FOIL *(Gets beer and goes to pinball machine.)*

CLEO Newspaper said that the Southern Democrats are siding with Ike, and it was a good as law.

AVERY Senator Jack Kennedy runnin' for President and he'll head off that law or water it down so much it'll mean nothin'. He needs the Union vote, real bad come next spring, if he's still runnin' for President.

BUCK That rich, nigger lovin' Yankee ain't got a chance with me.

CLEO Don't think he needs your vote. *(Sardonic.)* He's a Catholic too. Some of my best friends go to the Catholic school.

BUCK Them Kennedy's never did have to sweat the mortgage.

MINNIE MAE Or pay for French underwear.

BUCK Give me a patriotic Southerner.

AVERY One of these days, Buck-a-roo, you'll learn that them good ole boys down at your Birch Society, don't butter your bread. Or, is it your Klavern, where ever it is you go in such a big hurry on the first and third Wednes-dees. I know it ain't Prayer Meeting or Choir Practice. *(Laughs.)* You a big shot under a bed sheet ... but you had better learn about these new ways ... And, who butters your bread and where your paycheck comes from. Or, you won't have a paycheck. Your patriotic Southerner ain't going nowhere in politics ... the way they always begging new industry to come down here, because of the cheap labor. Cause our unions are weak. Bullshit. *(Whispers.)* I'd best check out the stranger. *(Walks to pinball machine.)* Excuse me James Dean.

FOIL *(Says nothing, ignores Avery and continues to play pinball.)*

BUCK *(Turns to Cleo for small talk.)* Sunday night, I's telling you about how on Amos and Andy, how Kingfish come home driving a big long Cadillac and Sapphire wants to know where he got it ... *(Laughs.)* All hell breaks loose, Sapphire gonna go shopping to get even.

CLEO And get a new hairdo. *(Does a little dance.)* Shufflin' and jivin' and we're naturally comical too.

BUCK That's what I always say.

CLEO I know.

BUCK We get that pay scale we asked for in that new contract, even you can buy you a television set. I tell you, Amos and Andy is my favorite show on television.

CLEO And, some of my best friends are honkies.

AVERY *(To stranger at pinball machine.)* Whadda you think about Mississippi State winning the Southeastern Conference title and lettin' Kentucky go to the tournament out in Kansas. *(Receives no response.)* Nigras. *(Receives no response.)* *(Turns to point.)* That one over there, just like family. Why, his Daddy use to do my heavy lifting when my back went out ... and then after my hernia operation. His Daddy, Big Cleo, use to help run this here Waterin'Hole, too. Yeah, Doctor said I's givin' into the pain so long, I started walking in a stoop, and then bingo, my back goes out. Your back ever gone out? Yeah, they don't make 'em, like they made Big Cleo. Sweetest fella you'd ever see.

FOIL *(Ignores Avery.)*

AVERY If my back goes out, I hope it ain't from heavy lifting. *(Sexual/Elvis hip thrust.)* Right?

FOIL *(No response.)*

AVERY You see Elvis on Ed Sullivan? They cut out his wiggling ... now that'll throw your back out.

FOIL Army ... he's in the Army now.

AVERY By God, you can talk. Yeah, he's in the Army now. Rather my back go out while I's bumping the fuzzy than crawling around with a rifle. Right? *(Looks at Foil. Long pause.)* You're not real talkative, you know?

FOIL Supposed to have something to say.

AVERY Bought my boys '57 Chevolets ... blue green ... got a good deal on 'em.

BUCK *(Looks over shoulder at Minnie Mae.)* Minnie Mae, these here are good chairs, where did you get them?

MINNIE MAE Big Cleo got them when they shut down that Polio Hospital.

BUCK Umh. Umh. Umh. *(Backs off.)* There's been a lot of sadness in these chairs.

MINNIE MAE That's why Big Cleo got such a good deal on them.

CLEO I miss Big Cleo, he always wanted me to go places.

MINNIE MAE Got you through Ullman High.

BUCK Problem now, two Ullman High School students want to transfer to Phillips High. Read it in the paper, just yesterday, Whadda you think of that?

CLEO Whadda you want me to think?

BUCK Well, they'd better watch out. You ought to think of transferring out of your Mama's house. Gets you more joy that-a-way. *(Laughs.)*

CLEO Joy? Can't afford that. Trying to make my paycheck go around … til my brothers and sisters get outta school. We hope my little brother, Alfonse, be able to go down to Tuskegee.

AVERY That schooling is expensive. Way I figure it my turnaround boy got a good chance at All State and to go play for the Bear, and the other boy hell bent on going to college too … he plays football but he's lot more interested in his slide ruler. Says football just a game. Don't have his heart in it. No, that Boy was raised in the shadow of his Granddaddy's house, and he'd rather read a book than to run a foot race.

CLEO Me too.

BUCK *(Gets out checker set to play with Avery.)* Just wait until Oak Knoll plays Attalla next fall… you're gonna have one boy playing center for one team and the other boy playing nose guard for the other team. Who you gonna yell for?

AVERY *(Serious and playing checkers.)* Both of 'em.

BUCK And, why did you see fit to name 'em both Avery Joe, Jr.?

AVERY I told you, it's a good name and it frees up my mind for other things.

MINNIE MAE That's gonna catch up with you. You worse than that candy lady down at the Mary Ball … can't tell the cream from the nuts.

AVERY Joe Junior is a real brain … always worried about the Russians and Sputnik. Says only reason he goes out for football is so he can get a date during football season … guess, I ought to be glad he dates girls … him being such of sissy with that slide ruler of his.

BUCK *(To Minnie Mae.)* He's real bookish.

AVERY He's running for President of the Student Body this Spring. Guess he needs him a real nice date for political reasons…same reason he plays football. But, you know he can hike the ball pretty good… and if you don't make mistakes that's ninety-nine percent of the game… mistakes will kill you in high school ball.

MINNIE MAE Who's keeping count.

BUCK He could do like they do down at Auburn and hike it over the punter's head.

CLEO They the National Champions.

AVERY That was over a year ago. Just you wait and see what the Bear does. I heard tell, that when the Tide loses a game, on Sunday morning about four-thirty or five in the morning, he gets his boys outta bed and dresses them out in full pads and takes them to the five-yard line on the practice field. Puts the first-string offense on the five-yard line against the first-string defense ... and then says, boys you score ... talking to the offense ... and to the defense he says boys you stop 'em. Then he climbs up to his tower and watches. *(Rubs hands together.)*

FOIL Scars.

AVERY When Joe Junior heard about that, he licked his lips and changed his mind about going to Auburn ... said he's going to play for the Bear. Gonna be a Marine, too.

CLEO Joe Junior? Which one?

AVERY *(Perturbed.)* My ball playing Joe Junior over in Attalla ... he's the ball player.

MINNIE MAE Still Avery, Baby, ain't you got enough problems without calling them by the same name?

BUCK That's what I told him.

AVERY Naw, it sort works out best ... frees up my mind to think about other things. If I call the wrong boy, the wrong name in the wrong house, I'd be worse off than that bitch down at Mary Balls Candies mixing things. *(Triple jumps in checkers and laughs. Then, looks over shoulder at stranger.)* Buck, why don't you go speak to our friend.

BUCK Don't seem too friendly to me. Seems right strange.

AVERY Go on, I got to help Cleo with his safety rules.

BUCK *(Gets up and walks to stranger.)* Good thing Mississippi ain't going to Wichita. There are somethings more important than a ballgame... like our Christian way of life.

FOIL *(Says nothing.)*

BUCK You know much about politics?

FOIL *(Says nothing.)*

BUCK Republicans gonna run Nixon next year. Democrats do good to run Lyndon Johnson outta Texas. What do you think?

FOIL *(Says nothing.)*

BUCK You ain't Catholic? Are you?

FOIL Orthodox pervert.

AVERY Orthodox pervert. *(Laughs and pulls roll from pocket.)* Minnie Mae, put a round of drinks on the Union social fund. Even give James Dean over there a Pabst Blue Ribbon on the Union. Orthodox pervert … that's a good one.

MINNIE MAE *(Pours round and exits.)*

BUCK What business you in?

FOIL Agriculture.

BUCK My granddaddy was a farmer.

AVERY *(With roll of money present… talking to Cleo.)* You Mama need any money with them babies?

CLEO We manage. Mama's ironing picks up with spring and the twins started cleaning house for this lady on the weekends. And, with my paycheck. And, Aunt Minnie helps a lot.

AVERY *(Pulls twenty from pocket.)* Your Daddy … Big Cleo was a fine man. He saved my job many a time. He'd even do my consist for me if I needed him to.

CLEO I know. *(Cleo has heard this before, but listens to be polite.)*

AVERY Consist just the cars that make up the train with numbers as long as a whore's dream. When I had too much medication. When I was not up to par Big Cleo would do the consist for me. He couldn't read a word, but Big Cleo knew his numbers. *(Hands him a twenty.)* You take that to your mama. Tell her all we got is our future generations and we need to give them plenty to eat. That Depression been over for a full two decades or so now … the way I figure it … but down here some of us still worrying about getting enough to eat.

CLEO Couldn't Mister Avery.

AVERY Hush, that Mister Avery shit. Just take her the money and tell her she can send me some fried chicken on Monday… I like the way she does that pully bone. Tell her she don't have to use up one of her yard chickens … she can go to the A&P … believe chicken on sale for around twenty-nine cents a pound. *(Pulls out small book)* Now let's get to work. Coupling and Uncoupling …

(INSERT: The Whistle Stop Fugue, a tone poem of sorts, follows. The feel and/or sound of train wheels, much like early Johnny Cash under the Sun label, should underpin the fugue. Generally, lights should be dimmed and/or turned blue, to show that something strange, albeit different, is going on. In theory, we're just going into the characters' heads for a few minutes. It's like when a room falls silent every twenty minutes or so and one wonders what folks are really thinking. CLEO *reads from safety rules while* FOIL *snaps his fingers to beat of the music … train wheels on tracks. Other characters intersperse and overlap with thoughts. Director, actors and tech have lot of latitude as to mood, tone, timing and overlap.)*

FOIL *(Snap. Snap. Repeat.)*

CLEO *(Reads.)* When uncoupling the steam hose, the greatest care must be used to avoid being burned by the steam. Or, hot water. When coupling cars or locomotives Keep clear of tracks and face moving engines or cars. *(Repeat in a whisper as if committing to memory while others speak.)*

AVERY Um, huh. *(Pause.)* Good. *(Repeat in half tone while others speak.)*

BUCK Strikes and kids. It's tough. Say what you wanna, boys are easier to raise than girls.

CLEO Avoid being burned by steam or hot water. If lever should be inoperative cars should be stopped before pin is lifted by other means.

AVERY Strikes tough on kids. Depression tough on me. Cleo, you gonna do okay. Let you move up. Give a kid a ball and let him run. Whiskey makes me sad.

FOIL *(Snap. Snap.)* I was a prayed for child. Don't think it worked. Sputnik circling, looking down on us … shhhhh … *(Snap. Snap.)* We gonna die.

AVERY Life is a terminal illness.

CLEO Avoid being burned by steam or hot water. Do not use hands or fingers to force sticking lock pins. Cars should be stopped before pin is lifted by other means. *(Repeat in whisper.)*

AVERY Other means. You only live once. Took the boy to Sears and Roebuck must have been four or five. War was over and buying stuff again.

FOIL *(Snap. Snap.)* Heroes dead or dying.

BUCK Lil' Imogene's a freshman cheerleader. All four girls on cheerleading squad. *(Cheerleading routine with hand clap.)* Go! Hueytown Golden Gophers! Go! Boys carry the name but girls carry the heart.

CLEO Avoid being burned by steam or hot water. Do not stand on ends of cars to open or close knuckles or to adjust drawbars. *(Repeat in whisper.)*

FOIL *(Snap. Snap.)* Heroes dead or dying.

MINNIE MAE Love is not a hero's game ... try hard ... never a hero. Closest hardest to love. Honeymoon over. Honeymoon all the time. Love's a game of inches. *(Laughs.)* Tallywacher turnaround joke.

CLEO Avoid being burned by steam or hot water. Do not operate couplers release levers of car or engine other than the one being ridden. *(Repeat in whisper.)*

AVERY I's on the Extra Board. Need the overtime. Saving, paying for two Chevys and other necessities.

FOIL *(Snap. Snap.)* Where's the promised pony? *(Snap. Snap.)*

BUCK Debbie Lou spent money on pretty thangs. Gonna buy a weddin' ring.

CLEO Avoid being burned by steam or hot water. Do not use hands to adjust drawbars, knuckles or lock pins while cars or locomotives are in motion or while couplings are about to be made. *(Repeat in whisper.)*

MINNIE MAE Almanac says plant on Good Friday. Strike coming. Better not wait. Cabbage, mustard greens, collards, turnips, okra, squash, beets, corn, cucumber radishes tomatoes, watermelons and pumpkins for the fall. Gotta feed the fools and their innocent children.

AVERY Took the boy to Sears and Roebuck. Basket full of balls ... footballs, basketballs ... all kinds balls. Little white boys and little Black boys playing with the balls in the aisles. Crowd laughin'. War over.

FOIL Earth Mother eats it all ... scars, eyeballs, tongues. *(Repeats. Snap. Snap.)*

AVERY Stop! Stop! Stop playing. Ball cost four dollars. We walk away looking back.

MINNIE MAE Hopes take over ambitions. Good Friday or not. Sow perchance to reap.

FOIL *(Snap. Snap.)* No daddy ... child labor. Machines. *(Snap. Snap.)*

BUCK Marry them girls off one of these days. Too late for a son. Debbie Lou gettin' old.

CLEO Avoid being burned by steam or hot water. Employees required to control cars by brakes must know how to operate the type brake they are used to. When uncoupling the steam hose, the greatest care should be used to avoid being burned by the steam or hot water. Avoid being burned by steam or hot water.

AVERY Umm. Good. Good.

End of mood and tone poem.

CLEO Mr. Avery, I thought they got rid of them steam engines.

AVERY Most of 'em are gone, but you still got to learn that stuff … if you run across an old steam engine you don't want to get burned.

BUCK *(To FOIL.)* Avery over there has got him a pet nigger … trying to teach him the Safety Rules if they ever let Coloreds move up to conductor.

CLEO *(Angry. Gets out of chair.)*

FOIL You confuse me with somebody who gives a shit.

BUCK Says, he knows niggers are faster than we are.

CLEO *(Looks at Buck.)* Gonna adjust his smart mouth with my … *(looks at fist.)*

AVERY Hold on, don't do what they expect. Do the unexpected. Learn the fucking Rules. *(To Buck)* You damn right, they are faster than you are.

BUCK Avery claims he use to foot race with Jesse Owens.

FOIL And, I grow marijuana up behind Sportsman's Lake. Good cash crop.

(Lights joint.)

AVERY Jesse won every time but one.

MINNIE MAE I've heard about Jesse Owens … forty … fifty times. *(Turns to Foil.)* Wish you would not smoke that wacky tobaccie in here.

AVERY Back in the Thirties, when Jesse was overseas showing off for Hitler … *(Stares at Buck.)* I's down in Tuscaloosa running the mile in the state finals … I ran the mile in under five minutes. Use to run with Jesse all the time, we even raced a train up near Courtland once. Way up in the hills of North Alabama, we didn't worry too much about color … the race went to the fastest, not the prettiest. *(Laughs.)* Yeah, when I'd spend my summers with my Grandma outside of Oakville, I'd slip over the ridge and do some fancy foot racing with Jesse. We'd outrun horses, rabbits, trains, you name it. *(Sighs.)* Only beat him one time ... when he stepped in a gopher hole. *(Laughs.)*

BUCK *(To Foil.)* See, he's been a nigger lover all his life.

AVERY At least I love, instead of hate. Hate reduces my positive energy.

BUCK And, I can pee up a rope.

AVERY You son-of-a-bitch, you accusing me of lying. *(Starts to fight.)*

BUCK Watch what you call my Mother ... you nigger loving asshole. *(Starts toward Avery with clenched fist.)*

AVERY Your mama wears Army boots and works at the Tutwiler.

(Overlapping.)

CLEO Hold it Mister Avery. *(Reaches for Avery.)*

(Overlapping.)

BUCK You scab sucking, scum bag. *(Throws a fist...hits Cleo.)*

AVERY Don't you even say the word "scab" around me.

MINNIE MAE *(Shouts.)* Hold your horses... ain't gonna fight in my establishment. *(Gets in middle and checks out Cleo.)* Look what you done.

CLEO *(Wipes blood from mouth.)* I'm okay. *(Looks at blood.)* Can't feel a thing.

MINNIE MAE You just numb.

BUCK *(To Avery.)* Look what you made me do. *(Takes another swing.)*

MINNIE MAE You calm down or get out. *(Pulls handkerchief from pocket and blots blood.)* Y'all nervous as chickens on wire and you ain't even out on strike yet. You fight among yourself, how you gonna fight the company?

BUCK See what she says.

AVERY Next time the son-of-a-bitch falsely accuses me ... I'll ...

MINNIE MAE Mister Righteousness sit you pink butt down and cool off.

AVERY *(Shocked.)* But ...

MINNIE MAE Don't but me ... if that strike last as long as it did last time, ain't gonna have you fussing and fightin' on the first day.

CLEO Not even the first day yet.

BUCK And, you, you Mister Big Spender already dipping into that big wad of

Union cash.

MINNIE MAE You cool down … you the one who started throwing that fist of yours. *(Shakes her head.)* Can't you see, it's just tension … and you not even out on strike, yet. Lord, Lord, the times are tough enough without you boys bustin' up the place like it was a roadhouse or something.

AVERY *(Hiding behind Minnie Mae.)* And, your wife is working at the Tutwiler Hotel this weekend.

BUCK Don't you talk about another man's wife. *(Goes after him again.)*

CLEO Y'all don't fight. *(Gets in middle, again.)*

AVERY *(Fight with Buck and Cleo in middle.)*

MINNIE MAE *(While trying to break up fight, she falls.)* I've had it. You Boys, just pay up and leave. Now!

FOIL *(Fires gun over the head of brawlers.)*

AVERY *(Stunned.)* Jeepers, that shit's loaded.

MINNIE MAE Hold your horses big shot. We got enough tension in here without you stirring things up with that firearm.

(Overlapping.)

AVERY Be careful with that thing, I've got young boys.

(Overlapping.)

CLEO Believe he means business.

BUCK You seem like a nice enough fella, what can we do for you?

MINNIE MAE *(Whispers to Avery.)* He may be one of them mental patients that escaped from down at Bryce's Hospital.

BUCK What do you want?

FOIL *(Stares.)*

BUCK How 'bout some of the Union social fund. *(He reaches for Avery's bib pocket.)*

AVERY No, you don't. *(He pulls back. Hits Buck with hat. Switches money to shirt pocket. Whispers to Buck.)* One minute you trying to protect our money and the next minute you trying to give it away, Dumbass.

BUCK Circumstances have changed.

AVERY You hard to figure, Buck-a-roo.

CLEO No, he ain't.

AVERY *(Whispers.)* I believe James Dean there is a little touched in the head.

MINNIE MAE *(To Foil.)* You gotta want something...let me get you a drink of whiskey. *(She goes behind bar.)*

FOIL Where the keys? *(Points with gun to pinball machine.)*

MINNIE MAE Believe jukebox man got the only key. *(Reaches below bar.)*

FOIL No. No, you don't. *(Waves gun for her not to reach behind bar.)*

MINNIE MAE *(Pulls up key.)* Child, I's just checkin'. He left me an extra pinball key. *(Hands key over bar.)*

FOIL *(Looks at key and throws it to Cleo.)* Open that machine.

CLEO Not me. *(Backs to machine.)*

FOIL Yes, you.

MINNIE MAE Who you think's gonna win the Oscar now that James Dean is dead?

AVERY Oscar, what are you talking about?

MINNIE MAE Motion picture shows. *(Looks at Avery.)* Wasn't talking to you, Fool.

FOIL *(With gun, points Cleo to pinball machine.)*

BUCK *(Whispers loudly.)* Why is he fucking around with the pinball machine, when you got that Union social fund?

AVERY *(Pulls hat off and whacks Buck across the head.)* Would you kindly shut up.

BUCK *(Loudly, to Foil.)* Did you hear what I said?

AVERY Would you leave well enough alone.

MINNIE MAE *(Walks toward Foil.)* Figure it's between *Cat On A Hot Tin Roof* and *The Defiant Ones*. What do you think?

FOIL *(Watching pinball machine and Minnie.)*

MINNIE MAE Paul Newman is about as good as we got now that James Dean is dead.

FOIL (Stares.)

MINNIE MAE You ever go to the picture show?

FOIL Yeah, what's it to you?

MINNIE MAE Just trying to strike up conversation.

FOIL Well, I don't like talking.

MINNIE MAE Too much talk-in' around here anyways.

AVERY That's what I always say … some of us just got more to say than others. They say if you ever want to change the subject, just start talking about yourself. *(Walks toward Foil.)*

FOIL *(Real crazy.)* SHUT UP!

BUCK See, his bread didn't get done.

AVERY One brick shy of a load.

CLEO *(Opens pinball coin box and a modest amount of dimes roll across the floor.)*

MINNIE MAE *(To Foil.)* Pinball man gonna be mad at you for making a mess.

CLEO I'm sorry. *(Starts picking up dimes.)*

FOIL No tricks.

AVERY Maybe he just likes to play pinball and he needs the dimes.

BUCK Reckon so?

AVERY Ole Buddy, I can help you out. *(Reaches in pocket.)*

FOIL *(Waves gun.)* Hands up … no tricks. *(Looks around.)* Take them overalls off … no tricks. Y'all got too many pockets.

BUCK What?

FOIL *(Waves gun.)*

CLEO I can't take my britches off. Not in front of Aunt Minnie.

MINNIE MAE Do what the man says … he could be dangerous.

CLEO I just can't.

MINNIE MAE Lord Child, I use to change your diapers.

AVERY It's not gonna be too easy for me to comply with your security request, Sir. In fact, it will be impossible, because I quit buying underwear for economic reasons.

BUCK If he ain't seen a little goober, he won't know what it is. *(Laughs.)* And, if he has, it won't be nothin' new.

FOIL Hush up! Shirts too, anything with pockets.

AVERY *(To Buck.)* You dying to show off your new French sling shot.

MINNIE MAE He's serious. I don't want the place shot up any more than it already is.

CLEO Are you sure Aunt Minnie?

MINNIE MAE Sure about what? Gettin' the place shot up.

CLEO No, me taking my overall off, like he said. I didn't wear my new underwear and you know what you use to say about nice underwear and car wrecks.

MINNIE MAE Best thing we can do is to get shed of him. *(Pauses and makes step toward Foil.)*

FOIL *(Fires gun at floor.)* Y'all gonna talk or do what I say?

CLEO Hold it. *(Unbuckles his straps.)* I been doing what the Man says all my life. *(Stands in well-worn boxers.)*

AVERY Ain't gonna be so easy for me. You might just have to shoot me.

FOIL *(Shoots again, at floor in front of Avery.)*

BUCK Avery, you a Fool. *(Undoes straps.)* Your buckles work just like everybody else.

FOIL *(Laughs at Buck's underwear as he pats discarded clothing for money and railroad watches.)*

BUCK Don't tell nobody.

MINNIE MAE *(Laughs.)* Now, who is he gonna tell?

BUCK Wait a minute that's my Daddy's railroad watch.

FOIL *(Points gun at Buck and then waves gun at Avery to take off overalls.)*

AVERY Are you sure? *(Undoes straps and overalls fall to floor. Tries to cover himself with shirt tail.)* Sorta drafty in here.

FOIL *(Picks up overalls and pats for money and watch.)* Thank you gentlemen. *(Looks to Avery.)* Pity.

BUCK Did he say puny?

AVERY Shut up.

FOIL Just a minute, where's that roll of money? *(Points gun.)* Give me them shirts too. You too good at switching pockets.

BUCK & CLEO *(Remove shirts.)*

AVERY Hold it now. I ain't got nothing on under here and there's a lady present.

FOIL SHUT UP! *(Points gun and pulls back hammer.)* You the one trying to hold out.

AVERY *(Takes off shirt and tries to hold on to Union money.)*

BUCK Minnie Mae, throw Avery a dish rag.

FOIL No monkey business.

AVERY *(Throws money and reaches for box of Easter candy.)*

MINNIE MAE *(She hands Avery the Easter candy.)*

CAST *(A scramble, but Foil comes out holding Union money and backs everybody to stage area where the table is with the bag of explosives under it.)*

AVERY *(Tries to hide behind candy.)* Now if I could get that money back from you… it ain't mine.

FOIL That's for sure. *(Waves at Cast…they move in unison based on FOIL's random gun movement. He point gun at Cleo.)* You load them clothes in that bag. Ain't got time to sift through no more pockets. *(Laughs crazy like.)* Don't figure you boys will chase after me looking like that. *(Waves gun.)*

BUCK *(Whispers to Avery.)* Son-of-a-bitch is crazy.

FOIL Whatta you say?

AVERY He said this is wild and crazy … he likes showing off his new underwear. *(Pretends to help Cleo with packing the bag, but carefully palms Zippo that's atop a pack of cigarettes and makes sure fuse is hanging out of bag.)* Now if I could just get my britches back.

FOIL *(Looks at Avery's rearend up in air.)* And, spoil my view.

BUCK Avery, you better quit messing with him … he might start messing with you.

AVERY Sir, I really do need that money back. It belongs to a lot of folks.

BUCK Like his bookie and Smiling Sam's Used Car Lot.

AVERY Shut up, whose side you on anyways?

BUCK Mister that money ain't gonna do you no good.

FOIL Try me.

BUCK Stuff has got bad luck all over it.

AVERY Minnie Mae put a jinx on it.

FOIL *(Looks at Minnie Mae.)* I'll take my chances. *(To Minnie Mae.)* You can keep your dress on just lay face down.

MINNIE MAE Floor dirty and I ain't gonna lay down for no body. You better take that money and run along or I'm gonna get real angry.

BUCK Better do what she says.

CLEO Yeah.

AVERY Might leave us a little cash for the beer.

FOIL *(Backing to door.)*

BUCK *(Moves suddenly.)*

FOIL Now, y'all get down on the floor.

AVERY *(In the scramble, lights fuse cord hanging out of bag.)*

FOIL Don't want nobody to move for ten minutes, just like in the movies.

CLEO, AVERY AND BUCK *(Lay face down on the floor.)*

AVERY This linoleum is cold.

BUCK It's dirty.

CLEO It's sticky.

FOIL *(Points gun at Minnie Mae.)* Git down.

MINNIE MAE I'm not gittin' on no dirty floor for nobody … and that includes you … you Pinball Cowboy. *(Reaches for broom.)* Now go on and git while your gittin' is good.

FOIL *(Looks around, picks up bag and exits.)*

AVERY *(Starts getting up.)*

BUCK He said to stay down for ten minutes.

AVERY How's he gonna check up on us … he busy high tailing it outta here.

FOIL *(Foil sticks his head back in door and fires bullet that hits juke box and Train of Love comes on by itself.)*

AVERY Go, go on git! *(Falls to floor.)*

FOIL *(Exits.)*

CAST *(Lies real still for a few seconds.)*

OFF STAGE *(An explosion that causes the windows to light up yellow, rattle and shatter. And, dust comes under door.)*

End of Act One

ACT TWO, Scene One

AT RISE: *Deputy Sheriff enters carrying one brick. Minnie Mae seated snapping beans. A bowl of fresh oranges on bar.*

DEPUTY Minnie Mae, did you forget me?

MINNIE MAE Doyle, Baby, it's been a while. *(Looks at brick.)* What you doing cowboy, building houses.

DEPUTY Minnie, there wasn't your regular cash contribution to my Children's Fund under my brick. *(Points out front door where brick was.)*

MINNIE MAE Look, Doyle, Honey, that strike been going on so long, the Union boys done quit buying ... I should say quit paying for their beverages. Ever since that James Dean fella got blown off the face of the earth last spring, I been rethinking, my ways. I'm only in the beer business now, not in the payoff white lightnin' business. Beer is nice and legal.

DEPUTY Whadda you saying?

MINNIE MAE I quit paying you, Honey. Quit feeding the Bulldog. No longer in the white whiskey business.

DEPUTY That fella who got killed last spring was my cousin and we's doing some business together.

MINNIE MAE He was in the agriculture business? Wacky tobaccie?

DEPUTY Alfalfa. Yeah, he was growing some things. But, was not as good with explosives. Them homemade bombs he was making from fertilizer must have turned on him and splattered him all over the side of your establishment. But that don't mean you can quit paying the Children's Fund.

MINNIE MAE Time we all got legal. Might-as-well, ain't gettin' paid anyway. You on both sides of the law. You know what I mean.

DEPUTY You need to rethink what you just said.

MINNIE MAE I just did. Got my own child to take care of.

DEPUTY I don't even like coming around here no more. *(Picks up brick.)*

MINNIE MAE Suits me. I'm tired of that brick.

DEPUTY *(Exits.)*

MINNIE MAE *(Talks to self as resumes tasks.)* Payoffs eats into the profits. At least they use to.

AVERY *(Enters with Cleo, both are carrying worn picket signs.)* That was close. That cowboy still building houses with them pay off bricks? Ain't been the same since James Dean died. Minnie Mae, could you sell us a couple shots of your white whiskey … real cheap?

CLEO Not me, I'm tired of that stuff.

AVERY Minnie Mae, your boy here says he's tired of the devil's nectar, so you can pour his in my glass. *(Goes to ash tray and looks for a butt to smoke.)* Poor me, I can't even afford cigarettes.

MINNIE MAE Poor me. Pour me. pour me another double shot of free whiskey. *(Gets Mason jar of white whiskey.)*

AVERY Put it on my tab and make sure I get the happy hour discount.

MINNIE MAE If you NOT paying don't matter what it costs.

AVERY That's what I always say money is only good for what it can buy.

CLEO Believe, I'll have me a R.C.

MINNIE MAE Fresh orange be better for you. Nobody's paid me in over a month. And, I'm not the one on strike.

AVERY Times they are hard. Even my bookie went broke when Tennessee beat Auburn last weekend.

CLEO *(Gets orange and bites hole in top and sucks juice.)* That was something else. That field goal went right through the uprights, sure did.

MINNIE MAE How do bookie's go broke… thought they had it figured out.

AVERY Auburn a pretty good favorite, and everybody around here bet on

Tennessee for some reason. *(Throws back drink and motions for another.)*

CLEO Tennessee won it all with that field goal. Three to zero.

AVERY That ball game was fought in the trenches. *(Gets used newspaper from table.)* Alabama won too, and Bear is here to stay. Already had one of his assistants over at Attalla looking at my boy play ball. You know the one that's pre-season All State. He's gettin' close to twenty tackles a game.

MINNIE MAE Avery, Baby, we love you, but you been talking about that boy for two months now. That whiskey ain't got to you brain? Heard down in Mobile, when them stevedores stay out on strikes too long... some of them would go wet brain. You better watch out.

AVERY *(Reads paper.)* Look here Attalla number one team in the state in their division. I told you. *(Reads.)* Course, Oak Knoll still undefeated ... they ranked eighth. Come Friday night, there's gonna be a shoot-out.

MINNIE MAE And, you gonna change sides of the field at half time? If you make it to Friday night.

AVERY Hadn't figured that one out yet. But, I figure I'll get to go home with the winning team.

MINNIE MAE Them womenfolks ain't figured you out, yet?

AVERY I tell my turnaround woman, I'm divorcing my church wife as soon as the strike is over. *(Pause.)* And, I tell my church wife that I got a lot of Union business over at the turnaround. *(Throws back drink and reads paper.)* Says here Khrushchev and Ike gonna get on with their talks in Gettysburg.

CLEO *(Peels fresh orange, tearing it open to eat.)* Cuba already turned Communist. Buck says it's just a matter of time until...

AVERY Buck hadn't had an original thought, since he started scratching his nuts.

CLEO Says it's just a matter of time until the ....

AVERY *(Annoyed because he's reading.)* Time for what. Scratching your nuts?

CLEO 'Til the Communist takeover ... Buck says Communist everywhere.

AVERY Communist make a lot of sense, if you've been on strike as long as we have.

CLEO Says Communist in the labor unions and Buck thinks all Coloreds are communist.

AVERY Cleo, your problem is that you are too sweet. You suppose to walk off when an asshole like Buck is talking on and on. And, trying to get you to agree with everything he says. Make that everything they say down at the Klavern. Buck has yet to have an original thought. *(Reads.)* Good, thing you don't work down around Montgomery, Minnie Mae. Says here that the Klan intimidating a restaurant out in the Normdale Shopping Center for hiring Nigra help. Folks got to work ... thought that's why they brought you over here in the first place.

MINNIE MAE Next time they can pick their own damn cotton.

AVERY *(Laughs.)* Says here that the harried restaurant owner done shot one of the Klan boys ... Heavy set dude who worked for the Power company.

CLEO Buck was down in Montgomery, yesterday.

MINNIE MAE Buck probably got right in the middle of it.

AVERY Buck was not on the picket line. Remind me to fine his ass. *(Reads.)* Hurricane Gracie out in the Atlantic and dropped down to seventy miles per hour.

MINNIE MAE *(Pours another drink.)* Them women folks gonna turn into hurricane force, if they ever catch up with you.

AVERY You know, Thelene been telling me that my smart boy, the snapper back, been having nightmares all week long about playing against my All State boy, the nose guard.

MINNIE MAE She knows you got another boy over in Attalla?

AVERY *(Knocks back drink.)* She just knows Joe Junior gonna have his hands full playing against a All State nose guard. That's all.

CLEO Both of them boys pretty good from what you tell me.

AVERY *(Continues reading.)*

MINNIE MAE Lord, somebody that talks all the time apt to tell you most anything Cleo, Baby. *(Laughs and pours another drink, And, has one herself.)*

CLEO I gotta go pee.

MINNIE MAE Thank you for sharing.

CLEO Didn't want you to think I was rude by just walking out. *(Starts to exits.)*

MINNIE MAE *(Shouts.)* Don't use the new plumbing. Go out back to the garden and don't pee on my collards.

CLEO *(Sticks head back in door.)* Those the slick leaves or the curly one?

MINNIE MAE Collard greens is slick. Mustard greens is curly. Don't you pee on any of my greens. I have enough trouble gettin' the grit out of them.

CLEO When you gonna let me use that new plumbing?

MINNIE MAE New plumbing not working so good. Besides, ain't no need to clean up after you and that city water we connected to cost money. Pee on something growing, like my zinnias, but stay away from my greens, you hear?

CLEO Yes 'em. *(Exits.)*

MINNIE MAE Childrens are something else. *(Shakes head.)*

AVERY Sure are. *(Reads.)* Looks like that school integration out in Little Rock is working after all.

MINNIE MAE All that stuff just scares me to death, I hope nobody gets hurt.

AVERY Boy, if I was a Nigra, I'd be mean and mad as hell. I feel oppressed enough just being a union man out on strike. And, children are something else.

MINNIE MAE Sure are. We done screwed over our life, but our childrens ought to have it better. *(Looks at Avery and laughs.)* You done screwed all over North and Central Alabama. God must love poorfolks and yard childrens, because he sure made enough of us.

AVERY Ain't just the screwing… it's the pride they give you as they grow older. Faith that we'll have a better, stronger generation to come.

MINNIE MAE *(Laughs.)* You puttin' out some good bull now. You sound like a cross between Shakespeare and Thomas Jefferson. You must be paying more attention to what you saying.

AVERY No, I get all choked up about my boys… don't matter which one. I even wish Big Cleo was still here to see how Little Cleo is coming along on them rules.

MINNIE MAE *(Sees that Avery is serious.)* I appreciate all you been doing for Little Cleo. *(Nods in the direction of Cleo's exit.)* And, no body misses Big Cleo more than me.

AVERY Treat Little Cleo like one of my own.

MINNIE MAE I know.

AVERY He's smart as a whip.

MINNIE MAE I know.

AVERY Funny, how he's never figured out you his mama.

MINNIE MAE Best it stay that way. *(Pause.)* And, you make sure my baby's safe out on that picket line?

AVERY Picket line real safe these days. Rather be on the picket line than on a train riding across a tressle bridge. On the picket line, we're safer than the general public with all the cops watching and all the private security watching and the detectives up in the weeds taking photos. Hell, the Company the ones blowing up the bridges ... sympathy from the rich folks and the Chamber of Commerce.

MINNIE MAE Lord Jesus I hope there is gonna be a brighter day. A brighter day, Sweet Jesus. *(Pours another and sips.)* Course, we came to Birmingham looking for a brighter day and I end up with Little Cleo. Depression set in real bad and Daddy moved us up here to Birmingham from Gees Bend down in Wilcox County. I's thirteen years old and confused. Thirteen year old children don't have babies no more, and my cousin, Doris, she wasn't but about eighteen and already started her family with Big Cleo right after he hired on at the Railroad yard. Big Cleo was one of the sweetest men I knew ... all us young girls thought so. He kept Doris pregnant them first four or five years. She'd get on down to her last few weeks pregnant and he'd come a begging like a little wet puppy. Honeychild, you thought he had big feets and big hands. *(Laughs.)*

AVERY Make a white man walk backwards and slap his grandma to be able to trade places just on Saturday night ... I mean to have such a ... a freedom ... *(Laughs.)* ... Of a Saturday night.

MINNIE MAE Ain't it the truth?

AVERY Seems like you all had more fun.

MINNIE MAE Whadda you mean?

AVERY No so inhibited.

MINNIE MAE Watch your mouth. Some things you not supposed to say. But, when you work all the time, your pleasure comes in small spurts ... mightaswell make the most of it.

AVERY I heard about the drunk slave. Plantation owners would help 'em get drunk and have a little fun on a Saturday night. Then when they were hungover and sinful, the owners would put 'em back to work.

MINNIE MAE That's where Big Cleo came in handy ... for the fun, that is. Oh, he not afraid to work neither. Then along comes my baby and me just thirteen years old. Had to tell everybody, I found me a Turnaround man that said he'd be good to me for the rest of my life, but he left on the morning train for Chicago. Then along comes Little Cleo.

AVERY Healthy and crying with that mouth wide open wanting to be fed.

MINNIE MAE Lord, yeah. And, you know when the titty milk run out ... they gonna be ready for a beef steak ... as big as Big Cleo was.

AVERY How did you get to call him "Little Cleo?"

MINNIE MAE Nobody ever accused me of being slow. To this day Doris has not figured it out ... she'd read something about it being bad luck to name a boy after his Daddy. Some of her Pratt City Voo Doo ... had to be names fresh out of the Bible. They know I'm not too attached on the Bible. Anyways, we finally did figure out that "Cleo" meant glory, but best we could determine it came from Cleopatra ... Lord knows where Big Cleo's mama got it from. You ever tried to look up Cleodius in the book, the Bible or some such. One of Big Cleo's Aunties swears up and down that his real name is Cleopatra ... cause his mama thought "patra" meant father 'cause she had some neighbors that use to go to the Catholic church. And, she dreamed he'd grow up being called the glory father. Cleopatra the glory father.

AVERY No offense, Minnie Mae, but Glory Father would have been a good name for Big Cleo.

MINNIE MAE *(Lifts gold watch.)* This was Big Cleo's watch and I'm gonna give it to Little Cleo one of these days. *(Laughs.)* Right now me and Doris wearing it out, trading it back and forth. Hamilton watch and we careful not to wind it too tight. See here where the face is cracked ... that was when Big Cleo fell under the train. And, he was not cool off in the grave when Buck tried to buy the watch from me for near nothing ... said I wasn't no railroad man and didn't need such a fine watch. Right now me and Doris wearing it out. You see, she so good to be raising little Cleo and that house full of her own childrens. Well, now, she runs outta money from time to time and she'll come to me and hock the watch. And, I'll keep it for a while. Then, on those rare occasions when I takes me a nip or two of my whiskey. *(Pours self a drink.)* I'll get real generous and sentimental and give it back to her ... her having that house full of children and all. And, I never go back on my word, whether it's the whiskey talking or not. When I give it back to Doris, she'll try not to take it ... but then you can't out talk whiskey. *(Laughs.)* I can't give it to Little Cleo until all them other childrens gets through school. Doris needs the money and I needs a hand in raising my boy. I appreciate you taking him under your wing.

AVERY Wouldn't have it no other way.

CLEO *(Enters.)* Aunt Minnie, them greens sure are pretty.

MINNIE MAE Did you miss them?

CLEO *(Looks back at door.)* Ain't been gone that long. *(Catches breath.)* Mamma ask if you could spare one of your cabbage heads, she'd appreciate it.

MINNIE MAE Got your mama a whole basket back in the kitchen and don't you forget it on your way home.

CLEO That cabbage stinks.

MINNIE MAE Just when it's cooked. Tell your mama to make some cole slaw to go along with the catfish I sent her.

CLEO And hushpuppies. Yum.

AVERY *(Reading paper.)* Lookie here, ex-beauty queen killed ... found dead on top of a big black Cadillac. Mrs. Janice Drake, she sure was a pretty thing. They believe it was mob related. *(Finishes off drink.)* She sure was a pretty thing. Did I tell you my boys having nightmares?

MINNIE MAE That Mrs. Janice Drake one less pretty thing, you'll have to worry about. (Voo doo pause.) And, nightmares, them that come just before dawn, they the ones that tell the future. Them boys just worried about falling short of your expectations.

AVERY Expectations? Cleo, get your Safety Rules out ... we don't want to get rusty.

CLEO Mister Avery, we been on strike so long I done forgot. I don't know a box car from a baggage cart.

AVERY Freight car not box car.

CLEO See, I told you I was rusty.

AVERY I know, that's why we gonna practice.

CLEO Reckon we'll ever go back to work?

AVERY Sure. Just when you least expect it.

BUCK *(Enters, excited.)* Just went by the picket line and they got a warrant out for your arrest.

AVERY Me?

BUCK You and an unnamed Colored accomplice. And, that seems to be the problem. Description seems to fit Lil' Cleo, but I tells them, Lil' Cleo afraid of explosives. *(Looks at Cleo.)* Said, he even use to shy away from a cap pistol when he was little.

AVERY What they want to arrest me for? And, I don't need no accomplice to do nothing. And, that's exactly what I chose to do this time around. Nothing!

BUCK It's that same bridge down at Waxahatchee Creek ... the one you take out every strike. Don't you know you talk too much as it is. *(Catches breath.)* They done traced the same explosives that blew up that James Dean fella out yonder in the parking lot to the same kind of explosives you used down at the Creek ...

AVERY Watch what you say. I have not used any explosives down by any Creek. It's the company that's blowing up the bridges ... sympathy and the insurance money. *(Tries to drain empty glass.)* Have you been talkin' loose like this around your Buddies at the Klavern or the John Britches boys?

BUCK I don't think so? It's the Colored accomplice that gives them trouble. Like they needs a lynching and it don't matter much who it is, as long as, he's a ...

AVERY Jesus Christ! I don't tell LIES! Truth is I don't need no accomplice, one more loose tongue to worry with. *(Looks at glass.)* Minnie Mae, whiskey please? I tell only the truth, and the TRUTH is I did not blow up no bridge, this time.

BUCK They are worried about giving Coloreds explosives. You know, guns and communist rebellions. I'm sure I didn't call no names.

AVERY And, they know I'm a nigger lover, right?

BUCK Well, yes.

AVERY And, I'm good with explosives?

MINNIE MAE Wish you wouldn't even talk about explosives around here.

(Overlapping.)

BUCK Well, yes. You are good around explosives.

AVERY Goddamn. *(To Buck.)* You fucking fanatic.

BUCK Why you so mad?

AVERY Goddamn. You'd have to study real hard to elevate yourself to the status of stupid.

BUCK Whadda you mean?

AVERY Tell him Cleo.

CLEO When I talks to much, Mister Avery says I got to first put my mind in gear. Says it's like a game of checkers. It ain't so much how you move straight on … it's what you don't let slip up on you. That's why you always face the moving freight cars … but you got to know all freight cars gonna move at one time or another, so you be on guard. And, in checkers kings go both ways.

BUCK What's he talking about?

AVERY One track mind. You go to the Klan and you brag to 'em about our new explosives … Only you forget that we are this salt and pepper team. You are thinking through your hemorrhoids. And you say, *(Imitates Buck)* "Why that nigger lover treats Little Cleo like one of his own just cause Little Cleo is smart and Avery was on the train when Big Cleo got …"

BUCK You mightaswell go ahead and say it … when Big Cleo got his foot caught in the switch and y'all was bumping cars in the spur tracks out at United Chemical. The good ones gets killed.

MINNIE MAE Not now.

CLEO You talking about Daddy?

AVERY *(To Buck.)* Just how much did you tell your fellow fanatics?

BUCK I said when you got off your high horse and we was off strike, you might give them a lesson in them new plastic explosives.

AVERY You'd have to take a cram course to come all the way up to stupid.

BUCK Well, I thought you might.

AVERY Thought, hell. Maybe you could go to school out in Little Rock.

BUCK *(Looks at paper)* Ain't that awful?

AVERY Stupidity, carries a certain innocence.

MINNIE MAE Looks to me, you better quit your philosophizing and start looking for a hiding place.

BUCK That's awful. Mrs. Janice Drake sure was a pretty thing … you think the mob got her. Wonder for what?

AVERY Don't think too hard, you might throw a cog. Screwing! Why else does the mob kill a pretty woman.

BUCK That Mrs. Khrushchev standing alongside Mamie Eisenhower ... makes Mamie look sorta pretty. *(Shakes head.)* Debbie Lou says bangs is out.

AVERY Brains are out too.

MINNIE MAE There you go solving everybody else's problem, but your own. *(Turns to Buck.)* When the high Sheriff came out to the picket line looking for Avery, did they figure where else to look?

BUCK We all knew Avery would be here, but nobody told the Deputy to come here. I don't think.

AVERY I don't think? *(Imitates Buck.)* Don't go to Minnie Mae's Waterin'Hole out near Boyles Yard in Tarrant City ... just off the intersection of Highway 79 and the Old Warrior Road. Hell, Deputy Doyle has already been by here collecting payoff bricks.

MINNIE MAE Did they say they was gonna keep looking for him or just wait for Avery to show up on the picket line?

BUCK They did ask where he lived.

MINNIE MAE And? *(Goes to bolt door.)*

BUCK We had to tell them something, so they wouldn't think we's in on it. Just where he lived... that's all we told them.

MINNIE MAE And?

BUCK They was right amused that he had two wives ... I mean two addresses.

AVERY What?

BUCK We thought that would distract them.

AVERY Thinking? When you start thinking, everybody else needs to run for one of them new fallout shelters.

MINNIE MAE *(Looks out window.)* Lord Jesus. Run for it. Deputy Doyle and another car just come over the hill. *(Looks around.)* Buck you and Avery go outta the back door. Cleo you stays here like nothing happening.

BUCK Accomplice? Not, me?

MINNIE MAE You ain't Colored, either.

AVERY What about the ball game?

MINNIE MAE Go on and git. Or, you'll be listening to it in the jail house. Hide out in that Bangor Cave up at Blount Springs 'til I figure out something.

AVERY & BUCK *(Exit as if the Marx Brothers.)*

MINNIE MAE *(At window.)* Lord, Child what's the world coming to.

CLEO Aunt Minnie, I got something I got to tell you.

MINNIE MAE No, you don't. Only one lie at a time. *(Looks out window and laughs.)* Deputy Doyle just waves at Buck and Buck just waves back. Avery must be hiding in the floorboard of Buck's car. God is doing for us what we cannot do for ourselves. *(Laughs.)*

DEPUTY *(Tries bolted door then knocks.)* Minnie Mae is Avery still in there?

CLEO What we do now?

MINNIE MAE *(Opens door length of chain.)* No, Avery is not in here. No, Avery been called outta town on business. And, in case you wondering why his car is out there, Avery just lettin' Little Cleo drive his car while Avery outta town. *(Whispers.)* Cleo, Baby, play like nothing happened. Get your Mama's vegetables and play like you in a big hurry to gets to the picket line. *(Unchains door.)*

DEPUTY *(Shouts off stage.)* I got it boys. Two of you circle around back and you other boys, y'all watch that car, he's slippery. I'll take care of the inside. They know me. *(To Minnie.)* You sure Avery Joe Johnston, Senior, still not in here? *(Grabs Cleo by arm.)* Got some questions for you too, Boy. *(Looks around.)*

MINNIE MAE Little Cleo afraid of cap pistol. I've known Little Cleo since he was a ... baby.

DEPUTY Now, Minnie Mae, you know I don't like to make arrest during a strike ... my brother-in-law is a union man out at T.C. and I., but sometimes we don't got a lot of choices. Strikes ought to be between the Union and the Railroad and leave law enforcement out of it. And, the High Sheriff got word out at the picket line that this Avery Joe Johnston, Sr. is not only good with explosives, he must be good with women too. Two wives? *(Shakes head.)*

MINNIE MAE Some of us have to hold down two jobs. Didn't you say you was also into agriculture? You and your James Dean cousin, all splattered up side the place? You not still growing wacky tobaccie up on the other side of Sportsman's Lake? Now are you? Lot of us got two tales to tell.

DEPUTY Well, tell Avery Joe Johnston, Senior, if you see him that bigamy is just a Class C felony and carries less than ten years ... but then he'd probably enjoy the rest and relaxation down at Kilby prison. And, Minnie Mae, you know how I hate to make an arrest with both Avery's boys playing football on Friday night. Seeing that Avery is so smart, he's got enough good sense not to show up to the game. And, Minnie Mae you might ought to think about puttin' a little something under one of my Children's bricks out yonder next time you gets the chance. *(Exits and shouts off stage.)* Boys he ain't in here. Done skipped town. Lettin' the Colored boy use his car. Little Cleo is afraid of cap pistols, so he ain't messing in no explosives.

CLEO *(Runs hand across hair.)* White folks can grow some hair.

MINNIE MAE Don't you know it.

ACT TWO, Scene Two

AT RISE *Nighttime and the bar has been twirled with crepe paper and radio coming in over static. On stage: Minnie Mae, Avery, Cleo and Buck. Everyone but Avery in fresh clothes to indicate a few days later.*

RADIO VOICE Welcome Ladies and Gentlemen to this broadcast of spectacular high school football with this week's game coming from the most lovely hamlet of Oak Knoll, Alabama on the banks of the Black Warrior River. The sky carries a brisk chill under a radiant Harvest Moon. But, sports fans what is really in the air is football — serious, down in the trenches football. At pre-season no one would have bet that this game, fairly early in the season, might very well carry all the marbles for the state two-A championship. But, hold on sports fans that's exactly what you have in store for you tonight. We have the cross state rival, and number one team in the state, the Huns of Attalla in town to defend their number one ranking. But, then, we have the Oak Knoll Hurricanes that like Hurricane Gracie that just hit Charleston, South Carolina, this week they are picking up speed and if they are at full gale force they could give the Huns of Attalla a game. The Canes are undefeated and have just this week moved into the state's top ten. *(Breath.)* With a little gametime excitement and inspiration Cinderella may show up at the ball ... make that the ball game ... and dear hearts and dear listeners it's anybody's ball game. And when you get that inspiration under them shoulder pads, you can move mountains. But, first a word from our sponsor. Delicious ... *(static)* ... *(Overlapping thirty seconds of* *commercial, static and a high school band.)*

MINNIE MAE Avery Baby you nervous as a turnaround woman in Church. They say God don't give us more than we can handle. *(Pours some white whiskey from fruit jar.)*

AVERY Hiding out in them caves is scary. Did you call my wife … wives? Afternoon newspaper had my boy's tackles all wrong in that article. Junior's got closer to twenty tackles per game instead of just sixteen.

MINNIE MAE Afternoon paper also say they looking for Avery Joe Johnston, Senior. Avery Baby, you got one foot on the dock and the other in the boat.

(Overlapping.)

CLEO Heap of tackles. Attalla is so good the other team is lucky if they gets the ball sixteen times.

MINNIE MAE Both them wives say, both them boys having nightmares and falling outta bed … the snapper back and the nose guard having nightmares. That one over in Attalla too heavy to pick up, and Miss Eileen lets him sleep on the flo.

AVERY They just worried about the game. What did you tell 'em?

MINNIE MAE The truth.

AVERY Oh, God, anything but the truth.

MINNIE MAE The truth I could get by a party line. Told 'em you was on Union business and would miss the ball game tonight.

(Overlapping static and Radio voice.)

RADIO VOICE And, now Ladies and Gentlemen please stand for our National Anthem.

(Cast pauses for Stars Spangle Banner . One stanza overlaps until next RADIO voice.)

AVERY *(Picks up after only a bar or so.)* Did you tell her, my wife … wives … I's hiding from the law?

MINNIE MAE I told you, I's on Doris' party line, you think I'm as dumb as Buck?

BUCK Whadda you say?

MINNIE MAE I say dumb as dirt. I say, "You think I'm as dumb as dirt?"

BUCK Looks like to me Junior is not playing nose guard so much as he's trying to play linebacker to get more tackles.

AVERY And, he's All State. What's the problem?

BUCK With a good quarterback draw, he'd be too fast and off balance and they'd fake him outta his jock strap.

AVERY Who you think you are? Bart Starr?

BUCK Even one of my girls could bump him outta the play if he's hot-dogging like a linebacker. .

AVERY Did you say one of your girls gonna hump him outta the play? *(Starts to fight.)*

BUCK You sorry S.O.B. *(Fights.)*

AVERY How you think they get elected cheerleader in the first place.

CLEO Stop fightin' y'all, they fixin' to kick off.

MINNIE MAE I'll call the law. *(Breaks up fight.)* You boys gonna be outside listing to that car radio if you don't calm down.

RADIO VOICE So, if these Canes get the adrenaline pumping and play inspired ball against the mighty Atillas from Attalla … we gonna have us a ball game. *(Radio sputters to silence.)*

BUCK Adrenaline pumping alright.

AVERY What happened to the radio. *(Goes to whack it.)*

MINNIE MAE Calm down.

BUCK You win either way. If one of your boys gonna win.

AVERY Damn radio is out.

MINNIE MAE Quit beating on it.

BUCK You don't know nothing about machinery and radio waves.

MINNIE MAE Cleo Baby, you turned off the outside lights and put out the closed signed.

CLEO Aunt Minnie, you already ask me that ten or twelve times.

BUCK Look whose nervous.

RADIO VOICE *(Sputters back on.)* The Captains are in the middle of the field for the toss of the coin. Junior Johnson for the Huns calls the toss. Looks like the Canes won the toss and the Huns will defend the South end zone. *(Static.)*

There is just a light breeze here tonight … barely lifting Old Glory and the Stars and Bars off the flagpole.

(Static and radio blinks out.)

AVERY Goddamn! *(One final whack.)*

BUCK Calm down, don't take it out on the radio.

MINNIE MAE *(To Buck.)* Hush up and run on down yonder to the Esso station and borrow their radio.

BUCK *(Drains drink.)* Why me?

MINNIE MAE You the only one who's not a fugitive.

BUCK How can you be a fugitive here at the Waterin'Hole?

MINNIE MAE Easy … just figure it out on your way to the Esso station to borrow their radio. Take 'em a jar of my whiskey.

BUCK *(Gets whiskey and exits.)*

MINNIE MAE *(Pours Avery a drink.)* Calm down Honey … what's gonna be is gonna be. And, it's gonna be a long one, tonight.

AVERY Why has it come to this. I ain't at the greatest event of my life. That game means so much to both them boys and me. We's all having nightmares and falling outta bed.

MINNIE MAE *(Rubs Avery on the shoulders.)* We can't keep puttin' them back in bed. They on their own now.

AVERY Minnie Mae, what am I gonna do?

MINNIE MAE *(Looks at Cleo.)* Childrens are something else. You can only take them to water, but you can't make them tote it. *(Sighs and a little hateful.)* Maybe instead of teaching them to look both ways before they cross the street … maybe, just maybe, we should tell them that there is traffic out there and it's gonna get you, so go deal with it … go play in it if you wish. Avery Honey, if I had any of the answers I'd go on the television set. *(Rubs Avery's shoulders.)* They gonna be okay, Avery Baby.

AVERY You think so? *(Puts head down on table.)*

CLEO I think those Gentlemens at the Esso station needs they radio. There's a boxing match out of New York City tonight.

(Lights fade to indicate passage of time.)

BUCK *(Enters with radio.)* Sorry it took so long, but I had to get 'em half drunk before they'd let me have the radio. *(Laughs.)* Seems like there is a Friday night fight out of New York City. *(Goes to plug in radio and looks around.)* What's wrong … somebody spray this place with nerve gas? We got us a ball game … it was zero to zero at half-time. Now it's well into the fourth quarter and still zero to zero. And that announcer is going crazy, and the whole town is coming out to the ball field and the radio keeps on talking about the war in the trenches and how the battle is between the Johnson's boys. That announcer is too excited. Course that announcer is easy to get excited.

CLEO You joking. Zero to zero now that's a ball game. Just like Auburn and Tennessee at half time — ain't fancy — but that's a ball game.

AVERY *(Looks at Buck.)* Turn on the fucking radio.

RADIO VOICE Score zero to zero and the Hurricanes are seriously moving the ball for the first time of this contest.

AVERY What's happening?

BUCK The score is zero to zero and the Hurricanes are moving the ball for the first time of this contest. Listen.

RADIO VOICE This announcer is impressed with the battle in the trenches… these boys have come to play ball. Speaking about Cinderella stories that Joe Johnston for the Canes has snapped the ball in the end zone at least a half dozen times … the snaps have been high and Beavers, the punter, has done an outstanding job of leaping for the ball and kicking it outta the end zone. Averaging a good thirty yards a kick. Then the Huns run it down to the goal line. The Cane's defense holds and those goal line stands are for the history books. Cane's offense has been stagnant all evening but now it's moving three or four yards a clip. The Huns seem to be on their heels. Dear hearts, everybody likes an underdog but the favored Huns.

BUCK Not when our favorite Hun is going for scholarship money.

MINNIE MAE Hush.

AVERY Leave him be. Buck is good a kicking you when you down.

BUCK How can you be down? You got a boy on both teams. You win either way.

RADIO VOICE The Canes' center just got knocked a little woozy, lost his helmet and maybe a cracked jawbone … but he won't let the Coach take him out. Johnson boy is reeling a bit but he can still snap the ball. And, the quarterback for the Canes has been brilliant, but somebody put molasses on his shoes.

AVERY What's he talking about?

CLEO They got a smart quarterback but he's slow …

AVERY No. No. About my boy?

BUCK Which one?

AVERY The one that is hurt.

MINNIE MAE He may have a broken jawbone but he ain't hurt.

AVERY Whadda do you mean. Not hurt?

MINNIE MAE Seems to me like his juices are flowing and he don't feel no pain. Moving with a power greater than his own.

RADIO VOICE Play has resumed. Johnston for the Canes is over the ball and McFee receives the snap. Glory be, it's the banana peel pass play made famous by the Tennessee Volunteers. The ends are going long. Long. Long. The line is holding this time and the ball is in the air. McFee may be slow of foot but he's got an arm and can fling the pumpkin. It's in the air. In the air. Hold it. Hold it. It's almost intercepted.

AVERY What happened?

RADIO VOICE Coach Smith went for all the marbles with that banana peel play sending both ends deep arcing to the outside, a pattern just like two bananas. A play made famous by the Tennessee Volunteers, but sport's fans this is high school football. Blalock off tackle for three as the score board clock ticks down. Less than a minute. Looks like Coach Smith is going to settle for a tie and not risk an interception. That's right … McFee takes the snap from center and drops to one knee… and sports fans this ball game is over and the state's top ten is in a jumble tonight. The fierce Hurricanes from Oak Knoll zero and the mighty Attila the Huns from Attalla zero. It ain't pretty unless you're a defensive coach or maybe Bear Bryant that new coach down at Bama. But, Ladies and Gentlemen, it has been high school football game for the ages. Zero to Zero.

BUCK A dog fall.

CLEO Like kissing your sister.

MINNIE MAE Watch who you go kissing on. Big Cleo was bad to kiss around. *(Gives Avery a hug and lets him cry on her shoulder.)*

ACT TWO, Scene Three

AT RISE: *Next morning, bar in after party debris, with Avery asleep in booth wearing a pink bathrobe and having a nightmare. He gets up, pours whiskey and eats pickled egg. Minnie Mae enters with newspaper, milk and a grip for Avery.*

MINNIE MAE It's a frosty morn in Dixie. Honey it's the first day of the rest of your life. *(Starts coffee.)* That coral pink color looks real nice on you, sorta matches your skin tone. But I brought you some running clothes and a bus ticket. I figure since they didn't find you at that football game last night, they'd be hot on your trail this morning. They bound and determined to arrest who blew up that bridge. And, they ain't gonna over look your favorite Waterin'Hole much longer. I put a crisp Benjamin under one of Deputy Doyle's bricks. He might look the other way for a while.

AVERY Minnie, how bad was my boy hurt?

MINNIE MAE Both of 'em got bruised up pride, but they okay.

AVERY I mean Joe Junior, the one that got hurt on the radio?

MINNIE MAE Avery, Baby, I said his pride got hurt more than his jawbone and that was your other boy that hit him going after the quarterback or the corner back or some such. Don't make sense to me.

AVERY Radio man, said something about his …

MINNIE MAE His jawbone went out when he got hit on that play … couldn't even eat the T-bone steak the rich team doctor bought the boys after the game was over. It was your boy, the snapper back or was it the nose back, who hit him again on the last play when they went after a tie ball game. That was when the corner back or the quarterback going down on his knee. And, he won't praying. Confusing if you ask me.

AVERY Which boy did what? Minnie Mae you're not making a lot of sense.

MINNIE MAE *(Haughty.)* Honey, don't blame the confusion on me.

AVERY I need a drink.

MINNIE MAE Want!

AVERY Want?

MINNIE MAE You WANTS that drink You don't NEEDS any drink. *(Pours whiskey.)* If you plans to stay ahead of the law, this whiskey will just slow you down.

AVERY I didn't do it ... and I'm tired of running from everything. And I feel guilty, but I didn't even blow up that bridge this time.

MINNIE MAE Guilt ain't no feeling ... you either is guilty or you isn't ... guilty.

AVERY I just feel out of sorts.

MINNIE MAE You just confused with all them signals God's sending down.

AVERY *(Takes a drink.)* Signals? Zero to Zero tie. Goddamn dog fall. *(Nervous laugh.)* Minnie, can you inherit nightmares?

MINNIE MAE Believe so. Believe I read somewhere, you can also inherit that whiskey habit, too!

AVERY You say, you call my wife ... wives. They doing alright? I mean with me being gone.

MINNIE MAE Even with that ball game over, they worried to death. But, like good white women they don't let on.

AVERY Whadda you mean by that?

MINNIE MAE Just about what I said.

AVERY You not got some sorta sixty-four thousand dollar question up your sleeve?

MINNIE MAE Figuring out women are the last of your concerns. *(Pause.)* I brought you a pair of Big Cleo's clean overalls.

AVERY Don't like wearing a dead man's overalls, don't care if they are clean.

MINNIE MAE Big Cleo been dead almost a year now ... besides dead man's clothes should be the least of your worries.

AVERY Worries? Worries is all I got and you won't even tell me how my wives are.

MINNIE MAE They worried to death?

AVERY Is Joe Junior hurt bad?

MINNIE MAE He's hurt, but not bad. He's just a kid, he'll bounce back.

AVERY Good. *(Knocks back another drink.)*

MINNIE MAE Oh, them wives worried sick about you, but they been worried sick about you for some time. *(Pause.)* They sorta happy how that ball game come out.

AVERY Thought nobody was happy with a tie?

MINNIE MAE Joe Junior, your turnaround boy, gonna get more scholarship money than God. Your wife, Eileen, said he got enough advanced money from one of them rich alumni to get his Chevrolet back from the repo man.

AVERY Good. I just couldn't make them last payments.

MINNIE MAE God works things out when we done messing with them. *(Pause.)* How much you love your boys?

AVERY More than anything in this world ... why do you think I been out on strike... for over six months now.

MINNIE MAE When's the last time you told them?

AVERY They know. They know.

MINNIE MAE Avery, Baby ...

AVERY Men don't ...

MINNIE MAE Men better start ...

AVERY I mean, they know ...

MINNIE MAE They may, they may not, ain't like hearing it from the horse's mouth. You don't want them growing up and having them childhood flashbacks. Nightmares.

AVERY Nightmares?

MINNIE MAE Big Cleo not afraid to tell a child that he loved him. *(Sighs.)* Course, Big Cleo told just about everybody he loved them.

CLEO *(Enters carrying a bag of clothes. Excited.)* Mama was able to find some of Daddy's overalls. Figured Mister Avery needs a change of clothes. Boy, that was some football game, sure was. Went by the picket line and Buck trying to tell the Deputies you still up in the caves. But, I don't think it's gonna work. Buck also told them that you didn't know how to figure out a zero to zero tie. So, Deputy knows you're around here somewhere.

MINNIE MAE Lordy, Avery Baby, with Buck on your side you better hurry. Change clothes and pack that grip and Little Cleo will take you to the bus station. Got you a ticket just this morning.

AVERY Why am I running. I didn't do nothing. *(Exits while picking up jar of whiskey.)*

MINNIE MAE 'Cept run your mouth.

194   FLAWED GOOD PEOPLE

CLEO Aunt Minnie?

MINNIE MAE Yes child?

CLEO Avery's right.

MINNIE MAE What? How do you know?

CLEO I'm the one who blew up the bridge.

MINNIE MAE You what?

CLEO I said, I was the one …

MINNIE MAE You didn't.

CLEO Yes, Mam, I did. I said …

MINNIE MAE I heard you, but … but where was Avery?

CLEO He wasn't there.

MINNIE MAE Cleo Baby, you just excited.

CLEO No. I'm the one who blew up the Waxahatchee Bridge this time around. Mister Avery tells me how it's best to worry the Company and getting them to guard all the bridges, but the gentlemen on the picket line thought it was a good idea to blow up just one bridge. Avery was pulling their leg, like we was gonna take it out. But, Avery said the only bird that don't sing be a jailbird …and he had too much ahead of him with that boy of his gonna play for the Bear and all. He don't want to go to no jail,

AVERY *(Appears up stage, in Big Cleo's overalls, but is undetected.)*

CLEO Well, the gentlemen on the picket line thinks it's a good idea to take out the bridge and Avery he's done trained me real good with them plastique explosives… you talk as much as Avery, you gonna do some talking. Avery said we needed a hoax to get the Company all confused so they'd spend a bunch of money guarding all the bridges.

(Avery disappears in upstage exit to kitchen.)

Well, I'm brand new to this Union business and I blew up the bridge … I mean … he showed me where the security parked and all. I'd been down to the bridge early on in the strike with Avery. And me and Avery would throw a watermelon in the weeds and watch the security mens shoot at the watermelon. *(Laughs.)* And, THAT night, I went down there by myself, and the security mens was gone like we'd been waiting on. I walked out on that trestle in the dark of night.

Moon behind the clouds. I hooked up me a long fuse and I was a mile or so away when it blew… Avery ain't the only one who can run fast. *(Proudly.)* I did a pretty good job, too. Only I dropped that second bag of explosives down by the Creek … and they didn't go off.

MINNIE MAE No. No. Honey, you didn't.

CLEO Yes Maam, I did. I dropped that second bag.

MINNIE MAE Not talkin' bout no bag.

CLEO You don't go back when it's about to blow.

MINNIE MAE Lord Child, what are we gonna do.

CLEO Avery, say when the strike is over the law will forget about the bridge.

MINNIE MAE Cleo, Baby, you the wrong color for the law to be forgetting anything.

CLEO But, Aunt Minnie, you told me not to lie. *(Squirms.)* I gotta go pee.

AVERY *(Enters and Cleo counters to go to restroom.)* These garments are a little airy, don't exactly fit.

MINNIE MAE Cleo's so young. *(Anger.)* He's just following along in the footsteps of his White Savior. Yeah, Avery Baby, you his hero the way you teaching him them Safety Rules. But, you gone too far this time.

AVERY *(Laughs to defuse.)* Boy, he's hurtin' for a hero if he settled on me. And, what are you talking about?

DEPUTY *(Knocks on door.)*

MINNIE MAE That bridge. *(Looks out window.)* You better hide and then go out that back door when I give you the high sign.

AVERY What?

MINNIE MAE Deputy sheriff.

AVERY *(Grabs whiskey jar and grip and exits to kitchen.)*

CLEO *(Flushes and enters.)* Aunt Minnie, I been thinking.

MINNIE MAE Quit thinking and just shut up. Don't open your mouth, you hear? *(Opens door.)* Did you read the sign? We closed. Too early to be drinking and you still in uniform.

DEPUTY Miss Minnie, we got word down at the picket line that Avery Joe

Johnston, Sr. might be up here at the Waterin'Hole.

MINNIE MAE Honey, we not open yet. Not seen Avery in a week or so now. Think he got religion and quit the union and he quit drinking and got religion or went to the AA or somewhere.

CLEO Aunt Minnie …

MINNIE MAE Cleo Baby, your Mama waiting on her vegetables. Get her a mess of collards. *(Points toward kitchen.)*

CLEO *(Exits toward kitchen.)*

DEPUTY Not so fast, there is an unnamed Colored accomplice, if we find him with Avery we can arrest him to.

CLEO *(Stops exit to kitchen.)*

DEPUTY Mind if I take a look around. Figure Avery will put the pinch on your Colored boy when he figures the score out.

MINNIE MAE That score was zero to zero. What you talking about? And, we closed. We not cleaned up yet. Can't you see this place is dirty.

DEPUTY Looks like you had a football party here last night.

MINNIE MAE This time of year, everything is a football party.

DEPUTY I know. Figure Avery might not be in them caves after all. Minnie, I stalled as long as I could. *(Pulls papers from pocket.)* To make it easier on you, I got a search warrant.

MINNIE MAE Cleo Baby run along. *(Shouts to back.)* Time to pick the collard greens.

DEPUTY Hold it! *(Puts hand on gun.)* What are you doing?

AVERY *(Appears washed up with hair combed.)* I'm Avery Joe Johnston, Sr.

DEPUTY Saw your boys play ball last night, and I hate to, but we got a warrant for your arrest.

AVERY What took you so long?

DEPUTY Says here you had a Negro accomplice. Could you help us out, now that the strike is about over. The Judge might go easy if we could officially get the name of the Colored accomplice. *(Looks at Cleo.)*

MINNIE MAE Railroad hired couple hundred Coloreds. And, Cleo here is my Baby.

AVERY Accomplice? You sell me short cowboy. What would I need with an accomplice. I can take out that Waxahatchee bridge with one hand while you turn your back to pee. *(Deputy puts handcuffs on Avery.)* That plastique explosive is pliable like silly putty. French used it when they were fightin' the Algerians …easy to handle … with a fuse of any kind. I personally like the long fuse and some swift feet. Did I tell you about the time in my youth when I use to foot race Jesse Owens. Now why would somebody like me want a remote detonator? An accomplice would just slow me down. That bridge is only a hundred and three feet long and a small bag full of well-placed charges on each side of the rail will do the trick and you don't have to worry about nobody else's fear, sweats or lack of speed. *(Turns.)* But, I did drop a bag of explosives this time. *(Pause.)* Seldom make a mistake. Yeah, cowboy, you sell me short. If my recollection serves me correctly that was the same Waxahatchee Bridge some un-apprehended criminal took out during the Fifty-five strike.

(Exits with Deputy.)

MINNIE MAE *(Goes to bar to pour a drink for herself and one for Cleo.)*

~ END OF PLAY ~

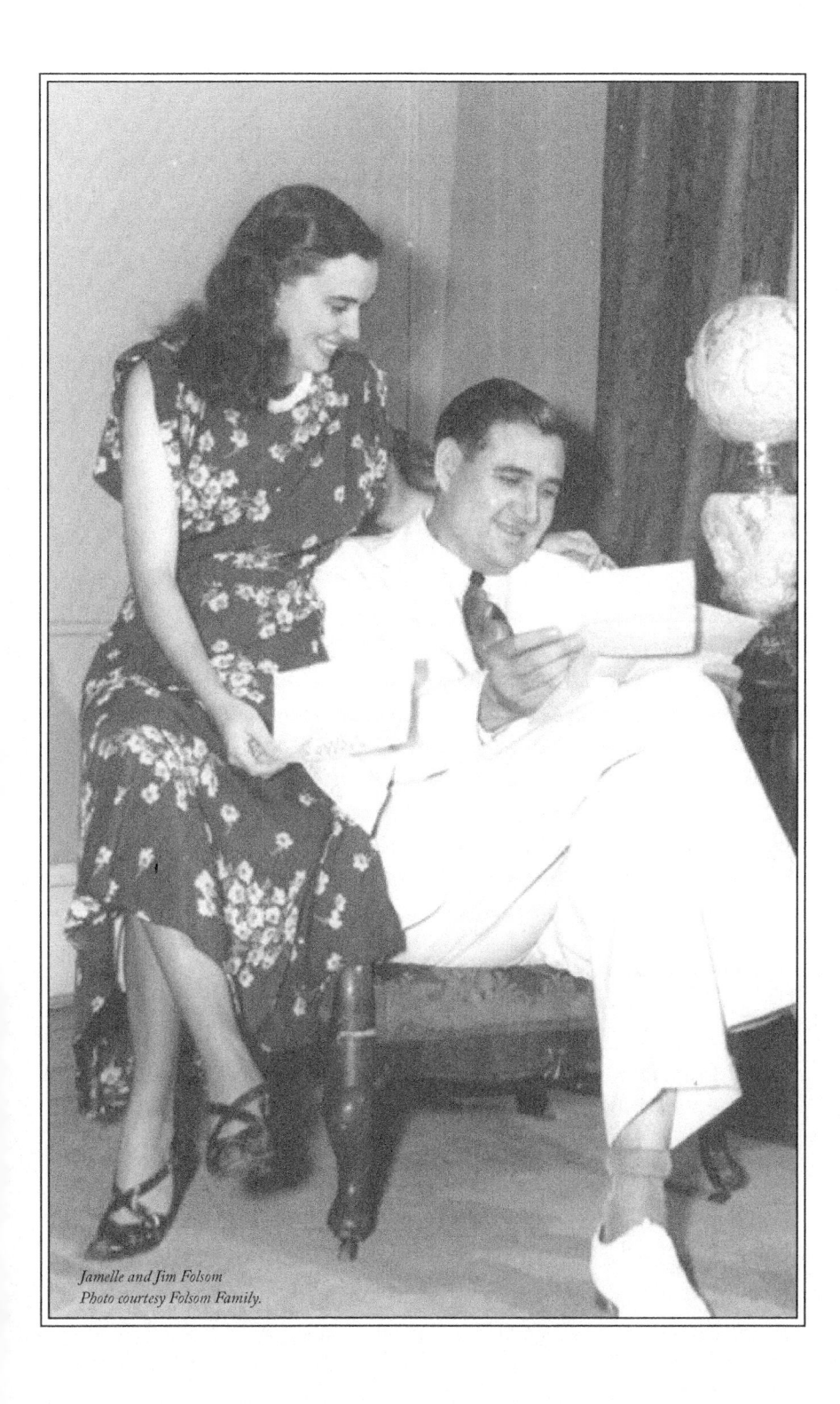

Jamelle and Jim Folsom
Photo courtesy Folsom Family.

Jamelle, Alabama's Teenage First Lady

In 2016, this play enjoyed a workshop reading in Cullman Alabama among the Folsom clan with JAMELLE read by Marsha Folsom, also an Alabama First Lady. Musicians Micah Simpson and Bill Strandlund shared the role of HONEY bringing back memories of the original Strawberry Pickers.[38]

TIME

November 2012.

CAST

JAMELLE: elderly (85 y/o), but spry, defying age with coal black hair and ebullient spirit. (Note she is in pain but in "denial" of her cancer that will take her life on November 30, 2012.)

HONEY: Guitar Player/Country Singer. Mature male, with suggestion he was a former (perhaps want-to-be) Strawberry Picker. (Non-speaking, except for "optional" brief epilogue.)

VOICE OVER (from old radio): Governor Folsom's voice and/or historical news casts … via Jamelle's imagined recall. (Epilogue may come from either the radio or Honey. To make this a literal one-woman play, the character Honey may be dropped using the radio for the songs with adjustments in Jamelle's dialogue.)

ONE SET

Traditional, North Alabama suburban living room, with large mirror, '40s upright radio, comfortable chairs and cluttered tables, family photos and scrapbooks from Governor's Mansion days, books, crocheted dollies and other collectibles adorn the set. Upstage there is an opening to a kitchen. Stage right opening to the dining room with sideboard laden with heavy silver tea set, chafing dishes and large serving pieces, all wrapped in plastic. Stage left exit hallway to bedrooms. Jamelle enters from "outside" so she may mingle with the audience.

At Rise: HONEY *in spot picks and sings SHE WAS POOR[39]*:

> SHE WAS POOR BUT SHE WAS HONEST, HONEST, HONEST
> NO VICTIM OF A RICH MAN'S WHIM
> 'TIL SHE MET THAT SOUTHERN GENTLEMAN, BIG JIM FOLSOM
> AND, SHE HAD A CHILD BY HIM.
> IT'S THE RICH WHAT GET THE GLORY
> IT'S THE POOR WHAT GETS THE BLAME
> IT'S THE SAME THE WHOLE WORLD OVER, OVER, OVER
> IT'S A DIRTY-GOSH DARN SHAME.
> NOW HE SITS ABOVE THE LEGISLATURE
> MAKIN' LAWS FOR ALL MANKIND

JAMELLE: Enters downstage (or back of theatre) from running errands, e.g. trip to doctor, bank, beauty shop, bakery and Elks Club … in light coat, handsome suit and bright scarf, carrying box of cookies from Duchess Bakery and poinsettia from Elks Club. Listens to but "ignores" song while greeting audience members.

HONEY:

> WHILE SHE WALKS THE STREETS OF CULLMAN, ALABAMA
> SELLING GRAPES FROM HER GRAPEVINE.
> SO, YOUNG LADIES, TAKE A WARNING
> AND DON'T EVER TAKE A RIDE
> WITH ALABAMA'S CHRISTAIN GENTLEMAN,
> BIG JIM FOLSOM
> AND YOU'LL BE A VIRGIN BRIDE.

JAMELLE: Honey, I wish you would not play that hateful tune … not a word of truth to that song. (*Pause.*) 'Cept, of course, I was a virgin bride … but then that song is not about me. (*To Audience.*) No, that that political ditty was about Big Jim's fooling around before he ever met and married me *(winks)* and I settled him down. (*To Honey.*) That song was an old college drinkin' song. Speaking of drinkin' you Strawberry Pickers were a bad influence on my Man. (*Shakes head.*) And, I inherited a handful.

HONEY: (*repeat*)

> SO, YOUNG LADIES, TAKE A WARNING
> AND DON'T EVER TAKE A RIDE

> WITH ALABAMA'S CHRISTAIN GENTLEMAN, BIG JIM
> FOLSOM
> AND YOU'LL BE A VIRGIN BRIDE.

JAMELLE: Well, now, everybody knows I took a ride with the Governor. He wasn't Governor yet ... he was running for Governor. And, I was still in high school ... just before graduation ... seventeen years old. But, nothing happened on that ride, but a lot of talk. Not only was there a lot of talk inside his car that night, but I suppose there was a lot of talk outside that car. Folks like to speculate. Some call it their gossip.

HONEY:

> WHILE SHE WALKS THE STREETS OF CULLMAN, ALABAMA
> SELLING GRAPES FROM HER GRAPEVINE.

JAMELLE: (*Stage whisper to audience.*) Since it is just us and I don't want to talk outta school, but I was told the Governor had him some wild times before he met me ... and I settled him down ... as best I could. Boys will be boys. And, Big Jim was such a sweet man, and all boy. He was something else, him being so plain talking and big. *(Pause.)* He wore a size eighteen shoe ... no maybe eighteen was the size around his neck ... collar size ... believe his shoe size was closer to a sixteen ... still pretty big ... you get the picture? (*Dreamlike.*) Two Term Governor, James E. "Big Jim" Folsom, Alabama's Kissin' Governor ... but all that kissin' was before he met me. They say, Big Jim was not just kissing babies on that campaign trail ... or so I was told. (*Laughs.*) Later on before we were married you could see him kissin' movie stars and other pretty young ladies on the pages of LIFE MAGAZINE. (*Pause, thinks, laughs.*) He wasn't exactly on the pages of LIFE MAGAZINE, he was actually in Hollywood and later in New York City where they took a photograph of him kissing those pretty models staying at the Barbizon Modeling School, but as I said that was before we married.

Lordy, I was just graduating high school, when he started chasing after me. I met him over in Berry my hometown when he was campaigning for his first term in 1946 ... he was a widow-man ... and I was just graduating high school that May. One night I did take a ride with Big Jim and we talked to the wee hours ....

HONEY: (*sings an aside.*)

> SO, YOUNG LADIES, TAKE A WARNING
> AND DON'T EVER TAKE A RIDE

JAMELLE (*Looks at Honey.*) Nothing happened! Not even a good night peck on my cheek. But, that night we took that ride and we talked to the wee hours. Nothing romantic took place at all. (*Laughs*) I didn't even know the Governor was courting me … me being so young and him being a widow-man with two young daughters. Lord, he was almost twice my age.

You can say I was Alabama's child bride … I was just 19 when we married. But, I'm getting ahead of myself. (*Thinks and repeats.*)[40] Originally I didn't even know we were dating, me about to graduate from high school and him running for Governor. That was 1946, but it seems like yesterday to me.

Oh, by the way, I am Jamelle Dorothy Moore Folsom … wife of the Two Term Governor and Mother of another. Mother of another … sorta rhymes. Jim, Jr. served as Governor after they sent Guy Hunt to jail … back in 1993. They caught Guy using the state plane to go off preaching. I guess, when you get the calling to go preaching, you have to get there as best and fastest way you can regardless of the law about state airplanes. (*Pause.*) Jesus has been dead over 2000 years; don't know why Guy was in such a big hurry he had to jump on a State plane.

(*Shakes head.*) Alabama has gotten so hateful, once you serve as Governor they … the other party tries to indict you and send you off to the jail house as soon as they can. Tried it with Little Jim, but it didn't work. Doesn't matter what party it is … guess it doesn't matter much anyway … everybody says they are Republicans nowadays … except us Folsoms! Obama ought to give us one of them Freedom Medals remaining Loyal Democrats in Alabama all these years and we're not even Colored … I mean African American. (*Shakes head.*) You give a good 'ole boy a pick-up truck and a bass boat and he thinks he's a rich Republican.

Governor always said we's Yellow Dog Democrats, with the big "D". He meant Big D as in Democrat, not as in Dog. But nowadays, they got blue dogs, red dogs and purple dogs in politics … I can't keep up … but back then we always said we'd vote for a Yellow Dog before we'd vote for a Hoover Republican. Governor said Nixon went after the old Dixiecrats after they got mad at LBJ for them Civil Rights Acts. (*Shakes head.*) Big Jim had no use for them old Dixiecrats and said the Republicans could have the Kluxers. But, I'm getting ahead of myself.

Anyway being a Democrat in my part of North Alabama was a Depression thing back in the '30s that's when the Depression was. Yes, the 1930s when I was just a baby (*laughs at self*) don't go doing the math you'll know how old I am. Back then I was very young and I am young at heart now, except I been getting a lot of acid reflux of late and I'm in some pain. They say gettin' old is not for sissies. I just take me another nerve pill but don't go around telling that out of school. Folks don't like to worry over us "Old Ladies." (*Winks.*) Folks like it when you put on a happy face ... no one wants to listen to your aching joints and how your digestive track is working or not. Troubles ... and Lord, we have had our share. (*Smiles. Fishes pills out of purse and takes pill going upstage for bottle of water.*)

Governor Folsom and I got married mid-way through his first term way back in the late forties. Everybody wanted to warn me and tell me about all those wild women. But, when somebody wants to talk about those "wild women" the Governor flirted with back then ... before he met me ... I just change the subject and talk about what I want to talk about .... What is it called when you just change the subject? Whatever it is, I learned that from the politicians. It's a technique. Can't remember what they call it. When you don't want to talk about something, change the subject, and just talk about what you want to. Right Honey?

Honey: (*Startled, hits a chord and sings.*)
 DON'T EVER TAKE A RIDE

JAMELLE: (*To Audience.*) You remember what they call it when you change the subject? (*Adlib if an answer; otherwise, thinks. Snaps finger.*) "Deflecting" that's what they call it when a politician gets a question she doesn't want to answer and then says whatever she wants to say. That Sarah Palin was good at it. Deflecting!

(*To Audience.*) Please, make yourself comfortable. Did we offer you something to drink? Something besides a bottle of water. (*Adlib, if drinks in theatre. "Don't you love white wine?" "You won't need coffee to stay awake, Honey, I'm gonna tell some secrets." "I know it's five-o'clock somewhere, but we are only serving 7-Up and spring water." If drinks are not allowed in theatre ... would offer you something to drink but the last visitor had a little too much to drink and ruined the carpet. You ever tried to get red wine outta a light colored carpet?"*)

(*With Box of Cookies.*) Have a cookie. After my doctor's appointment, had to run down to the bank and the beauty shop this morning and the Bakery is just across the railroad tracks. Bakery been here as long as the town has ... Duchess Bakery. Here have a cookie ... baked fresh daily.

(*Adlib ... "Com' on Honey (audience member), you don't have to worry with your weight." "We're not supposed to talk about our girth." "It's almost Thanksgiving and we all are thankful for our sweets." "Have one ... oh, you can have two." "You look modern, looking like next year with that fashion." "If I'd known you were coming, I'd gone by Starbucks and got you a pumpkin latte." "Yes, we even got a Starbucks now.")*

Lord, those Germans really know how to bake. Did I tell you this town, Cullman, Alabama, was settled after the Civil War by the Germans. They were laying the railroad tracks from Nashville to Birmingham. Not sure the Germans were laying the track — they were probably the engineers who told the workers where to lay the tracks.

And, I'm told there wasn't much to Birmingham back then, so I guess they were running the railroad to what was to become Birmingham? So, the Germans were coming down from Ohio or somewhere up North and they got off on this pretty little plateau of Sand Mountain. Cullman, Alabama.

And, Honey ...

HONEY: (*Reacts when hears his name, hits an arbitrary chord.*)

JAMELLE: Honey, I wasn't talking to you. I call everybody "Honey." It's confusing, I know, but I guess that is the way it is. (*Laughs.*) Where was I? Oh yes, as I may have said, this Hill Country is not the Old South, like in the movies. You see, during the Civil War, when Sherman and those other Yankees marched through Alabama, there wasn't nothing around here to burn except a few pine trees, as the Governor always said. He loved his history. Said if we don't remember history we are doomed to repeat it or it rhymes or some such.

Anyway, back when the Governor was living, there was a stream of history professors always dropping by and Governor would bend their ears, especially after he turned blind. You don't have to have good eye sight to sit in an easy chair and pontificate. Lord, the Governor could do some pontificating.

He'd always pointed out that this county, Cullman County, was part of the Free State of Winston during the Civil War. I was born and bred in Berry, Fayette County, just on the western side of the Free State of Winston. So, you can say we all belonged to what they called the "Free State of Winston!" Now what exactly was the "Free State of Winston?" Governor always said, "Hillbillies got us a mind of our own and at our core we may be Yankees." Don't worry, he was just making a point.

So, when Jefferson Davis stood on that gold star on the Capitol steps down in Montgomery to break from the Union and officially join up with the Civil War ... the good folks of Winston County gathered at Old Looney Mill Tavern (*points*) just over there in what's left of Winston County and we seceded from the South, when the South seceded from the Union. (*Pause*.) It didn't actually happen but a lot of folks acted like it did. They say, Winston County had more men fight for the North than fought for South. Figures because there weren't any plantations in these foothills.

But we don't sound like Yankees; now, do we? But we may be. (*Laughs*.) It's all good.

Big Jim loved talking about our history and how our ancestors ... the dirt farmers ... had a lot of common sense and wanted to sit out the Civil War. No one around here had any slaves and when you think about it war is not such a good idea anyway. Did I tell you that these parts have some strong headed folks? (*Pause*.) I guess I just did. (*Snickers at self.*) Governor said the Germans are strong-headed too.

(Pause, looks at cookies.)

Where was I? Well, regardless of war and politics, the Germans are real good bakers and we all get along real good. Germans mostly Lutheran, but we are good Southern Baptist. So, many Baptist Churches around here. Use to have to attend two or three Church services on a Sunday back when the Governor was running for office.

Don't you love the cookies? There's a funny story about the Duchess Bakery. Well, Big Cookie who ran the Bakery ... don't remember his name and I'm sure I called him "Honey." But let's just call him Big Cookie for now. Well, Big Cookie was also the bootlegger or one of the several bootleggers the Governor used from time-to-time. You see, Cullman County is dry ... believe it has been since the Great Depression. The City of Cullman only recently voted "wet."

Where was I? Dry doesn't mean it's hot as in arid ... well it can get real hot in the summertime but we got a lot of humidity that's wet and sticky. (*Laughs*.) Where was I? You didn't come here for a weather report. (*Pause*.) I was talking about liquor. You see, "dry" means they don't sell whiskey. At least they don't sell it legally. And, if you were like the Governor, you'd enjoy a nip every now and then. (*Pause*.) Actually, the Governor drank full measure and said he did not trust a man who would not likewise drink a full measure. Could not be a sissy with your drinking, if you hung around the Governor. Well, when you drank full measure in Cullman, Alabama, you'd have to have a bootlegger ... or two.

Big Cookie, the baker, was a friendly man and almost as big as the Governor.

And, like the Governor he was a back slapper. (*Laughs.*) I could tell when the Governor had bought him a bottle from Big Cookie, Governor would come home with a big ole white hand print right there on the back of his blue serge suit coat. (*Laughs, shaking head.*) And, I knew the Governor was not at the Duchess Bakery buying cookies.

Governor's drinking was not as bad as those rumors his political enemies always circulated. Big Mules and Lying Daily Newspapers were just slinging mud. When the "mudslinging" got bad, Governor said just let the mud dry and you can flick it off. Between all that dried mud and that flour dusting on the back of his suit jacket, I had a collection of them little thing-a-ma-jigs that you roll on a suit jacket to keep it looking fresh.

(Fishes lint roller out of purse and demonstrates on her coat.)

Don't you love these little things. Work pretty good.

(If audience accessible, consider demonstrating on nearest audience member with moment of adlib. Looks at poinsettia.)

Poinsettias not my favorite Christmas plant. You can't smell 'em. They not even a flower. I like a Christmas plant that smells sweet, like them paper whites. But, I drove by the Elks Club this morning and they were unloading a truck load of Poinsettias that they give us widow-women each Christmas. Usually they hand them out at our Thanksgiving Dinner, but I bragged on them like they were my favorite Christmas plant and how they brighten up a holiday house.

Maybe, I mentioned that I had not been feeling too good lately and hoped that my hair was not a mess. *(Adjust hair.)* Told 'em I might not be able to make Thanksgiving Dinner. The Elks put out a big spread at Thanksgiving ... dozen turkeys with all the trimmings. Well, then they up and gave me a poinsettia. Sorta forced me to take it. I did allow how it would brighten up the house and make me feel better. The Elks put out a big spread on holidays, for those of us who don't cook much.

It's no big secret, when Cullman was dry the Elks Club was wet ... real wet and that's an understatement. Elks Club where Big Jim and his buddies would tip a few, as they said. And when he got home and said he'd had just a few at the Elks Club, I thought just a few Mason jars full. As our reward for puttin' up with the foolishness, widow-woman of a deceased Elk, get a poinsettia at Christmastime each year. (*Sighs.*) I guess it's close enough to Christmas and it does brighten up the room.

I'm living with my change-of-life baby, that is my baby daughter Melody and her husband Doug. This house is nice but it's no mansion. Melody and her husband own A J's Steakhouse on Highway 31 just north of town, where you can get a good steak at a reasonable price. Melody was born in 1970. Don't do the math, but it was when I was pretty sure I was officially out of the baby birthing business. *(Winks.)* "Baby birthing business" say that real fast and you can get all twisted up. Melody and Doug are real sweet and I get to babysit my grandbaby Abigale Jamelle, hence A.J. like the name of the steakhouse.

Yes, Lord. The Governor said he kept me barefoot and pregnant. You know, your feet do swell when you are with child and Camellia made sure those floors in the Mansion were waxed slick as glass. I went barefoot most of the time because I didn't want to slip and I was pregnant most of the time. *(Turns on radio.)*

RADIO VOICE: (*Voice of Governor Big Jim Folsom running for office, circa 1946.*) Yes, my fellow citizens of the Great State of Alabama, as a people we are proud and we have been through a lot, the Great Depression and the Second Great War. We have survived a lot. Now we got to get down to the business of helping each other. I'll pave your roads so you can get your crops to market. Increase teacher's pay, so your youngins' will have a better future. And, we need an old age pension, cause we're not getting younger. Vote for Big Jim. Y'all come! You hear. Vote Big Jim. There's a brighter day a comin'.

JAMELLE: They called Jim the Little Man's Big Friend. I just love this old radio. One of my grandbabies is into music and stereos and all the new stuff. Well, she fixed it up for me, so I can just punch a button and it plays the Governor's old radio addresses, some of the old songs. With the sound coming out of that old radio cabinet, I feel like I am sitting in a living room — fifty or — I guess — maybe sixty years ago listening to the Governor. Oh Lord, there you go doing the math. *(Smiles.)* And, there was always music. *(Starts humming.)*

JAMELLE *Sings with* HONEY *on guitar plays YOU ARE MY SUNSHINE*[41]

> THE OTHER NIGHT DEAR, AS I LAY SLEEPING
> I DREAMEND I HELD YOU IN MY ARMS
> BUT WHEN I AWOKE DEAR, I WAS MISTAKEN
> AND, I HUNG MY HEAD AND CRIED.
> *(Sing up tempo.)* YOU ARE MY SUNSHINE, MY ONLY SUNSHINE
> YOU MAKE ME HAPPY WHEN SKIES ARE GRAY.
> YOU'LL NEVER KNOW DEAR HOW MUCH I LOVE YOU
> PLEASE DON'T TAKE MY SUNSHINE AWAY.

RADIO VOICE: The good folks of Alabama been through some hard times and there's a rain cloud on the horizon. From time to time it's gonna cloud up but it ain't gonna rain.

JAMELLE: Governor loved telling that story when he was on that flatbed campaigning. Alabama had been through some hard times. Some folks not over the Depression to this day. Well, when the Governor was a boy down in Coffee County, his Pa had him plowing in the hot summertime and Jim always looked out for them rain clouds so he could quit plowing, take the afternoon off and maybe go fishin'. One day he saw a rain cloud out on the horizon and he pulled the mule off the row of cotton. Then, his Pa said, "Jim, keep on plowing!" His Pa pointed. "It may be gonna cloud up, but it ain't gonna rain! Keep on plowing!" Governor would tell the crowd we's gonna keep plowing and clean up Montgomery.

The crowds loved it when he talked like that. I never knew exactly what he meant because rain is good for the crops. I know that from my work with the Agriculture Department. But, the crowds knew Big Jim would keep on plowin' to clean up Montgomery and sweep out the Big Mules. *(Pause.)* I keep talking about Big Mules like everybody these days knows who I'm talkin' about. Big Jim said that in a pasture all the mules follow the biggest mule. And, in the State of Alabama the industrialist in Birmingham and the plantation folks in the Blackbelt and the County Agents thought they run everything, so Big Jim called 'em "Big Mules." Some of you looked as confused as I use to be. Like what do County Agents have do with anything? Well, back then through some government program they told farmers just how much cotton they could plant and still get some government money on the side or some such. You might have guessed it, the County Agents told the farmers how to vote if they wanted a generous grant. Jim even had him a big ole mop and suds bucket to clean up the mess the Big Mules made in Montgomery. I always laughed at the Governor saying with all your plowing and the mess the Big Mules left, floors gonna get good and dirty and you'll for sure need that mop and suds bucket. *(Laughs.)* It's a little inside joke about Jim having his own mess to clean up too.

HONEY:

> YOU'LL NEVER KNOW DEAR HOW MUCH I LOVE YOU
> PLEASE DON'T TAKE MY SUNSHINE AWAY.

JAMELLE: Goodness gracious, that song does bring back the memories. My voice was young and only fair back then, but I use to sing it with the Governor when we were on the campaign trail. I was kinda shy but he'd call me on that flatbed. The Strawberry Pickers would crank up the tune. We loved everybody and the crowds loved us back. We were elected twice, once in 1946 and again in 1954.

I told you I met the Governor when he was running in 1946 and I was just graduating high school. My Daddy was into politics and he was working on the Governor's campaign and Mama was home trying to make sure I didn't grow up too fast. Mama even called me "Ja-Baby." Mama called me Ja-Baby 'til the day she died. *(Picks up framed photo of younger Jamelle.)* I sorta knew I was attractive but there were a lot of other girls in Berry, who were just as pretty as me. *(Coy.)* Don't know why the Governor picked me out of the crowd. Well, that day, I went to see all the commotion. They'd come to town in a caravan of cars with car horns blaring and a big ole speaker on one of the cars announcing a rally to be held down by the Bank. The Governor traveled with the Strawberry Pickers on that flatbed truck and they could draw a crowd with all that racket they'd make.

There was music and excitement in the air. It was all new to me, but I could see the Governor eyeing the crowd and you sorta know when you catch somebody's eye. Then out of the blue he stopped thanking all the local politicians and said, "You folks have some good lookin' chillen' here in Berry, Alabama!" If that wasn't enough … him eyeing me and all, after his speech, he walked right up to me and asked: "Honey, do you want to get married?" *(Pause.)* I was beyond startled and did not know what he was talking about, so I said, "Someday." I did want to get married someday but graduating high school and maybe going to college was on my mind. Then he noticed my friendship pin, some of us girls wore, and he must have thought it was a fraternity pin or something, because then he asked, "Are you attached?"

(Smile.) You can imagine, it took me a while to figure out what he was talking about and I'm sure I told him I was not engaged to be married or anything like that and that I was busy graduating high school. He was tall and handsome, but so old with two little daughters to rear. Then he asked me to the drugstore for a Coke Cola. And, I went thinking there were a lot of other pretty girls at the rally but *(winks)* I sorta felt special. Then, he asked me to go the rally at the Courthouse in Fayette that night. County seat is Fayette and it was sixteen miles away from Berry. So, I told him I could not go out at night without my parents' permission.

Then he decides to go to my house. *(Laughs,)* Big Jim going to my house would have been funny even if I had not been right in the middle of it. I mean, the scene at my house when the Governor went asking permission to take me to the Courthouse that night. Well, this six foot, eight inch tall man came a callin' to ask me out. Daddy was sorta impressed because Daddy was into politics and he was a Folsom man and had been working on the campaign. Don't think Daddy thought Big Jim was trying to court me, though.

But, Mama was another story. She said "No" and if she'd been a cussing woman, she'd said "Hell, No!" Then, she said, "No, my Ja-Baby, can't go. Big Jim you are as old as I am!" Meaning Big Jim was as old as Mama. Did I tell you Mama always called me Ja-Baby like I was still a babe-in-arms. And as I had learned to do as a teenager, I turned to Daddy when Mama didn't give me a good answer. He said he didn't see any harm in me going to the Courthouse for the rally. So, I guess that was my first date with the Governor.

That afternoon, I was so excited, I changed outfits three times and settled on a soft-green suit. And, worked on myself, primping for a couple of hours. I went to a lot of trouble while pretending I was not dating a man about twice my age, and about twice my size. He sent a driver, Bill Lyerly, this good lookin' muscle guy about twenty-one years old, who let me know he'd take me home if I was uncomfortable traveling with the Governor after the rally. I told Bill that I'd be okay and I wanted a good seat in the balcony at the Courthouse so I could take it all in.

Well, after the rally, Big Jim did ask me to the reception at Dr. Robbin's house. When we got to the reception, Dr. Robbin said I could have anything to drink that I wanted. (*Laughs.*) I asked for a chocolate milkshake. At first I didn't know why they were laughing. Dr. Robbins was real nice and made me a milkshake. They still laugh about when I ordered that milkshake. The men folks were not drinking milk shakes. As with most of us good Southern Baptist, Mother did not allow whiskey in the house and when Daddy wanted a drink, he'd have to go out to the back of the house. Folks having cocktails in their living room was sorta new and exotic to me.

Big Jim insisted on driving me home that night. Halfway home, Big Jim allowed as how sixteen miles was not enough time to get to know me, so he pulled off to the side of the road and we talked and talked and asked each other every question we could think of. We talked and talked well past Mama's midnight curfew. Here I was falling in love with a widow-man with two small daughters and me not out of high school yet.

Big Jim kept on campaigning that spring and the Strawberry Pickers kept drawing big crowds. Big Jim kept calling me and trying to court me but he was a busy man with that campaign and all, and I was busy graduating high school.

HONEY: *(Sings OH! SUSANNA.[42])*

> I COME FROM ALABAMA WITH A BANJO ON MY KNEE,
> I'M GOING TO LOUISIANA, MY TRUE LOVE FOR TO SEE.
> IT RAINED ALL NIGHT THE DAY I LEFT,
> THE WEATHER IT WAS DRY
> THE SUN SO HOT I FROZE TO DEATH,
> SUSANNA DON'T YOU CRY
> OH! SUSANNA, OH DON'T YOU CRY FOR ME,
> FOR I COME FROM ALABAMA WITH MY BANJO ON MY KNEE

JAMELLE: *(Thumbs through scrape book and old newspaper clippings.)* That spring, I graduated from High School and Big Jim got in a runoff with Handy Ellis, one of the Big Mules. And the Big Mules must have been running scared, because they cooked up a plan to kill Big Jim. I was right there that night in Jasper, Alabama when everything got real strange from where I sat. Big Jim was running strong in the runoff. It was the Democratic Primary, and if you won the Democratic Primary, you were a shoo-in come November. Not many Republicans in Alabama back then and what few Republicans there were seemed to be all in Winston County. I'm sure the Big Mules wished they were Republicans but they ran as Democrats because everybody else did too.

But in 1946, the Big Mules must been running scared. You see, this lady newspaper reporter happened on the plot to kill Big Jim 'cause he was running against the Big Mules' pick Handy Ellis. Well, Big Jim's caravan was traveling around the state and the last day of campaigning was a Monday before the runoff election on a Tuesday. Jim had stops in Hamilton, Winfield, Carbon Hill and Jasper. The last stop was over in Jasper and I made sure that Momma and Daddy took me to that rally in Jasper. I wanted to sit down front to show my support. Before the rally got started good, Bill Drinkard just comes over and told me that the Governor could not see me after the rally that evening, because he had to leave the rally in a hurry because of some business.

I later learned that the Big Mules were going to way-lay him on the road back to Cullman. They suspected he'd travel Highway 69 by way of Bug Tussle, Cold Springs Mountain and Bremen back to Cullman. But, after the rally, they put Jim's big old Stetson hat on another fella and put the fella in the Folsom car pretending to be Big Jim. Then the caravan headed out of Jasper and took the Highway 69 fork to Cullman. Jim slipped out to another car and back tracked to Birmingham ... the long way around, if you ask me, but it turned out to be the safer way to get back here to Cullman.

Then, when the Folsom caravan, without Big Jim in it, reached Bremen, all hell broke loose. A car barreled out of a side road and cutting off the Folsom car. Bill Lyerly broke out of formation and began passing the cars in front of him. Another car dashed from a side road but the Folsom car suddenly stopped and the assassins' car plowed into the Folsom car, killing the driver. The Sheriff and a Deputy piled out of the Folsom car and arrested the would-be assassins.

The next day, that lady reporter wrote in the Tuesday newspaper, the paper that came out on election day: *(Puts on thick-lens glasses and reads clipping.)*

RADIO VOICE & JAMELLE (overlay) "Last night an attempt on Folsom's life failed. One dead, three in custody. None of the men in the Cullman County jail are talking. There is no evidence that the attempt on Big Jim's life came from the Ellis camp. The Folsom organization is not talking much about the incident that took place on Highway 69 near Bremen, Alabama. The only comment from the men arrested was that it was just a bad traffic accident."

JAMELLE: *(Takes off glasses quickly.)* The runoff turnout was heavy and the Folsom camp smelled victory ... victory sweet as a paper white narcissus. Election night around midnight Handy Ellis conceded and the Folsom crowd whooped and hollered at the Redmont Hotel in Birmingham. It was a landslide victory.

That January, my parents and I quietly attended the inauguration festivities in Montgomery. Jim's sister Ruby stepped in and started running the Mansion for the Bachelor Governor and calling herself First Lady ... when she was only a First Sister. But, to her credit and in spite of her drinking, she was raising Jim's daughters, Rachel and Melissa, while raising her own children, Cornelia and Charles Ellis, Jr. (Laughs.) No kin to Handy Ellis, that Big Mule who lost to Big Jim.

I didn't go to the University of Alabama as my folks had hoped I would. No, I went to business school to learn typing and bookkeeping and later moved to Montgomery. Mama followed me to Montgomery and got an apartment to be near her Ja-Baby. I got a job with the Highway Department as a receptionist and the Governor kept courting me. Or, trying to court me ... with Mama right in the middle trying to protect her Ja-Baby.

When the Governor's long black car would pick me up for a lunch date all the Highway Department employees would run to the widow and wonder why this young, new employee was datin' the Governor.

After a year or so of having lunch with the Governor, and him beggin' me to marry him. One day at the Sahara Restaurant, he made it clear that he was askin' to marry me one last time. Sorta forced my hand, saying you know now if you want to marry me or you never will! Of course I said yes.

Mama didn't take it too good, so we eloped to Rockford. Well, it wasn't much of an eloping with Rockford being so close by. We got the marriage license from the Probate Judge. I was all dressed up and I'm a good Baptist, so I put my foot down and said I was not going to marry at a courthouse. So, we found this pretty little Baptist Church in Rockford ... Church even had a rock façade on the outside, just real pretty. Big Jim found the Baptist preacher and we were married in a church service.

HONEY: (*Plucks a few bars of "Here Comes the Bride" or "Rock of Ages."*)

JAMELLE: Our wedding was May 5, 1948, almost two years to the day that I first met Big Jim. For the Honeymoon, Jim borrowed a friend's place on Lake Martin ... real nice lake house, with a tin roof and big front porch overlooking the Lake. Well, that tin roof sounded real nice in a soft rain. But, that night when I was in the back bedroom primping up, getting ready for our wedding night, there comes the biggest racket you ever heard on that tin roof. It was like all the fireworks you ever heard going off all at once on the Fourth of July. Heck it could have been World War III for all I knew. Scared me to death.

Big Jim in just his shorts went out to see what it was. I was in my new frilly nightgown and matching robe, but I was not about to go out on that porch. *(Laughs.)* You know what it turned out to be? They have a word for it. *(Thinks.)* It was his cronies ... cabinet members and drinking buddies ... throwing rocks on that tin roof, shooting off fireworks, scaring me to death. Back then, they called it something ... like .... *(Asked audience.)* Do you know what they call it? It's an old fashioned word and they don't do it much now-a-days. I'll think about it in a minute. Don't you hate getting' ol ... maturing. Like when you go in a room and look around and ask yourself, "Why am I in this room?" You have to think for a minute. Then if you're lucky you'll remember you're lookin' for the car keys. *(Pause.)* Does anybody know what they call it when your friends and neighbors make a bunch of noise and interrupt your wedding night? *(Interact with audience, if responsive.)*

Anyway, his cronies ended up giving us all those big silver pieces. *(Points to sideboard.)* Real nice serving pieces, but the stuff needs polishing all the time and when you are in the Governor's Mansion, the staff keeps it bright and shinney. Now, if it gets polished, I'd have to do it myself ... so I just keep it wrapped up in plastic.

(Snaps finger.) "Serenade!" That's what they call it when the groom's buddies disturb the bride and groom on their wedding night. *(Winks.)* They hadn't disturbed nothing yet. I was still primping. *(Adjusts hair while looking in mirror.)* And, Jim just in his shorts, goes out on the porch and invites the boys in for a drink. I stayed in the back bedroom thumbing through a magazine. *(Laughs.)* Probably a Bridal Magazine about what to wear on your wedding night.

Lord, you got to love Big Jim, he was an original and all boy.

(Lifts a wedding announcement from scrapbook.) Back in Montgomery, I let Mama announce the marriage: *(Takes out glasses and reads.)*

Mr. and Mrs. Earnest Melvin Moore
Announce the marriage of their daughter
Jamelle
To
The Honorable James E. Folsom
Governor of Alabama
On Wednesday the 5th of May
In the year of our Lord nineteen hundred forty-eight.
Montgomery, Alabama

JAMELLE: Big Jim took me over the threshold and posed for the camera. *(Holds up photo.)* You can see how much bigger he was than I was. The Governor's Mansion was like a fairyland to me. There was a valet, driver named Winston, who would make sure the Governor was ready for every occasion. My favorite house keeper was Camellia who help raise all the children. *(Picks up another photo.)* You see we had a house full of children ... I love to say we had a Mansion full of children.

When we first married, I just bumped around that old Mansion with nothing much to do. The first Mansion was an old Brownstone that's where that Interstate Highway is now. But, there was one big problem and it wasn't termites.

No the problem was over six-feet tall and she was Big Jim's sister. Yes, Ruby had parked herself in the Mansion and got use to calling herself "First Lady." Lord, that sounded like incest, to me. On second thought, maybe she called herself First Hostesses. Whatever she called herself, I said she was at best First Sister and she was a handful. But, she got use to life in the Mansion. So Ruby had a way of turning my Fairyland into Purgatory.

(*Laughs*.) You know, they say, up North they hide their crazy folks in the attic, and down here in the South, we put our crazy folks on the front porch and stick a cocktail in their hand. Everybody on Perry Street knew Aunt Ruby, as the children called her. I should be more kind, she tried to be good for the children: Big Jim's daughters by his first wife and her own children. You know Ruby is Cornelia's mama. And Cornelia ended up marrying George Wallace, who we called little Bantam Rooster when we were being nice. But, I get ahead of myself. Back then George Wallace was a Folsom man and he was married to Lurleen. There are even stories about him and Lurleen visiting the Mansion back then and seeing little Cornelia on the stairway playing with the Folsom girls Rachael and Melissa. Years later after Lurleen died of cancer, George married Cornelia. She was real pretty and athletic too. Cornelia and Melissa skied professionally down at Cypress Gardens. Anyway, you may remember Cornelia from the cover of *Life* or maybe it was *Look Magazine*. That was when she was all bloody after that white boy tried to kill George Wallace in Maryland that time.

(*Shakes head and then laughs*.) But, Ruby was the mess. Shortly after Cornelia married George Wallace, Ruby told some reporter that George Wallace was not titty high. We all knew that and did I tell you we called him Little Bantam Rooster. Turns out if you got Folsom in your blood, there was no way you could respect George Wallace no matter how much he flipped and flopped and made sure Alabama had plenty of junior colleges and trade schools.

Oh, they loved Ruby on those T.V. programs ... she'd arrive at the station after she had a few cocktails and talk about her latest trip to rehab. All that would have been funny, if she had not been family. But, I get head of myself. When I moved into the Mansion, Ruby would take her cocktails in her room. Reminds me, it's time for my medicine. Excuse me. *(Exits.)*

Honey: *(Sings MOUNTAIN DEW.[43])*

    MY BROTHER BILL RUNS A STILL ON THE HILL
    WHERE HE TURNS OUT A GALLON OR TWO
    AND THE BUZZARDS IN THE SKY GET SO DRUNK

THEY CAN NOT FLY
JUST FROM SNIFFING THAT GOOD OLD MOUNTAIN DEW
(Chorus) THEY CALL IT THAT GOOD OLD MOUNTAIN DEW,
AND THEM THAT REFUSE IT ARE FEW
I'LL HUSH UP MY MUG IF YOU'LL FILL UP MY JUG
WITH THAT GOOD OLD MOUNTAIN DEW
MY AUNT RU-BY HAD AN AUTOMOBILE
IT RAN ON A GALLON OR TWO
IT DIDN'T NEED NO GAS AND IT DIDN'T NEED NO OIL
IT JUST RAN ON THAT GOOD OLD MOUTAIN DEW

JAMELLE: (*Returns.*) As I was saying, Ruby was a mess. I'm telling this out of school but she was tipsy most nights and did not like me moving into the Mansion and taking over the duties of First Lady. She'd go up to her room at night upset and with her vodka. Lordy!

I told Jim there was not room in the Mansion for two First Ladies or First Hostesses or whatever she called herself. And I finally told Jim that she had to go. It took him a while but Jim eased Ruby out of the Mansion. Got her a house just down the street.

Rachael and Melissa, Jim's daughters by his first wife, really liked having me around when they were still little girls. Jim and I would be sitting at that long dining room table eating our dinner and Melissa would be up under the table playing with my feet. She was the youngest ... only four or five years old. I was sorta their playmate at first. I got along real good with the girls until they turned teenagers. If you know how a step-mother can handle teenage step-daughters, let me know. For that matter what mother ... natural or not ... can do right by a teenage girl when they have their Daddy wrapped around their little finger? They run to Daddy ever chance they get. (*Sighs.*) I should know, I got real good getting second opinion from my Daddy when I needed one. With all my duties as First Lady and me and Jim having our own children, I just had my hands full to be a mama to teenage girls. I wasn't much passed being a teenager myself. (*Extended beat.*)

I told you the Big Mules did not like Jim winning the governor's office and they made sure politics got real messy. That's when the Blackbelt farmers and the Birmingham big shots got together. Blackbelt farmers didn't pay taxes on their plantations. Big Jim said those boys would vote pine trees and livestock but they would not let our Negro Citizens vote. You see, they were use to running things their way. The Big Mules and even the County Agents started all sorts of rumors about Big Jim.

(*Whispers.*) One rumor was about Jim having an illegitimate … love child. Late at night, I'd ask Jim about those rumors and he just say it was a bunch of lies about him before he met and married me. I didn't let on and it is just between us, but I read a lot of newspapers back then.

Alabama is famous for having famous folks, like Jim Nabors … Gomer Pyle... he was from down around Sylacauga … And when he wasn't acting like a hillbilly … he could sing like an opera star. Makes you wonder?

(**Honey** *plucks "Stars Fell on Alabama."*[44])

But the worst of our native sons, was William Bradford Huie who was from just up the road there in Hartsville. *(Points.)* He got famous by moving to New York City and writing a book about some girl in Paris France or somewhere. Well, back in the '40's before Jim and I married, Bill published that hateful article in a New York paper about Jim having that bastard child. Then, on television one time I heard Bill say that that boy was the prettiest child Big Jim ever sired. Makes you wonder? 'Cause my Bama was a beauty queen. (*Adjusts hair and glances in mirror.*)

You know resentments will kill you? You have to let them go or they will eat you up on the inside. Forgiveness is about you, not the hateful person who offended you. But, when you do forgive them, it frees up a lot of time for more important things … like making sure you stylist gets you hairdo just right. (*Winks, looks in mirror and pushes up hair.*) Yes, resentments will kill you on the inside.

HONEY: *(Plucks and sings.)*

> SHE WAS POOR BUT SHE WAS HONEST, HONEST, HONEST
> NO VICTIM OF A RICH MAN'S WHIM
> 'TIL SHE MET THAT SOUTHERN GENTLEMAN, BIG JIM FOLSOM
> AND, SHE HAD A CHILD BY HIM.

JAMELLE: When I asked Big Jim about those rumors of him having that child out of wedlock, Big Jim just told another story. I know the times have changed and a lot of children are living together before they get married. But, back then a love child was a big problem, especially if you was a politician.

Anyway, Big Jim said when he was running for Governor the first time, a

Probate Judge down in Montgomery called him in his office one day. The Judge said he liked Big Jim and said he had happened on plot hatched up by some of Big Jim's enemies, the Big Mules. Judge warned Jim that the Big Mules had gone to New York City and got one of them a pretty model and fixed her up with the finest fashion from Paris France, including perfume, high heels and all. And, they were gonna set her loose on the streets of Montgomery, Alabama lookin' for Big Jim. (*Laughs*.) Jim said, "Hold on Judge. You mean they, my worthy opponents, are goin' hire that pretty woman and outfit her real pretty and set her loose on the streets of Montgomery, Alabama?"

"Yes," the Judge said.

"And, she'd be looking for me," Jim said.

"Yes," the Judge said.

"Well," Jim said, "Judge, if they are going to go to that much trouble, and set a trap like that and bait it with bait like that. They gonna catch this old boy every time!"

Jim told that story out on the stump when he was campaigning, but he was careful to point out to me that he was just … deflecting. Jim told me that child it was just a rumor and it was before he started courting me … when the rumor started.

Governor always said, a high tide lifts all boats. There was always stories going around about how progressive the Governor was. He always said it didn't matter what you called him as long as you called him to dinner. But you didn't call him a Dixiecrat. He said he was always grateful that back when Nixon and the Republicans inherited the Dixiecrats with their Southern Strategy. Said after integration the Republicans didn't even need a "strategy" to take over. Southerners are not stupid, but some are blinded by their anger. But, I get ahead of myself.

Back in our day, some of the Dixiecrats were real flirts and kindda cute until they opened their mouth. They'd always come at you sideways with their hateful politics. Dixiecrats like Strom and Jesse were against Blacks … African Americans.

Big Jim said the Dixiecrats were just Ku Kluxers in business suits. At night they's put on their hoods and bed sheets. Governor made it illegal for the Klan to wear their hoods. Wearing a bed sheet without a hood would look sorta silly. "Ku Kluxers" is what Big Jim called the Klan. He always said: "As long as the

Negroes are held down by lack of opportunity, the other poor people will be held down alongside them." Said he never knew why the Kluxers didn't figure out they were in the same boat with the Blacks economically speaking. In Alabama back then nobody had a pot to pee in or a window to throw the pee out of, that's what he said. Lordy, the Governor would preach and preach history and politics. He loved it. Democracy fixes everything that needs fixin'. Always said that he wanted to be viewed kindly after he was gone.

Nineteen-Forty-Eight was an up and down year for Big Jim. *(Thinks.)* I know that was the year we were married, but I mean up and down politically. Some had encouraged Big Jim to run as Truman's vice president because he ticket needed some life. Some even wanted Jim to seek the Democratic nomination for President himself. But, back in 1948 some of the rumors by the Big Mules, were taking hold. Jim lost the election to be a delegate to the National Democratic Convention in 1948 and he'd get real sad about losing the confidence of the people.

Back then Big Mules and Dixiecrats were about the same thing and they were all against Big Jim. Even tried to recall him, impeach him and knock him out of office. He kept me protected from most of this. I couldn't even go downtown Montgomery to shop for a new outfit. No, the department store would box up an outfit, with matching shoes and purse and send it to the Mansion. That was fun opening those pretty boxes, but I sorta missed going downtown to shop. Trying on a variety of pretty things.

Well, back in 1948 when the Dixiecrats marched out of the National Democratic Convention because of the race questions, the Dixiecrats held their own convention in Birmingham and nominated Strom Thurman.

(To audience.) You know what happened next? *(If response, adlib.)* When the Dixiecrats marched out the National Democratic Convention? Well, Big Jim marched right in the Convention as Loyal National Democratic and a favorite son candidate for President. And, you know who else marched in the National Convention right beside Big Jim? *(Ask audience. Adlib if response.)* You're right, was none other than George Corley Wallace, our little Bantam rooster. How's that for strange bedfellows? Actually they didn't march … they were already seated in the Convention and held on to their seat while they waved good bye to the Dixiecrats.

Lordy, we weathered many storms, the recall petition, the Dixiecrats, the rumors about the love child and moving Ruby out of the Mansion. And, we never know how history will treat us. I'm looking for Big Jim's 1949 Christmas message. Excuse me, I need another antacid and maybe that book is in the back. (*Exits for book, pill and water.*)

HONEY: (*Plays "Oh Little Town of Bethlehem."*)

JAMELLE: (*Enters with copy of William Safire's LEND ME YOUR EARS, GREAT SPEECHES IN HISTORY … thumbs to page 718.*) Here's a book by Mr. William Safire who use to write for the *New York Times* back when he was still alive and it's a collection of great speeches in the history of the world … LEND ME YOUR EARS, as in Friends Romans and Countrymen Lend Me Your Ears. This book is heavy and Big Jim is keeping some pretty important company: Lincoln, Churchill, Martin Luther, and Martin Luther King, Jr., the Kennedys … even Jesus Christ. They all gave important speeches.

Well it was 1949 and Jim did not care much for the Big Mules who were oppressing ladies and gentlemen of color, who we called Negroes back then.

Today, I try to remember to say "African Americans" out of respect. What do they call it? Political something. But, I sometimes have a hard time keeping up with what folks want to be called these days. Back then I learned not to say "Nigra" because some thought it was disrespectful and not politically (*thinks*) politically correct. But to me "Nigra" was just a softer way of saying "Negro" and I meant no disrespect. Just trying to soften up the word. Back then, if somebody wanted to be hateful, they had a word for it. But, not in this house. If the children ever came home from the playground saying that word or any other word of blasphemy, they got their mouth washed out with soap.

It's hard to describe what it was like back then. Nineteen-forty-nine was sixty something years ago, and Big Jim was way ahead of time when it comes to racial equality. In his Christmas Message that year, the Governor starts off remembering the season: (*Reads, puts on glasses.*)

HONEY: (*Strums 'Silent Night' as background to Message.*)

RADIO VOICE AND JAMELLE (*Overlap*): "This is the greatest day, the most revered day, of our entire calendar. It is the birthday of Christ, who was the greatest humanitarian the world has ever known.

"This is a day to talk about loving our neighbors, lending help to the less fortunate, and bringing joy to others by good work."

JAMELLE: Then he talks about the Blacks, the African Americans …

RADIO VOICE & JAMELLE *(Overlap)*: "Our Negroes, who constitute 35 percent of our population in Alabama — are they getting 35 percent of the fair share of living? Are they getting adequate medical care …."

JAMELLE: He had compassion for all people: (R*eads p. 720*)

RADIO VOICE & JAMELLE (O*verlap*): "As long as the Negroes are held down by deprivation and the lack of opportunity, the other poor people will be held down alongside them.

"There are others, too, who should share in our thought of the neglected — wounded veterans, the blind, the shut-ins, the crippled, and on and on. *** The job for us here in Alabama is a *positive* one. It is time for us to adopt a *positive* attitude toward our fellowman."

JAMELLE: And, I would like to add "our fellow-women." Mr. Safire and all those history professors said Big Jim was ahead of his time on the race situation. He was a dreamer and such a good man. I mean Big Jim was a good man … I don't know much about Mr. Safire.

(Shakes head.) When Big Jim mentioned health care in that speech, he had no idea he'd need open heart surgery and turn blind before his death back in 1987. *(To audience.)* Don't you wish all of us, could be remembered with such kind and thought out words as was in that speech. I never did understand why one group of people would want to hate another group of people because of the color of their skin … unless they didn't get that playground bully out of their system when they were young. *(Sighs.)* And, I suppose, they didn't listen when their Sunday School teacher taught the Golden Rule. Or sang about all the World's children being all different colors.

(Picks up picture frame of Big Jim, Jamelle, children and Camellia in front of Mansion.) Big Jim said his real job was to keep me barefoot and pregnant. We did have us a house full of children. All my boys were born while we were in the Mansion. I should say Mansions, plural. *(Pensive.)* No Mama should have to bury a child, and I have had to bury two of my boys. Excuse me if you will, I'm not feeling too good and need a few minutes to myself. Make yourselves at home. *(Forced smile.)* Talk among yourselves. *(Exits.)*

    End of Act One

ACT TWO

HONEY: (*Picks and sings Y'ALL COME.*[45])

WHEN YOU LIVE IN THE COUNTRY
EVERYBODY IS YOUR NEIGHBOR
ON THIS ONE THING YOU CAN RELY
THEY'LL ALL COME TO SEE YOU
AND NEVER, EVER LEAVE YOU
SAYIN' YOU ALL COME TO SEE US BY AND BY
Y'ALL COME! (points to audience: Y'ALL COME!)
Y'ALL COME! (points to audience: Y'ALL COME!)
WELL, YOU ALL COME TO SEE US NOW AND THEN
Y'ALL COME! (points to audience: Y'ALL COME!)
Y'ALL COME! (points to audience: Y'ALL COME!)

JAMELLE: (*In fall outfit for Thanksgiving Dinner. Enters carrying large box from department store, books, MAGIC, Cookbook of the Junior League of Birmingham, AL, LIFE MAGAZINE September 15, 1947 and ALABAMA'S FIRST LADIES AND THEIR GOVERNORS by Patsy Riley.*) Lord, my bedroom is full of memories. I should clean it out sometimes. I told you I loved the Governor's Mansion ... actually we lived in two Mansions. The first one was an old Brownstone, the one we had to move Ruby out of. Then Jim talked the State into buying that nicer Mansion on Perry Street that was ready for our second term. That old Brownstone was there until Ike's Interstate coming in from Atlanta got that old Brownstone back the '50s. We enjoyed a second term in the new Mansion and filled it up with children. In 1962 Jim tried for a third term and lost to that (whispers) Pissant George Wallace. (*Whispers.*) That's what we really called him. But, I get head of myself.

My first two boys Little Jim and Jack, Andrews Jackson Folsom, were born while we lived in that first Mansion. And, while Big Jim would go on his walks through the neighborhood he'd see this handsome old Southern mansion ... neoclassical and graceful ... and he befriended the widow woman who owned it, Mrs. Ligon. (*Coy.*) He didn't befriend her that way, no he just admired her stately home and said it would make a better Governor's Mansion than that old Brownstone. The Ligon home was what they call neoclassical and it had a grand staircase and majestic columns. The Ligons were a political family and Mrs. Ligon ... I believe her name was Aileen ... anyway, Aileen after the death of her husband started spending a lot of time out of state with her daughter. (*Pause*) I recall her daughter was Emily. Before Big Jim left office in 1950, he established a Commission to look at buying another Mansion. Aileen heard about the Commission and allowed as how she'd be honored to sell her home to Alabama … for a price.

About that time we left Montgomery and moved back to Cullman, Big Jim had to convince Governor-Elect Gordon Persons to buy the Mansion for a $100,000 which was a record back then. Gordon thought it was too much money, but he went ahead with it after Jim talked him into it.

Well, we did move back here to Cullman and enrolled the girls in East Elementary, just across the street from our home in Cullman. Jim eventually built a tennis court on the property next door. We like to pay tennis. I was young and quick and could scoot around and hit the ball. When we moved back to Montgomery after the 1954 election he build a tennis court out back of that new Mansion. We even had Poncho Gonzales visit and play on our new tennis court.

But, I get ahead of myself. I told you that Little Jim and Jack were born while we were in Montgomery during Jim's first term. Well, when we moved back to Cullman we had some more babies: Jamelle Alabama we call "Bama"; Thelma Ebelene "Scrappy"; Layla; and I told you about my change of life baby, Melody, who was born much later. Joshua "Josh" was born while we were in Montgomery during Jim's second term.

Big Jim said it was like a poker game, "With our seven children — we have three sons and four daughters — then two by his first wife." He'd joke like in a poker game, "have seven and raise two." Then, he'd say something about a full house.

(Pause, look through photo album and picks up old baseball hat with an Alabama "A" on it.) I told you that a Mama should not have to bury a child. I had to bury two of my boys. Buried two of my boys within 11 months of each other.

Josh was working construction up in Alaska. He loved to hunt and fish. He was the real outdoors man … sorta looked like the Marlborough Man. *(Pause.)* Don't think he knew that Palin clan but he stayed in Alaska that winter. Most winters he'd come home … home to Sweet Home Alabama during the winter and thaw out down in Gulf Shores or somewhere. But that winter he stayed in Alaska to fish. He was by a stream living in his little bitty camper and the propane heater leaked and he died of carbon monoxide poisoning in the cold Alaskan winter when he should have been down in Gulf Shores enjoying our warm sunshine. *(Shakes head.)*

And, Andrew Jackson Folsom died of a strange, quick flu … virus … new-ma-cockle something. Jack died down in Birmingham. Real quick onset and his cute little wife, Cullman City Councilwoman Jenny got him down to Birmingham but they could not do a thing for him. (*Pause.*) Jack should have been the politician … he loved to talk politics. Ran unsuccessfully for Public Service Commission once. Jack took after his Paw, the way he read everything put in front of him. Liked everybody. He'd drive his Paw around the State after Big Jim turned blind.

No Mama is supposed to bury a child. I buried two of my boys, within the same year … eleven months apart. Excuse me. (*In pain, takes another pill with water.*)

(*Long pause, turns to forced ebullience .*) I told you all three boys were born in the Mansion, two different Mansions. A week after Josh was born and we were in that new Mansion with its grand staircase. Then, Jim had his office calls me and says that the photographer from National Geographic was coming to take pictures. (*Laughs.*) The First Lady and a nursing mother had less than an hour to put on that ball gown. I met the Governor on that grand staircase and managed a smile. The photo did turn out okay.

(*Displays photo of Jamelle in gown with Governor at bottom of stairs.*)

I was so mad at him when I first started down those steps. I was breast feeding Josh and could barely get that ball gown zipped up the back. Oh, was I mad. (*Pause.*) But when I saw how handsome Big Jim was in his Tuxs and he reached out his hand for me and said 'I love you,' I forgot how mad I was. I just love this photograph.

Back then before all that internet stuff, folks read magazines. Here's a LIFE MAGAZINE from 1947 when they had Big Jim out dancing with movie stars and charming the ladies. Turns out when he met a pretty girl back then he ask, "Do you want to get married?" Most of us were shocked by the question, but I guess he could tell a lot about the answer if we came out of the shock. And, Jim knew how to relate to regular folks, like eating barefoot and taking tub baths for the photographers.

(*Fishes instamatic, throw-away camera out of purse.*) That reminds me, I forgot to take a picture while y'all are here visiting. (*Points camera at audience.*) Now if you are here with somebody you're not supposed to be with or if you are just playing hooky or if you are just shy and don't want your picture taken for history, just hold that program up in front of your face. (*Checks camera, points.*) Now say "cheese" but think sex! (*Clicks photo.*)

You probably guessed by now that Big Jim won a second term as Governor.

HONEY: (*Picks and sings BACK IN THE SADDLE AGAIN.*[46])

> I'M BACK IN THE SADDLE AGAIN
> OUT WHERE A FRIEND IS A FRIEND
> WHERE THE LONGHORN CATTLE FEED
> ON THE LOWLY JIMSON WEED
> BACK IN THE SADDLE AGAIN
> ***
>
> WHOOPI-TY-AYE-OH
> ROCKIN' TO AND FRO
> BACK IN THE SADDLE AGAIN

JAMELLE: I don't recall Big Jim having a lot of trouble winning that second term, but as he said I was barefoot and pregnant most of the time except when National Geographic photographer showed up and I had to put on shoes … and that inaugural ball gown.

Big Jim loved his New Mansion. He loved entertaining and the music. When we were inaugurated in 1955 and moved in the new Mansion the first thing Jim noticed was that the piano was missing. Someone had donated that piano to the University of Montevallo by mistake and the new Governor made sure we got it back. Had to get it un-donated. There was always music.

HONEY: (*Few bars of Stars Fell on Alabama.*)

JAMELLE: We'd have big dinner parties. We'd entertain politicians, Supreme Court members. The ladies in long dresses and the gentlemen in tuxedos. We just loved having formal dinner parties. It wasn't much trouble to throw a party because the staff at the Mansion could really cook and the food was so good.

(*Pause. Pulls out MAGIC, The Cookbook of the Junior League of Birmingham, AL, 1982 and turns to page 217.*) I don't cook much, but they could even make cabbage taste real good. Here it is. It's even called, "Governor's Mansion Cabbage." (*Reads receipt.*) You take a head of cabbage, a stick or two of melted butter, some flour, two cups of milk, Worcestershire sauce, two hard boiled eggs, cup of grated sharp Cheddar cheese and toasted slivered almonds. And, mix it all up and it would make old smelly cabbage taste like ambrosia. Big Jim loved that dish, but he said don't tell his doctors and to list it a green leafy vegetable.

I could not cook a lick. One time when we moved back to Cullman, the help had the day off or maybe it was when we fell on hard times and didn't have any help. So, I decided to cook, and I popped open a can of those grocery store biscuits and ran them under the broiler. Burnt on top and dough on the bottom. Children still laughing about me trying to cook those biscuits. My boy Jack laughed about "my biscuits" 'til the day he died. (*Thinks.*) But, I did learn somethings. You see, the cooks at the Mansion when they made that cabbage dish they'd make that French sauce ... becha ... something like that. You know which one I'm talking about? *(Adlib if audience says "bechamel" brag on their culinary knowledge and thank them.)* Whatever you call it. Anyway, I did learn that most southern cooks don't fuss with making a fancy French sauce. No, they just use a can of Campbell's Cream of Mushroom Soup. You heard it from me. But, Lord, don't go telling folks you're taking cooking hints from me. I did manage a big breakfast for the Governor. (*Laughs.*) After Big Jim died and I spent my year in mourning, I decided to start looking around again. *(Whispers.)* I don't tell just anybody that.

Nowadays, when a widow-man comes available in Cullman, I like to take him some homemade beef stew with fresh vegetables. (*Goes to Kitchen and shows audience a cast iron Dutch oven.*) Now, I need for you to keep this a secret. *(Gets agreement from audience.)* I don't think it's too dishonest, but when a widow man becomes available and his mourning time passes, I know he'd like a good home cooked meal. You may not believe this, but I go up to Shoney's and get their beef stew. Then, I put it in this Dutch oven and go a calling on the Widow Man. Shoney's beef stew is just as good as homemade. Men folks sure like to eat, or at least they use to.

Back when we were in the Mansion eating that Governor's Mansion Cabbage and other heavenly dishes, our waistlines began to spread. With having babies and all, I was not fitting in those pretty ball gowns or those department store suits either. I hate the word "matronly." Don't you?

Back in the '60s Metrecal came out to help you lose weight. The Governor and I would eat our lunch and then drink a can of Metrecal. We thought that's how it worked (*Laughs.*) We did not lose a pound. In fact, I believe we gained a few.

I told you, we loved that new Mansion but the politics was turning bad on us. That School Board decision came down from the Supreme Court saying that the schools had to be integrated. Privately, Governor said it was about time and he believed that democracy could take on most anything. Big Jim once told *Life*

Magazine that three arguments never end. Religion, politics and race. Then he told the reporter, "Just say, I'm for everything that's good and against everything that's bad."

But, the rest of Alabama was angry about that School Board Decision. I should say most of white Alabama was angry ... the Kluxers and the Dixicrats got real mad ... like they were gonna start another Civil War. That all hit about the time Governor's second term got underway in 1955. Then Montgomery had that Bus Boycott.

(*Picks up handsome department box.*) I told you that back during the Governor's first term, I could not go downtown Montgomery to shop because of all the hateful politics. Well, it got much worse after that School Board decision and the Bus Boycott. I was literally locked up in the Mansion ... having babies and playing a little tennis when the doctors would let me.

Thank, God, the department stores kept sending me matching outfits. (*Holds up dress and looks in mirror.*) The suits were always so nice and the shoes and purses to match. (*Shows audience.*) Every now and then, I'd get a note in the suit pocket, saying, "We sure like what the Governor said like in his Christmas Message." I figured the seamstress put the note there. Those seamstresses had all my measurements and they were good at adjusting for child birth. (*Holds up dress and looks in mirror again.*) Don't even think it ... I told you I hate the word "matronly."

To occupy my days in the Mansion, I'd have tea parties, mostly for the children and I worked for the March of Dimes. Always make sure the Mansion was set for entertaining, if not for some surprise visitor the Governor would bring home at the last minute. I learned to stay dressed-up, a habit I keep up until this day. I keep getting those jogging outfits from my children at Christmas ... I just thank then and later I re-gift them. I don't feel right if I am not dressed up even when I am feeling down.

(*Laughs.*) And, one day I had the surprise of my life. Well, it wasn't exactly a surprise because I told Jim that the help would feel uncomfortable serving one of their own, another Colored person. Then, I opened the front door of the Mansion and there he was ... handsome as a movie star and with an entourage lined up behind him no less. Yes, Winston was escorting The United States Congressional Representative from the Great State of New York, the Honorable Adam Clayton Powell. I know it's not politically correct, but that was a first for me back then, and I was still pretty young. Just like having cocktails openly in the living room, entertaining an African American in your home was not done in Alabama back then.

(Shakes head.) Apparently, I just stood there with my mouth open. The Congressman was so nice and he was dressed to the nines. I wasn't at all dressed up like I should have been. The Governor had said something about a Congressional visit and I expressed my doubts that we'd be up to the task. But apparently I forgot. Standing there in real time, it just caught me off guard.

Not even sure I had put on my makeup and I probably had on one of my shapeless maternity smocks, so I just stood there holding the door open and I heard the Congressman say. "You must be the Lovely Lady of the house. You gonna catch some of these Alabama flying bugs with that pretty mouth open …"

Embarrassed to death, I welcomed the Congressman and pointed him and his entourage to the Governor's study. Then, I went upstairs so embarrassed I could have died. Governor said he didn't care what color a person's skin was, all U.S. Congressmen are welcome in the new Alabama Governor's Mansion. Come to think of it, the Governor did say the Congressman was coming for cocktails but I must have forgot what exact time it was with all the babies to tend to. I was just caught off guard. Anyway, Governor said the Congressman thought I was cute with my mouth opened. I was so embarrassed. After that I always stayed dressed-up around the Mansion, and most everywhere else for that matter. You never knew whose gonna show up when the Governor was around.

Well, the hateful folks got wind of the Congressman visiting in their New Governor's Mansion and heard that the Governor and the Congressman were drinking scotch whiskey on the front porch under those stately southern columns. Governor would just laugh it off and say, "Everybody knows I don't drink scotch whiskey on the front porch, I drink my bourbon … cheap rot-gut … Early Death on the back porch." Governor was good at deflecting. *(Laughs.)* Governor always said, "Those that are 'fer you will love and stick by you. Those that are again' you, won't ever be happy with you."

Governor never did deny hosting Congressman Powell. Maybe that's what killed Big Jim's political career, like that Governor down in Florida hugging Obama. Honey, I'd hug and even kiss the President of the United States, if he'd give me a bunch of stimulus money.

The day Congressman Powell came a calling, I don't exactly know where they drank their whiskey or what kind of whiskey it was. I was upstairs embarrassed to death for not being properly dressed up for the Congressman. Big Jim said the Congressman told those students at Alabama State he would not have enjoyed such fine hospitality from the Governor of the Great State of New York.

(Picks up LIFE MAGAZINE.) Governor always talking about true democracy and how it can fix all that is broken in society. Then he told that reporter he knew about hot topics and he learned to avoid idle talk of politics, religion and race. Told that *Life Magazine* reporter just to say he was for what was good and he was against what was bad.

That racial stuff interfered with what Big Jim wanted to get done for Alabama. Then along came Autherine Lucy and that mess at the University of Alabama. Politicians down in Montgomery just stayed mad at one another and didn't do much good, little bit like it is today, everybody always bickering. Jim said 'bout all he got done in his Second Term was the Tennessee-Tombigbee Waterway. *(Laughs.)* His opponents called a big ole drainage ditch.

Sorta sad how hateful the Dixiecrats and the Kluxers got when they started running George Wallace for Governor. *(Feels pain.)* Big Jim ran again for Governor in 1962 until …. Excuse me, I need to take me another pill. Honey, you remember the election of 1962? We did real good until …. *(Exits.)*

HONEY: *(Sings Y'ALL COME.)*

> KIN FOLKS A-COMMIN'
> THEY'RE COMIN' BY THE DOZEN
> EATIN' EVERYTHING FROM SOUP TO HAY
> AND RIGHT AFTER DINNER
> THEY AIN'T LOOKING ANY THINNER
> AND HERE'S WHAT YOU HEAR THEM SAY
> Y'ALL COME! (points to audience: Y'ALL COME!)
> Y'ALL COME! (points to audience: Y'ALL COME!)
> WELL, YOU ALL COME TO SEE US NOW AND THEN
> Y'ALL COME! (points to audience: Y'ALL COME!)
> Y'ALL COME! (points to audience: Y'ALL COME!)

JAMELLE: *(Enters a little off her game.)* Everyone always said, the Governor and I were a cute couple … him six feet eight and I was about half his size and about half his age. I told you that we kept the Governor's Mansion full children and he worked for the good people of Alabama. I loved his speech about the sunshine. "It's gonna cloud up, but it ain't gonna rain."

Sometime rain is good for the crops, but sometime you don't need more rain. Last spring Nashville was under ten feet of water, flooded the Grand Ole Opr-ie before the Tennessee River had time to crest. And, those tornadoes ... I spent April in the basement. If the terrorist don't kill you, the weather will. Times have really changed.

Back then, politicians spoke sideways when they had to. But, when the Governor was lying, he told you he was lying. Most of the time it was him just "deflecting" and he'd get around to the truth when he needed to. But he loved democracy and freedom for all.

I told you, Big Jim always drank full measure, but losing that 1962 election nearly killed him. After he lost he disappeared to Buck's Pocket over in Guntersville and licked his wounds with a whole lot of likker. And, that turncoat Judas headed to Mexico.

Even with all that integration stuff, in 1962 Big Jim was running ahead of everybody. Ryan had been killed in that airplane crash. And, George Wallace was showing his fanny talking about segregation this and segregation that and segregation forever. Governor always said as long as the Negro is held down, all working folks — Black and white — will be held down with them. But, Big Jim was forced by the times to poke fun at the Freedom Riders. It's always safe for a politician to get after Yankees. But, privately he told that he'd like to be on that freedom bus because it was headed in the right direction for history. He'd love to wave at the likes of old Strom, Bull, George and the whole lot as that Greyhound slid through the South. He got real sad when the Klan burned that bus in Anniston and the Freedom Riders got beat up in Birmingham. Another black eye he'd say.

Then he'd get run into a corner and the same folks who burned the bus would force Big Jim to say he was for segregation if he wanted to get elected governor again. But, he'd tell me that the Black-folks knew where he stood and they knew he didn't mean nothin' bad with his political talk. Privately he'd say he was a Jim Crow liberal, keep your friends close and your enemy closer.

As you may know that T.V. show back in 1962 did us in. The night before Election Day Jim was supposed to go on T.V. in Birmingham. And, I was to get all the kids dressed up and we were to be there too. Well, the T.V. station in Birmingham was on a union strike and we all turned away at the picket line. Ended up in Montgomery for the telecast.

Jim rode in a separate car with his aides and one of his aides had been bought off by the Wallace crowd. Big Jim made the mistake of taking a drink of whiskey. He'd been off the bottle the whole campaign, but I guess he was tired. Well that Judas character must have spiked his whiskey with some powerful drugs, 'cause Jim was not in good shape when he got to the television station in Montgomery.

Some of us tried to get Jim just to take a nap and have the T.V. Station run one of his campaign films, but he'd have none of it. So, he gets on television and he is not in good shape. Did not remember the children's names exactly right. He was slurring his words like he'd been drugged. We just froze as it went out on the airwaves the night before the election.

The election was the next day and we did not have time to tell the good folks of Alabama the Governor had been drugged. (*Shakes head.*) We lost that primary election to George Wallace. Back then the Democrat always won in November and George Wallace became Governor of Alabama.

Now, Jim was hard put to defend his television appearance, 'cause he sometimes bragged about taking a nip of his Early Death. But, one of his top aides, the one that turned Judas on him, high-tailed it to Mexico the very next day. We are sure he's the one who put the mickey in the Governor's drink and I know the Wallace crowd was behind drugging Big Jim.

Governor never did put that loss behind him. What a different the State of Alabama would have been if Big Jim had been elected to a third term. That's like saying if the Supreme Court had given the 2000 election to Al Gore, instead of Bush, we would not have that mess in the Middle East. "If." Now that's a funny word. Governor always said, *if* a frog had wings it would not bust its fanny when it jumped.

But, it was especially hard losing that Governor's race to that Pissant … excuse my language but that's what we called George Wallace when we were being hateful. Then, years later Big Jim had to go down to Montgomery and beg Governor Wallace for our pension money. When you lose a race in Alabama, the winner tries to take everything away from the loser. It's more than flicking a little dried mud off your suit coat. (Pause.) My acid reflux is getting worse. (*Exits.*)

HONEY: (*Slow tempo sings YOU ARE MY SUNSHINE.*)
    THE OTHER NIGHT DEAR, AS I LAY SLEEPING
    I DREAMEND I HELD YOU IN MY ARMS

BUT WHEN I AWOKE DEAR, I WAS MISTAKEN
AND, I HUNG MY HEAD AND CRIED.
YOU ARE MY SUNSHINE, MY ONLY SUNSHINE
YOU MAKE ME HAPPY WHEN SKIES ARE GRAY.
YOU'LL NEVER KNOW DEAR HOW MUCH I LOVE YOU
PLEASE DON'T TAKE MY SUNSHINE AWAY.

JAMELLE: (*Enters & sighs.*) After Big Jim went blind, I had to go to the legislature again and beg for our pension. And, after Jim died, A.W. Todd appointed me as an officer with the Alabama Agriculture and Industry Commission. I really enjoyed going around to County Fairs and judging the canned goods. But, when A.W. lost, that Republican tried to eliminate my post.

I am grateful for my agricultural job, because I needed the money. Be nice to all those you meet when you are going up the ladder, 'cause you don't know whose fanny you have to kiss on your way back down. Lord, I did not have to kiss A.W.'s fanny. Lordy, I have to be careful how I say things. (*To Audience.*) Now, you are not going to go tell things about me out of school? Now, are you?

Where was I? We had some hard times. When Melody was a baby and the Alabama legislature was jerking Big Jim's pension around. Excuse me, they did not jerk it around; no, they eliminated it all together and we were broke. We would not have had food on the table except for the Welti Store that let us buy food on credit. (*Laughs.*) The children had a hard time believing we were broke and their spending habits were hard to break. Big Jim installed a pay phone in the den, because the children would come through and make long distance phone calls without thinking about it. Governor always said it was the children but he'd pick up that phone and call all over the place. You know you are broke when you cannot not even afford long distance telephone calls. Nowadays, folks just flip open their cell phones and call all over the place.

It's hard to be broke and try to live with your head held high ... being a Governor and a First Lady you have to try.

Every four years after he lost that election to George Wallace, Big Jim would scratch up the qualifying fee and run for Governor again. Every now and then a reporter would show up along with those history professors and Big Jim would talk and talk. Lord, Lord, what could have been if Big Jim ....

Excuse me. I'm not feeling too good. My children want me to go to the Elks Club for their Thanksgiving spread. (*Takes pills.*) But, I have got to perk up some. (*Beat.*)

Big Jim never did get use to his blindness ... he'd walk around the house hitting the furniture with that cane and trip over the furniture with those big feet of his. But he liked riding around Alabama and letting the fresh air from an open car window hit him in the face. That is when he could find somebody to drive him. He wore most of us out. But, we loved him dearly.

He died of heart failure on November 21, 1987, almost 25 years ago to the day. He was 79 years old. He had a big stately funeral at First Baptist Church right here in Cullman. They said the small airport north of town filled up with private airplanes flying in from Washington D.C. and other important places. I believe that all the good Democrats — state and national — were just realizing what a friend they had lost in Big Jim.

(*Laughs.*) The Family gathered in the living room before the funeral and before we went to the church. Out of the blue Little Melissa came in the living room hold out the telephone receiver. We Folsom keep using the same name for our children over and over. We have several Bamas and several Melissas. Little Melissa, I believe was Rachael's daughter. Anyway, she comes into the living room, holding out the phone and asked, "Does anybody know an Al?" We laughed and then she said. "There's an Al Gore on the phone." I took the call and Al was real sweet. Everyone was real nice how they were paying respects to Big Jim.

When we got to the church, it was full ... somebody had filled the choir loft with dignitaries so everybody could see the dignitaries, I guess they'd run out of church pews down front. The church was packed. Everybody loved Big Jim. Don't remember much of what was said at the church service. At Cullman Cemetery, graveside, after the preacher said a few words of comfort, that Highway Patrolman played his bagpipes under that far off oak tree.

HONEY: *(Strums, sings with Bagpipe music out of Radio.)*
    AMAZING GRACE, HOW SWEET THE SOUND,
    THAT SAVED A WRETCH LIKE ME.
    I ONCE WAS LOST BUT NOW AM FOUND,
    WAS BLIND, BUT NOW I SEE.
    T'WAS GRACE THAT TAUGHT MY HEART TO FEAR,
    AND GRACE, MY FEARS RELIEVED.
    AND GRACE WILL LEAD ME HOME.

JAMELLE: To this day, I have not been able to afford a proper tombstone for the Governor. *(Takes a pill.)* I'm still not feeling too good … believe the pain has gotten worse. I hate to disappoint the children, but I don't believe I can make it to the Elks Club for Thanksgiving Dinner this year. First time I missed a Thanksgiving Dinner … in I don't know when. (*Lies down on sofa and closes eyes. Extended beat.*)

HONEY: When the children came to get Jamelle for Thanksgiving Dinner, she was worse and they rushed her over there *(points)* to the Cullman Medical Center, where she died of cancer on November 30, 2012. If she knew about her cancer, she told no one. Wonder how she put up with all that pain and didn't let on. *(Pause.)* But, that was Jamelle.

~ END OF PLAY ~

Poster by JaiCreations, Inc., Tampa, Florida

BAPBOMB
[CODE BAPBOMB]

Development History: In 2004 Gypsy Productions, Inc. under the direction of Trevor Keller stage read BAPBOMB in St. Petersburg, Florida and Key West, Florida during Hemingway Days.

BAPBOMB (Renamed CODE BAPBOMB) was produced by Stageworks Theatre at the Gorilla Theatre, Tampa, Florida, January 11-28, 2007. BAPBOMB was directed by Producing Artistic Director Anna Brennan; with Managing Director Peggy Huey; Set Design by R.T. Williams; Lighting and Technical by Keith Arsenault; Set Construction by International Arts and Entertainment Group; Master Electrician Chuck Bowen; Costumes by Michael Jevorkian; Sound Design by Tracy Borgatti; Stage Managed by Lynn DeBree; and assisted in many ways by Gorilla Theatre coordinator Bridget Bean.
The Cast:
    HAMBRIC - Oliver Dill
    OX - Steven Clark Pachosa
    SLAW DOG - Jim Wicker
    BOAT - Slake Counts
    EULA - Rhonda Easton

TIME
August 31 & September 1988.

PLACE

Law firm, Birmingham, Alabama.

SET

Boat's office. A window or floor-to-ceiling doors to thin balcony overlooks historic Kelly Ingram Park. The desk/table is open revealing desk chair. On the desk there are files, books and speaker telephone. The office is appointed with client chairs, vintage computer (optional), a few law books, fax machine, dictation machine, and modern art.

Opposite entrance, adjacent to Boat's office is a workroom/storage area, downstage, there is an old, law-firm safe and telephone. (The "space" between office and safe should suggest division, but should also permit quick, fluid on stage transitions to safe, downstage.) A banquet table, with an "End-the-Hate in '88" banner, may be used briefly at top of Scene 1, Act Two.

CAST

BOAT Boatwright: Male lawyer, Caucasian, 45 y/o, and mid-level partner.

EULA Tyler: Female, African American paralegal, 30-40 y/o. Eula is also a Boy Scout leader and dresses as such during weekend work.

HAMBRIC Smith-Davis: Male, African American, former associate lawyer, 30 y/o, who plays a specter/hallucinatory image of himself and is Ox's conscious. While singing *Birmingham Sunday*, Hambric wears choir robe with stole of Kente fabric.

OX Oxford: 65 y/o, male, Caucasian, senior partner of the firm. Wears safari outfit in Act I, before and after "African trip." Otherwise lawyer outfits or the lack thereof.

SLAW DOG (Given name long since abandoned): Male, 50 y/o, Caucasian, law firm's go-fer, flunky and private investigator. Wears overalls and tool belt.

Quote: *"The hottest places in hell are reserved for those, who in times of great moral crisis, maintain their neutrality."* Dante

ACT ONE Scene One
August 31, 1988

At Rise: Ox in "safari" outfit, at safe with two reel-to-reel tapes, large manila envelope containing "medical records," his passport and a scrap of paper with combination to safe. Opens safe prior to putting tapes and records in. Upstage, Hambric appears.[47]

HAMBRIC *(Sings BIRMINGHAM SUNDAY.)*

COME ROUND BY MY SIDE AND I'LL SING YOU A SONG.
I'LL SING IT SO SOFTLY, IT'LL DO NO ONE WRONG.
ON BIRMINGHAM SUNDAY THE BLOOD RAN LIKE WINE,
AND THE CHOIRS KEPT SINGING OF FREEDOM.[48]

OX *(During song, hears but tries to dismiss.)* My doctors warned me about you. *(Pause.)* You are a mere figment![49]

HAMBRIC Whatever. *(Pause.)* Oxford, do you remember Birmingham Sunday?

OX Hambric, you bastard, I'm trying to forget. Normally, I'd trust this old safe … to be "safe." *(Looks at "Medical Record" envelope in hand.)*

HAMBRIC Oh, what a tangled web we weave when we first set out to… conceive.

OX *(Dismisses voice, places tapes and envelop in safe, closes safe. Stands, looks at passport, placing it on safe.)* I am large and I contradict myself. This old safe contains multi … multifarious-ness ….

HAMBRIC *(Finishing thought for Ox.)* Multitudes.

OX Multitudes, that's right. *(Looks at scrap of paper.)*

HAMBRIC That's right, Mr. Oxford, your memory returns if you focus. And, sometimes it helps if you squint your eyes and concentrate.

OX These days I don't know where my quotes come from. I'm getting so old, some of the quotes seem like I wrote them myself. *(Perplexed, squints eyes.)* Isn't Hambric supposed to be dead?

HAMBRIC Yes, Hambric is dead and you are supposed to be in Africa or someplace?

OX I am? That's right I got a plane to catch. *(Looks at passport and puts scrap of paper in mouth, chews.)* Now, that Walt Whitman was a complex fellow.

HAMBRIC If you judge him by his poetry, he was complex.

OX We are all judged by our poetry. *(Goes to Boat's office.)*

HAMBRIC Pathos and paradox? Oxford, you have spent a lifetime putting out highfalutin sounding "Oxshit" expecting your entourage to nod that you are profound.

OX Surely, that is an exaggeration. *(Coughs.)*

HAMBRIC Are you okay?

OX I'm fine. *(Coughs, looks at papers on Boat's desk.)*

HAMBRIC Why are you in Boat's office?

OX I need to leave him a note. *(Ox starts methodically searching Boat's desk and reading notes looking for clues.)*

HAMBRIC Looks like you are snooping through Boat's files. *(Points to Boat's desk.)* And, you need a drink of water.

OX No. No. I'm fine. *(Finds note pad.)*

HAMBRIC No, you are not. You ate the combination to that old safe. *(Points.)* There some water right there on Boat's desk.

OX Hambric was married to a Congressman's daughter over in Atlanta.

HAMBRIC You were at the wedding.

OX Atlanta, one of Martin's old churches. Three or four summers ago … hot as blue blazes. *(Gulps water. Writes note.)*

HAMBRIC It was hot, that you remember.

OX Had Hambric made partner here at the Firm? *(Ox finds letterhead looks for Hambric's name.)*

HAMBRIC Sir, you don't remember?

OX Me? I guess I don't remember.

HAMBRIC No, Hambric had not yet made partner. Hambric had just finished his sixth year and there was a vote, but ….

OX The Firm has grown so large, so fast, I lost track. *(Preoccupied writing a note.)* But, I remember my partners were impressed with Hambric on our firm dove shoot.

HAMBRIC Such a massive effort for so little meat.

OX *(Ox picks up "Parade Permit" file from Boat's desk and heads to storeroom.)* I like a man who kills what he eats. *(Puzzled, stops for a moment.)* Or, eats what he kills? *(Turns, kicks gas can.)* What's that? *(Misplaces file.)*

HAMBRIC A gas can. You'll remember Hambric found that can in the back seat of his locked car the day before he was shot.

OX Shot? I thought Hambric's death was self-inflicted ... a suicide, pardon the expression. *(Opens can, pours out a red and white fishing float/bobber.)*

HAMBRIC Unexplained death does make some people uncomfortable, but why the fishing bobber?

OX Damn things can be used to detonate a bomb, if they use the drip method.

HAMBRIC The church bomb that killed the four little girls ... on Birmingham Sunday?

OX The F.B.I. said **no** detonation devices were found at the crime scene, but that may have been just another one of Edgar's cover-ups.

HAMBRIC That's right; you and J. Edgar Hoover were *tight*.

OX It's not what you know; it's who you know. And, Edgar covered up more than he exposed and prosecuted. You see, Edgar had a long time male companion, whom I met back during the War. (Pause.) Good man. But, when you are in the spy business, one male companion is one boyfriend too many.

HAMBRIC The Klan blackmailed Hoover because he was gay?

OX Nobody could blackmail Hoover, but *(looks out window)* those Negro demonstrations were costing the taxpayers their hard earned tax money. *(Crosses back to Boat's office to read Boat's phone messages, looks for file.)* And, nowadays that AIDS will cost taxpayers dearly.

HAMBRIC Your mind is jumping around quite a bit, and why did you change the subject?

OX Subject? *(Squints, confused.)* Last year, when Ron called me to the White House, we were having one of our private chats on the balcony. *(Looks out window/balcony.)* There on the Mall was that quilt the size of a football field.

HAMBRIC A lot of people have died.

OX I asked Mr. President what he thought, and he said our buddy Rock Hudson should have kept his *butt* in his britches.

HAMBRIC And, Just Said No! *(Beat.)* Remember we are focused on that gas can and the fishing bobber?

OX *(Crosses back to desk and can.)* Klan used these fishing bobbers instead of a cheap alarm clock. Metal is indestructible, easy to trace the parts. But, plastic could be part of a child's play toy.

HAMBRIC Oxford. *(Pause.)* The 16th Street Baptist Church bombing? *(Beat for response. None.)* Remember, the FBI code named it "BapBomb." Code BapBomb!

OX Don't say that!

HAMBRIC Ah, you don't like that reminder. Do you? But I see your selective memory is coming back. *(Pause.)* Birmingham Sunday?

OX Of course, I remember the bombing. *(Looks toward safe)* I was downtown that Sunday morning the 16th Street Church blew up. Downtown, eating my sandwich and reading the *New York Times*.

HAMBRIC And, taking your nerve pills.

OX There was a wonderful old drugstore where this building is now. Gladys would squeeze fresh limeade right there at the counter, and her pimento cheese was homemade.

HAMBRIC The bombing must have been horrible?

OX Old drugstores are a thing of the past ... no more lunch counters like in the old days.

HAMBRIC The church bombing must have been horrible?

OX Demonstrations closed down the lunch counters, I suspect.

HAMBRIC Oxford, this is Hambric, I am inside your head and I won't go away. One more time, the church bombing?

OX Horrible, yes, but also predictable. Detonating dynamite was part of their job. Klan Boys worked in the mines.

HAMBRIC Did you just tie the church bombing to those fishing bobbers?

OX A wire and a fishing bobber act just like the gizmo in the back of a toilet... when the water runs out the detonator is tripped. BAMB! The rest is history.

HAMBRIC So these little symbols of your past appeared in the back of my locked car the day before I was murdered.

OX Murdered? Now, that's harsh. *(Takes a pill with water.)*

HAMBRIC Harsh is an understatement. *(Pause.)* But, what did that can of gasoline mean?

OX You think the Klan was trying to tell **us** something? *(Pause.)* The Attorney General has reopened the church bombing case.

HAMBRIC Now, just what would the Klan try to tell **us**?

OX *(Evasive.)* Are they still burning the Nig-ra churches down in the Projects?

HAMBRIC They say we "Nigras" are burning our own churches.

OX That's what they said back then. These days, the Ku Klux Klan is nothing more than an ideology, not a vigilante club.

HAMBRIC It's difficult for me, who happens to be Black, to accept the Klan as a mere ideology.

OX *(Finds misplaced file.)* Why is Boat filing that Klan Parade Permit in your stead?

HAMBRIC Sorry, I did not get around to filing that Permit before I was murdered. Perhaps, I was dragging my feet thinking ….

OX *(Interrupts.)* Boat should not be snooping around in my files, with that particular client.

HAMBRIC Oxford, Boat was just trying to help me. But, he is as confused as you are demented. You are his super-Uncle, and he found himself covering for you.

OX I take umbrage with that statement. And, as you full well know, Boat has gone off in a strange direction, since his law school friend died of AIDS out in San Francisco.

HAMBRIC What we don't understand, we avoid. And, just why was it so important for me, your African American protégé, to file for the fucking Ku Klux Parade permit?

OX Klan is just a free speech club these days, much like the ACLU. *(Ox takes can and Boat's file and hides them in store room.)*

HAMBRIC Now, that is a brain fart.

OX Our First Amendment freedoms are absolute, and a client disserves a vigorous representation.

HAMBRIC Excuse me, but a simple parade permit did not require a vigorous representation.

OX *(Ox returns to making notes on Boat's desk.)* I was judging your timber ... your devotion to the law ... before that partnership vote.

HAMBRIC Boat said you vetoed me.

OX That was highly inappropriate of Boat.

HAMBRIC Oxford, you no longer have to blow smoke up my ass. I am dead.

OX But, I had nothing to do with your death!

HAMBRIC Are you sure?

OX *(Beat.)* We are in jeopardy of losing our hard fought freedoms, unless we welcome...

HAMBRIC *(Finishes sentence.)* ... Unpopular causes.

OX Your Daddy and I worked out the integration of the lunch counter down at Woolworth's. *(Pause.)* You know, I haven't seen your Mama and Daddy since that wedding over in Atlanta.

HAMBRIC Daddy was at my funeral.

OX Well, there were so many dignitaries at that funeral, I lost track, and you should be proud.

HAMBRIC "Pride" does not immediately come to mind. But, I am new at being dead, and all.

OX Reckon' I can get your Daddy down here for that End-the-Hate Breakfast Award?

HAMBRIC Why don't you ask him?

OX Mighty fine. "End-the-Hate in Eighty-Eight!" It's my year for that Breakfast Award and I'd like your Daddy to introduce me. When all was said and done, he instructed me on man's inhumanity to man.

HAMBRIC And women too. Inhumanity to women also.

OX What are you talking about?

HAMBRIC Daddy appears, when the student is ready. *(Pause.)* Now, what was on those old tapes you put in that safe?

OX Tapes? *(Spooked, but recalls.)* I don't exactly know. What does Boat know? What do you know?

HAMBRIC Remember, I'm dead, but what exactly did you know?

OX Back in the Sixties, I represented the newspaper and we … they wiretapped the civil rights preachers and the Klan. But, I got rid of those tapes … hundreds of them… after that Watergate mess. *(Pause.)* Then, just last week another two reels cropped up. I was helping the new Attorney General when he reopened the case and the Klan seemed to misunderstand.

HAMBRIC Are those the tapes you just put in the safe?

OX The contents of that safe are of no concern to you or anyone else for that matter. I forgot the combination and threw away the key.

HAMBRIC Excuse me, Oxford, you just *ate* the combination. And, you got a plane to catch.

OX That's right! I got a plane to catch? *(Pause.)* I need to make sure that safe goes into the lake?

HAMBRIC Into the lake? A bit of overkill, surely? Couldn't you just destroy the tapes?

OX We didn't think of that. Besides, I am humoring the Klan. With the safe in the lake, the Klan will stop their threats and this place will be out of harm's way.

HAMBRIC That makes about as much sense as anything else around here. Why don't you dial Eula's extension and leave her a message?

OX Good idea. *(Goes to wall phone in storeroom, dials and leaves message.)* "Eula, while I am in Africa, I have asked Slaw Dog to come by and get this old safe in the store room here and throw it in the lake. The safe will make an artificial reef for crappie. Be sure to remind Slaw Dog for me. *(Pause. Squints.)* Oh, yes, when Eric Bob calls, tell him the safe is in the lake. Be sure to tell Eric Bob that the safe is already in the lake, as in past tense. Like it's already in the lake. Get it? Now, I got a plane to catch." (Exits.)

ACT ONE, Scene Two
A Week Later, September 7, 1988

At Rise: Boat at fax machine and Slaw Dog enters without knocking wearing bib-overalls, a hardhat and a tool belt pushing a heavy-duty dolly.

SLAW DOG Boat, look at you. A new fax machine? *(Pause.)* Honey, you know nothing about machinery.

BOAT I do know that Uncle Oxford has been in Africa only a week, but he called from the airport just this morning.

SLAW DOG I know, he left me a message too, but wasn't sure which airport he called from.

BOAT My point is: Oxford only spent **one** week in Africa?

SLAW DOG *(Rubs Boat's shoulder.)* And, you are tense.

BOAT Dog, please, not here. I'm not that tense. *(Pushes button to send fax.)*

SLAW DOG Here at the firm? I forgot, no touching according to HR and everybody is turning Republican. Boat, you are the one sporting a new earring and running around beating on tom toms with your shirt off.

BOAT New Age freedom of expression as I was forced to explain at the last partnership meeting but no one listened. And, just what is your job description today — Uncle Oxford's gofer, detective, telephone technician, or holistic New Age neck masseur?

SLAW DOG Jackoff-of-all-trades. I'm just here to remove that old safe and drop it in the Lake.

BOAT Are you late? *(Pause, no response.)* Last week, before he left, Oxford left me several notes that it was urgent that you remove that old safe ASAP.

SLAW DOG Duh. I must be late.

BOAT And, we rearranging the deck chairs on Oxford's pontoon boat?

SLAW DOG That and throwing shit in the lake. Oxford also mumbled something about the '63 Church Bombing and those old civil rights tapes.

BOAT Old civil rights tapes?

SLAW DOG Attorney General reopened the 16th Street Church Bombing case.

BOAT My God, Dog, we had to bust our ass to keep him out of Dynamite Bob's trial back in the '70s, so why pray God, would Uncle Oxford again try to insert his fading legal expertise into …?

SLAW DOG Officially, Oxford helped elect the new Attorney General.

BOAT That I know. And?

SLAW DOG Officially, he should not be involved, but he is getting old and needs a legacy.

BOAT Isn't his "legacy" already baked into the cake? Or, not?

SLAW DOG Boat, he not tracking.

BOAT While we pretend not to notice.

SLAW DOG Oxford swore he destroyed all the tapes after Watergate.

BOAT Sure and Uncle Oxford also swore he taught Richard Nixon to record history. *(Pause.)* Wasn't it just urban myth, that Oxford tape recorded the Civil Rights Movement?

SLAW DOG Oxford did not exactly tape record the Civil Rights Movement. We merely did back-up tapes to protect the newspaper in the event of litigation.

BOAT Back-up tapes? Uncle Oxford did not authorize illegal wiretaps?

SLAW DOG "Illegal?" In the words of Bull Connor, our esteemed Public Safety Commissioner, "Down here we make our own laws."

BOAT Bull Connor also said, "Whites and Negroes shall never segregate together." Yes, the City was governed by lunatics, but ….

SLAW DOG … But, Ox had me double checking by recording the fuck-ups, so we could keep it out of the newspaper or spin it if we had to. So, by the time, Dr. King arrived at the Park across the Street *(points)*, wiretapping was an art form.

BOAT Slaw Dog, you had personal knowledge of all of this?

SLAW DOG Verification knowledge only, and I am in the information business, remember? *(Puts utility phone to ear.)* It was spring, April 1963, and Reverend King was headed Downtown here. *(Speaks to receiver.)* You Klan boys got your pants down around your ankles. *(Pause.)* Who am I? Who do you think I am? I am the Dog!

BOAT The Klan didn't know who you were?

SLAW DOG The Klan didn't care, and the idiots assumed everybody was on their side. Shall I continue?

BOAT Yeah.

SLAW DOG *(To utility phone receiver.)* Now, whom do I have on the phone? Let me guess: the FBI, the River Klan and Bull Connor. Now listen up White Trash everywhere, operation "C" for Confrontation officially arrives Downtown tomorrow. *(Pause.)* You heard that right. Preacher King is in Downtown Birmingham. All the little school children will play hooky and march from the church… across the Park… right down to City Hall to get a drink of water… cool clear water of righteousness, right out of a proper white folks' water fountain.

BOAT *(Points to phone.)* Did they have that equipment in 1963?

SLAW DOG Close. Back then we spliced wires, and used alligator clamps. Had little rubber stoppers for the receivers that went straight to the tape recorder.

(They go to safe.)

BOAT Did Uncle Oxford preside over all this?

SLAW DOG On one of his good days, the Ox might deny it… but Boat Honey he was in the middle of everything. J. Edgar himself would send the Ox the latest equipment. Back then, the Ox was way too cutting edge for 'Bomb'ingham. Ox knew Hoover's boyfriend. *(At safe, picks up passport and puts in pocket.)*

BOAT Dog, did you know too much?

SLAW DOG Honey, all Republicans have boyfriends on the side. *(Tries to wedge dolly under safe.)* Then, in April of 1963, after Bull brought out the fire hoses and police dogs, Oxford suddenly changed. He went from sounding like George Wallace to sounding more like Gandhi. But there were glitches. *(Struggles with safe.)* This won't budge.

BOAT That explains some of his inconsistent…. *(Pick up gas can.)* What's this?

SLAW DOG A gas can filled with *(shakes can)* a fishing float.

BOAT I don't want to know this either? Do I?

SLAW DOG Boat, there is a long list of shit you do not want to know. *(Squats at safe, twirls knob & listens.)* Be a lot easier to open this safe, than to haul it to the lake.

BOAT And, if the tapes are in there?

SLAW DOG There were hundreds of tapes, but Oxford said he destroyed those tapes. Or so he thought.

BOAT Or, so he thought? Assume worst case scenario.

SLAW DOG Worst case we do not want to assume.

BOAT *(Angry.)* Enough of the fuckin' game, what's in the safe?

SLAW DOG *(Angry.)* I said I don't fuckin' know!

BOAT Shh! What?

SLAW DOG All I do know is that the Ox called with his shorts in a wad, and wanted me to drop this old safe in the lake on an emergency basis. *(Pause.)* Then he mentioned that old reel-to-reel tape recorder.

EULA *(Enters on last sentence wearing a cordless telephone headset and plugs into wall unit. Dials operator.)* Darlene, Eula, here. Put my calls through to extension 109, I'm working in the storage room next to Boat's office. *(Pause.)* No, tell that *New York Times* reporter, that the Oxford has jet lag from his trip to Africa. We don't know when he'll be in the office. And, his schedule is mostly full when he does get in. Got to run. *(Clicks off phone and looks through files.)* Strange you all talking about that old tape recorder. I dug it out of basement storage a few weeks ago, for the Oxford.

BOAT Eula, did you listen to those old tapes?

EULA Are you kidding? After I scrounged around and nearly ruined my new pants suit. Besides, he didn't want me around, so I did not linger. *(Looks at gas can and screams.)* What's that?

SLAW DOG A gas can.

EULA I know it's a gas can, but what is it doing here?

SLAW DOG Beats me.

EULA Hambric found one just like it in his car the day before he died.

SLAW DOG What is so strange about that?

BOAT Dog, it is a gas can with a fishing bobber. Now, that **is** strange!

EULA It totally freaked Hambric out… he came to me worried about how it got in his locked car and who put it there. Then, he went in to see the Oxford.

SLAW DOG You know, the Klan has started burning churches again.

BOAT The Klan says that Blacks are burning their own churches, but no one believes that except old white guys.

SLAW DOG And, the last time I checked old white guys were still in charge. At least for now. Right Eula?

EULA Leave me out of that one. *(Pause.)* You seem to be an authority on the Klan.

BOAT Has anyone tried to connect the dots? Safe in lake. Gas can in car. Incriminating Civil Rights tapes. Burning churches.

EULA Well, you knew that Hambric was slow to file the Klan parade permit and that Mister Oxford vetoed him on the partnership vote.

BOAT That I knew. But, none of that struck me as having life or death consequences.

SLAW DOG Usually, the truth is hidden right there in plain sight. Let's hypothecate: the Attorney General is reopening the Church Bombing case, hence, the Klan is naturally nervous with rumors of a death bed confessions floating around. The Klan assumed incriminating information on those old tapes.

BOAT That's a hell of a lot of dots. Your point is?

SLAW DOG Ergo, the Neo-Klansmen assumed the Ox's African American protégé knew way too much.

BOAT Even if he knew 'way too much,' I can't believe Hambric committed suicide.

SLAW DOG Oxford said Hambric was cleaning his huntin' rifle.

BOAT Hambric didn't have a hunting rifle.

SLAW DOG Shot gun, whatever. It's just a euphemism for suicide.

EULA Every old southern family has someone who accidentally shot himself while cleaning "his huntin' gun."

BOAT Why would Hambric kill himself?

EULA I don't know that he would.

SLAW DOG It is not a rational act.

BOAT But, suicide?

SLAW DOG Permanent solution to a temporary problem. I thought you'd have some New Age Boat Babble to cope with the situation.

BOAT Well, I don't.

SLAW DOG *(Pulls the Ox's passport from pocket.)* Guess what I found on top of this old safe.

BOAT *(Does not see passport.)* A gas can, some fishing bobbers and our pathetic history.

SLAW DOG That and the Ox's passport. *(Waves passport.)*

BOAT What?

EULA Give that to me. *(Reaches for passport.)*

SLAW DOG Just how did the Ox get to Africa without a passport? *(Holds passport out of Eula's reach.)*

EULA Some people have several passports. *(Reaches again.)* I believe the Oxford even has one from Saudi Arabia. *(Phone Ring.)* Eula speaking. *(Pause.)* Darlene tell him I don't have time. *(Pause to Boat.)* You two, hush, your mouth about our history. It's embarrassing. *(To headset.)* No. No. Darlene, I wasn't talking to you. *(Laughs.)* But, it's time you hush up and hang up too. *(Clicks phone off, and finds "Parade Permit" file.)*

BOAT Eula, will you get rid of your head phones, I never know who you are talking to.

EULA My head phones are not your problem, Boat, Honey. *(Phone rings.)* Eula, speaking. *(Pause.)* I don't have time, but put him through. *(Pause.)* Yes, Eric Bob, the Ox is back in town. *(Pause.)* Yes, Slaw Dog is here to remove that old safe. *(Pause.)* Well, he's running late. *(Pause.)* If you are no longer at the farm, where can I send your supplies? *(Pause.)* No. No. Bye. *(Clicks phone off.)*

BOAT Supplies?

EULA Fertilizer, ammonium nitrates, nitroglycerin, and plastique stuff.

SLAW DOG *(Laughs.)* Blasting gelatin?

EULA That's nothing new. We've been ordering supplies for Oxford's farm for years.

BOAT Oxford has you ordering these supplies? And, who takes delivery of them?

EULA Well, usually it's Eric Bob.

BOAT Eric Bob who?

EULA I don't exactly know. Just, Eric Bob. He's pretty new in town. Says he is working down at Oxford's farm.

BOAT What the hell are you talking about?

EULA I don't exactly know, but when Hambric was alive we sent the invoices through the Oxford Foundation. Some tax angle, but it looked mostly like ordinary chemicals ….

BOAT Sure? And, blasting gelatins?

SLAW DOG And, Ox said to tell them Hambric was George Washington fuckin' Carver and into science and hobby farming.

EULA Said they would not question anything. Said if they did, send them to the tax boys.

BOAT They? Who?

EULA The Authorities. Said it would look like the Oxford was fertilizing his horse farm, maybe removing some stumps with dynamite like in the old days.

BOAT Those generic "Authorities" are troublesome.

EULA Said the little Make-a-Wish children could go to his farm and ride horses, and he would deduct the whole thing.

BOAT The tax department bought into this?

EULA Well, yes, I suppose. The tax lawyers didn't talk much to Hambric before he died.

BOAT I'm sure they didn't.

EULA Oh, Boat, will you still help me with that Parade Permit that Hambric didn't file?

BOAT I said I would, but my file has been missing of late.

EULA It's right here. *(Hands file to Boat.)* You know, the Klan has already made plans for their big parade.

BOAT How, after all these years, did Oxford manage to reunite with the Klan?

EULA He joined that Federalist Society and I believe the Klan found him.

BOAT I'm not sure he was ever lost to the Klan.

SLAW DOG He's lost alright.

EULA You know Oxford says "a client, is a client, is a client."

SLAW DOG As opposed to a rose ... a rosy butt ready for the jailhouse.

EULA Said we could make out the Parade to be an ACLU thing ....

BOAT What?

EULA The right to march and all.

SLAW DOG Like Skokie, Illinois. Another liberal opportunity. What else?

EULA I told him the Klan is burning those old churches too.

SLAW DOG A gas can is flexible but it does smack of arson.

BOAT And that's before we get to the fertilizer ... explosives. *(Sits at desk.)*

SLAW DOG The Ox hasn't been confiding in me lately. Now, Eula, you run this place. What did Ox tell you?

EULA Huh.

SLAW DOG My God, Eula, your family has been wiping his ass for three generations and he groomed you to be his super paralegal and the Ox told you nothing?

EULA Nothing, except he wanted that old tape recorder in his office, and for you to get rid of that old safe.

SLAW DOG Well, the Klan wouldn't have left that gas can as a warning to Hambric unless they thought Hambric knew something. Excuse me. *(Exits.)*

EULA But we still have to file the damn Permit. *(Crosses to store room, plugs in headset and dials.)* Eric Bob, Honey, I could not talk earlier. But, listen there is a warrant out for your arrest. *(Pause.)* Because you been a Klansman all your life and you don't keep it much of a secret. (Pause.) Yes, yes, that old safe is still here. Slaw Dog could not budge it. That's on the q-t because Ox said to tell you the safe was already in the lake. But, you know Slaw dog he'll be late for his own funeral. *(Pause.)* Ammonium nitrate? Joe Bob, you can't blow up that old safe while it is still in our building, here. You are joking?

(BOAT crosses to store room, over hears.)

EULA Eric Bob, Honey, now, you are talking crazy; now where are you? *(Pause.)* I got your car phone number. But where are you staying? *(Pause.)* There are Limestone Caves all over the place. *(Whispers.)* Okay, you did not hear this from me, but there has been an death bed confessions or some such and that's why the Attorney General is opening up the Church Bombing Case. *(Pause.)* I said death bed confessions, because a lot of you bad boys are dying. *(Pause.)* I don't know what's on those old tapes.

(Sees Boat; changes subject.)

We will need at least three German chocolate cakes for the Boy Scouts' Bake Sale.

BOAT Does Eric Bob, Honey, teach the Spelunking Merit Badge? Or, is he into lawn maintenance?

EULA Just organizing the Boy Scouts' bake sale. *(Turns off phone.)*

BOAT And. Eric Bob is German and bakes a tasty cake.

EULA I am the Assistant Scout Master. Appreciate that my hands are full and need all the help I can get.

BOAT Eula, it's me, Boat.

EULA Attorney General has issued some new arrest warrants base on the confessions.

BOAT Good for him.

EULA Eric Bob thinks we might turn him in. Just trying to help Oxford.

BOAT What?

EULA He's gonna get caught eventually, so I might as well cash in on the reward.

BOAT Eula?

EULA Some call it reparation, if that makes you feel better.

BOAT Bounty hunting on the telephone can get you in trouble.

EULA Hey, I am a single mother and college for my Jeff will be expensive.

BOAT Eula?

EULA Jeff is twelve and college will be here before you know it.

BOAT Eula?

EULA Honey, they are the criminals, I'm just trying to catch them.

BOAT Unless, you become an accomplice-after-the-fact. *(Pause.)* But, there seems to be an accomplice behind every fake ficus around here.

EULA The Oxford says once the check clears, no one cares. Besides, with all these lawyers around here, I can get immunity.

BOAT Speaking of too many lawyers, Uncle Oxford's African trip was quite short for such a long flight. I thought safaris were at least a week or two. I guess he used his Saudi passport.

EULA Oxford brought back a cargo of African art.

BOAT So he was just buying up culture? Not killing the fauna? (Pause.) Of lost tribal customs, is anything coming across Ox's desk that would ….

EULA After the Attorney General reopened that case, the Klan went a little crazy. Oxford called some of the Klan Boys into the office and tried to calm them down.

BOAT So, it is more than just a parade permit?

EULA Mmmm, Klan wanted to get rid of the tapes. At first Oxford just laughed at the Boys and said he didn't have any tapes, but then he agreed to put them in the safe, I think?

BOAT You think? Did you get any idea of what they might do next?

EULA Well, I was talking to Eric Bob when you came in, and I think they want to blow up that old safe. *(Shakes head.)* Klan is crazy. For example, they have accepted that I am Black, but out of the blue, now, the Klan wants to get rid of homosexuals and abortions too.

BOAT What?

EULA As I said, the Klan is crazy. They say, "Gay is the new Black." Klan says it's about time they bombed gay night clubs … get rid of the plague.

BOAT The plague does thrive on chaos and body temperature.

SLAW DOG *(Enters.)* Chaos and body temperature, sounds hot to me!

EULA Slaw Dog you shouldn't make light. There is a committed couple at my church, very good Scout leaders, who are trying to adopt a Foster child, a cocaine baby that nobody else wants. *(Shakes head.)*

BOAT Eula, tell Slaw Dog about your friend Eric Bob.

EULA Mr. Boatwright, Eric Bob is not my friend. And, Slaw Dog, I just wish you were a real detective. I believe Eric Bob had an accomplice.

BOAT Besides you? *(Pause to Slaw Dog.)* Tell Eula she is flirting with (disaster here.)

SLAW DOG Eula while you are flirting with this Eric Bob character, kindly get me a good price on an assault rifle? *(Pause.)* And, Boat did not switch sides, he is just a New Age Metro Man. Confusing, I know.

EULA No one cares what you do, as long as it is in private. *(Phone rings.)* Darlene, I don't have time for a *New York Times* reporter. *(Pause.)* Once it's in the *New York Times* you won't recognize it, embellished or not. *(Pause.)* Honey, I know the Oxford is back already. *(Pause.)* Did he get me that carved ivory necklace with matching earrings … the ones with the elephants dangling down, like I requested.

BOAT Ivory?

EULA Politically correct, around here? You got to be joking. *(To headset.)* Okay, girl, I'll be right out. *(Switches off headset.)*

SLAW DOG Some Great White Hunters are above the law.

EULA Besides ivory trinkets are getting hard to find. And, I might lose my heritage.

SLAW DOG Heritage, hell, you are from down below Demopolis.

EULA Well, at some point, I go back to Africa. Boat, I still need your time sheets and your reporter friend from the *Times*' Atlanta Bureau …(is here).

BOAT What?

EULA He says he is a friend, and he is in town.

BOAT Who, what are you talking about?

EULA Well, he says he is a friend of yours or knows a friend of yours, who use to work for the Newspaper here and then down at the *St. Pete Times*.

BOAT Huh uh?

EULA Anyway, he said he was only in town for a few hours. When you weren't in, he asked to talk to the Ox to get comments on reopening the Church Bombing case. *(Pause.)* I said, the Oxford wasn't in from the airport yet.

SLAW DOG Thank God.

EULA Besides, the Oxford knows when to quote and when not to quote, but I don't think he wants it appearing in the *New York Times*, again.

BOAT My friend at *The New York Times* is in Washington … he is no longer in Atlanta.

SLAW DOG It's all smoke and mirrors. *(Crosses to safe to try combination.)*

EULA This place is crazy. *(To Boat.)* Here are your new messages, and Honey, you need to catch up on things, 'cause some things are coming down real fast around here and you seem to be in slow motion. Shall I call Dr. Morgan?

BOAT No, Eula. I think it's just temporary. Anyway, I don't have time. *(Cross to safe.)*

EULA Honey, if you are not careful, all you are going to have is time. *(Exit opposite.)*

BOAT *(Boat watches Slaw Dog.)* Do you think the tapes are incriminating?

SLAW DOG Your guess is as good as mine. But, I repeat myself. It'd be easier to destroy the tapes than to move the whole fucking safe.

BOAT The tapes?

SLAW DOG Remember Dynamite Hill?

BOAT I was just a kid in Mississippi, but yes I heard about Dynamite Hill.

SLAW DOG Just a foundation here and there. That was the rule. Scare the hell out of the new Negroes, the civil rights preachers and protestors. No one was to get killed.

BOAT Until.

SLAW DOG In the Spring of 1963, after the protest in the park, the City struck a deal to hire a Black cop. BAMB! The Klan bombed the Motel where they thought Dr. King was staying, but King had already left or had changed rooms to the back side. Then, the Klan was given clear instructions to stick with just a foundation here and there. The same was true at the Church bombing.

BOAT Did the Klan get the message?

SLAW DOG What do you think? It mostly pissed the Klan off, but the Brotherhood had been warned that if they killed anybody that Civil Rights Act would be forced down their throat like a big old slimy prison dick. The party line was that the New Negroes were blowing up their own churches for northern sympathy. The Ox recorded all the wiretaps just in case the leaders needed exonerated. Then, the fuck up that Sunday morning. Klan was supposed to blow out the foundation early before Sunday School even began. But the fucking fishin' bobber got stuck and there was Klan chatter about retrieving the dynamite that had their finger prints all over it, when the blast occurred. According to the Ox, those little girls were not supposed to be in that lower level restroom.

ACT ONE, Scene Three
Later the same day, September 7, 1988.

At Rise: Ox in safari outfit in Boat's office, seemingly lost.

HAMBRIC *(Enters with African mask and is heard only by Ox.)* Oxford, this is one handsome artifact that you purloined from my African ancestors. Feel the Love. But, Boat is getting nosey and he found out about the explosives.

OX I know nothing about explosives!

HAMBRIC Oh, yes, you do. Remember?

OX They are just removing stumps on the farm and clearing trails down by the River for the little Make-a-Wish children.

HAMBRIC They who? *(Hands Ox the mask.)* Oxford, that is weak.

OX What is weak?

HAMBRIC No one is buying why you needed explosives down on the farm.

OX Is there a problem? And, that new Civil Rights Institute across the Park will need some additional parking. Most of that area is blighted and demolition is expensive. *(Pause to think.)* Klan Boys are real good with explosives... they worked in the mines. I plan to save the Civil Rights Institute demolition cost.

HAMBRIC I can't say it more clearly. Your lame excuse is not working. Questions are being asked and you are not tracking.

OX You are just trying to confuse me.

BOAT *(Enters on last sentence.)* Welcome back Uncle Oxford. Who were you talking to just now? *(Looks at mask.)*

OX What? *(Looks at mask and hands it to Boat.)* Here.

BOAT So, you brought back a cargo of African Art. Are you honoring your departed protégé, with whom you were representing the Klan?

OX What is wrong with that? *(Looks at Boat.)* I mean what's wrong with you?

BOAT Oxford, you just handed me this mask. I don't know that anything is wrong with me.

HAMBRIC *(To Ox.)* Boat told me to laugh at the Klan Parade. Said in their satin robes the Klan would look like a lost gospel choir in drag.

OX A gospel choir in drag.

BOAT Oxford, are you okay?

OX Okay? What do you mean? Okay? *(Pause, squints.)* Explosives are necessary to remove stumps and boulders to make new bridle paths so the little Make-a-Wish children may ride horses.

BOAT Eula said something about explosives going through the Oxford Foundation.

OX How much does she know?

BOAT Why don't you tell me?

OX Hambric was not supposed to find out about the partnership vote until …

HAMBRIC But, I did.

BOAT We don't hire idiots … and they hang around here seventy hours a week.

OX I'd hoped to find a good placement for Hambric, even though I found his little protest with that Parade Permit to be reprehensible. *(Looks in direction of Hambric's voice.)*

BOAT And, why are you still hung up on that Klan parade?

OX Freedom of Assembly.

HAMBRIC Oxford, the Klan's got you by the gonads?

BOAT Freedom of Assembly, bullshit. Why after all these years, did the Klan show up here at the firm?

OX The Attorney General, will need some additional information when he reopens that case.

BOAT We know you have a new friend, the Attorney General, but we are more concerned for your wellbeing … as in aiding and abetting?

OX And, some of your partners are concerned about you too.

BOAT You know what I mean.

OX That earring pushed us too far.

BOAT You expect me to dignify that with a response?

HAMBRIC It's just an earring Oxford and Boat is a touch sensitive right now.

OX I don't care how sensitive you are, my friend, a lot of us work very hard, so you may do as you please. And, I haven't seen you refusing any pay checks of late.

BOAT How does my paycheck, or my earring for that matter, push you too far?

OX Well, for example, at the Country Club, they say you have a boyfriend.

BOAT Oh, I know, and one boy friend is one boyfriend too many.

OX Only if it gets out.

BOAT It's just a New Age Men's Group. And, I don't have a boyfriend, but on the other hand, I no longer give a shit what they say at the Country Club.

OX Why didn't you tell me?

BOAT Tell you what? Telling you things has become increasingly difficult.

OX I am family, and we know your proclivity, among other things.

BOAT Proclivity? One earring, and I am supposed to be what?

OX Committed.

BOAT Committed? What the fuck are you talking about?

OX You forget I took you on a dove shoot when you were a kid, and I knew you'd rather be skipping rope. Do you have a permanent companion?

BOAT Permanent companion? Like J. Edgar Hoover? I have a permanent earring, but not a permanent companion? *(Laughs, recalls what Ox may be thinking.)* Slaw Dog and I went on that New Age Men's Gathering up on Lookout Mountain with Robert Bly. We ran around half naked and beat on drums, but it was not ….

OX Slaw Dog? *(Laughs.)* He'd screw a circle chainsaw if he thought he could get by with it.

BOAT *(Joins laughter.)* We don't have an elephant in the living room, we have the whole pachyderm palace.

OX The whole frigging zoo. But, the toughest thing we do around here is cover up a morals charge.

BOAT So don't cover it up, it is just a fucking earring and a New Age retreat.

OX You forget that I am as modern as they come and a random circle jerk ….

HAMBRIC But, one boyfriend is one too many, so is one bombed church, one bombed abortion clinic, one bombed gay nightclub.

OX No one is going to bomb anything, take my word for it.

BOAT How did you go from a circle jerk to a bomb?

HAMBRIC Oxford, you are starting to sound like Dr. Strangelove.

OX *(To Hambric.)* What are you talking about?

BOAT Just trying to understand.

OX You are in no position to understand.

BOAT I'll give you that, but I would settle for a modicum of truth.

HAMBRIC Truth, that's a novel concept around here. Change the subject.

OX Don't sell me short. I found a good placement for Hambric.

BOAT *(Confused..)* It's a little late to place Hambric, but the placement was to be good for whom? *(Pause.)* And, why did you veto him?

OX It was for his own good.

BOAT Come now Oxford, you don't do anything unless there is an angle.

HAMBRIC Oxford, we are waiting for the truth.

OX The Klan had resurfaced and Hambric needed to be placed faraway. His Daddy knows everybody in Washington D.C.

SLAW DOG *(Enters with sniper rifle[50] in case and proceeds to open it.)* Oxford here' your new gun.

BOAT Oxford, last time I checked, Hambric was still dead.

HAMBRIC Roger that. Boat doesn't understand the Klan. Slaw Dog is here with your new gun, the gun that you didn't take to Africa.

OX I liked Hambric, knew his father and I had a good placement for him. *(Looks at Slaw Dog and gun.)* My rifle.

SLAW DOG Speaking of Great White Job Hunters. *(Pulls rifle out of its case.)*

BOAT Hambric no longer needs a job, but I am concerned about the Klan. *(Looks at rifle.)* Just what we need, a safari rifle.

OX My huntin' rifle in Africa was accurate up to three hundred yards. *(Ignores Boat, tells Slaw Dog story of trip as he picks up rifle.)* There were hoof prints at the salt lick and I say to my trusted guide, Kawando "We seem to be going to the mountains for the buffalo at the precise time that the antelope, the mighty kudu, come to the salt lick and vice versa. Poor timing, Kawando."

BOAT Oxford, we were just talking about the Klan, and now you have gone to La La Land. Just where were you, Uncle Oxford? *(Facetious.)* The Zoo? Busch Gardens?

HAMBRIC Oxford, I don't think that Boat is buying into your African trip.

OX What is he talking about?

HAMBRIC You forgot your passport.

SLAW DOG More Boat babble.

OX *(Dazed.)* Should I be concerned?

SLAW DOG Why start now. *(Puts gun to Ox's shoulder.)*

OX Guns ... *(points gun)* ... I get a rush.

BOAT Drugs are less cumbersome.

SLAW DOG Easy, Boat.

HAMBRIC Oxford, your story is not working. Kick it up a notch.

OX Slaw Dog, as the kudu were coming up on the salt lick, a rotted out Mercedes truck driven by a German lawyer came out of the blue and scared the kudu off one more time... one more time the mighty antelope had eluded us.

BOAT Now that's *Out of the Green Hills of Africa.*

SLAW DOG What are you talking about?

BOAT Hemingway!

OX What did he say?

SLAW DOG Having-our-way ... with the wild animals.

HAMBRIC Oxford, you'd screw up a one scoop ice cream cone. Excuse me. Now, you are on your own. *(Exits.)*

BOAT Speaking of endangered species, excuse me while I go pee. *(Exit.)*

OX Boat seems confounded. How much does he know?

SLAW DOG Your literary German friend did not go over too well. *(Pulls out flask.)* And, you forgot your passport.

OX I'm bad to lose it. But, I have several passports? *(Pause.)* I worry about Boat. *(Drinks from offered flask.)*

SLAW DOG Oxford, this is the Dog here ... I know you are worried about Boat.

OX *(Looks around room.)* My deepest fear is that he will go off and try some of them new drugs, maybe catch AIDS.

SLAW DOG He says he quit. *(Takes flask and drinks.)*

OX Quit what?

SLAW DOG Whatever. Come with me. *(Crosses to safe with gun that he puts on shelf.)* Now, I need your help with this old safe.

OX Wait a goddamn minute! that old safe should be in the Lake.

SLAW DOG Damn thing is heavy, already bent one dolly. Besides, I hear it contains important history.

OX It's important that it be destroyed.

SLAW DOG Wouldn't it be easier to destroy the contents? The tapes?

OX They can even read ashes these days. I want that safe in the Lake.

SLAW DOG Calm down. They can also fish shit outta the lakes. *(Takes drink and offers to Ox.)* Now, what could be so important? Incriminating?

OX Old tapes and some records. Now, you do as I say.

SLAW DOG The safe is heavy. Give me the combination and I'll destroy the tapes. Why are they such a big deal?

OX Old civil rights tapes. Been so long, I don't know what's on 'em.

SLAW DOG Ox it's the Dog here. You know exactly what was on them. But, there were hundreds of tapes.

OX I destroyed those tapes years ago, but I came across two more reels.

SLAW DOG Alright, that is what I am trying to understand. Why would you come across two more reels?

OX They were in the closed file. I saved them for some reason, maybe our alibis.

SLAW DOG Leave me out of this white man. Oxford, you are not thinking clearly. I don't care if that new Attorney General is your new Buddy; yester-year's alibi can become tomorrow's Grand Jury indictment.

OX Don't sell me short. There is more in the safe than just the tapes.

SLAW DOG What?

OX I am more worried about the medical records … remember?

SLAW DOG Oxford, what's in the fuckin' safe?

OX *(Reluctant.)* When I was a young man, I sired a child for a married woman.

SLAW DOG Oxford, you told me that thirty years ago. Did you take the medical records out of your safety deposit box at the bank and put them in this old safe?

OX I did? *(Confused.)* No one is to be privy to that information.

SLAW DOG Are you losing your mind? Those records could be important after you are dead and gone.

OX Never!

SLAW DOG Buck up old man. What's right is right.

OX That's not the point and you gave me your word.

SLAW DOG My word? I said I would make those records known if and when the records were medically needed. You know what the fuck I said.

OX No one is to ever know of those records, and that is the end of that.

HAMBRIC *(Enters.)* Oxford, you are not thinking clearly. Boat just wanted some answers and apples don't fall too far from the tree.

OX *(To Hambric.)* Boat was a pretty good lawyer when he caught fire.

SLAW DOG Yes. *(Looks at gas can.)* But, fire might not be a good metaphor around here.

HAMBRIC Yes, Boat was a pretty good lawyer and made a difference sometimes, in spite of himself. Remember, Boat was a volunteer liberal at the ACLU and the Legal Aid helping us little Black children.

OX I saw some spunk in Boat when he was younger but like most of his generation, he got side-tracked.

HAMBRIC Oxford, remember my friend, the Negro who got his scrotum shot through? *(Pause and laughs.)* Boat never knew if it was his ego or just youthful rebellion.

OX *(To Hambric.)* I suspect he just wanted to distance himself from the past.

SLAW DOG What are you trying to say?

OX At the Country Club, we told them that the law suit was about true justice for the Negro.

SLAW DOG What are you talking about?

OX *(To Hambric.)* Case back in the '70s, when your friend was shot in the nuts for stealing panty hose.

SLAW DOG He was Hambric's friend. I liked the kid but Hambric grew up with him.

HAMBRIC Shot in the nuts by an off duty white Birmingham cop. *(Laughs.)* They loved you at the Country Club.

OX We sure knew how to disrupt a pleasant party at the Country Club.

SLAW DOG Are you okay?

HAMBRIC Oxford, nod "yes" to Slaw Dog and grin. *(Beat.)* That was a classic case. You let Boat sue a cheap-ass Northern Negro Department Store, that could not believe they had hired an off-duty cop in Birmingham, Alabama, who was still shooting Negroes through the nuts with big ass handguns for stealing three dollar panty hose while the Negro was on pills ... big Reds. Young liberal white lawyer gets big verdict for Black citizen.

OX Verdict wasn't all that big. But, Boat, was quite the lawyer when he set his mind to it.

HAMBRIC Our white savior.

OX I don't know what happened to Boat.

SLAW DOG Thinking can be difficult. Save your energy. *(At safe.)* Again it would be easier to open this safe ... destroy the contents as necessary ... than to lug the fucker to the Lake.

OX *(Dazed.)* You want to open the safe? *(Pause.)* Nine, one turn to five...no one turn to fifteen.

SLAW DOG *(Tries to open safe.)* Goddam-it, Oxford, you were to destroy all of the tapes years ago. *(Stands.)* And, this is not working. Do you want me to call a moving company? *(Goes to Boat's office and picks up phone.)*

OX No, don't call anyone.

HAMBRIC *(To Ox.)* And, you should tell Slaw Dog about the *New York Times* reporter.

OX *(To Boat's Office and speaks to Slaw Dog.)* That *New York Times* reporter did not know his ass from a hole in the ground. Pretends to be from around here.

SLAW DOG What are you talking about? *(Stops dialing.)* A reporter where? You didn't.

OX ... Didn't what?

SLAW DOG Oxford, you ain't got Alzheimer? Have you?

OX I don't think so. *(Checks fly.)* Just a little sub-acute organic memory loss.

SLAW DOG You mean organic brain loss? Are you being blackmailed?

OX The Klan is pissed off, but I got enough money and memory to set things straight. *(Boat enters as Ox zips fly.)* Something else, that reporter from the *New*

York Times wanted to know about those wiretap tapes back during operation Confrontation during the Civil Rights Movement.

HAMBRIC You have screwed up now.

BOAT What? There was the reporter in Africa?

SLAW DOG Reporter? In Africa?

OX *(Incredulous, but edifies.)* The reporter was at the airport here, not in Africa!

SLAW DOG Ox, I know we, the power structure back then, and we knew it all. But, remember our Gentlemen's Agreement of Silence? We haven't told anybody lately … have we?

OX Just that *New York Times* reporter.

BOAT Oh, shit! *(Laughs.)* You two are too much.

OX That expatriate friend of Boat's knows nothing. I had to set him straight.

SLAW DOG Ox it was a set up. He didn't know anything but he is talented.

BOAT *(Laughs.)* As they said in law school, here is a dime, go call your mama and tell her you don't want to be a lawyer. *(Flips coin, Slaw Dog grabs it.)* Or, here is a quarter go call the *New York Times*, and tell them that old *status quo* white men are still in charge, but their Conspiracy of Silence is about to hit Page One of the *New York Times* again. *(Laughs.)*

SLAW DOG *(To Boat.)* Why are you so amused?

OX Does Boat's friend know that I am always off the record? That I'm not on the record, until I choose to go on the record and specifically so state that I am no longer off the record.

BOAT Welcome to the Mad Oxen Tea Party, but you got it backwards.

HAMBRIC Oxford, Boat does not understand your righteousness.

OX *(To Hambric.)* I like to review my quotes before publication. *(To Boat.)* You know exactly what I mean.

BOAT No I don't, everyone is on the record, unless they go off the record.

OX I am not to be misquoted without my permission. *(Smacks desk.)* There were hundreds of bombings all over Dynamite Hill going all the way back to the thirties.

HAMBRIC Whence the name … Dynamite Hill!

OX We specifically told them not to kill small children, right Slaw Dog?

SLAW DOG Can't argue with that, but leave me out of it when you talk to the press.

OX And, I made it clear, that if I thought I was on the record, I would have declared myself off the record.

BOAT Excuse me, I'm getting a bit dizzy. But, be sure to tell the *New York Times* reporter that you could have prevented a lot of bloodshed and arson, even the church bombing … if the Kennedy Boys had just called you.

OX *(Angry.)* The Kennedy Boys should have called me. Remember, I was at a Rotary Convention in Tokyo and there on the front page of that Japanese Newspaper was Birmingham and the Park there. *(Points toward window.)*

HAMBRIC A photo of Ol' Bull Connor's police dogs chewing the ass-end outta the britches of that Black man, as the fire hoses scooted little school children across the sidewalk.

OX *(To Hambric.)* Right. Fire hoses. *(To Boat.)* I could not read a word of Japanese, but I could read "Birmingham" and that photograph did not lie.

HAMBRIC You ran into my Daddy on that trip.

OX *(To Hambric.)* Yes I did. *(To Boat.)* I ran into Hambric's Daddy on that trip to Japan, and we saw that photograph we fell to our knees in prayer. Yes, Bobby and Jack fucked up when they did not call me, Young Man.

BOAT Young? *(Angry.)* My youth has gone up in flames with everything else around here.

SLAW DOG Young Man, don't take a butter knife to a gunfight.

OX History took care of those Kennedy Boys. *(To Boat.)* And Boat, my boy, perhaps you are no longer happy here at the firm.

BOAT Happy? What's my happiness got to do with anything?

OX Getting shed of you would be easier than shooting caged animals.

BOAT The only kind you shoot.

HAMBRIC Easy, Oxford, you have enough to do and you are not tracking too well.

OX Watch your tongue, my job is to keep the place swept out.

BOAT You son-of-a-bitch. *(Goes for Ox.)* So, now I am trash?

SLAW DOG Careful! *(Steps between Ox and Boat.)*

HAMBRIC Ease up, Oxford, you do not need any extra problems right now.

OX Don't tell me what to do.

BOAT No one is telling you what to do… as if that would do any good. But the next time you go to Africa, it might be well to take your passport.

OX Is that your best shot? I want everything you say and do around here, cleared with me first. And, you may start by bringing me your active files. *(Exits followed by Hambric.)*

BOAT *(Shouts to Ox.)* You can't treat me like a child.

SLAW DOG Boat, don't let it get to you. There are some things you don't know.

BOAT Growing up I would look forward to his visits, then the visit would be awkward and brief. *(Pause.)* When I first got to the firm he was charming and powerful … totally different than I suspected … but then his marvelous façade wore thin … and I was just as perplexed.

SLAW DOG Here, here. *(Gives Boat a consoling hug.)* You know the game.

BOAT The game?

SLAW DOG Play along.

BOAT Why? For what? The money?

SLAW DOG Don't go there. You'll just beat yourself up.

End of Act One.

ACT TWO, Scene One
Thursday, September 15, 1988

AT RISE: Oxford seated down stage at End-the-Hate breakfast table.

HAMBRIC *(Enters as specter, heard only by Ox, then sings.)* "This Little Light of Mine, I'm gonna let it shine. Let it Shine, Let it Shine, Let it Shine." Oxford, my Daddy regrets that he could not make it here today for your esteemed honor, and if I could, I would introduce you.

(Taps on a glass and stage whispers facetiously as if introducing the Ox.)

Ladies, gentlemen, fellow Africans, the assembled Press, and distinguished politicians. *(Clears throat.)* I give you the Honorable John "Ox" Oxford, Esquire, founder of the United Negro Church Fund, Inc. a veritable urban renewal project that is designed to give our new Civil Rights Institute some ground level parking. The Oxford and my Daddy forced Bull Connor to turn off the fire hoses and to muzzle the police dogs. But, through historical oversight, a young, inexperienced, President Kennedy did not invite the Ox to the Church of the Advent here in Downtown Bombingham to unite this beleaguered City. And, through much travail Mister Oxford, Esquire, assured the passage of the Civil Rights Act by making sure his Boys stayed in the headlines and otherwise stayed on top of things.

OX *(Eula enters, but Ox preoccupied stands and speaks.)* Thank you, thank you, but perhaps I should not take all that much credit for the passage of the Civil Rights Acts. *(Sees audience and is confused.)*

EULA *(Whispers.)* Mister Oxford, are you okay?

OX *(Ignores Eula, turns to Hambric.)* You know, the Kennedy boys did not do much for Civil Rights. My friend Lyndon did all the heavy lifting. You see, Lady Bird owned some property down near my farm in West Alabama and we were thick.

EULA *(Whispers.)* Not so loud. Mister Oxford, are you okay? You do not want to start without a proper introduction. *(Getting no response, taps water glass, looks at audience and starts introduction.)* Welcome to our annual End-the-Hate Breakfast, on this the 25th Anniversary of the most horrific of hate crimes. In our beloved City on September 15, 1963, a hateful blast, heard around the World ripped through the foundation of the 16th Street Baptist Church, taking four precious, young lives. We must remember, lest we forget.

My name is Eula Tyler and it is indeed a privilege to introduce our honored guest this morning. *(Pause.)* Yes, only one-score and five years ago there was apartheid in our All American City. For example, my Granddaddy did yard work for the Oxford family, and when Grand-Mom Oxford picked up my Granddaddy in her new Coupe de Ville Cadillac, she did not make him sit in the back seat of her car. No, Grand-Mom Oxford made him get in the trunk, because his work clothes might soil her fine leather seats. On hot summer days, Grand-Mom let my Granddaddy keep the trunk lid cracked open for a little air. Sometimes at traffic lights he would open the lid and frighten white-folks, but that's another story. *(Clears throat.)* In the name of progress, our honored guest put an end to that demeaning practice of his mother transporting persons of color, in the trunk of her long hot Cadillac. Because it was wrong, it looked bad and it frightened white folks at traffic lights. Now, that was Progress!

HAMBRIC *(Whispers.)* Oxford, that was mighty white of you.

EULA Progress! I was the first in my family to go to college and now I am employed at the law firm of Oxford, Oxford and Boatwright, again thanks to our honored guest. Mr. Oxford's Charities include: The Little Make-A-Wish-Children; the founding director of The United Negro Church Fund, Incorporated, and Facilities Chairman of a proper Civil Rights Institute parking area to be constructed downtown here in our historic Colored district. So, it is indeed a pleasure that I give you the Honorable John Oxford, Esquire *(Applauds.)*

OX *(Stands.)* Thank you. Thank you. Ladies and Gentlemen. Just a few weeks ago we were befallen with tragedy when my bright young protégé *(looks at Hambric)* died of an accidental gunshot wound while cleaning his hunting rifle. But, in death we must celebrate life, celebrate our Freedoms. And, young Hambric loved our Freedoms.

HAMBRIC Oxford, tell it like it is. All about our little "f" freedoms.

OX And, young Hambric loved our Freedoms! To deny Freedom to the least of us, is to deny Freedom to all of us. Injustice anywhere is injustice everywhere. As we learned from Dr. Gandhi, I mean Gandhi, and Dr. King, Civil Disobedience takes the law into its own hands in the face of an oppressive government. Here, I speak to the Vigilante Spirit and the Right to March in our beloved South, regardless of the Cause. John called it "Good trouble!"

(Eula starts fidgeting and Ox stares at Hambric.)

For example, the modern Ku Klux Klan was resurrected in this fair City in 1915 by a drunken, broken, fallen Methodist minister from Atlanta, who saw the nightriders return in an alcoholic hallucination.

HAMBRIC Hallucination ... apparition ... that would be me.

OX We forget that the Klan was the insurgent wing of the Democratic Party in this State, to drive out the carpet bagging Northerners.

HAMBRIC *(Laughs.)* The Klan was an insurgent wing of the Democratic Party? And, I am a nigger lacrosse player.

OX Do you want Willie Horton doing your yard work? No one has the right to tell us how to treat our Negroes. *(Eula increases fidgets.)*

HAMBRIC Our Negroes? Thank you, Massa Oxford, Esquire, for letting my people out of the trunk of that long, white-hot Cadillac.

OX Right! *(Thinks and becomes aware of audience.)* Wrong! Carpetbaggers cannot occupy another's homeland for any length of time, with any degree of success. *(Eula gets up.)* My point is …. *(Eula gently gets Ox's arm.)* Where was I? Oh, yes, everyone has the right to march or no one gets to march! *(Eula prods to exit.)* I don't care what the Nig-ras at City Hall have to say! *(Eula hustles Ox off stage as lights fade on breakfast table.)* The Klan gets to march!

ACT TWO, Scene Two
Saturday Morning, September 17, 1988

At Rise: Slaw Dog and Boat are packing boxes. Fax machine prints parade permit.

SLAW DOG You are being a little righteous, cutting and running after all these years.

BOAT You heard him fire me. *(Reads fax.)*

SLAW DOG Ox did not fire you, assuming he even knew what he said. You heard his jumbled-up thinking and watched him fuck up that Hate Breakfast.

BOAT In a sad sort of way, it was worth the price of the ticket and getting up early on an otherwise beautiful morning in Dixie.

SLAW DOG The Ox, who is one order of fries short of a Happy Meal.

BOAT That's Uncle Oxford.

SLAW DOG If you are going to act to your own foolish detriment, I will not stop you.

BOAT Will Uncle Oxford even notice that I'm gone?

SLAW DOG A lot gets past him these days. *(Pause.)* And, just what will you do for money?

BOAT Aunt out in Texas left me a small trust fund.

SLAW DOG Still you are pretty high maintenance.

BOAT Aren't you more concerned about losing a playmate?

SLAW DOG I don't even remember the old Boat.

BOAT "'Freedom' is just another word for nothing left to lose."

SLAW DOG Thank you Janis.

BOAT The Old Boat has now officially fucked with the Klan parade. *(Hands fax to Slaw Dog.)*

SLAW DOG May I be of help? *(Reads.)*

BOAT I suspect, you will do what entertains you.

SLAW DOG Ah, Boat?

BOAT Okay, remember, Oxford stuck Eula and Hambric with filing the permit. Even when Hambric was alive, I planned to file that stupid permit to let 'em off the hook.

SLAW DOG And, deprive the Ox of the irony?

BOAT He is easily amused.

SLAW DOG Ox rationalized that the Klan parade was an ACLU thing.

BOAT And, everyone has the right to counsel. Bullshit!

SLAW DOG Bullshit is knee deep around here. Isn't that a course in law school?

BOAT Yesterday, I faxed the Klan parade permit to the all-white County Sheriff's office. I only needed the color of law.

SLAW DOG Clever venue shopping. *(Waives faxed Permit.)* You didn't need Colored City law; you needed white suburban law.

BOAT Looks like the High Sheriff immediately signed the permit, as if he were already dressed up in his satin bed sheets and hood to be the Grand Marshall in the parade. Got a faxed signed copy just this morning. Surprise. Surprise.

SLAW DOG Do the Africans at City Hall know the parade will snake through their fair City?

BOAT I faxed a copy to City Hall begging forgiveness that the firm may have filed in the wrong jurisdiction. But noted the overlap stating that the City is within the County.

SLAW DOG Citizen Boatwright you are a geographical genius. I am so proud of you. Asking forgiveness and all gives you a tinge of righteousness.

BOAT Now, the Klan will have the element of surprise in reverse.

SLAW DOG Ambushed by Black cops on horseback.

BOAT You think?

SLAW DOG Bad ass Negro cops with mean ass police dogs, too. *(Pause.)* I like that. It's a 1963 Bull Connor-in-the Park sort of deja vu thing in reverse.

BOAT We can laugh, but I still have a problem with Hambric's suicide over this petty crap. I suspect his suicide was faked.

SLAW DOG Why open that up?

BOAT Oxford was too quick with that hunting gun story.

SLAW DOG It's southern folklore.

EULA *(Enters.)* If you are serious about leaving, I'm supposed to collect your active files, Boat, Honey. The Oxford says it's for your own good, but he doesn't believe that for one minute. You can change your mind if you want to.

SLAW DOG Boat is seeking a relationship with himself … that makes him a tri-sexual.

EULA Tri-sexual?

SLAW DOG *(Laughs.)* Yeah, he'll try anything.

EULA Would you two be serious. *(Pause.)* That New Age Animal stuff …

SLAW DOG Anima.

BOAT New Age Anima.

EULA Whatever it is. It does not go over around here. Forget me. The Senior Partners just don't understand.

BOAT You think?

EULA You're gonna leave me in the middle of this mess. I wish you would not go.

BOAT For now, I'm going to my therapist. I pay her to understand. *(Exits.)*

SLAW DOG Eula, Boat is doing the best he can for now, but is Oxford okay?

EULA Lord, I was about to ask you the same thing. *(Thinks.)* Best I can figure: the Klan might be blackmailing Oxford.

SLAW DOG Why would a defunct Klan blackmail the Ox?

EULA Klan was about to go out of business but then they thought the Oxford leaked some information to the Attorney General from those old tapes.

SLAW DOG Klan thinking? That can be dangerous.

EULA But, when Boat helped me get that permit, the Klan turned happy as a pig in sunshine, like they had the Old Oxford back.

SLAW DOG God forbid.

EULA Oxford is having his moments,

SLAW DOG Okay, I no longer understand how the Klan resurfaced after all these years. But, why was Ox trying to protect Boat, one minute, and trying to run him off the next.

EULA Oxford is not all there.

SLAW DOG You think?

EULA The Oxford is worried sick about Boat right now. And, it's not the ear ring and you two messing around with that New Age animal stuff.

SLAW DOG I get it, but Ox kept saying that Boat was never to know about his passive participation in the wiretaps but then he tells the free world by talking to the *New York Times*.

EULA Klan boys were extremely worried about those old tapes, but when Hambric passed, they seemed to ease up some on the Oxford. *(Pause.)* Now, Oxford seems more worried about those old medical records, the ones in his safety deposit box.

SLAW DOG I believe that Ox took the medical records out of the safety deposit box and put them in that old safe. *(Pause.)* Do you know?

EULA It's a big secret, if I do know. But, how would you know?

SLAW DOG I know, that those medical records are important, and Ox seems to be fading fast.

EULA Write down what you know. And, I'll write down what I know and we can turn it over at the same time. *(Hands out paper.)*

SLAW DOG Wait a minute, that makes no sense. What if it is different… what we know?

EULA You are his confidant. *(Writes.)* And if he asked me, if I told you, I can say no.

SLAW DOG Oh contraire, you are his confidant. *(Laughs. Writes.)* But, I like your little flash card idea. It has a certain grade school charm to it.

(Turns card: "Ox is Boat's Daddy.")

EULA *(Turns card at same time: "Boat is Ox's Boy.")* I knew you knew.

SLAW DOG Why the game? *(Resumes packing.)*

EULA Confidants don't tell secrets! Speaking of which let me see if I can find that combination to that old safe, after I make some calls.

ACT TWO, Scene Three
Sunday Morning, September 18, 1988

At Rise: Jukebox music Hank Williams, Sr. "I'm So Lonesome, I Could Cry." Ox at safe: Wearing just Fruit of Loom briefs and a robe with NYT under arm. Struggles with combination to safe. Gets hot, removes robe and continues at safe. Hambric enters.)

OX *(Senses Hambric's presence.)* It's hot in here. Why is the air conditioning off?

HAMBRIC Oxford, it's Sunday morning.

OX Run downstairs and get me a limeade and my sandwich.

HAMBRIC Oxford, I'm a thing of the past. And lunch counters are also a thing of the past.

OX Lunch counters are a thing of the past. I miss my old drugstore.

HAMBRIC Yes, Oxford, lunch counters have faded into our past. When I was a child, holding my Daddy's hand, we went to Woolworth's in downtown Greensboro, North Carolina. At the lunch counter there were faded cheeseburger posters and photos of hot fudge sundaes that were larger than I was. Bright red stools spun around like whirly gigs on a playground. I cried out for ice cream, but I really just wanted to spin around on those bright red stools. One day, I broke free of Daddy's hand and took a couple of twirls on the stool before the waitress could stop me. *(Puts pencil behind his ear.)* She shouted: "Git that Nigger baby out of here!" Daddy said, Mama was waiting supper and ice cream would spoil my appetite. I cried. The stool kept spinning bright red, as he pulled me away. Daddy never did get over that. *(Laughs.)* A few weeks later I was on one of them stools, and eating ice cream while flash bulbs popped…and I was spinning. *(Exits.)*

EULA *(Enters in Scout leader uniform, looks out at park.)* Lord. Lord, it looks bad. *(Plugs in headset, dials.)* This is Eula Tyler. *(Pause.)* I am the Assistant Scout

Master is who I am and the troop has no business in the Park. *(Looks at Park.)* Nobody is going to buy lemonade from the Boy Scouts, I don't care how big the crowd is. I told you, it was a bad idea.

OX *(Crosses to office, trying to put on robe.)* Eula? Eula?

EULA *(Shouts.)* I'm in here Mister Oxford, Honey. *(Looks at Park.)* Lord, help us! *(To phone.)* Well, you can march the Boy Scouts right back to the van and get them out of the Park. *(Pause.)* This place is crazy. Get my Boy Scouts out of the Park, now! *(Clicks phone off.)*

OX Where is my newspaper? *(Looks for paper while struggling with robe.)* Why are those policemen in the Park?

EULA Sweet Jesus, you too old for this. *(With eyes diverted, covers Oxford, ties robe.)*

OX I miss my old drugstore. Lunch counter would do a good business with that commotion in the park. Lunch counter is a thing of the past.

EULA Lord let me get you dressed up for the parade.

SLAW DOG *(Enter opposite.)*

EULA Dog. *(Points to Oxford.)* Look.

SLAW DOG It's Sunday morning, but Ox, Honey, you are a little too casual. *(Looks at Ox.)* Oxford, are you in there somewhere.

OX Gladys would fix me homemade pimento cheese on toast.

EULA My God, Honey, that was over ten years ago.

OX Fresh squeezed ... limeade, pimento cheese, lies and the *New York Times*. I could skip church and read lies about me in peace and quiet. *(Shouts.)* Gladys, hold the Mayo.

SLAW DOG You got it, no Mayo. Hold the frigging Mayo! Gladys! *(Gets close to Oxford.)* Oxford are you in there? *(Whispers.)* Are you really gone, or is this a guise?

(Last word overlap.)

OX Lies? *(Looks around.)* Where's my *New York Times*? I just read about how that young Texan got the death penalty just for killing a queer telephone repairman?

SLAW DOG Jesus! *(Does a double take.)* Easy Oxford!

BAPBOMB 277

OX Stabbed him 15 times. Hit him with a hammer 17 times. Where's my paper?

EULA Under your arm. Don't know why you still read that newspaper. Just makes your blood boil. *(Walks Ox to window.)* Look, Klan Boys are getting lined up in the Park and the Brothers are getting lined up on horseback and in riot gear.

SLAW DOG *(Looks out to Park.)* Also, dogs and fire hoses, like the good old days.

OX Good. *(Takes off robe looking for paper.)* Where's my paper?

BOAT *(Enters with NYT in hands.)* Who invited Emperor No Clothes?

EULA You're back?

BOAT Heard there was a parade. And, the Ox is all over the *New York Times*. *(Reads.)* "The Negroes have been burning and bombing their own churches for decades now. Gay nightclubs and abortion clinics are symbols of decay. Strategic urban renewal is needed, blah blah blah …" *(To the Ox.)* Is someone upstaging you, like JFK did?

EULA *(Putting the robe back on Ox.)* Don't tease him and don't bring up that old stuff.

BOAT I wish it were old stuff. *(Reads NYT.)* "Klansmen have a right to express themselves."

OX How could you hammer somebody to death, even if he was queer?

SLAW DOG Freedom of expression, I suppose.

BOAT *(Reads)* "Everyone gets to parade, or no one gets to parade, a sacred ACLU principle."

OX *(To Boat.)* What are you talking about?

BOAT The quote is attributed to you, Uncle Oxford. *(Reads.)* "City police, who are predominately African American, will arrest members of the Ku Klux Klan when they march this afternoon." The *New York Times* concludes despite Lawyer Oxford Bradford's freedom expression admonition. *(Laughs.)*

SLAW DOG Oxford you would fuck up a one car funeral.

EULA Boat, you filed the permit.

BOAT We filed the permit, but it looks like….

SLAW DOG Oxford, can you call off the parade?

OX I told the Klan, their parade permit was illegal and they should back off.

(Pause.) Then, they just laughed and started making threats, again.

SLAW DOG Threats to you? No, way?

BOAT Hello? Threats are their business.

EULA *(Looking out balcony.)* Streets down there are getting scary.

BOAT Oxford do your remember asking Hambric to file the Klan Parade Permit and then telling Eula you were being blackmailed.

EULA *(Whispers to Boat.)* He can't even remember to dress himself.

SLAW DOG Don't get too righteous, Boat, you are the one who notified … (City Hall).

OX Where would the First Amendment be without us?

BOAT Right there between the body of the Constitution and the Second Amendment… the right to bear arms, detonate bombs. *(To Slaw Dog.)* Bombs? Oh, Shit.

OX Where would we be without the First Amendment?

SLAW DOG Let's get you dressed up for the parade. *(Exits with Ox.)*

BOAT *(Preoccupied, starts exit.)*

EULA *(Ignoring Boat, dials phone.)* Eric Bob, you need to return to the farm and stay out of the mess downtown here. *(Pause.)* And, yes, Mister Boatwright filed for that parade permit in the wrong place. *(Pause.)* And, you may assume that Slaw Dog threw that safe in the lake, I believe, just yesterday.

BOAT Eula, who are you talking to?

EULA Nobody.

BOAT Eula?

EULA *(To headset.)* Eric Bob, I have got to run now. *(Hangs up, then to Boat.)* Well, the Klan did threaten to blow this place up with the safe still here, then I lied about the safe being in the lake.

BOAT That I heard.

EULA But I told them we'd be out of reach, being on an upper floor and all.

BOAT Out of reach of what.

EULA Lord knows.

BOAT Eula, what have you … we started?

EULA I just said only the Lord knows.

BOAT Is the Ox still with us? Or, is he completely gone?

EULA Lordy, lordy, where to start? Here, read this for yourself. *(Pulls letter from file.)* Ox wasn't in Africa.

BOAT I knew it.

EULA He's been up in Rochester, Minnesota visiting the Mayo Brothers in that Clinic.

BOAT Is his demise imminent?

EULA Careful, he helped you the best he could, when you'd let him and you should be grateful.

BOAT If he was helping me, I'm in trouble.

EULA *(Points to letter.)* He's not exactly got Alzheimer's. But, there is sub-acute organic brain atrophy syndrome according to that report. That means he is in a gray zone between delirium and dementia, but it is persistent and progressive. Comes and goes like a brain hiccup. He may be doing the best he can.

BOAT Yes, but have you noticed that through his dementia, Oxford confessed criminal knowledge of the Church Bombing? *(Lifts NYT.)* It's right here in the *New York Times*.

EULA What do you mean?

BOAT Eula, Oxford confessed to monitoring the bombing! Here: *(Reads and points.)* "By 1963 there had been dozens of reported bombings all over Dynamite Hill, and each bombing was invariably just the foundation, away from human habitation. No one was to be hurt until." *(Reads, then summarizes.)* Then, the Sunday the Little Girls were killed, Oxford just happened to be downtown for the explosion, he was skipping church and having a pimento cheese sandwich and fresh squeezed limeade. Then he concludes: "But, No one was supposed to be hurt!"

EULA *(Looks at paper.)* No one was supposed to be hurt? *(Beat.)* That is horrible.

BOAT Oh, Eula. *(Tries to comfort her.)*

EULA Wait a minute. *(Goes to safe, Boat follows.)* I had no idea what this was all about. *(Rummages through old boxes, finds combination to safe and hands it to Boat.)*

BOAT *(Looks at combination.)* What's this?

EULA The combination to that old safe.

BOAT Did you know where it was all along?

SLAW DOG *(Enters.)*

EULA No, it just occurred to me where it might be. Excuse me, I need some time by myself. *(Exits.)*

BOAT *(Holds up paper.)* The combination.

SLAW DOG *(Reaches for combination.)* Here give me that. *(Takes paper, crosses to safe, reads.)* Nine-fifteen-sixty-three. *(Shakes head.)* He is losing it.

BOAT Past tense. He has lost it. Are you sure we want to open that thing?

SLAW DOG *(Turns knob.)* Remember, you don't give a damn. *(Clicks safe open.)*

BOAT Perhaps, we had rather leave those tapes alone.

SLAW DOG *(Pulls out medical records and tapes.)* I knew it.

BOAT Knew what?

SLAW DOG *(Looks at tape.)* This one is dated nine, fourteen, sixty-three. The day before the Church Bombing. Oxford stumbled on the Klan's plan to blow the foundation of the 16th Street Church. *(Beat.)* Oxford commissioned me to tell the Klan that their alibis were not holding up. That the FBI knew they were popping valium before they took the lie detector tests. Somehow, the Ox thought that would give him some leverage with the Klan. Then he wanted them to make sure all the little children were upstairs in Sunday School, far away from the foundation. We begged them to change their minds and pick a time when no one was in the church but they wanted to scare people, not just a building.

BOAT Did anyone think to call the cops ... the FBI?

SLAW DOG Where have you been? Boat, it was 1963, law enforcement had the same information we had. Bull and his cops were corrupt to the man. Dynamite Bob thought he was doing Bull a favor and would get promoted by the City. We were trapped by too much information. *(Picks up medical records.)*

BOAT Too much information? At least Uncle Oxford was consistent.

SLAW DOG Too much information. There's more.

BOAT Is that old reel-to-reel tape recorder still in Oxford's office? *(Shouts off stage as he Exits.)* Eula where is that old tape recorder?

SLAW DOG Eula, do you know where I can find a good lawyer?

ACT TWO, Scene Four
Later Sunday Afternoon, September 18, 1988

At Rise: Eula in Boat's office on phone, parade music from Park.

EULA *(Talking to headset.)* Eric Bob, I know you are stuck in traffic, I can see you from here. That Brother on horseback is looking at your rig real funny like. *(Pause.)* Sure, you're gonna tell the Cops you are into lawn maintenance and they are going to believe you? *(Pause.)* But, a Volvo with a car phone pulling a U-Haul now that was clever.

OX *(Enters dressed without pants: White shirt, yellow tie, dress socks with garters, wing tips and briefs.)* Eula, who's that?

EULA Who? *(Spits words.)* Eric Bob, one of your Klan Boys has gone into lawn maintenance. *(Facetiously.)* He says he is going to blow this place up, safe and all. But, he is stuck in traffic. *(Pause.)* Got to run, Eric Bob. *(Exits to get Ox's pants.)*

OX Very well. *(Is lost in thought.)*

HAMBRIC *(Appears to Oxford.)* Code Bapbomb, the FBI cold case file box BB-63-674, had a pair of little girl's shoes, patent leather, with low-heels, the kind pre-teens get for Easter. Also, there was a note in the file that suggested that the only mistake the little girls made that Sunday morning, was going to the restroom downstairs in their Sunday best, perhaps to act grown-up and dab on a hint of lipstick. *(Exits.)*

OX That is sad.

EULA *(Enters on last sentence with pants.)* Sad? *(Looks at Ox.)* Yes, it is all sad. And, Mr. Oxford you may be the saddest of all.

BOAT *(Enters pushing cart with tape recorder, and plugs it in.)* Does this work?

EULA Honey, doesn't matter if it works or not, you don't want to listen to it.

BOAT *(To Eula.)* Do I have a choice?

OX Eula, we had a tape recorder just like that in the old days.

EULA *(Points.)* It's a mess in the Park. I'd like to get Eric Bob a little closer to the commission of a crime before I call the FBI.

BOAT Has it occurred to anyone that we set all this in motion?

OX Commission of what?

BOAT Who knows? Read your *New York Times* article. *(Reads.)* Look, a neo-skinhead hammered to death a Black gay transvestite over in Atlanta near Little Five Points.

OX Hammered to death? Eula, do they make Black trans … trans … whatevers?

EULA Not in my neighborhood. But ….

OX Those gay bars in Atlanta are in a blighted area, like west of the Park here.

BOAT A hammering death seems more primal than an ordinary lynching.

OX What? We put a stop to lynchings!

BOAT Hammering is more direct and it lets out pent up energy.

EULA He doesn't understand. You might as well be talking to a fence post.

BOAT Dear Fence Post, Eula has rented a U-Haul full of ammonium nitrate, and your Klansman Eric Bob could demolish those blighted buildings west of the Park while we have an assembled crowd to witness his big bang.

EULA It's not Eula's U-Haul. It's rented by an employee of the Foundation. And, if Mr. Oxford was thinking clearly, he'd get a piece of my mind. *(To Boat.)* You are not thinking too clearly, either.

HAMBRIC *(Appears.)* Oxford, start talking politics or something. Distraction!

OX George Bush will be your next President, mark my word.

BOAT What?

OX LBJ lost the South forever when he signed that Civil Rights Act. Told me so himself.

EULA Oxford, that Civil Rights stuff was at least twenty-five years ago and you don't want to go there.

HAMBRIC God, Guns and Gays. We need some new victims to let my people off the hook.

OX God, Guns and Gays. You can buy the Jesus freaks with their own righteousness. *(Pause as if to hear himself.)*

BOAT What brought that on?

OX I don't like your friends.

BOAT I'm not sure I do either.

OX Those expatriates.

BOAT Everybody who left town in the last twenty years is an expatriate.

EULA Once again, that old stuff will haunt you. *(Points to Park.)* Hello? We got an illegal parade mounting in the Park.

OX No one quotes me without my permission.

BOAT Who are you talking to?

OX That friend of yours didn't know his ass from his elbow.

BOAT I love my imaginary friend. Have you ever thought about an invisible rabbit?

HAMBRIC Oxford, Boat is confused.

OX Boat, you are confused.

BOAT You can say that again.

OX Boat, you are confused.

HAMBRIC Oxford, he didn't mean for you to correct him. Try to listen.

BOAT Oxford, I thought you went to the Newspaper and listened to the wiretaps to sift through the legality. I had no idea you were an active participant. You actually knew about the bombing. Did any of that strike you as wrong?

OX Everybody wire-tapped everybody else back then.

BOAT That we have established. *(Reads.)* And you tried to stop the church bombing. Almost worked, it should have been just the foundation. The little girls should have been upstairs in their Sunday School classroom. You "should have" all over yourself.

OX What? *(Looks in his pants.)*

EULA Boat, Honey, you are wasting your time, and forgiveness is selfish act. Frees up your bitterness so your heart can look for better things. *(Phone rings, to headset.)* Mr. Boatwright's office. *(Pause.)* Eric Bob, I know you are stuck in traffic. *(Exits.)*

BOAT Good God, Eula, quit working both sides of the street.

OX Working the streets? Is that what she is doing? I never know who she is talking to.

BOAT Neither do I.

OX Eula, just said you were wasting your time. Have you gone back to day dreaming?

BOAT Dr. Morgan calls it 'Mixed Anxiety-Depressive Disorder,' but 'day dreaming' sounds better. *(Looks at Ox's blank expression.)* Remember when you took me on my first dove shoot?

OX How could I forget? I thought a dove shoot and a shotgun would help make you a man.

BOAT That Dove shoot was awful… hot and dusty. I wounded a bird. Innocent big black eyes, wings flapping in the dust and chest heaving. I put it in the back of my hunting vest, thinking I would take it to some animal rescue shelter and confess. But, you saw it flapping, pulled it out, and rung its neck.

OX Had the cook fry it up for you to eat.

BOAT The buckshot got stuck in my braces. Were we having fun yet?

HAMBRIC Ox, did you say Boat was your Boy?

OX Afraid so.

HAMBRIC When you gonna tell him?

BOAT Oxford, you may not be able to hear me and I suspect the next time we communicate will be when I arrive amongst the settling dirt and dying flowers to piss on your grave.

OX At one time you had a bright future. I can put a spin on most anything, if you let me know ahead of time.

BOAT You don't even know who I am, yet you want to fix me to conform to ….

OX I suspected that giving your mother a child, would eventually take on complications.

BOAT What?

HAMBRIC Mother-fucker, we need a parade! *(Exits.)*

OX There was a lot of mutual respect and love.

BOAT *(Disbelief.)* Spare me, please!

OX Your father and I were good friends. And, we both loved your Mother. She was such a gay blade, a free spirit … in the South of France before the War. *(Beat.)* After you parents died, I didn't want to leave you with your Aunts in Tupelo.

BOAT What did you say about giving my Mother a child?

OX Your father was sterile.

BOAT Tell me you are delusional … and this is a product of your brain atrophy.

OX Your father loved life and quick fixes.

BOAT Jesus Christ!

OX We were all so proud of you. *(Fishes for letter.)* Here's a letter from the Mayo Clinic. I was the only male in your life, between the time I dropped you off in Tupelo with your aunts and I came to drive you to college in Chapel Hill. I regret not being there for you when you were growing up. *(Beat.)* Pretty soon I'm gonna just sorta fade away. Doctor says, at first, I'll lose my memory, then my speech and last my motor skills… then I'll just fall over like a bowling pin.

BOAT Why didn't you tell me?

OX I just learned about it.

BOAT No, I mean, being my biological father?

SLAW DOG *(Enters and listens.)*

OX If you need evidence we've got old Doc McWhorter's records. Sealed and certified. *(Tries for a hug.)* I'm going to die. *(Boat dodges hug.)*

BOAT This is fucking stupid. My therapist said I needed a father growing up. Now, out of the fucking blue I have a screwed-up father who is fading fast. *(Pause, while anger fades slightly.)* Appreciate that I am finding it difficult to play along. *(Exits.)*

SLAW DOG So, Dr. Faustus, you just up and told him. *(Laughs, adjust Ox's tie.)* Why was it ever such a big secret?

OX It is Biblical that my sins should be visited upon him… my son. *(Pause.)* I saw my passion in Boat when he represented the Nig-ra with the one nut. I watched Boat catch fire in the courtroom when he truly believed in his client… usually a client who was damaged.

SLAW DOG Isn't it a little late for the chip-off-the-old-block horseshit?

OX Loyalty to the client and vigorous representation is our noble calling.

SLAW DOG Oxford, you represented the fucking Ku Klux Klan and the bastards came to own you.

OX You make it sound harsh. And you know full well we tried to turn them around.

SLAW DOG Yes, and it did not work.

OX I did not want Boat to bear the burden of my passive participation in....

SLAW DOG Passive participation! Honey, your whole life has been on big Ox-y-moron.

OX Then, I guess, I just blurted out that I was his father.

SLAW DOG That you did. *(Pause.)* Oh, come on. Just blame it on a moonlit night on the Cote d' Azur. *(Adjusts Ox's lapels.)* Looking good, for an old Sperm Donor.

(Slaw Dog exits, Ox crosses to Safe.)

EULA *(Eula enters Boat's office with pimento cheese sandwich and limeade, placing them on desk, then looks out to Park. Engages phone.)* Yeah, Eric Bob, Honey, you could set a whole bunch of stuff straight, if you could just get out of that traffic jam. *(Pause.)* Sure, sure, I hear you. Now, you stay stuck in traffic, while I make a few telephone calls. *(Clicks phone off.)*

OX Eula? Eula? *(Crosses to Boat's office fully and handsomely dressed.)*

EULA I'm right in here Oxford, Honey. I've been in the break room praying for forgiveness for all of us. *(Helps Ox to chair.)* Brought you a nice pimento cheese sandwich and some fresh limeade.

OX Much obliged.

EULA Mister Oxford, I don't know exactly how to say this. And, I really appreciate all you have done for me over the years, and I know in my heart that I have to love the good and reject the bad in you. *(Pause.)* But, client or no client, I do not approve of that Klan and what you did back then. I'm not even sure you know what I am talking about, but I need to say it. You could have stopped the church bombing! *(Beat, no response.)* When you called in the Klan thinking you were helping that new Attorney General, you put this whole place in jeopardy. *(Pause.)* And, fooling around with those old tapes and that parade permit killed Hambric as if you had pulled the trigger yourself. Yes, that's what I believe. Just to be honest, I must tell you, that I am going to do all in my God given power to get Eric Bob arrested and put the Klan out of business. Client or no client. *(Understated Anger.)* I know you felt trapped back then, but at some point we have got to stand up for what is right. Attorney-client privilege don't extend to crimes, you once taught me. *(Pause.)* You don't remember. I'm trying to pray away my anger and bitterness. You can call it forgiveness, if you want to, but it's ...

OX You and Slaw Dog are my only friends.

EULA It's difficult. *(Pause, deep breath.)* Slaw Dog sure dressed you up nicely. *(Looks at sandwich.)* I almost forgot, you like your sandwich cut sideways. *(Cuts sandwich.)* Yes, you are something else. But, Lord knows, you have been good to me and I appreciate that extra vesting in my pension plan.

OX Now, take care of that boy of yours.

EULA It'll be there for Little Jeff's college.

OX Eula, you are a wonderful person.

EULA Now, you sit here and eat while I make some telephone calls.

BOAT *(Enters on last sentence.)* Don't let me disturb you.

EULA *(To Boat.)* I now know filing that parade permit in the wrong place was your act of civil disobedience.

BOAT I notified City Hall.

EULA And, it's going to be a mess out there in the street and you are no Dr. King.

BOAT Is my civil disobedience stepping on your civil disobedience?

EULA What do you mean?

BOAT A U-Haul full of fertilizer headed this way.

EULA Revenge is best served up ….

BOAT Cold?

EULA Try hot. *(Points.)* Now, watch the Oxford while I phone in for my reward.

BOAT As I said, don't let me disturb you. *(Looks at Ox.)* Is he still with us?

EULA Why don't you ask him, he is sitting right there. *(Pause.)* If I can forgive him, it wouldn't hurt you to try.

BOAT Forgiveness? Is that what you call it?

EULA Frees your heart up for better things.

BOAT Saw that you are full vested in ….

EULA He's not a bad man, but he lived in a bad time. *(Kisses Ox on cheek. Exits.)*

OX Thank you, Eula. It's a struggle, but we do what we can.

BOAT Father Dearest, are you planning your defense or just eating a pimento cheese sandwich?

OX I wish that were all I had to do.

BOAT *(Conflicted.)* Excuse my frustration. But what are you talking about?

OX A jealous God, visits the sins of the father on the son.

BOAT That doesn't make sense nor does it frighten me. Aren't you more worried about my sins?

OX No one cares what you do.

BOAT It's just a New Age Men's Group. .

OX Professor Kinsey said it may pass.

BOAT What?.

OX And, I liked how you jumped in and helped Eula with that Klan permit. But I also noticed that you produced a commotion today, by notifying City Hall. *(Nods then smiles.)* Working both sides of the street, are you?

BOAT *(Sarcastically.)* Like father, like son.

OX But, the more dastardly form of incompetence is to get trapped in the middle.

BOAT I am not trapped, but how would that be incompetent?

OX At first you embrace the middle, having everyone coming to you for advice, both ends against the middle. *(Pause.)* The fanatics trap you. *(Pause.)* You shout compromise. Then, you only want to keep things quiet. Then you lose control.

BOAT I hate it, when the conspiracy of silence falls apart.

OX *(Ignores Boat's remark.)* Oh, you hope no one gets hurt, but then, it becomes a cover-up. Too late you shout, Stop! But no one hears you. Then, it blows up. *(Points.)* Go ahead and play those old tapes.

BOAT Are you sure? *(Presses play button on reel-to-reel recorder.)*

RECORDED TELEPHONE *(Recorder static, then ring.)*

MALE VOICE: FBI, Central District, Musgrove speaking.

OX *(Younger and a little drunk):* Is this the Code Bapbomb of the Birmingham Division of the Federal Bureau of Investigation?

MALE VOICE: Yes.

OX: This is Oxford Bradford.

MALE VOICE: Oxford, this is Agent Musgrove. I know who you are.

OX: Musgrove, you Boys might as well give up. Edgar said there would be no federal prosecution. I tried to tip you off and you did nothing. I have it all on tape! Now, your Klan informer has been trapped in the bombing. You play your cards right, no white jury will convict your informer. Double agents got double agents. I warned the FBI and you did nothing and you too will need a good lawyer. *(Static. End of recording.)*

OX Few weeks ago, I screwed up the tape, because Eric Bob called in when he was not supposed to. But I taped him too.

HAMBRIC *(Appears.)* Yeah, Oxford, your old Klan buddy appeared just before I died but maybe it was the FBI informer. Anyway, dead is dead. And, I'm getting good at it.

RECORDED TELEPHONE *(Static, break, then a newer cleaner tape. Older more sober Ox.)*

ERIC BOB: Oxford what the fuck is going on?

OX: Why did you ring in on this number? Damn things can be traced.

ERIC BOB: That nigger lawyer knows too much?

OX; Just put a gas can in his car, scare him a little.

ERIC BOB: Just a gas can?

OX: I do not want him hurt. He is kissing my ass wanting to be a partner.

ERIC BOB: You old fool, I am getting tired of this fuckin' cave. If you don't do something soon, I may blow up that shiny office building of yours.

OX: Suit yourself. And good luck finding another lawyer. The Feds are bound and determined to use that new Death Penalty of theirs. Besides I may not be around much longer and you won't have a lawyer. *(Static & end of recording.)*

BOAT Won't have a lawyer? Who was that character? *(Fiddles with tape recorder.)*

OX Eric Bob. I just told you who he was. *(Watches Hambric beyond Boat.)*

HAMBRIC So, Oxford the gas can was your idea?

OX No. *(Pause.)* It was for your own good.

BOAT My own good? *(Puzzled.)* You said it was "Eric Bob"? *(Looks at Ox and gives up.)*

HAMBRIC Yes, Oxford, I was murdered, by your buddy, Eric Bob, who feared he would spend the rest of his pathetic life in prison. My death was totally unnecessary, because I knew nothing. *(Smiles.)* After all these years, I guess, the Klan got paranoid.

OX Paranoid?

BOAT Are you paranoid? Is that part of your diagnosis? *(Gets no response.)*

HAMBRIC Yes, Oxford, you were the catalyst for my death.

OX *(To Hambric.)* How did you know?

BOAT *(Responds.)* I don't know. You are the one who brought up paranoia.

OX *(Stares at Boat, then in the direction of Hambric's voice.)*

HAMBRIC Being dead you see shit. *(Sighs.)* My death was gratuitous. I was killed by Eric Bob in a UPS outfit, who walked right past the receptionist saying he had a special delivery for you, Oxford. He detoured, fed me the shot gun blast, and then escaped down the back stairs in the commotion that followed.

OX *(To Hambric, beyond Boat.)* I hate that it happened.

BOAT *(Puzzled.)* Me too.

HAMBRIC Me too. I hate that it happened at all.

BOAT Oxford, I wanted to believe that you were on the sidelines back then.

OX You get trapped bit-by-bit. *(Looks at sandwich.)* When they come after you, you're brain is fading and you're about to fall over like a bowling pin. And, I could not depend on law enforcement to hold the party line.

HAMBRIC Shit happens, when conspiracies fall apart.

OX It fell apart, but our South will repeat in fifty years, or so, mark my word.

BOAT What are you saying?

OX I'm saying, you learn to wait, with caution. My foolishness gave certain permissions to the Klan, but mind you it was early on and just a foundation, here and there.

HAMBRIC And, I hate it when white folks fuck up.

OX Then, the Klan Boys killed those little girls by accident. *(Looks at hands.)*

HAMBRIC Some fuckin' accident!

OX I never intended that children get hurt.

BOAT What did you intend?

OX *(Suddenly aware of Boat.)* What?

BOAT Setting in motion a culture of bombings and then trying to stop the bad one is not sufficient. The arsonist does not get to put out the fire. *(Shakes head.)* There is no statute of limitations on murder. If you were guilty then, you are guilty now.

OX I never intended.

BOAT No one gives a shit what you intended. Eat your sandwich, Dad. *(Beat.)* From time-to-time, I feared all of this, but I told myself to pretend it was not true. But then you were only my Uncle.

OX If I had it to do over again. *(From the Park louder band music, dogs barking, car horns and helicopters.)* Where is it? *(Crosses to storeroom for gun puts in bullets.)*

PHONE RINGS

BOAT *(Pushes speaker button.)* This is Boat, may I help you?

PHONE VOICE Boat, this is Agent Musgrove with the FBI. I called Oxford about that *New York Times* article, but Eula said he was busy and then she told me she had a Klansman with a U-Haul full of explosives. Do you know what's going on?

BOAT Not exactly. What exactly did Eula say?

OX Tell Musgrove, the FBI was in on it too.

BOAT *(To Ox.)* Shut up! *(To phone.)* Seriously, Oxford is not thinking clearly.

PHONE VOICE Careful, Boat, don't force me to read you your rights, too. But, listen, we have to take Eula seriously this time, and this Eric Bob character with the U-Haul trailer has disappeared into your building's parking garage. Bomb unit is on its way but traffic is jammed. So, we need you to very calmly but promptly evacuate the building. Make sure everyone is off your floor and out of the building, then call me.

BOAT Are you in your office?

PHONE VOICE Yeah. Hurry.

BOAT Okay. *(Pushes phone button, looks at Ox who has the gun.)* No!

OX Shoot me, please. *(Forces gun on him.)*

BOAT *(Takes gun.)* Don't tempt me. I can't.

OX Show me you are a man, shoot me!

BOAT No.

OX *(Dives for gun, noise from Park gets louder.)* For once, act like the son I wanted you to be.

BOAT *(Blocks him.)* You wanted me to be what?

OX Shoot!

BOAT No.

OX Please, I don't want to go through this.

BOAT I wished you'd thought about that years ago.

OX Lawyers act on behalf of our client.

BOAT Clients? You tried to control both sides from the middle.

OX Sides? We don't choose sides, Son.

BOAT Don't pretend to be my father now! It's too late.

OX I didn't intend that it end this way.

BOAT I'm sure you didn't. *(Conflicted...lowers gun.)*

OX Shoot!

BOAT No.

HAMBRIC Oxford, Boat is not going to shoot you.

(Overlap.)

OX Shoot!

(Overlap.)

BOAT No.

HAMBRIC Shoot! Don't shoot!

OX Shoot!

(Overlap.)

BOAT No.

HAMBRIC Chip off the old block. But doing nothing.

BOAT I can't. *(Lowers gun.)*

HAMBRIC Tell him you love him.

OX I love you! *(Pause.)* Now, shoot!

BOAT What? *(Pause.)* Appreciate that I am … not going to shoot you.

HAMBRIC Eric Bob is in the parking garage and you'd best get your pink butt out of here. I'm already dead and I'm leaving. *(Exits.)*

BOAT Let's get out of here. *(Ox does nothing.)* Hurry! *(Grabs Ox and exits.)*

OX *(Stage is clear, after extended moment with offstage commotion of Ox struggling with Boat, Ox returns to stare at safe.)*

BOMB BLAST, VIBRATIONS, FIRE BALLS, DUST.

(Noise fades to emergency vehicles coming to scene while stage is dark.)

HAMBRIC *(In dark Hambric sings last three verses of "Birmingham Sunday")*[51]

> ON BIRMINGHAM SUNDAY A NOISE SHOOK THE GROUND.
> AND PEOPLE ALL OVER THE EARTH TURNED AROUND.
> FOR NO ONE RECALLED A MORE COWARDLY SOUND.
> AND THE CHOIRS KEPT SINGING OF FREEDOM.
>
> *(LIGHTS SLOWLY UP ON DUST COVERED HAMBRIC.)*
>
> THE MEN IN THE FOREST THEY ONCE ASKED OF ME,
> HOW MANY BLACKBERRIES GREW IN THE SALT SEA.
> AND I ASKED THEM RIGHT WITH A TEAR IN MY EYE.
> HOW MANY DARK SHIPS IN THE FOREST?
> THE SUNDAY HAS COME AND THE SUNDAY HAS GONE.
> AND I CAN'T DO MUCH MORE THAN TO SING YOU A SONG.
> I'LL SING IT SO SOFTLY, IT'LL DO NO ONE WRONG.
> AND THE CHOIRS KEEP SINGING OF FREEDOM.

~ END OF PLAY ~

BACKSTORY

AS A PLAYWRIGHT I REMAIN IN AWE OF THE PREPARATION SOME ACTORS, DIRECTORS AND TECHS undertake in prepping and presenting their craft for the stage. In BAPBOMB the actor playing the elder lawyer became enamored with "his clients" the industrial barons of Birmingham and I lent him a five-hundred page tome THE STORY OF COAL AND IRON IN ALABAMA (Armes, Beechwood Books, 1987) which he devoured. The director of the staged readings of WINSTON DRIVES BIG JIM at Jacksonville State put my research to shame at a time when I thought I had exhausted all sources. First, in the University's towering library she found FIGHTING THE DEVIL IN DIXIE, How Civil Rights Activists Took On The Ku Klux Klan in Alabama (Greenhaw, Lawrence Hill Books, 2011) that reminded me that Governor Big Jim Folsom slipped Winston Craig cash to pay poll tax for Blacks wishing to register to vote over a decade before the Voting Rights Act of 1965. Also at the staged readings the director extended the plays ending of Dr. King's "I Have A Dream" speech to include his reference to little Alabama children both Black and white playing together and being judged by the content of their character and not the color of their skin.

I gratefully accept deep dives into these characters, their history and gleefully appropriate efforts to bring them depth. I justify the randomness of these backstory observations because I do not know what is important to actors, directors and techs. Selfishly, these look-backs provide residual benefits, e.g. moments of self-discovery, good and not so good, the obvious with the attendant blind spots of white privilege. Perhaps a future generation will conclude that we were not all of one mind and one's ancestors were complex. Hence, today's youngsters don't have to follow the loudest voice in the tribe, the proverbial drunk uncle at Thanksgiving dinner.

SHORT STORY TO PLAY

I began writing these plays in the 1980s when I converted a short story THE DIAMOND BUTTERFLY into the play WEDGES. The short story won an Alabama State Hackney Award that was presented to me by Erskine Caldwell during a Writing Today Conference at Birmingham-Southern College (BSC) circa 1984. Mr. Caldwell did not select the short story as a winner and over dinner asked me why it was so long. His wife Virginia was kinder with her comments. Apparently, the Writing Today Committee asked Mr. Caldwell to skip his afternoon nap to hand me the award. The moment of the award, Mr. Caldwell's presence and his wife's kindness were and remain special.

As mentioned in the Introduction, I started these plays as an apology that we were not all of one mind back then with some whites trying to do good — perhaps not enough — but arcing toward good. During this process I have tried to define "Jim Crow Liberals" while asking if there is any redemption in today's polarizing woke-ness, excuse the pun, black and white thinking. Some call it our Cold Civil War. Though he may whence at the title, Mr. Caldwell was an early Jim Crow Liberal exposing the South during our era of apartheid. Of course it was easier for a writer to write harsh truths about our beloved South and then ex-pat themselves to a safe enclave in New England or somewhere out West near Hollywood. Obviously, it is more difficult to speak those truths while remaining among the locals, behind our "Clay Curtain" as we use to call it.

Jim Crow Liberals are seldom perfect, for example: Governor Big Jim Folsom in 1949 as a New Deal Democrat asked for racial equality, but later in his career he began to water down his call for racial progress in an effort to get elected after *Brown v. Board* in 1954. When facing and ultimately losing to George Wallace in 1962 Big Jim gave lip service to segregation. What was his truth? Was he just trying to win an election? How strong was his belief in true democracy?

As a college student in Birmingham in the early 1960s and a hometown Cullman, Alabama boy, I knew that Big Jim did not have his heart in segregation because among other reasons segregation prevented all citizens from voting, the cornerstone of democracy and a more perfect union. Back then before Big Jim officially announced for office he'd go out of his way to woo the sparse minority vote, a rarity among southern politicians. So, when Bill Maxwell on July 4, 2010 writing for the *St. Petersburg* (now *Tampa Bay*) *Times,* lumped Big Jim with notorious segregationists e.g. Wallace, Lester Maddox, Jesse Helms, Strom Thurmond, *et al,* part of my world crumbled.

Why? It's complicated and perhaps irrelevant today among the uber-woke crowd, but the arc of the moral universe — that bends slowly according to Dr. King — has to start bending somewhere. The new indoor sport among the woke, the remotely righteous, seems to be taking pot shots at Jim Crow Liberals of yore, including among their targets Atticus Finch of TO KILL A MOCKING BIRD. "Nuisance" may be too much to ask, but it adds depth to flawed characters, as we try to understand them in their time, perchance to put them on stage.

WEDGES THE INSPIRATION

Like my short story that Mr. Erskine Caldwell thought to be too long, my first play WEDGES had the same four characters and divided nicely into two acts.[52] Its central character a domestic I named "Sadie" came to me via a real law-life experience. My mentor at the law firm chaired a grievance committee of the Birmingham Bar Association when the committee received a complaint that a member lawyer had stolen diamonds from a client.

Circa 1950, the real African American domestic "found" the diamonds after a drunken brawl in a Palm Beach Florida mansion, kept them for twenty plus years when she returned to Birmingham for family reasons. While in Birmingham she wanted to return the diamonds to their rightful owner, a socialite who seasonally switched between Palm Beach, Florida and Newport, Rhode Island. But, the errant Birmingham lawyer she consulted took the diamonds for himself while assuring her all was taken care of. Then the maid writes the socialite in Newport expressing relief that the diamonds had been returned.

Oops, the plot thickens. As a young associate lawyer my mission was to take a statement from the domestic for the grievance committee. Her shotgun house was on Village Creek, that spewed an industrial stench that I remembered well from my college days in that end of town. It was August and several degrees above hot. About the same time, I was volunteering some Saturdays at the local legal aid office. While at the firm I was being trained to keep rich folks rich, but I was lousy at solving problems of folks who could not afford a lawyer. Hence, the narrator in WEDGES.

As an aside, the Walker Percy southern malaise that was heavy on the narrator in the short story turned out to be negligible in the early production of the play. If it's not on the page, it's not on stage, so I take blame or credit for the lack of the southern malaise. But, for an actor wishing a deep dive into the Smith character, I recommend Mr. Percy.

For another script note, my writing mentor, Jesse Hill Ford, read an early draft of the short story and suggested that I prolong, albeit stretch, the moment the diamonds appear to build suspense. I found writing this "literary delay" to be difficult and a bit disingenuous as in gimmicky, but for the play the roll out of the diamonds became much easier — by putting knots in the strings of the old tobacco pouch containing the diamonds. Here the actor, director and techs also carry the burden of suspense.

In WEDGES after the lawyer/narrator gets saddled with the diamonds he needed someone to help return the diamonds perchance to soften the consequences for Sadie. (The story was set in the mid-70s, and I had not yet moved to Florida. Thank God. After I moved to Palm Beach County Florida in the late 1990s, I attended a Duke University Alumni gathering at Mar-a-Largo, originally the Post breakfast cereal family mansion situated between the Atlantic Ocean (Mar) and Lake Worth (Largo). Had I gotten close to the setting of the real drunken brawl, that is, a Palm Beach mansion, I fear the story would have been a different story, one for the opulent trash heap.)

However, serendipity solved my "white savior" problem for the return of the diamonds. Enter the Governor: One may never fully appreciate one's hometown until one moves away or until someone from New England gains a new admiration for one of its characters. In the mid-70s a writer friend reversed migrated to the South, from Vermont to Birmingham. With George Wallace-ism spreading north, this friend became fascinated with Big Jim Folsom and his early call for racial equality. So, I arranged an interview with Big Jim when the Governor was broke, blind but full of his hope for the Constitution and its experiment with representative democracy. After the interview, I had a renewed appreciation for the Governor, and he became the perfect character to solve my "found" diamond problem in WEDGES. The Governor provided the ending — a surprise even to me when my old IBM Selectric II first stumbled onto it. At the risk of sounding too artsy, the characters talk and I record them.

As an aside, the day my friend and I interviewed Big Jim in the mid-1970s there was a dreaded Klan parade forming in downtown Birmingham. Knowing I was a lawyer and that our mission was "progressive" Big Jim set about to quiz us: Does the Constitution permit that Klan parade? Townsfolk love to quiz Birmingham lawyers and writers from New England.

WATERIN'HOLE THE INSPIRATION

Similarly, the characters in WATERIN'HOLE came about by accident. When I was a young lawyer, the Maitre d' of a private club, The Relay House, on the top of our office building asked if I were kin to Hubert Grissom who worked for the L&N Railroad? Well, yes, that's my father. The Maitre d' once worked on the railroad and said my father would take him to Cullman to buy shoes. What? Tell me more. Turns out that Cullman had a popular discount shoe store and Blacks felt more comfortable shopping with a local white guy. Then I learned that Black and white railroad workers in the 1950s drank together after work in the backroom of a Fultondale bar/restaurant in defiance of Jim Crow laws. Pursuing this, I learned that Daddy Hubert coached Blacks in their railroad cub exam, and otherwise helped them move up on the railroad. That imagined barroom became the set for WATERIN'HOLE.

JAMELLE THE INSPIRATION

The late Carl Stewart, founder of Terrific New Theatre in Birmingham and director of my earlier plays, first suggested a play that became JAMELLE, ALABAMA'S TEENAGE FIRST LADY. Jamelle Folsom was a fictional character in WEDGES, played with flare by Ruth Speake, and Mrs. Folsom attended the opening of WEDGES at TNT. With her coal black hair and tailored outfits Jamelle was always the vivacious First Lady with a little flirt. So, Carl suggested a play with Jamelle in the lead. Acting on Carl's suggestion, I interviewed Jamelle with an announced intention of writing a play about her. When I asked Jamelle about Big Jim's love child by another woman (the subject of "She Was Poor" a famed college drinking/folk song back in the day), First Lady Jamelle Folsom went into full deflection mode. She patted her hair and adjusted her bright scarf, letting me know that she kept her man happy. But, the love child was before you and Big Jim were married ... still no response. Next subject.

Early November 2012, Jamelle dropped by Mother's 96th birthday party, dressed to the nines and in full First Lady ebullient mode. So, I was shocked that three weeks later Jamelle Folsom died of cancer that she kept secret from the family. During the production of WEDGES, I got to know Roland Johnson one of the original Strawberry Pickers and was inspired to have a picker as a foil to Jamelle in her "one-woman" play. In development of JAMELLE, ALABAMA'S FIRST LADY I was fortunate to have a reading in Cullman attended by the Folsom clan with Marsha Folsom, also an Alabama First Lady, reading the lead. I am grateful to Ben South and my sister Jenny Folsom for making the reading possible.

CODE BAPBOMB THE INSPIRATION AND DEVELOPMENT

After its 2007 production, I renamed the play "CODE BAPBOMB" when a local Tampa reviewer said the name sounded like "Be Bop," a harbinger that early Alabama civil rights history was fading, especially in faraway Tampa. Initially I thought "BapBomb" the FBI code name to be a mysterious combination of Baptist and Bombing that would attract the curious. Alas, "BapBomb" presented more confusion than intrigue; hence, the change.

In the 1960s with wiretapping being prevalent, who knew what? When? Why did no one stop the bombing? On that Sunday morning September 15,

1963 we could feel the vibrations from the bomb at the SAE fraternity house at Birmingham-Southern College approximately two miles away. Vibrations from bombs were nothing new in Bombingham back then, but the horror of the death of the innocent young girls was a defining moment. Early on, white folks were led to believe that the Klan being familiar with dynamite from working in the coal mines always planted the bombs on Dynamite Hill and at the Gaston Motel in the front of the dwelling just to scare Blacks who were always in the back of the dwelling. Somehow no one got seriously hurt. Somehow this was okay? Then the young girls in their Sunday best wandered down to a lower level restroom in the 16th Street Baptist Church, Birmingham, Alabama.

Recently, a 1960s television special on CNN concluded that President Kennedy's assignation on November 22, 1963, was a defining moment in our nation's history. True but coupled with the church bombing in Birmingham two months earlier this college student wonder if our nation would survive.

While in college during on campus political gatherings I had the privilege of meeting Birmingham's progressive lawyers, e.g. David Vann, Chuck Morgan, Vernon Patrick, who in an effort to get rid of Bull Connor were instrumental in changing Birmingham's form of city government. And, later as a lawyer got to know the establishment who like most of us found it convenient at times to talk out of both sides of our mouth. Even the clergy the subject of Dr. King's Letter from the Birmingham Jail were clothed with a bit of righteousness when they ask Dr. King for more time to let Birmingham's change in city government take place. (As of March 5, 1963, the citizens of Birmingham voted in a new mayor and city council form of government that was to rid the City of the old commissioners.) Although the clergy, also Jim Crow Liberals, had their moral justification, Dr. King was politically smarter, because he knew he needed Commissioner Bull Connor — albeit old racist Birmingham with police dogs and fire hoses — for the cameras and the national/international news coverage. Dr. King's Letter from the Birmingham Jail became famous and often quoted as the moral justification for "good trouble" needed to effect change.

CODE BAPBOMB is set when Dynamite Bob's fellow Klansmen were being investigated for the 16th Street Church bombing, a time that God, gays and guns were political hot potatoes.[53] It was a few years before domestic terrorist Eric Robert Rudolph bombed abortions clinics in Birmingham and Atlanta in addition to bombing a gay night club and Atlanta's Olympic Park. In the play, an old law firm safe contains secrets thought to be long ago buried that may tie the firm's patriarch to the church bombing. CODE BAPBOMB is set in a time when flawed white people knew too much and did little, but were asking for a modicum of righteousness while rationalizing where they were during their time of moral crisis.[54]

THE WISDOM OF BLACK WOMEN

On December 8, 2022, I watched Trevor Noah in his final show as host of The Daily Show on Comedy Central and joined his amen corner when he praised Black women for their abiding wisdom. Four of the five plays included in this collection carry strong Black women characters and their wisdom. In my first two plays Donna Thornton took these characters to heights well beyond my puny writing. (After a performance of WEDGES at TNT, the late Alys Stephens, as in UAB Performing Arts Center and a popular beach community in Florida's Panhandle, took me aside to praise the enormous talent that Donna brought to the character of Sadie.) With the help of her daughters Regina Craig Avery and Rita Craig Rose, and her niece Gail Barlow I hope I have brought depth and understanding to Ruth Craig in WINSTON DRIVES BIG JIM.

I would be remiss if I did not confess how I learned of and grew to appreciate the wisdom of Black women. When my children were young, we lived in a lumbering old house in the Redmont section of Birmingham and we employed an African American housekeeper who doubled as a nanny for the children that I now realize included me. Ruthette Tyler, who we all called Ruth, would time any ironing of the day so she could watch her stories (the Soaps) with my daughter Lauren at her elbow — an education not approved by Lauren's mother. Once, when Lauren was quite young we were driving to the Gulf Beaches (to integrate seafood restaurants in Gulf Shores, AL and Pensacola, FL). Ruth and Lauren were sitting next to each other in the station wagon when I hear Lauren ask Ruth: "Why is my arm pink and your arm brown?" I almost drove the station wagon in a ditch, but as I righted the vehicle, I heard Ruth respond: "Skin pigment." Enough said. And, when Lauren was about ten, it fell my duty to explain slavery to Lauren. We had a policy of trying to be age-appropriate but honest, and all I remember after I finished my explanation was Lauren screaming that slavery was not true. I wish and I don't envy teachers when they address our original sin in our critical race history.

THE PAST IS NOT EVEN PAST

TO KILL A MOCKINGBIRD is set in an Alabama courtroom similar to the courtroom in Mississippi that freed the Klansmen who lynched Emmett Till. THE ALABAMA STORY, a play set in 1959, protests the banning of a book that featured white rabbit marrying a black rabbit. Does MAGA Republican Ginni Thomas and her husband Justice Clarence Thomas come to mind? President Obama's parents? THE ALABAMA STORY claims to be an Alabama cousin of MOCKINGBIRD, with characters inspired by good (and bad) Alabamians. Of course WINSTON DRIVES BIG JIM depicts historical characters and events in Alabama's civil rights history that back-drop both MOCKINGBIRD and STORY.

By choosing plays set in a previous era, one may pick and choose dramatic moments, that tend to prove Mr. Faulkner's adage that the past is now. Charles Dickens concluded: "It's in vain to recall the past, unless it works some influence upon the present."[55] At the end of the first scene in WINSTON DRIVES BIG JIM, after Winston and Big Jim have watched a replay of George Wallace's "Segregation Forever" speech and Wallace's subsequent "Stand in the School House Door," Big Jim laments: "Winston, God help us we already fought one Civil War." When I wrote that line, I could not have imagined the insurrection of January 6, 2021. More recently Georgia Congresswoman Marjorie Taylor Green suggested, "We need a national divorce." One wonders if Ms. Green is fully aware of our previous Civil War (April 12, 1861 – April 9, 1865) and the carnage that pitted my great, great grandfathers against each other. I do recall from my youth that Rome, Georgia, that abuts Alabama and is in Ms. Green's district, was where an underaged couple could get a marriage license.

JIM CROW LIBERALS AND OUR MESSY MIDDLE

I've often wondered what it was about my upbringing including my education that let me escape being a full-blown racist like many of my generation in the South. (On my walks in the Florida sun, I wear a Mission Cooling Scarf so my neck won't get too red.) In my fledging attempt to define (perhaps to make excuses for) "Jim Crow Liberals" I've arrive at the wishy-washy, messy middle that defies a clear and concise definition but where many voters reside. There's an old Texas saying that there is nothing in the middle of the road except white lines and dead armadillos. But does it taste like chicken?

I fancy myself an equal opportunity curmudgeon, fussing at the woke almost as much as I disdain the MAGA crowd. Political extremist may win primaries, but seldom win the general election. For example, on the Democratic side after a hard fought primary sometimes the Bernie Bros rebel by sitting at home while the other side wins. A "what if" example was found in the 2022 midterms in

Colorado's 3rd Congressional District when woke Dems stayed at home rather than vote for a moderate, resulting in our modern-day Annie Oakley, gun-toting, MAGA Republican Lauren Boebert winning by only 546 votes after recount. After her narrow victory, Ms. Boebert's first "legislative" proposal was to permit House members to attend committee meetings fully armed. Will gun fire be the modern substitute for 19th Century Congressional cane-ing? Did 547 ski country elites sit at home in 2022?

More endemic, have the super woke created a generation of non-voting, sit-at-home acolytes? Professor Cornel West with his singsong delivery frequently blasted President Obama for not doing enough for minorities. I could facetiously point out that Obama is half white, but seriously did Dr. West's rants create a generation of hopeless non-voters who watched Trump get elected? Is there a lesson to be learned from Congressman Jim Clyburn's support of moderate Joe Biden in the 2020 South Carolina Democratic Primary?

WHITE SAVIOR

Another Catch 22 presents when Jim Crow Liberals of yore come across as "paternalistic" and never doing enough, e.g. not marching. Did Big Jim Folsom or Atticus Finch wake up one morning and say: "I'm going to go advocate for a minority today because they need help and I'm their benevolent parent, their white savior." Or, perhaps unequal treatment of a citizen ran afoul of Big Jim's concepts of true democracy. Or, maybe Lawyer Finch felt his client deserved a full and vigorous representation in a system that claimed equal justice for all under law.

WHY HISTORY? WHY 1955? WHY GO BACKWARDS?

Presumably the Make American Great Again (MAGA) crowd want to go back to an earlier time although the precise time for their return remains vague. Beyond the fact that some citizens (on both sides) seem only happy when they are angry, the MAGA meme has a substantial racist component. Act Two of WINSTON DRIVES BIG JIM opens in 1955 with Big Jim's 2nd inaugural speech after which Winston Craig tells the Governor that his speech was not as clear on individual rights for Blacks as his 1947 speech had been. What happened? *Brown v. Board of Education of Topeka* happened in 1954 and whites did not want their children mixing with Blacks and risk going to inferior schools that the white power structure had put in place.

AUTOMOBILES WITH TAILFINS

As a newly minted teenager (only six months younger than Emmett Till), 1955 was great for this white boy. I was transitioning from riding my Schwinn around town to learning to drive one of Daddy's nearly new, gently used cars. My childhood and teen years looked like I was suspended in a series of Norman Rockwell paintings: The Cub Scouts, later an Eagle in the Boy Scouts, pretending to hunt squirrels with my pellet gun in the woods where the shopping center is now, catching tadpoles in the creek with a tea strainer, fishing with a cane pole sans the red bandana, picking blackberries while shooing snakes with my bare feet, munching sun ripe tomatoes from Paw Paw's showcase garden, playing football on a ranked high school team and, yes, riding my bike all around Cullman, Alabama. I even had a sprinkling of freckles across my nose and two pairs of blue suede shoes. But, in the 1950s around midday I'd have to come inside and lie down under the window fan, to cool off so I would not catch Polio.

By 1955, World War II rationing was far away in the rearview mirror and Daddy filled the driveway with a new Ford Fairlane and assorted used cars. It was a time, when new automobiles were sprouting tailfins. The homestead of the family who owned the Ford dealership in Cullman was in my neighborhood, just across the street, and in late summer an early demo of next year's (brand spanking new) Ford would be delivered to the Mitchell's garage and "hidden" under a tarp. Of course, it was no problem for neighborhood boys (and sometimes girls) to sneak into the garage and lift the tarp and check out next year's tailfin weeks before the official unveiling. Next year's new model car was a big deal like when Marilyn Monroe visited Ava Marie Grotto at St. Bernard College on the eastern edge of town. Alas, Ford tailfins (or the lack thereof) were always a disappointment especially when compared to Elvis' Cadillac. In grade school when asked what we wanted to be when we grew up, most of us said Governor. Why did we skip past lawyer, doctor, police, firefighter, school teacher, etc.? I now surmise, that in the mid-50s when Big Jim Folsom was at the height of his power, we kids saw a continuous entourage of shinny late model cars parked around the Governor's house across the street from East Elementary.

Obsessed with cars, I was unaware that 130 miles to the south in Montgomery, African Americans were having to walk to work and school in all sorts of weather during their Bus Boycott. It was a time when Big Jim was slipping cash to Winston Craig to pay poll tax for African Americans trying to register to vote.

EDUCATION IS WHERE ONE FINDS IT

It is axiomatic that teenagers are self-absorbed and care little about the world beyond theirs, beyond our driveway filled with cars. Although a provincial education was readily available at the Pure Oil Station and the barbershop, Cullman High School was better than average academically (or so we were told) with a college prep curriculum before it was called "AP." What also became known as STEM was important to us because Sputnik was circling above and Huntsville, Rocket City, was just forty-five miles away. We were going to save the World from the Russians, the USSR, by learning math and science while ducking and covering from the atomic bombs. I facetiously suggest that we didn't bother to duck and cover — no, we practiced yoga. Being equal distance from Rocket City and industrial Birmingham, if the Russians dropped atomic bombs we'd need enough flexibility to kiss our ass goodbye.

Looking toward college, I became obsessed with going to Vanderbilt, but Vandy required a foreign language in high school. Oops! Too much science and math. So, the summer of 1959 before my senior year, I arranged to take Latin 101 at St. Bernard College. One day we were hic, haec, hoc-ing, when in walked an African American student. The monk/professor introduced the new student and explained that he was a pre-seminary student in route to St. Louis, Missouri. I vaguely wondered if his sitting in our all-white class was legal in Cullman, Alabama and/or if we'd be arrested or some such. (I repeat, it was 1959 and I was a teenager.) I also knew the Benedictine monks had an autonomy on their 800 acre campus, so I returned my focus to the hopeless task of learning Latin on an accelerated basis. The Black student, who's name I have long since forgotten, became a friend, and after class we'd go back to his dorm room and he'd try to teach me Latin. He had the advantage of hearing Latin read in church back then and was a good but unsuccessful teacher. So, later when at the barbershop or the Pure Oil Station, I heard the puny theories as to why Blacks should not go to school with white children, I felt like saying that a Colored guy tried to teach me Latin because he was smarter than I and I'm a member of the National Honor Society, Cullman High Chapter. Dante[56] would not approve of my silence while getting a haircut, but the barber had a razor.

DOES HISTORY REPEAT?

In 1848 at the National Democratic Convention in Baltimore, William Lowndes Yancey, Alabama's fire eating slavery advocate, presented a proposed platform with a plank forbidding the federal government from restricting the expansion of slavery in the territories. One hundred years later, almost to the day, in 1948 the Dixiecrats walked out of the National Democratic Convention in Philadelphia, because among other reasons Hubert Humphrey had introduced a civil rights plank in the platform. All of the Mississippi delegation walked out of the Convention and a few in the Alabama delegation, including George Wallace, did not walk out. Later that year the Dixiecrats held their Convention in Birmingham nominating segregationist Strom Thurmond of South Carolina. (At age 100 Senator Thurmond did not seek re-election and MAGA Republican Senator Lindsey Graham inherited his seat.)

To paraphrase Maya Angelou when a racist tells you that he/she is a "racist," believe him/her. Extreme racist make good foil characters but generally they have little depth of character and are best used for cheap laughs. In WATER-IN'HOLE, Buck's modern wife has him wearing French bikini underwear, but when he needed a night out with the boys, Buck mindlessly stumbled into a Klan meeting instead of say a meeting of the Rotary Club.

Our history illustrates the hiccups of racial progress: The Emancipation Proclamation of 1863 freed the slaves but it also spawned the founding of the Ku Klux Klan on Christmas Eve 1865 in Pulaski, Tennessee. Reconstruction ensued but fifty years later in 1915 during the Jim Crow South, a drunken Methodist preacher had a vision of the fiery cross and the "modern" Klan was reborn and celebrated at Stone Mountain, Georgia. Another fifty years later in 1965 President Lyndon Johnson signed the Voting Rights Act. Almost fifty years later the Supreme Court in *Shelby County (Alabama) v. Holder* (2013) gutted the Voting Rights Act.

The beat goes on. In 2022 newly appointed Supreme Court Justice Ketanji Brown Jackson had to lecture lawyers for the State of Alabama who suggested that race could not be considered in undoing Alabama's gerrymandered redistricting plan. At issue in *Merrill v. Milligan* was the gerrymandering of Alabama's 7th Congressional District that covers Alabama's Blackbelt but also manages to snake a hundred plus miles away into Downtown Birmingham. Justice Jackson on oral argument noted that the Civil War Era Amendments (13th, 14th & 15th) to our Constitution were in fact race based. Madam Justice was just sticking to our critical race history, the real version.

In 1963 I registered to vote in the old courthouse in downtown Cullman and was offered an official courthouse flunkey to help me pass my "citizen test" as a prerequisite to voting. I rejected the offer of assistance letting the gentleman know that I was a history and political science major at Alabama's most prestigious academic institution and if I could not pass the test something was amiss. As I recall, the test was awkwardly worded and replete with double negatives or the like and I wondered if my arrogance had been misplaced. But, I was white, passed the test and got to cast a futile vote for Representative Carl Elliot in Alabama's 1964 Democratic primary.

THE MAKING OF A JIM CROW LIBERAL

Alabama's history, specifically as viewed through the eyes of Governor Folsom, became the alpha and omega of these plays. The "Governor" was fictionalized in WEDGES, but over the years Folsom's 1949 Message continued to haunt. Why? 1949? So early for an Alabama politician to call for racial equality? After World War II, a Truman Executive Order followed FDR's lead by desegregating the military, but Big Jim did not support Truman and even considered running against him. Maybe there was a simple explanation: if Blacks fought for freedom on foreign soil in World War II, they should enjoy freedom at home.

Again I wondered, why Big Jim and his Elks Club drinking buddy my father Daddy Hubert were not full-blown racist like many of their fellow white male Alabamians? As a kid, I recalled a favorite Uncle telling me to bury the fact that we had Cherokees in our family tree and just say we were Scot Irish. Scot Irish? What fun was that? I cheered for the "Indians" at the Saturday morning picture show and later in the Brotherhood of the Order of the Arrow in the Boy Scouts, I ordered and assembled a war bonnet kit complete with a full length trail of feathers. And, in the Folsom's den there was a photo of an ancestor who appeared to be Native American. My high school classmate and Big Jim's daughter Melissa said the ancestor was Choctaw. So, I concluded that if one had Indigenous people in one's family tree it was difficult to be a full-blown racist.

Additionally, much of North Alabama was in the foothills of Appalachia, an area that did not lend itself to the sprawl of fertile acreage needed for plantations and the antebellum myth that all Christian white men were land barons who sat on their wrap-around verandas sipping mint juleps while listening to their slaves sing happy ditties in the cotton fields of Dixie. In fact, during the Civil War, Cullman County was part of the "Free State of Winston" that proposed seceding from the Confederacy when Alabama seceded from the Union. Toward the end of the Civil War, my great, great grandfather, the Methodist Preacher Armstead Blevins, swam across the Sipsey River in Winston County and the Tennessee River in route to Nashville to join the First Alabama Calvary, a Union (a/k/a Yankee) fighting force.

Okay, on the same side of my maternal family as the Rev. Blevins, there was my other great, great grandfather Smith who was conscripted into the Confederate army. Beyond wondering what dinnertime conversations were like back then, I've tried to understand the lost cause myth in which one substitutes valor (of the soldier-ancestor) for victory. Alas, honoring this "valor" became a part of Jim Crow when the Daughters of the Confederacy erected their memorials across the South decades after the Civil War. Does the South, albeit fly-over country, still feel this lost cause insult? Do coastal elites talk down to these loser insurrectionist and insult without even knowing it? Do those who are happily angry get even more riled up when they are talked down to by the woke? What do Blacks feel when they walk by one of these public displays that reminds of slavery?

Early in his first term, Governor Folsom had some political setbacks. In 1948 he lost an election to be a delegate to the Democratic Convention in Philadelphia. The "Big Mules" (industrialist, joined by planters and county agents) sponsored recall (impeachment) petitions attacking Governor Folsom at a time when Big Jim had a paternity suit filed against him. ("Love children" out of wedlock back then were thought to be political death nails.) So, by 1949, I concluded that Big Jim had nothing to lose politically when he called for racial equality in his Christmas Message and he probably enjoyed gigging the *status quo* Big Mules. But, wait, there had to be more.

Daddy, a railroad union man, and Big Jim were FDR New Deal Democrats again not the loudest voices in white Alabama after *Brown v. Board of Education*. Politically, as a ten year old I came home from East Elementary one day and announced, "I like Ike!" Daddy let me know in no uncertain terms that we belonged to the other political party and I silently felt my supper to be in jeopardy. The tribe had spoken and I couldn't even spell "Adlai." Years later I concluded that I liked alliterations more than political affiliations. Being a Mickey Mantle Yankees' fan in North Alabama presented an additional set of problems but that's another story.

After the tribe spoke, I became at age ten a Yellow Dog Democrat. Forget the red and blue hues of today, back then a FDR Democrat would vote for a yellow dog before he/she would vote for a Hoover Republican. FDR's (TVA) electricity and Big Jim's paved farm-to-market roads brought rural North Alabama into the 20th Century.

And, back then it was easy to be a Democrat in Alabama because there were no significant number of Republicans. President Eisenhower had to look long and hard to find a Republican to appoint to the federal bench; however, our history is blessed that he found and nominated Winston County Republican Frank M.

Johnson, Jr., who became a constitutional champion of the emerging Civil Rights Movement, desegregating the busses of Montgomery in 1956 and after Bloody Sunday ordering the voting rights march to continue from Selma to Montgomery in 1965.

THE PROGRESSIVE SOUTH?

When and why did the "progressive movement" start in the South? In addition to the New Deal, World War II helped get Alabama out of the Depression. But, my Democratic heroes Justice Hugo Back and Governor Bibb Graves, both Alabamians, were Klansmen in the 1920s when President Woodrow Wilson was showing BIRTH OF THE NATION in the White House and thousands of Klansmen were marching down Pennsylvania Avenue. Of course, President Franklin D. Roosevelt (possibly nudged by the First Lady) encouraged Justice Black to renounce the Klan in a fireside chat when FDR appointed Justice Black to the Supreme Court. Later in the mid-1950s, Justice Black signed with the unanimous Court in *Brown v. Board of Education*. Thereafter, Justice Black was no longer welcomed in Alabama. As a college student, I learned that Justice Black was not invited to a cocktail party of Alabama lawyers because of his liberal ways. Cocktail parties were all too important to me back then, but as an academic offshoot I began to admire Justice Black for his simple reading of the Constitution especially his absolutist approach to the First Amendment and his stand on racial equality.

Until recently, I knew little of Alabama Governor Bibb Graves. But, in researching and writing WINSTON DRIVES BIG JIM, I learned that Winston Craig and Big Jim Folsom had a "conceit" that is, when Big Jim needed racially progressive advice from Winston, Big Jim would ask, "What would Governor Bibb Graves do?"[57] Why would Winston summarize racially progressive advice from a Klansman? I tried to connect the dots: In 1928 Governor Graves renounced the Klan and in 1938 Governor Graves with other progressives politicians, including Senator Peppers of Florida, held an interracial meeting of the Southern Conference for Human Welfare in Birmingham. As is recalled in WINSTON DRIVES BIG JIM, Bull Connor tried to break up the meeting and make the races separate citing a local Jim Crow law. After the Blacks and whites were required to sit on opposite sides in the Municipal Auditorium, First Lady Eleanor Roosevelt sat squarely in the middle of the center aisle with a corsage sprawled over her left shoulder. Apparently, Bull knew his limits and did not mess with the First Lady.

To repeat, this was 1938 and First Lady (later United Nations Ambassador) Eleanor Roosevelt was bending the moral arc of justice while sitting in the middle of an interracial meeting in downtown Birmingham.

Recently, Governor Graves name was removed from the Education Building at the University of Alabama, Tuscaloosa, with the building renamed "Autherine Lucy Hall" after an African American educator who first tried to integrate the University in 1956 and who makes an off-stage appearance in WINSTON DRIVES BIG JIM. While I applaud this renaming of the Education Building, at the same time I am heart-sick that most news snippets about the renaming recalled only that Governor Graves was a Klansman, with nary a mention that he resigned from the Klan in 1928 and set up the interracial Human Welfare meeting in Birmingham in 1938. Not all is lost, when the State of Alabama gets around to removing George Wallace's name from the plethora of buildings, public structures and institutions because of his racism, I will not begrudge mention of Wallace's staying in the 1948 Convention as a loyal Democrat when the Dixiecrats walked out and his late-in-life apology to Blacks when he was wheeled into the Dexter Avenue Baptist Church in Montgomery. Age and the assassination attempt caught up with Wallace. The last time I saw him was at a lawyer meeting in downtown Birmingham. I was getting off an elevator and almost bumped into his wheelchair where Wallace sat small and slumped with a sad, lost, far-off, glassy-eyed stare.

CULLMAN, ALABAMA

In the late 1930s a few years before I was born, my Mama Gracie, recalled that the congregation of the First (United) Methodist Church of Cullman, Alabama invited African American Methodist from the Colony (near Arkadelphia and Hanceville) Cullman County, to a joint worship service. Mother also recalled that a banker and the editor of the weekly walked out of the church meeting. Otherwise, my family and the rest of the congregation stayed to worship.

And there was the sundown sign in mostly all-white, German-settled Cullman: "N**** Don't Let the Sun Set on You Here!" Note I said mostly all-white; there were a few African Americans who lived in the City of Cullman. In the 1950s, I had a playmate Joe Lewis, who was African American, and his mother worked for the judge's family giving them a form of immunity, I suppose. Joe Lewis was tutored in the morning by the church ladies and spent early afternoon inventing clubs, e.g., daredevil bicycling, weightlifting, guitar/rockin' roll, clubs that we white boys would try to join when we got out of East Elementary around

3 pm. Concerned and curious, I asked my grandfather Hembree, about that sign. Paw Paw employed the Socratic method by suggesting that I rode my bike all over town and asked if I'd ever seen that sign? I surmised that because I'd never seen the sign, perhaps it did not exist. And, my sister Jenny Folsom recalls asking Mother about the sign. Mother suggested that maybe there was just a hand-lettered sign in the yard of a "low life" on the outskirts of town. (Mother would not have use the term "low life" but the inflection in her voice and placing the sign on the outskirts of town would communicate such.) To this day town folks of Cullman deny that the sundown sign existed. But, when I mentioned that I grew up in Cullman to a blind African American masseur at the Birmingham YMCA, he elevated his voice in disapproval letting me know the sign was quite vivid to him.

Beyond our neighborhood, Cullman had a strong Klan presence "on the outskirts of town," even one of the main Klan bosses, a wizard or some such, lived in Cullman. An elementary school chum's parents hired an African American domestic couple and promptly got a Klan cross burned in their yard. The couple left town.

OUR FAMILY'S BLACK SAVIOR

Years later, I asked Daddy why given the times we were not racist and why he helped Blacks buy shoes and move up on the railroad? Daddy said that when he had severe back trouble a Black brakeman help him with his heavy lifting, recalling for me the image of Daddy's metal back brace that resided for years in the attic and resembled a medieval torture device. Later recalling the heavy-lifting story to my sister, she added that Daddy's back trouble was so severe that the brakeman had to lift Daddy on to the caboose so Daddy could keep his job. That railroad paycheck paid a lot of tuition for my sister (Dr. Jenny) and me.

So, an African American brakeman on the L & N Railroad was our family's Black savior, but if I give full rein to my contrived woke-ness, I can look down on the white savior characters in my plays, especially Governor Big Jim Folsom, as not doing enough — not marching for civil rights to borrow an ultimate test. I thought of apologizing more dramatically by burying these plays, but LINCOLN, TWELVE YEARS A SLAVE and TO KILL A MOCKINBIRD are also panned by the extremely woke as featuring white saviors. In the same breath that President Obama suggested flawed people do good stuff, he was critical of this remote righteousness — it's too easy! Democratic advisor Jim Messina suggested that it is easier for the woke to Tweet than it is for them to "door knock."

WOKE-NESS?

I eat avocado toast, sometimes order a latte at Starbucks and arugula is a go-to salad green, so why am I down on woke-ness. Even worse, the current Governor of Florida has denigrated the term with his Stop Woke Campaign (own the Libs) as he bans books, yells at COVID masked school children, flies Latin American asylum seekers to Martha's Vineyard, defunds diversity, equity, inclusion programs and curricula in Florida schools. In his 2023 second term inaugural address flanked by flags and the candy-striped awnings of the Capitol, DeSantis proclaimed: "Florida is where woke goes to die."

As an Alabama ex-pat in Florida, when I listen to Governor DeSantis today, all I hear is George Wallace in his run for president in 1968 shouting at hippies to get a haircut and a job, in that order. Much like Senator Joseph McCarthy of the early 1950s, DeSantis denies that he is burning books[58] as he courts the MAGA base. But during 2023's Black History Month officials of the Duval (Jacksonville) County, Florida saw fit to remove kids' books about Black athletes, including Hank Aaron, Jackie Robinson, Roberto Clemente and Jim Thorpe, because those books might contain objectionable material.[59] Apparently, the history of athletes encountering racism in Jim Crow America as they rose in the pro ranks is too much for Florida children.

The beat goes on: May 2023, a Miami Lakes, Florida school banned *The Hill We Climb* that was read at the inauguration of Joe Biden by Amanda Gorman, our National Youth Poet Laureate. The ban was the result of one complaining parent who thought that the mention of slavery was "hateful" and erroneously thought Oprah Winfrey had published the book. The school "defended" its decision suggesting that it was only banned for elementary students, ironically, the intended audience.

The Governor's stop "woke" campaign also extends to higher education and in particular New College Sarasota that was founded on diversity and a free thinking liberal arts environment. DeSantis solved the "problem" of New College by loading its Board of Trustees with Christian conservatives, removing its president and appointing a Republican politician President at a premium salary.

In a failed attempt to be open-minded, I bought a copy DeSantis' bestselling, *The Courage to Be Free*, and learned that the Governor had a higher batting average while playing baseball at Yale than did President George H.W. Bush also an Eli rounder. While at Yale, DeSantis was most concerned about his fellow classmates who waved Russian flags, cheered for Che Guevara and supported the Soviets in the Cold War that ended a decade before DeSantis entered Yale with his limousine liberal classmates. The Governor's Soviet/Russian knowledge is not wasted, because under his leadership the 2023 Florida Legislature borrowing from Putin's playbook introduced a bill that would require bloggers who write about the Governor to register with the state or face a $25 per day fine.[60] I guess they did not teach irony at Yale in the late '90s or DeSantis was too busy with baseball and missed that class.

Permit me to reverse a cliché: "Keep your enemies (MAGA) close and your friends (woke) closer." While MAGA Republicans pander to their base, the extreme woke does their part in alienating middle Americans. One pundit suggested that the Democratic Party has a voice in Berkley, California and a voice in Cambridge, Massachusetts that are hell bent on giving MAGA Republicans ammo (in the form of bumper stickers) to use against moderate Democrats.

DEFUND THE POLICE? OR, THE DEATH OF WOKE?

Former Congresswoman and incoming Los Angeles Mayor, Karen Bass said "Defund the Police" was the worse slogan ever. In her unsuccessful 2022 run for Senate, Florida Congresswoman Val Demings (a former police chief in Orlando) was forced to disavow her fellow Democrats who would "defund" the police. After the 2023 murder of Tyre Nichols in Memphis there were renewed calls for police accountability and retraining.

Camden, New Jersey is credited with the origin of "defund the police" when it reorganized its public safety department by requiring cops to retrain, undergo psychological testing and reapply. This process got rid of the union that represented bad cops and resulted in a drop in crime, increased surveillance and produced a larger "police force" after the reorganization. Unfortunately "reorganization and retraining" is not catchy enough for a bumper sticker.

Back in the '60s Senator Barry Goldwater did not fare too well when he proclaimed "that extremism in the defense of liberty is no vice." But today extremism seems to be vogue on both sides and keeps the happily angry in business.

Recently, W. Kamau Bell in his CNN special United Shades of American traced the origin of "woke" to the Scottsboro Boys in a song by Huddie William (Lead Belly) Ledbetter that admonished African Americans to be "woke" when traveling through Alabama. In a Netflix special comedian Bill Burr suggested that white liberals accidentally heard Blacks using "woke" at a cocktail party and adopted it as politically correct therefore chic. Hence "woke" knows no limits and has migrated to the faculty lounge, corporate sensitive experts, moral gatekeepers of movies and other righteous censors. Recently, some progressive Dems finally caught on and declared "woke" passé especially when comedians make fun of them (us). Perhaps "woke" should be labeled "fake news"?

Just as I was editing my "woke rant"[61] worrying who in the MAGA crowd might consider me an ally, on February 15, 2023 (near the ides of Black History Month) the Reverend Al Sharpton appeared in Tallahassee to protest the Stop Woke Campaign suggesting that DeSantis was a racist and he was substituting "woke" for the "N-word." Then to my chagrin Rev. Al proudly proclaimed himself to be "Woke!" No. No. Not another bumper sticker. Then, I thought that "woke" had become so tortured that it had lost all meaning and perhaps Rev. Al was facetiously (as in passive aggressively) going back to the Alabama origin of the term, warning Blacks to be careful when traveling through Florida. Will DeSantis' stop-woke policy make Blacks uncomfortable when traveling in the Sunshine State? Will it create less woke tourist at woke Disney? Will DeSantis' admonishment help keep Florida beaches sugar white? A possible downside might prevent Florida colleges and universities from recruiting top tier professors and athletes. In the 2023 Session of the Florida Legislature bill HB 999 would permit the Board of Trustees (the "Donor Class") of Florida's colleges and universities to review tenured professors and presumably rid those institutions of the "woke." Forget top tier professors avoiding Florida, but top tier athletes are serious business. Here Florida coaches will need to take a lesson from Alabama Coaches Sabin and Bryant, who did/do not let race-baited politics interfere with their recruiting. Perhaps a new Florida bumper sticker should read: "Woke Okay, If You Play Ball!"

Okay, I was sarcastic — even self-amused — when I wrote the previous warning, but subsequently — as if on cue — the NAACP issued a Florida Travel Warning to African Americans citing the state's Culture Wars under Governor "Courage-to-Be-Free" DeSantis, who wants to Make America Florida where woke goes to die. Are red hats biodegradable?

GLADWELLIAN REMOTE RIGHTEOUSNESS

An early example of this cancel culture woke-ness was Malcom Gladwell writing in *The New Yorker* (August 3, 2009) when he concluded that the fictionalized Atticus Finch and the real Governor Big Jim Folsom were "just a part of the old southern courthouse crowd" albeit racists. Kudos to Mr. Gladwell who mined race history for his limited (erudite) purpose and pointed out the obvious short comings (flaws) of two Jim Crow Liberals. Chris Rock might call this "selective outrage." But, it seems useless to argue with superficial, point-and-click journalism and others have done better job of putting Mr. Gladwell in his place than

I could even with my teach-a-pig-to-sing metaphor. (See; "What Is Malcolm Talking About?" Isaac Chotiner, *The New Republic*, August 4, 2009.)

Was Atticus Finch inspired by Big Jim Folsom as some suggest? It's possible given the time of Nelle Harper Lee's Alabama years. In GO SET A WATCHMAN Atticus Finch attended and/or helped organize a White Citizen Council meeting. On first reading of WATCHMAN my bias rationalized that Atticus, a hero to many southern lawyers, attended the White Citizens Council meeting to make sure the fact-challenged racists did not lynch someone? More recently, I learned that Ms. Lee's father lawyer A.C. Lee once ran an integrationist preacher out of the Monroeville Methodist Church. (I doubt they were having a theological dispute over the Trinity.) Presumably, Ms. Lee's fiction imbued her father character(s) with values — some noble, some not — that changed from manuscript to manuscript and was based on the Alabama she lived in before moving to New York City. After the success of MOCKINGBIRD, Ms. Lee chose not to publish WATCHMAN during the bulk of her remaining lifetime and WATCHMAN was only "discovered" when Ms. Lee was elderly and frail with the economic value obvious to her caretakers. To repeat both Ms. Lee's books were fiction.

THE PARADOX OF JESSE HILL FORD

As I look at critical race history, I wish all my heroes, my fellow Jim Crow Liberals, had been pure back then, but they/we were not. A personal example is author Jesse Hill Ford with whom I had the privilege of studying fictive writing during an academic year at UAB in the late 1970s. Although Jesse studied under the Fugitives and Southern Agrarians at Vanderbilt and the University of Florida, Jesse was an early pragmatic writer of race relations in his beloved South and was hailed by some as the next Faulkner. His best-selling novel THE LIBERATION OF LORD BYRON JONES (An Atlantic Monthly Press Book, Little Brown and Company, 1964) was made into a movie with Roscoe Lee Browne and Lee J. Cobb, and depicted the range of southern personalities — from a starry-eyed progressive to an old white southerner to a wealthy African American in need of a proper divorce — in a small town coming to grips with itself in a changing South.

As a theatrical aside, Jesse also had some acclaim as a playwright. With encouragement from playwright William Inge, Jesse wrote a play with the TV script produced by CBS. THE CONVERSION OF BUSTER DRUMWRIGHT, the Television and Stage Script (1964 Vanderbilt University Press). The play depicted white Christian fundamentalist in the mountains of East Tennessee and while on a Fulbright Scholarship in Oslo, Norway, Jesse extended the play for the stage.

Much later, during the 1982 World's Fair DRUMWRIGHT was staged in Knoxville as a musical.

After much literary success in the '60s, Jesse's world crumbled when on a November night in 1970 he went out to his front yard, shot and killed George H. Doaks, a 21-year-old African American Viet Nam vet. In writing for *Life Magazine* (October 29, 1971) Marshall Frady summarized: "A tormented southern novelist kills a Blackman and is consumed by the demons his works deplore."

Jesse Ford was born in Troy, Alabama, and during his days in Birmingham in the late 1970s he was more than a teacher; we became good friends and I sometimes called him my surrogate brother. During a long, late night drive from Montgomery to Birmingham, and in a tone that was both pensive and sorrowful Jesse volunteered his recall of the night he shot Mr. Doaks. (No thoughts nor prayers nor anything that I may say will take away from the tragic death of Mr. Doaks and the loss to his family and friends.)

This is a personal recall. December in the late '70s, Jesse and I attended an advisory board meeting of the Alabama Film Office and later we had dinner with Rachael Folsom Lichtenstein (Big Jim's oldest) at the Elite Café when it was in downtown Montgomery. During dinner Jesse excused himself to go outside to a watch a holiday parade and to cheer the bands, floats and scout troops as they passed by.

That night after we said goodbye to Rachael, I drove us back to Birmingham. Perhaps it was melancholy and missing all that is good and innocent about a holiday parade, but on that drive Jesse volunteered his recall of the night he shot Mr. Doaks.

In the fall of 1970 the schools of Humboldt, Tennessee integrated where Jesse's son Charles was a football star and captain of the team. Just before homecoming the Blacks on the team missed a practice or violated curfew or some other rule and were suspended from the team, upsetting the Black community. As a result in the homecoming parade on Friday the 13th the convertible Charles Ford was riding in got stoned by some Blacks. To further set the scene, Jesse's foray into Hollywood provided ample cash for he and his then wife Sally to build their dream house at the end of a very long driveway. Local whites were already upset with Jesse's liberal novel turned Hollywood movie and those whites had been making threatening phone calls to the Fords' residence. After the Blacks were suspended from the football team, Blacks joined the chorus of threatening phone calls to the Fords' big house. So, at the end of that long driveway in the deep woods there was Jesse, the proverbial "one man island" with a family to protect.

Jesse's habits back then included getting up before dawn to write, which had him in bed early. So he was in bed around 10 pm on that November 16th night a few days after the parade when Jesse saw unexpected car lights lick his bedroom ceiling. He got his gun went to his front yard and seeing a car fired a warning shot and after seeing movement in the car shot and killed Mr. Doaks. Jesse in that moment felt his first shot was to detain the car until the law enforcement could arrive, but then he felt threatened by movement in the car. At his trial for murder, Jesse maintained the shooting was an accident and according to reports pander to the all-white jury of Humboldt, Tennessee. Jesse was found not guilty of murder.

Perhaps it is a stretch to list Jesse in my attempt to define Jim Crow Liberals, especially since his later op-ed writings for *USA Today* frequently had a conservative bent. In the early days of *USA Today*, Jesse's friend and journalist John Seigenthaler hired Jesse to write an opposing view to various editorials that usually left Jesse with only a conservative alternative. For me Jesse's writings for *USA Today* were sad on many levels including that it may have been a sympathy hire after Jesse's career plummeted and his opinions were dictated as if he were a hack writer.

On June 1, 1996, Jesse shot and killed himself a month or so after his open heart surgery. The late Professor Ann Chaney, his biographer, concluded for his *New York Times* obit on June 5 that after Jesse shot Mr. Doaks he struggled to finish his last novel THE RAIDER and never published another novel. After Jesse's memorial in Nashville, Ann, a good friend and college classmate, shared with me that when Jesse shot himself her recently published book THE LIFE AND LETTERS OF JESSE HILL FORD, SOUTHERN WRITER (1996 The Edwin Mellen Press) was nearby. We surmised that at the time of his death, Jesse may have been reading about his literary accomplishments and what could have been.

IMPERFECTIONS IN A SMALL WORLD THAT'S NOT LIMITED TO THE SOUTH

The world of Jim Crow Liberals was small and imperfections plentiful. In 1962, when Big Jim Folsom was running against George Wallace for governor, the Wallace billboards reminded the voters that during his second term Big Jim entertained Negro Congressman Adam Clayton Powel of New York in the Alabama Governor's Mansion. Such was true and in 1955 while visiting Alabama, Congressman Powell said that he would not have been invited to the New York Governor's Mansion for cocktails nor would he have been chauffeured in a New

York State owned car. When running for governor and pandering to his white base, Big Jim became a master of deflection that many of us found humorous. During his 1962 stump speeches Big Jim would acknowledge the "rumor" that he drank scotch whiskey on the front porch of the governor's mansion with Congressman Powell, but he would provide a counter slant by clearly stating to the crowd that his well-known personal habit was to drink only cheap rot-gut corn whiskey on the back porch. That was enough information for his white Alabama voters who applauded his alternative slant.

In 1963 when Dr. King came to Kelly Ingram Park in Birmingham, CBS News came to Birmingham-Southern College and filmed students and our opinions. At that time BSC had students who sat in at lunch counters with Blacks, but we also had our share of racists, with one pre-preach commuter student suggesting to the CBS cameras that black and white chickens did not mix in the barnyard, an early alternative "fact." During the CBS filming, I specifically recall a fraternity brother from the Queens, New York, pointing out that the boroughs of NYC had clear racial demarcation lines. Without justifying our Jim Crow South, I recalled Tony's comments to CBS News when months later Harlem burned. I understand when these characters of yore find one foot on the boat and one foot on the dock. One may love a place and the complexity of its characters without loving its prevailing politics.

THE N-WORD

This same dichotomy is true for use of the N-word. My upbringing did not permit me to use the word, although it was/is ubiquitous among many in the South. This usage was especially true among the "low-lifes" who in the words of LBJ yearn for someone to look down on. In the 1970s, I began to hear the N-word uttered among Black basketball players and Black comedians. To repeat, I knew that white folks should not use the word. Then, I read a "modern" short story by a white southern writer Barry Hannah who used the N-word not as a direct quote but to set a redneck tone. What are/were literary permissions, obligations? In WATERIN'HOLE I used a range of words to refer to Blacks to set a blue-collar, barroom tone/confusion in late 1950s Alabama. Back then the preference for a proper word to refer to an African American seemed to change as frequently as railroad workers changed their bib overalls. In fact, the main character describes himself as a "Nigger-lover" a fact that appeared to my chagrin in the heading of WATERIN'HOLE's review in *The Birmingham News*.

When WINSTON DRIVES BIG JIM was read at Jacksonville State University, I was asked to remove the N-word from the script. After the producing faculty heard me expand on my Endnote that the N-words used in the script were direct quotes from newspapers, Klansmen and politicians of the era, including George Wallace and *The Montgomery Advertiser*, I removed the N-word for the reading at JSU except when Winston gets angry after the castration of Judge Aaron. I rationalized without much personal conviction that if the University were protecting fragile, under-aged students and audience members, I would defer to its wishes. Then after the readings at JSU one of the young African American actors, shared with me that her aunt who had gone to a historically Black college was insistent that the family always use "Negro" in the full name of the aunt's college. I was honored that the young actor felt comfortable sharing her aunt's admonition with me and I concluded anecdotally that the student was not threatened by a word and was more interested in the history of the era, a critical race history her aunt lived through. Additionally, I surmised that the requested change asking for the deletion of the N-word came from the "faculty lounge" and not from the actors, who by definition seek drama. I shouldn't fault professors in the faculty lounge too much, because a half dozen fragile students in need of a safe place and a couple of helicopter parents can make the professors miserable. See, profiles in courage discussed below.

FREE STATE OF WINSTON

Although I was born and reared in Alabama, I am "woke" (as in aware) when I return to visit and especially when getting a haircut.[62] All aged white male Alabamian look like the friends and classmates I played high school football with in the late '50s. I have a hard time imagining them as MAGA Republicans, but polls suggest that some may be. A few years ago, the Mayor of Hanceville, Alabama, a hamlet in south Cullman County that was historically within the Free State of Winston, announced that his town would welcome all the unwanted Confederate statues that were being taken down across the South. But, what about the Free State of Winston? My ancestors? Still standing in front of the Double Springs, Winston County, Alabama Courthouse there is dual destiny statue, a ubiquitous Civil War soldier carrying both flags, the Stars and Stripes and the Stars and Bar. According to that memorial, more Winston County citizens/soldiers fought for the Union than fought for the Confederacy. Beyond whatever emotion it evokes, the Double Springs statue more accurately describes my family's (and Hanceville's) critical Civil War history. I'm sure the Mayor of Hanceville will tell me to go pee up a rope, because Alabama's current Fourth Congressional District that includes, Hanceville, Cullman and Winston County voted 81% for Trump in the 2020 election, the highest percentage for Trump nationwide. Trump even held a rally in a bucolic Cullman pasture.

THE PARTY OF LINCOLN?

What happened to the Republican Party beyond Trump's takeover? In WINSTON DRIVES BIG JIM, the Governor asks Ruth Craig if she still voted with the party of Lincoln? During the time of these plays, the two political parties performed a switcheroo as far as race relations were concerned. When LBJ signed the Civil Rights Act of 1964 he acknowledged that the Democratic Party would lose the South for a generation. (Make that at least two generations and still counting.) This did not escape Richard Nixon who expanded his "southern strategy" permitting the Republican Party to lap up, *inter alia*, the old Dixiecrats. Now that Alabama and Florida are ruby red, we know where the old Dixiecrats and their descendant tribes reside. (My chiding MAGA Republicans is at best superficial, but for a more in depth analysis featuring the MAGA Auburn Alum Caroline Wren I recommend Tim Miller's *WHY WE DID IT, A Travelogue from the Republican Road to Hell*, Harper Collins Publishers 2022.)

Flip flopping seemed the indoor sport for Alabama politicians. For example, in his early career George Wallace was a loyal Democrat but when he lost a bid for Governor to John Patterson in 1958, Wallace proclaimed that he would not be "out seg-ged" again. Wallace was true to his word and in his 1963 inauguration speech he proclaimed "segregation forever." Recently retired Senator Richard Shelby of Alabama started out as a Democrat then switched parties, the aforementioned trend for pols wishing to play it safe.

PROFILES IN COURAGE

In commenting on Liz Cheney's precarious future in the MAGA Republican Party, a pundit noted that *Profiles in Courage* was indeed a thin volume. I brag that my first Congressman Carl Elliot of Alabama's old 7th Congressional District was the first recipient of the Kennedy family's profile in courage honor. After the 1960 Census when Alabama lost a congressional seat, the state didn't bother to redistrict and congressional seats were subject to a statewide, at-large vote. Congressman Elliot survived the 1962 statewide vote as a Democrat, but in 1964 he lost in the George Wallace controlled statewide Democratic primary. Representative Elliot had championed education reform and was Chair of the powerful House Ways and Means, making him Alabama's most powerful congressman. But Congressman Elliot did not kiss the ring nor the backside of Wallace. In 1964, Alabama's congressional delegation went from eight Democrats to five Republicans and only three Democrats.

Déjà vu. More recently, Alabama unelected progressive Democratic Senator Doug Jones, substituting an old Auburn football coach, another industrial-strength MAGA Republican, who could not correctly name the three branches of our federal government. While speaking to a 2022 MAGA rally in Nevada, Senator/Coach Tommy Tuberville equated descendants of enslaved people to criminals. I almost went to Auburn and had a great admiration for its football coaches, but coaches have their limits and should stay on the gridiron between their hash marks. I'll skip the ironic racism in Georgia where the MAGA Republicans (with Trump's recommendation) ran football great Herschel Walker for Senate.

THE GIFT OF EDUCATION, IN THE CLASSROOM AND ELSEWHERE

My quest to define "Jim Crow Liberal" cannot be separated from the gift of education. After giving up on learning Latin, I returned to Cullman High School for my senior year took journalism, drama and speech, and recall debating a classmate in which I took the position that the Pope would not control the USA if John F. Kennedy, a Roman Catholic, were elected president. In the spring of 1960 our senior government class took a trip to Washington D.C. Beyond visiting all three branches of government, Mount Vernon and learning where we could sneak a beer, I notice that the high school students of our nation were divided into two camps, that is, if one were from the South one bought a rebel hat and from the North a union hat. A few years ago I came across the wide angle photo of my senior class in front of the U.S. Capitol and none of us were wearing a Civil War era hat. I don't know if the hats were too expensive, if our history too complex or if the chaperons had us remove the hats for the photo, but the photo looks nice for history.

I entered Birmingham-Southern College in the fall of 1960 when students were swallowing gold fish and stuffing telephone booths in addition to drinking beer at the Tide & Tiger down by Legion Field. For my first political science paper I chose to write about the John Birch Society and concluded that they sounded patriotic to me. My grade was lacking and my superficial approach pointed out. Academically, things got better, I became the editor of the yearbook ironically and/or appropriately named *The Southern Accent*, and in that capacity I became a "student leader." One such duty included attending a leadership retreat at Camp Cosby on the eastern end of Birmingham to discuss if freshmen should be required to wear beanies in school colors and in the name of school spirit. I recall being cynical enough to ask if little propellers should be attached to the top of the beanie? Wearing the beanies became optional.

Then it happened: That spring of 1963 returning from that silly student leadership retreat and traveling west to campus through downtown Birmingham I saw sprays from fire hoses cannoning above Kelly Ingram Park and thought it to be a carnival, perhaps a celebration. Afterwards I became aware of Dr. King's protest. That spring two fellow students sat in at the Tutwiler Hotel Lunch Counter with Blacks, and a series of underground mimeographed newspapers cropped up on campus calling for integration.

As background, the Board of Trustees of Birmingham-Southern College every now and then goof in selecting a president for the college and such was true my senior year. In turn the new president selected a "Student Advisory Committee," fed us a thin dinner steak, did not ask for advice and put us on stage as a backdrop when he advised the student body against demonstrating for racial justice. Perhaps I was sluggish from the steak dinner, and we were told that the Klan had the campus under surveillance. The president seemed worried about our safety and his *parentis locus* obligations. I was slow to learn that we were being duped. That year *Quad* the literary magazine was censored by the faculty because two short stories selected for publication suggested interracial sex. I used my "student leader" status to join with the editor of the weekly newspaper and protest the censorship of *Quad*. Our protest to the dean in charge of publications fell on deaf ears and the editor of *Quad* refused to publish without the two stories. That fall of 1963 College Theatre produced an absurd farce ONE WAY PENDULUM by N.F. Simpson.

No one thought to censor the yearbook. In the introduction to *The 1964 Southern Accent* our copy editor Howell Raines noted that in the spring of 1963 ten blocks from campus America changed when "hundred-year-old adversaries (met) in Kelly Ingram's park" and on November 22, 1963, President Kennedy was killed.[63] Howell's introduction was prophetic, so none of us were surprised that he became a major writer of our history winning a Pulitzer Prize for "Grady's Gift" (*New York Times Magazine* December 1, 1991) that recalled his formative years in Birmingham and lessons learned from his family's housekeeper, Grady Hutchinson. In our yearbook, black and white photos followed the theme of change in a blue-collar industrial city that did not always appreciate academia. Later I learned that several of us on the yearbook staff got credit for the anonymous underground newspapers calling for integration. I wish, but speaking for myself, I was too busy meeting yearbook deadlines. I do recall my favorite philosophy professor who looked like Socrates letting me know he was pissed at the contents of the yearbook. I did not pause to ask why? At graduation I gave our new college president a shit eating grin as he handed me my diploma and my family wanted to know why the college choir laughed.

In the summer of 1964 I took the money I got for graduation to buy an electric typewriter so I could rapidly type my law school notes and went to Washington D.C. I was in a tunnel under the Capitol when the House passed the 1964 Civil Rights Act after Senator Dirksen's amendments. Applause broke out. Later that summer a college friend and I investigated a "write-in" campaign for LBJ electors in Alabama because the "Democratic" electors were pledged to George Wallace under the white rooster, a segregation symbol. Then, September 1964 arrived and my college friend and I went out-of-state to graduate schools.

My first roommate in law school was from Washington State that enjoyed a true democracy back then, but I could regale for hours with stories from Alabama, its politics and its lack of democracy under George Wallace. On cue, that fall Wallace came to Durham, North Carolina for a White Citizens Council meeting that I attended with an integrated group of students from the Divinity School. Wallace thinly masked his racism with calls for states' rights and bellyached about the encroachment of the federal government. After his talk I went back stage to say hello to the Governor and tell him I was from Cullman. He mentioned he had recently attended the Cullman County Fair and wished me well in my studies. To this day, I don't know why I felt a need to say hello to Wallace. Keep your enemies close while giving them a shit eating grin? Maybe it was just that Alabamians greet each other on foreign soil? Perhaps I wanted him to know that I was with the integrated group of students? Or maybe, I was a little homesick for Alabama and law school had become difficult and a little scary? That same fall of 1964, I remember going to the Raleigh-Durham Airport and leaning over the waist-high chain-length fence to shake the hands with LBJ as he ran for a full term. On November 13, 1964, I was lucky to get a seat inside Page Auditorium at Duke to hear Dr. King speak, after which he received a standing ovation. I remember being slow to stand and applaud, as I always am with standing ovations thinking I should fully analyze the event's merit before standing and worrying what others might think if my standing were too zealous. But then I stood and it felt good. A month later Dr. King accepted the Nobel Peace Prize and his legacy immortal with younger generations knowing Dr. King to be a holiday, a monument and the name of an important boulevard in town.

The last time I saw Bull Connor I was home from law school on break and the Bull was on the streets of Cullman trying to find someone to talk to. I said hello letting him know I was going to law school out-of-state and that I was in college during his reign as Public Safety Commissioner, which translated that I may have been one of those Birmingham-Southern integrationist, a/k/a commies. There are no monuments to Bull in need of removal — the black and white photos of his police dogs and fire hoses have said enough for his legacy.

Rounding out my academic recall, while in law school the range of speakers included Stokely Carmichael, a leader of the Black Power movement, and Richmond Flowers, Sr. an Alabama Attorney General who opposed Wallace's racial segregation. And, I boycotted Richard Nixon's speech in the spring of 1967, when he returned to his law school as he resurrected his political career. I wish my boycott had been politically savvy, but it was not. Tricky Dick's speech was on a Saturday afternoon and after our Saturday morning classes, it was pitcher of beer time at the Ivy Room.

JIM CROW LIBERAL

After some soul searching and head scratching my best definition of a "Jim Crow Liberal" is a southerner who with a tinge of moral fiber sometimes did good, bending the arc of justice ever so slightly, but at times flawed by choosing his/her battles while living among the locals. Moments of good are far from perfect. Most Jim Crow Liberals did not march, but among the more distasteful quality of this wish-washy middle is that frequently our silence meant assent, when it just meant we were tired of lost causes — teaching a pig to sing.

Thanks for indulging me. Perhaps this recall, this history has been more cathartic for me than helpful to you. I wish we were all perfect but we're not. Flawed but with some good? This complexity has built-in conflicts, with, I hope, a cautionary note for the future while presenting compelling characters who need untangling. Put our messy democracy on stage. The past is now?[64] Teach a future generation, so they won't feel obligated to follow their angriest ancestor, the loudest voice at holiday dinners. Perchance the new gens will be free to find their own voices and vote!

ENDNOTES

THESE NOTES ARE AT BEST RANDOM, because halfway through the rewrites of WINSTON DRIVES BIG JIM (cira 2018) I realized that the events depicted in these plays came from many sources, e.g. published accounts, Folsom family lore, personal interviews and the like. I started adding Endnotes lest I forget the source. Historical context was always a goal, for example, when literary license is taken within private moments the characters are influenced by external historical events that I try to get correct as to time and place. Additionally, these Endnotes afford an opportunity to explain any technical changes made as a result of reviews and observations after productions. As promised in the Introduction the tone and characters of the plays have not substantially changed over the forty-year period they were written, stage-read and produced.

1   "Critical Race History" is an intentional reference and specifically not "Critical Race Theory" (CRT) that has become a false flag waved by the MAGA crowd with the hope that woke liberals will take the bait, run down a rabbit hole while trying to explain CRT to a faction that does not listen. Ronald Reagan famously suggested: "if you're explaining, you're losing." I'll risk it: Critical Race History should be taught at all levels with age appropriate lesson plans. On the other hand, CRT is not taught in grades K-12 and when taught it is at the graduate level, usually in law schools. As a lawyer over the years I've seen many experts testify in court and have concluded that theories may take different forms. But, history ... real facts ... Black and white facts are not subject to change or debate.

2   Regina Craig Avery noted that her mother Ruth Craig resembled her mother's cousin Rosa Parks in stature, age and other traits. RUTH & WINSTON Craig wear well-tailored, natural fiber outfits to contrast to the many "ritzy" outfits (or lack thereof) worn by BIG JIM and JAMELLE. (Note some of the Governor's many costume changes may be done on stage. And, his fresh from the bath scene was suggested by a photo that accompanied "Outsize Governor" LIFE MAGAZINE, September 15, 1947 p. 64.)

3   Southern Male may be played by one actor with multiple roles varied with hats, shadows, KKK hoods and other theatrical devices. However, multiple actors may more effectively delineate the Southern Male characters,

especially using a different actor for news reporter. Racists should be in the image of George Wallace, suggesting "they all look alike." If multiple characters are used they should be named in the credits as Southern Male One, Southern Male Two, etc. and allotted as the director sees fit.

4   Scenes frequently are tied to time changes but within scenes there are transitions from one set to another; hence, the need for fluidity.

5   Suggestion: extreme upstage above the dais, on top an (abstracted) capitol dome, there may fly the Alabama flag above the Confederate flag. If this set suggestion is used, the playbill/program should note that at the time of the play the flags were authentic; however, in 1993 during the term of Governor Jim Folsom, Jr. the Confederate flag was permanently removed and now only the Stars and Stripes and the Alabama state flag fly above the Alabama capitol dome.

6   Although not scripted, multimedia projections would greatly enhance the play, e.g. George Wallace's "Stand in School House Door." Playwright has available an **IMAGE APPENDIX** for additional scene enhancement: The emerging Civil Rights Movement, and the campaigns & inaugurations of Big Jim Folsom, much of which are available from Alabama State Archives and various media morgues/archives. See: **BIG JIM FOLSOM, *The Two Faces of Populism*,** a film by Robert Clem. Note: Broadway production circa 2008 of *All My Sons*, Miller, used visuals of WWII aircraft, for historical references. *All the Way*, Schenkkan, used banks of T.V. screens for period broadcasts, political signs, etc.

7   Music, *Y'all Come*.

8   Music: *Stars Fell on Alabama*.

9   "Colored" was an "accepted" term to refer to African Americans in 1947. "Negro" was a legal term that became offensive and was frequently pronounced "Nigra" by mushy-mouth whites. "Black" gained acceptance later during the Civil Rights Movement. "African American" usage was in the future beyond the time of this play. Use of the N-word was ignorant and/or hate-filled racism, and is used sparingly in this play, for example, a quote from a newspaper of the day, hateful usage by the "Southern Male" as bigot, George Wallace and Klansman, the Sundown sign, and by WINSTON when upset at the castration of Judge Aaron.

10. Applause fades to Music: *Happy Days Are Here Again*. A theatre traditionally decides how much house music and transition music to use, if any. Most music is in the public domain or just a few bars fall under fair use. Because this is a Montgomery, Alabama based play time appropriate Hank Williams, Sr. music would add to the play. In fact, the Strawberry Pickers were picking buddies of Hank Williams, Sr. who from time-to-time voiced his support of Big Jim. Transition music may also include Alabama Blues, e.g. the music of W.C. Handy.

11. *Swingin' Out*, '40s dance music.

12. The simultaneous reading is optional. A director may choose to have only one actor read the lines or the lines may be partially shared or read sequentially ... any staging device to entertain the audience with the actual words from newspapers of the time. Also, if videos/stills are projected on set(s), the theatre may choose to scroll the newsprint as it is being read.

13. Music: *You Are My Sunshine*.

14. As mentioned in footnote 2, Governor Folsom was featured in *Life Magazine* September 15. 1947.

15. Facilities at Maxwell Air Force Base, Montgomery, AL were integrated in the 1940s and several groups met there, e.g. a Committee for Justice for Ms. Recy Taylor, who was raped in Abbeville, AL in the early 1940s. This scene is approximately eighteen months prior to President Harry Truman's Executive Order 9981 of July 26, 1948 that desegrated the Armed Services.

16. Sims, *The Little Man's Big Friend, James E. Folsom in Alabama Politics 1946-1958*, The University of Alabama Press, 1985, p. 167.

17. The following short half-scene is a true story from an interview with Roy Drinkard, Cullman, AL November 2016.

18. The "Self-Starter" Amendment was supported by George Wallace; hence, beginning of his split with Big Jim, Wallace's early mentor. p. 194, *Big Mules & Branchheads*, Grafton & Permaloff. University of Georgia Press, 1985.

19. *She Was Poor But She Was Honest*, 1930 Billy Bennett recording is in the public domain. Lyrics adopted to fit Big Jim Folsom: "...'Til she met that Southern Gentleman, Big Jim Folsom and she had a child by him." Love children (bastards) were frowned upon on the '40s.

20 Excerpts from a statement by State Representative, W.C. Givhan, Dallas (Selma) County Alabama to Gessner McCorvey, January 29, 1949. Barnard, *Dixiecrats and Democrats, p. 128 & ff Ch.7, no. 5.*

21 Speech reprinted in *Lend Me Your Ears, Great Speeches in History,* William Safire, Norton p.718-21.

22 Suggested house music: *Oh Little Town of Bethlehem* as intermission ensues.

23 A few bars of "Y'all Come" Strawberry Pickers.

24 Grover Hall, *Montgomery Advertiser*, January 16, 1955. Quoted in *The Little Man's Big Friend,* Sims, p. 140. Slightly edited for clarity.

25 Sign projected: "Nigger Don't Let The Sun Set on You Here!"

26 1955 speech to Alabama Educational Assn. (AEA)

27 *Big Mules & Branchheads,* Grafton & Permaloff, p. 187, ff 42. *Montgomery Advertiser,* July 7 & 10, 1955.

28 The neighbor was William Singleton who was arrested for legal firearms by the plain clothes detective sent in by Folsom. *The Children Coming On…, A Retrospective of the Montgomery Bus Boycott,* Gray, Leventhal, Sikora & Thornton, BlackBelt Press, 1998, p. 45.

29 This is a reference to Caludette Colvin who was arrested in the spring of 1955 approximately 9 months before Rosa Parks' arrest. Some civil rights leaders thought Ms. Colvin, a teenager, was too young to withstand the pressures of being a test case.

30 *Stars Fell on Alabama,* plays. (Scene inspired by *National Geographic* photo.)

31 Raines, *My Soul is Rested, The Story of the Civil Rights Movement in the Deep South, The Story of the Civil Rights Movement in the Deep South,* 1977 Viking, p.170, ff 322. Governor Folsom sent state investigator Ben Allen to investigate the castration of Edward "Judge" Aaron and Allen got Klansmen to turn states evidence. Unlike the Emmet Till injustice in Mississippi, Alabama got a conviction in the Aaron case and four Klansmen went to prison in 1959 to serve a 20 year sentence. George Wallace's Pardon and Parole Board permitted the Klansmen to walk free after serving only four years.

32 *We Shall Over Come* may begin softly and crescendo after Dr. King's speech that ends the play.

33 OPTION: At curtain call any actor(s) may relate some or all of the fol-

lowing: (1) On September 15, 1963, 18 days after Dr. Kings speech at the Lincoln Memorial, the Klan bombed the 16th Street Baptist Church in Birmingham, Alabama, killing four young girls: Addie Mae Collins, Cynthia Westley, Carole Robertson, all age 14, and Carol Denise McNair, age 11; (2) In October 1963 less than two months after the time of this play, George Wallace's Pardon and Parole Board released from prison the Klansmen who castrated Judge Aaron; and (3) On November 22, 1963 President John F. Kennedy was assassinated and Lyndon B. Johnson became President. Civil Rights Acts followed in the summers of 1964 & 1965. Dr. King was assassinated in 1968.

34 My earlier attempt at Mrs. Graham's dialect lines sounded awkward as I read them thirty plus years later. There was an attempt to swing back and forth between "formal" speech when poised and more "base" dialect when excited. In the original production of WEDGES in 1991 Actor Donna Thornton did such a beautiful job I did not hear the awkwardness. Actors should adjust to their comfort level.

35 Some of these "stage instructions" may appear excessive, as if the playwright is telling the actor how to act. Guilty. Seriously, when wanting to set a pace, I sometimes put in "too many" suggestions, but when the scene is off book I assume that the actor/director have made their own choices as to timing.

36 Theatres using this suggestion should seek permissions from copyrighted songs or limit verses to fair use. The song suggestions are for a late 1950s barroom with many options from country to early rock and roll.

37 Foil and Deputy appear in different Acts and may be played by the same actor.

38 The Cullman reading was at the All Steak Restaurant in a remodeled building that during the 1950s was the Ford dealership and showroom. Back then during Cullman's Strawberry Festival the Ford showroom would be cleared for a dance. Perhaps, the original Strawberry Pickers played the same venue as the reading of JAMELLE.

39 See note 19 above. With the original author unknown SHE WAS POOR is thought to come from the 19th Century English music hall tradition and was sung by British soldiers during World War I.

40 Repeats designed to show "aging"... if not working some may be deleted.

41 YOU ARE MY SUNSHINE was published by Jimmie Davis and Charles Mitchell on January 30, 1940 and has been recorded by over 350 artist and

into 30 languages. If a production uses more than fair use or a specific artist's recording permission should be sought.

42 OH! SUSANNA by Stephen Foster was first published in 1848.

43 MOUTAIN DEW written by Bascom Lamar Lunsford and Scott Wiseman. First recorded by the Stanley Brothers, September 15, 1959.

44 STARS FELL ON ALABAMA: lyrics by Mitchell Parish, composed by Frank Perkins and early recording 1934 by the Guy Lombardo Orchestra.

45 Y'ALL COME, written by Arlie Duff and first recorded January 9. 1954 by Bill Monroe and his Blue Grass Boys.

46 BACK IN THE SADDLE AGAIN was the signature song for Gene Autry who wrote it with Ray Whitney and it was first released in 1939.

47 This version of CODE BAPBOMB contains "excessive" stage instructions/blocking, because a the end of the run of the play in Tampa in 2007 this copy coordinated with that production's sound cues. I did not edit out many of these instructions, hoping they may be more instructional than annoying.

48 In the January 2007 co-production of Stageworks/Gorilla, the playwright obtained copyright permission for limited verses of "Birmingham Sunday" by Richard Farina from Universal Music Group. Joan Baez, sister-in-law of Mr. Farina, first recorded "Birmingham Sunday" in 1963. Such was acknowledged in playbill.

49 Ox frequently plays with back to Hambric, and other devices are used to suggest Hambric as specter. In the January 2007 production, Hambric played extremely upstage on a thin ledge seven feet above main stage level, amongst church bomb debris.

50 The "rifle" should be a thirty aught six but a shotgun may be used and dialogue should be adjusted.

51 Next to last verse of "Birmingham Sunday" is from original Irish folk song.

52 It helps me to think of all drama in three acts: set-up, complication(s) and resolution. Theatre of yore was an all evening affair with three or more acts with multiple intermissions. Today, if there is an intermission, one is usually enough, hence the "Two Act" label finding a moment to divide the play for intermission.

53 In the late 1980s it was thought that gay night clubs and abortion clinics were the new targets of extremist bombs in addition to Black churches,

as symbols of African American culture. Some reviewers felt BapBomb attempted too much. After I bristled at the mixed reviews, I knew not to argue with a newspaper that buys ink by the gallons. I have modified CODE BAPBOMB slightly based on the reviews.

54 "The hottest places in Hell are reserved for those who, in a period of moral crisis, maintain their neutrality." Dante.

55 Dickens, DAVID COPPERFIELD, Chapter 23.

56 Dante at note 54 above.

57 See Endnote 16 above.

58 Due to unconstitutionally vague law and policies, educators in Florida are confused as to what may be taught and what books made available to students. "Why Some Florida Schools Are Removing Books From Their Libraries," Charles Bethea, *The New Yorker*, February 7, 2023.

59 Nancy Armour, *USA Today*, February 15, 2023.

60 The day after I wrote the sentence about bloggers having to register in Florida, Governor DeSantis said he never supported such a bill, but his office said he "might" sign it if it passes the Legislature. Seemed like he was doing a Youngkin pivot to the middle before he even announced for president.

61 As I approached the Ides of March 2023 with my Backstory observations, Fox Fake News and MAGA politicians blamed the failure of the Silicon Valley Bank on the Bank's woke polices, presumably inflicted by the HR Department. These financial pundits failed to mention that under the Trump Administration in a bipartisan vote Dodd Frank was repealed. Senator Elizabeth Warren warned of bank deregulations and likelihood of bank failure. To paraphrase Senator Warren, government work should be boring as it provides for our common good, and I hope that my anecdotal rants, e.g. bank failures, do not come to fruition. But, let our history serve as a cautionary note that the past may be now.

62 I owe an apology to the barbers of Cullman, Alabama, because I don't specifically recall their politics from the 1950s. My specific recall of barbershop (George Wallace) politics is from the late 1960s in Birmingham when I was a young lawyer. I could not wait for the 1970s so I could grow my hair long and get styled at a uni-sex salon.

63 1964 SOUTHERN ACCENT, (yearbook Birmingham-Southern College,

Birmingham, Alabama) Vol. 23, pp 3 & 4. The events of 1963 e.g. the Kennedy assassination, the Birmingham civil rights protest and the 16th Street Church Bombing had not benefited from historical reflection at the time the yearbook staff met our deadlines the last of which tolled in January 1964.

64 As I wrapped this effort on Memorial Day weekend 2023, I had the honor of seeing BEYOND GLORY, a play by Stephen Lang that was produced by Outcast Theatre Collective of the Tampa Bay Area. The play recalled the sacrifices made by millions to protect our democracy and how tardy the USA was in honoring the contributions of African American soldiers. Also on this Memorial Day, a highway sign near Clanton, Alabama was hacked with "Reclaim America" a white nationalist slogan. Here's hoping for a future Memorial Day, when anti-democratic memes become dated, irrelevant and forgotten much like the postproduction heap of trash of a disassembled set after the last performance. For now, we need to put our critical race history on stage.

ACKNOWLEDGEMENTS

FIRST, A THANK YOU TO ALL THE ACTORS, DIRECTORS, TECHNICIANS, AND OTHER THEATRE PERSONNEL who have been a part of the plays in this collection. Another thanks to theatres everywhere that take risks in developing, reading and performing new works and in my case, specifically Terrific New Theatre in Birmingham under the direction of the late Carl Steward and Stageworks Theatre in Tampa under the direction of the late Anna Brennen.

Next, I would like to thank my writing teachers, groups, grants and support organizations: Richebourg McWilliams at Birmingham-Southern College (BSC), James Mersman and Jesse Hill Ford at the University of Alabama, Birmingham (UAB). The Writing Today Conference at BSC and Jesse's Group that lingered after his departure from Birmingham. The Stageworks Playwright Workshop in Tampa under the direction of Bruce Rodgers and Jim Wicker, and the Writers Actors Group (WAG) of St. Petersburg, Florida. A special thanks to WAG members: Susana Darwin, a writer, director, filmmaker who graciously undertook an early line edit of WINSTON DRIVES BIG JIM (WDBJ); to James Rayfield who saw something in WDBJ and suggested its first staged reading; and to Sheila and Matt Cowley who held WAG together, even via Zoom during the early days of COVID.

Thanks to playwright competitions everywhere and specifically to the Southern Playwright Competition at Jacksonville State University and its Coordinator Joy Maloney. I'm grateful to the Hillsborough County (Tampa) Individual Artist Grant (2007) that sponsored my attending the Kennedy Center Playwriting Intensive, Advanced Tract, under the direction of Gary Garrison. Thanks to Lorian Hemingway and Carol Shaughessy of the Lorian Hemingway Short Story Competition, Key West, Florida for their support in many ways.

WDBJ would not have been possible without the help of the Craig and Folsom families. I thank Regina Craig Avery of Montgomery, Irma Craig Thomas of Birmingham, the late Regina Craig Manly of Chicago, Rita Craig Rose and Gail Barlow, both of Atlanta, for their gracious recall of those days of yore although these ladies were quite young back then. The Folsom family help was a lifelong process, but specifically I thank the late Jamelle Folsom for her generous recall; my brother-in-law the late Jack Folsom for his many stories; Rachael Folsom Lichenstein for recalling that she did not want Winston to drive her to school in the state

Cadillac; Melissa Folsom Boyen for specific recall, corrections and sharing the family's genealogy; Jim Folsom, Jr. for general source information and his memory of Congressman Powell's visit through the eyes of a six-year-old; Marsha Folsom for the reading in Cullman and helping with names and resources; Alabama "Bama" Folsom Hager for words of encouragement and digging boxes of photos out of storage; and sister Jenny Grissom Folsom in many, many ways by locating photos, proofing this collection and helping recall stories from our parents, Mama Gracie and Daddy Hubert.

I thank: Roy Drinkard of Cullman for his recall of early Folsom lore and Big Jim's sisters: "Thelma had her Bible and Ruby had her bourbon." I thank Shelia "Snookie" Flood for sharing the Smith family genealogy. Professors George E, Sims and Wayne Flynt who took my calls when I was stumped on a fact or two. I relied heavily on books by two BSC classmates in writing WDBJ: Act One relied on DIXIECRATS AND DEMOCRATS, Alabama Politics 1942-1950, by William D. Barnard, and Act Two was enriched by Howell Raines' MY SOUL IS RESTED, The Story of the Civil Rights Movement in the Deep South. THE STRAWBERRY PICKERS, Southern Arts Corporation, by Roy Baham, Jamelle Folsom and E. Jimmy Key, provided the music and politics of the era in the authentic voices of those who were there. The Alabama Department of Archives & History provided a wealth of information including photos of the era.

Thanks to Charles Varner, Jr. who was gracious with his time and knowledge that came, in part, from his chairing a program at Alabama State University's E.D. Nixon Institute honoring the life and legacy of Winston Craig, a Black Voice at the Governor's Mansion 1939-1959. Thank you to Jason A. Trawick, of the Archives at the Levi Watkins Learning Center, Alabama State University, Montgomery for his research of photos and articles of the era.

Thanks to Julian Cross whose encouragement and specific technical advice prevented me from tossing into Tampa Bay an old laptop with a detachable hard drive that contained my old plays in gnarly, random and dated formats.

A special thanks to Shawn Wright of Homewood, Alabama whose design and advice made this collection possible.

ABOUT THE PLAYWRIGHT

HUBERT GRISSOM WAS BORN IN CULLMAN, ALABAMA forty-seven days after the Japanese bombed Pearl Harbor, making him a member of the Silent Generation. He graduated from Cullman High School, Birmingham-Southern College and Duke University, School of Law, and studied under Jesse Hill Ford at the University of Alabama, Birmingham. In addition to writing plays, he practiced law in Alabama and Florida, and now lives in Tampa.

Playwright with his mother, Gracie Grissom, and Jamelle Folsom at opening night cast party of WEDGES, Birmingham, AL, May 1990. On the theory that every child gets a trophy, the ladies presented a plaque to commemorate the play's premiere.

ACCLAIM FOR FLAWED GOOD PEOPLE

"In these five lively and moving plays Hubert Grissom nails the zeitgeist of the civil rights era in Alabama. Like Grissom, I was there for part of it and these plays capture the odd mixture of messiness and nobility, of courage and evil, of despair and inspiration that characterized those years — and they do so splendidly."

Charles Gaines, Writer.
Author of the non-fiction bestseller *Pumping Iron*,
and novels *Stay Hungry*, *Dangler* and *Survival Games.*"

"As a fan of historical fiction, I find Hubert's characters very relatable and not difficult to portray. His use of appropriate language and characteristics of the period help create multi-dimensional characters that come from a place deep in his heart where he identifies the good in flawed people."

Donna Thornton, Actor

"Hubert Grissom is a Southern writer in the finest possible sense of the term. In his plays Hubert explores the region's dark history unflinchingly, but with compassion and humor. His characters are dynamic and nuanced. I've had the pleasure and privilege of playing the roles of two of his most compelling characters: Governor James E. Folsom in WINSTON DRIVES BIG JIM and the inimitable Slaw Dog in CODE BAPBOMB. Hubert's plays and his characters are a delight for both the actor and the audience."

Jim Wicker, Actor

ACCLAIM FOR PLAYWRIGHT'S EARLIER WORK

"May the future meet the promise of this place and produce prosperity ... for a man who kept the faith with Birmingham."
March 21, 1986

Charles "Chuck" Morgan, Jr.
author of *A Time to Speak*, The story of a young American lawyer's struggle for his city — and for himself.

Made in United States
Orlando, FL
09 August 2024